NEW VOICES IN IRISH CRITICISM 5

New Voices in
Irish Criticism 5

Ruth Connolly and Ann Coughlan

EDITORS

FOUR COURTS PRESS

Set in 10 pt on 12.5 Adobe Caslon for
FOUR COURTS PRESS LTD
7 Malpas Street, Dublin 8, Ireland
e-mail: info@four-courts-press.ie
http://www.four-courts-press.ie
and in North America
FOUR COURTS PRESS
c/o ISBS, 920 N. E. 58th Avenue, Suite 300, Portland, OR 97213

A catalogue record for this title
is available from the British Library.

ISBN 1–85182–855–9 hbk
ISBN 1–85182–856–7 pbk

SPECIAL ACKNOWLEDGMENT

This publication received a grant in aid of publication
from The Arts Council/An Chomhairle Ealaíon.

Printed in Great Britain
by MPG Books, Bodmin, Cornwall

Foreword

The first New Voices conference coincided with my return to Ireland to take up my first academic job after several years spent engaged in doctoral research in England. The sense that I had then, that the conference represented a sign of change and a new confidence among younger critics and scholars in Ireland, has been strengthened and confirmed by the continuing success of the annual conferences and the impressive publications they have generated.

This, the fifth such volume, is no exception. Although the papers, as has been the case in the earlier collections, focus for the most part on aspects of Irish history, culture and literature, the editors' section headings highlight the multiplicity of identities, histories and experiences that 'Ireland' encompasses – or fails to encompass. The papers engage with topics across three centuries, recover forgotten names and question received ideas, deal with Irish-language as well as English-language authors and consider the impact of locations such as Paris, Spain and Irish-America. If you find yourself mentally rearranging these sections, wondering (for instance) if Anne Devlin, Christina Reid and Maria Edgeworth might not very well tell us something about the gendering of Ireland, as well as Northern or Anglo-Irish perspectives, it is one sign that the contributors and the editors have done their job, reminding us that categories are critical constructs, rather than fixed and immutable signs of identity.

A multiplicity of methods and approaches further diversifies the field. The impact on Irish Studies of critical theory itself is the subject of one essay, while another highlights history as a method and a mode of enquiry. On the evidence of these essays, theory is used widely and with discrimination to inform the enquiries of the next generation of critics and scholars. It is evident however that postcolonial theory and criticism, specifically, creates its own set of questions and preoccupations. From the outset, a primary focus of postcolonial criticism in Ireland has been on establishing the grounds for Ireland's inclusion in what David Lloyd has called a postcolonial frame, and some of the contributions here provide additional perspectives on this question. The explanatory power of the postcolonial paradigm is however challenged, with arguments in favour of Derridean deconstruction and postmodern feminism as theoretical approaches which may enable us not only to find new answers, but to pose new questions. One of the most striking features of this volume is the number of essays devoted to women writers and questions of gender and sexuality. Following the publication of volumes 4 and 5 of the *Field Day Anthology*, Irish feminist criticism appears to be flourishing, and the critical possibilities uncovered by an attention to discourses of gender and sexuality are displayed in essays that focus on texts ranging from the plays of Frank McGuinness to the 1916 Proclamation and the Irish constitution.

Shortly after the first New Voices conference in 1999 the first ever state system of research funding for the humanities and social sciences in the Republic of Ireland was instituted, in the form of the IRCHSS Government of Ireland awards and scholarships. Prior to this very welcome but rather overdue development, the path in this country towards a doctorate in the humanities and social sciences was uncertain and strewn with sometimes insurmountable obstacles. A reader of this volume can appreciate the impact that these awards have had, given that the research of a number of contributors has been supported by the IRCHSS. Financial support is a necessary precondition for the creation of a vibrant and sustained research culture – and as society in Ireland becomes ever more complex, the necessity for a culture of critique and self-questioning, which emphasises dialogue and the exchange of ideas, becomes ever more urgent. Dialogue is best when conducted from positions of equality, and adequate financial supports do much to guarantee a form of equality, particularly given the international scope of scholarship and research. But as the editors here note, most humanities research involves a high degree of isolation and solitary effort, and thus the creation of a research culture demands more than the funding of individual researchers. The New Voices venture, originating in the initiative of graduate students themselves, and since maintained by the energy and commitment of successive graduate student organisers, is a tribute to the desire of younger critics and scholars to put their work into question, to listen to other voices, and to offer their ideas for debate. The publication of these essays thus gives good cause for celebration.

Dr Clíona Ó Gallchoir

Contents

CONTENTS

CONTENTS

Introduction

The opportunity to present one's work at a conference of peers is an important part of what can be the very lonely postgraduate world. The topics that are exciting the minds of young academics and the new avenues of study that they have chosen are traditionally foregrounded in New Voices conferences. Therefore, a theme was chosen which would allow interdisciplinary participation yet provide a focus for those young critics who were working in Ireland or in the area of Irish studies. The word 'Irish' was an obvious starting point as it provides the conference's unifying link whilst its own connotations and denotations have sometimes been neglected. This approach is a challenging one as the word 'Irish' may be perceived, on the one hand, as both overly restrictive in the context of the conference and, on the other, too volatile a term to withstand any critical engagement. However by returning to its etymological origins we can consider both its current usages and how it has changed over time.

The Oxford English Dictionary provided us with a relatively stable definition of our term. We found that a series of wide-ranging concepts had attached themselves to what was not simply an adjective that defined inhabitants of a geographical space, but a word whose meanings proffered a snapshot of the development of Irish culture: from its nod to Celtic settlements in Scotland, to the perception of Irish speech as composed of 'contradictory statements', the culturally held view that 'Irish' acted as a synonym for temper, and, most notably, the mutation and cross-fertilisation of two languages in a process where the Irish mastery of another tongue is held up for questioning. What is most striking is how the secondary meanings of 'Irish' connote emotion, inconsistency and confusion and therefore how the stereotypes of Irishness in fact inhere in the adjective itself. Investigating the roots of this perception and how it informs the image and representations of Irish society and culture concerns to some extent all of our contributors

Literary analyses dominate in the collection, but history, geography and critical theory help provide the crucial interdisciplinary dimension. If these papers illustrate anything, it is the importance of disciplines engaging with each other's materials and theories in order to produce a richer and more sensitive understanding of Irish culture, literature and history. Whilst the papers are grouped by similarity of content, an analysis of them identifies many overlapping concerns, themes and positions, which in turn allow us to discuss them not just within the assigned categories, but based on multiple correspondences.

One theme that persistently emerges, particularly in the writing traditionally classed as Anglo-Irish, is the concern with the colonised Other. In relation to *Castle Rackrent*, Ciara Hogan argues that Edgeworth borrows the voice of a Hiberno-English speaker in order to voice *Rackrent*'s Irish Catholic peasantry, whose idiom, through its use of repetition and omission, offers a powerful critique of its speakers' socio-economic plight. Shelley Meagher looks outside the geographical confines of Ireland in discussing Thomas Moore's *Lallah Rookh* and considers how the Irish imagined the Orient, the quintessential colonial 'Other' during the era of the Union. She is particularly interested in the links between Moore's oriental romance and his ambiguous views on British rule in Ireland which endorsed Catholic emancipation but not the repeal of the Union. Meagher notes parallels in Moore's treatment of political and religious resistance to imperial rule in *Lallah Rookh* and in his 'A Letter to the Roman Catholics of Dublin' (1810). In both texts Moore endorses religious tolerance but condemns the manipulation of political processes for the ends of religious bigotry, whether in the Arab-Islamic context of *Lallah Rookh* or in post-Union Ireland. Yuri Yoshino offers a close reading of Maria Edgeworth's novels *The Absentee* and *Patronage* as an 'Irish tale' and an 'English tale' respectively, which deal with themes of traditional landlordism, middle-class professionalism and national identity. Edgeworth offers in both novels a prescription for a benevolent and patriotic landlord which encompasses themes of meritocracy, multilingualism, and a receptiveness to other cultures, ideas and values. However, in the case of the Anglo-Irish heir, Colambre, this receptiveness is carefully circumscribed to ensure he remains focused on his economic rather than on his ethno-cultural links to Ireland and thereby affirms his rejection of a Romantic nationalism.

Anita Howard considers how the seventeenth-century Spanish playwright Calderon uses the Irish Christian image of St Patrick's purgatory in order to investigate the relationship between Christian belief, kingship and redemption. Howard demonstrates how Calderón's Ireland, presented as both alien and uncivilised, nonetheless comes to exemplify idealistic national regeneration. The potential of an island race is further developed in Mary Burke's paper. She considers John Millington Synge, an Irish writer during the Revival and his portrayal of the Aran Islanders as intuitively bohemian. She argues that Synge's work recognizes the Islanders' inherent and unique qualities, while simultaneously distancing them from their fellow Irishmen on the mainland.

The political outsider gives way to the cultural outsider and to those who defy the cultural expectations of their gender. Tina O'Toole introduces a neglected group of nineteenth-century women writers, and within this group she isolates one common theme: their problematisation of gender identities. O'Toole explores Sarah Grand's contemporary bestseller *The Heavenly Twins* (1892) and highlights Grand's use of the device of female transvestism to question the limits of women's social, intellectual and sexual boundaries. Kenneth Nally discusses how the critical reception of Frank McGuinness' plays has treated the theme of same-sex desire as a metaphor for nationalisms. This limited perspective has meant a concomitant critical neglect of McGuinness' challenge to contemporary assumptions about homosexuality , aestheticism and effeminacy in his plays of the 1980s, particularly in his representation of the Italian Renaissance painter Caravaggio in *Innocence*.

The complexities of a writer's response to the cultural and historical conditions of their time form the backdrop to another set of papers. These contributors place particular emphasis on the writer's role as a cultural innovator and as an arbiter and participant in important political debate. The influence of the historical context on the act of writing provides the foundation for Mary Pierse's interpretation of the career of the late nineteenth-century writer, George Moore. In her paper she considers the stances taken and methods employed by Moore as he sought to challenge the prevailing Victorian ethos governing his art form in order to achieve literary freedom of expression. Anne Oakman examines how Sommerville and Ross engaged in dialogue with the activists and dramatists of the Irish Revival, exploiting their own deliberately marginal position within it to survey and criticize its discourses of Irishness. In their eyes the Revival's stage representations of the Irish were idealized stereotypes lacking in both nuance and verisimilitude. Their own evocation of a Hiberno-English dialect and culture was intended to convey the unique and hybrid identity of the Irish and Anglo-Irish and to offer a counter-challenge to the stage-Irishry of the Revival dramatists. Seán Kennedy shows how Beckett's text, 'Yellow', serves to analyse the Anglo-Irish response to an evolving social structure. The continued Protestant performance of identity after the collapse of the political foundations of their world underpins the actions and perceptions of Beckett's main character, Belacqua Shuah. Kennedy focuses on Shuah's reconciliation with his class in the penultimate tale 'Yellow' as an ironic counterpoint to Beckett's own failure to do so.

The theme of crises of identity in a changing society also informs Ann Walsh's analysis of Robert Lowell's work. Lowell's identification with the American aristocratic tradition is a fundamental aspect of his poetry. However, Walsh points out that as Lowell gives voice to the dissolution of this aristocratic tradition and his struggle with this void, he also voices his belief that immigrant groups like the Irish are unable to uphold or enter into this tradition. Frank McGuinness also draws on antithetical and subversive identities but uses them to critique rather than reaffirm establishment prejudices. In David Cregan's discussion of *Carthaginians*, he argues that McGuinness uses the queer aesthetic to revisit the events of Bloody Sunday and re-examine the cultural trauma inflicted by violence from the perspectives embodied in the idea of camp.

Another crucial issue for contemporary scholars is how a writer reinterprets his or her sources in suit differing social, political and personal agendas. Coilín O hAodha, in his paper, considers the case of the 'Rimes of the Ancient Mariner'. Despite Coleridge's revisions to the poem over time, O hAodha argues that the search for stable meaning limits the potential contained in each version of the poem. Textual instability may be seen as a positive opportunity to explore the change and development of the poem's meaning and concerns and to reflect the poet's shifting sense of literary authority. David O'Shaughnessy explores changing notions of literary authenticity in his study of the editions and translations of the influential Irish text *An tOileánach*. O'Shaughnessy argues that Padraig Ua Maoileoin's edition of *An tOileánach* supplies a significantly altered version of the original work in order to present the text as a significant literary work rather than an orally-based biography or autobiography. In so doing Ua Maoilean is entering into dialogue with Robin Flower's English-language translation of the text, which stressed the simplicity, directness and non-literariness of the source text. O'Shaughnessy argues that this re-imaging of *An tOileánach*, through its ideological reinscription as literature rather than autobiography, marks an important milestone in Gaelic literature's transition from an oral to a written tradition.

Lynne Maes' paper makes a close comparative reading of three texts: Joyce's *Portrait of the Artist as a Young Man,* and Beckett's *Film* and *Krapp's Last Tape.* She examines how *Krapp's Last Tape* parodies the artistic epiphany contained in *Portrait* but notes that Beckett then returns to the topic in *Film* to examine, in more serious vein, the interrelationship between art and subjectivity. Catherine Kilcoyne provides another perspective on Freud's theory of fetishism and applies this to a close analysis of Seamus Heaney's 'Maighdean Mara' and Nuala Ní Dhomhnaill's poem 'An Mhaighdean Mhara'. Both poems draw on the fable of the mermaid and examine her struggle to conform to the expectations of femininity she finds on land. Both poets represent this experience as causing permanent damage to her psyche, ensuring that on her return to the sea she never fully experiences her former happiness. Kilcoyne argues that in Heaney's reworking of the mermaid folktale, the figure of the mermaid is fetishised, that is, objectified, silenced and thereby idealised whereas Ní Dhomhnaill's version allows the mermaid/fetish to speak and challenge her own representation.

Examining the means and methods of nation-building produced valuable insights into the ideology and self-perception of the new Irish state. Judith Pryor considers how the founding moment and future promise of a nation are preserved for the inhabitants of the state. She offers an analysis of an historical text, the 1916 Proclamation, and shows how this text equated the concept of the nation with both an ethnic definition of Irishness (the Irish Republic) and a set of geopolitical boundaries (the Republic of Ireland). The unity proclaimed by this text retrospectively justified both the violent action that brought the state into being and its vision of unity invokes both a tradition of resistance and a promise of a Gaelic communalism to come. John-Paul McCarthy analyses the other founding document of the Irish state, the 1937 Constitution. The philosophical basis of this text, he argues, is a tense fusion of nationalism, Enlightenment liberalism and Catholic social thought and the aim of its draftsmen is the expression and demonstration of Irish political autonomy and the collective ethos of the Irish state.

Kalene Nix-Kenefick analyses the contemporary literary critique of this vision. She shows how Irish society during the period of cultural and social change of the 1950s was reflected and debated between the covers of *The Bell* magazine. Kenefick focuses on the magazine's female short-story writers and examines how they articulate their concerns about societal controls on women's bodies and sexuality. These texts, Kenefick argues, are both at variance with and symptomatic of the sexual and emotional repression experienced by young Irish women in the first half of the twentieth century. The ongoing project of nation-building informs Laura Kane's paper. Here Kane suggests this project cannot be conceived of as a linear and logical process but as a continuous concern that requires negotiations with the deeds of its people. Kane sees the Northern Irish playwrights Anne Devlin and Christina Reid address the themes of misogyny and entrenched nationalism as obstacles to the construction of a new community and, by extension, a new nation. Thomas F. Halloran interrogates Ireland's status as a postcolonial nation and draws on Joyce's *Dubliners*, *Portrait* and *Ulysses* to demonstrate the potential for developing new national identities. In these texts Irish people's ability independently to create a national consciousness is undermined by the discourses of colonisation and nationalism. It is through Bloom's rejection of binary identities and his embrace of different nations and religions that Joyce offers the possibility of circumventing this false choice.

Mapping, space and place concern another group of contributors and, as Neal Alexander reminds us, the representation of a place is both informed by and informs outside perceptions of that place. Alexander traces how Belfast has achieved its current image of a tough city encased in its own history and concerns. He then challenges this depiction and presents an alternative reading of the city that allows us to view Belfast as a place created by, and supportive of, dynamism and creativity. As with Neal Alexander, an open and progressive approach informs Francesca Bovone's perception of Northern Ireland. Bovone's philosophical position is inspired by a fundamental belief that Belfast has more to offer than the statics of a war-torn city. Glenn Patterson's and Ciaran Carson's works offer Bovone the fictional space wherein the Belfast of the late twentieth century is depicted as a dynamic city, one which recognizes and lives with its past and brings this knowledge to bear on the new themes of its present and future. Edwina Keown uses the images of compass, map and palimpsest in order to excavate the hidden depths and subtextual links of *The Last September* using Bowen's psychological connection with her characters, her experiences of Irish and English landscapes and the overlap of past and present in her writing.

The overt and covert rejection of an Irish tradition from a number of perspectives concerns our last group of critics. Brendan McNamee argues that

Banville, whilst rejecting the traditional belief in the mimetic qualities of language, still recognizes the necessity of societal myths for the creation of reality. McNamee draws on Heidegger's concept of *aletheia* (unconcealedness) to elucidate Banville's conception of the interrelationship between myth and history and the vital importance of achieving a balance between the too-comfortable certainties of the former and the terrifying exigencies of the latter. Claire Bracken grounds her work in a discussion of the limitations and possibilities of a critical theory. She interrogates Irish post-colonial theory's use of the term 'liminality' and challenges its attempts to inform our understanding of identity politics using this concept. She offers postmodern feminism as a more suitable framework through which liminality can support our understanding of moments that can be simultaneously oppositional and connected. The poetry of Catherine Walsh provides the textual space in which she develops this idea. Eoin Flannery also critiques postcolonial theory but praises some Irish theorists for avoiding the 'post-structuralist murkiness' of international theoretical waters and their ability to challenge the apparent cooption of radical cultural theory by the forces of institutionalisation and respectability. Sian White comments that Irish studies has been preoccupied with the significance of the past and she offers an alternative view through Trevor's work. Her project is aided by the use of Cixous' theory of language to examine the binaries contained in Trevor's novel *Felicia's Journey*. Finally, Michael O'Sullivan critiques the conference name as a means to analyse the postcolonial habit of referring to consciousness as voice, a metaphor which poststructuralism and deconstruction has successfully challenged.

The impressive scholarship of all these papers means that the volume as a whole offers authoritative and insightful comment on wide-ranging aspects of Irish culture, literature and history. It represents the approaches, opinions and perspectives of a new generation of scholars who collectively appraise and critique Irish identity whilst retaining a sense of its complexities and ambiguities. We hope that this book offers readers a sense of their achievement.

We would like to thank all of our contributors for their excellent and insightful papers and for their patience during the editing process. We would also like to offer particular thanks to Dr Clíona Ó Gallchoir and Dr Andrew King of the English Department in UCC and to all those who gave of their time and expertise in chairing the conference sessions. We are also indebted to our readers. We appreciate their time and expertise. A special acknowledgement must go to Professor Tom Dunne, of the History Department, UCC for giving us a stimulating and fascinating plenary discussion.

Ruth Connolly and Ann Coughlan*

* Ruth Connolly is completing her doctoral research at UCC. She is an IRCHSS Government of Ireland scholar. Ann Coughlan is a tutor with the English department at UCC.

'Somewhere in the Briny Say':
an imaginative geography of Belfast[1]

NEAL ALEXANDER, QUEEN'S UNIVERSITY, BELFAST

Belfast has traditionally been thought of – if it has been thought of at all – as a hard-nosed, flinty, intractable sort of place. This attitude has gained further credence in recent years as 'ideological divisions have increasingly become a concrete part of the physical environment'.[2] Indeed, with the rise of the 'Troubles' thriller, Belfast has frequently been reduced to a 'tribal map',[3] wherein the city is charged with dangerous potential at the same time as it is rendered static, self-enclosed, and hermetically sealed from the forces of history. Arguing against such depictions, this paper will attend to some of the dynamics informing both Belfast in history and the history of its representation.

I want to begin by observing that Belfast is the only city in Ireland to have a significant industrial history, a distinction that tends to generate very mixed reactions. Mr and Mrs S.C. Hall, who visited the town in the early 1840s when industrialisation was beginning to take hold, were emphatically positive: 'As we drew near the only manufacturing town of Ireland – alas, that it should be so! – its peculiar character became apparent. It was something new to perceive, rising above the houses, numerous tall and thin chimneys, indicative of industry, occupation, commerce, and prosperity.'[4] The only implied complaint that the Halls make is that there are not more Belfasts in Ireland, yet this sense of the city's singularity is not, they realize, without its complications: 'The cleanly and bustling appearance of Belfast is decidedly unnational. That it is in Ireland, but not of it, is a remark ever on the lips of visitors from the south or west.'[5] Belfast's anomalous position as 'the only manufacturing town in Ireland' tends, therefore, to make it both economically and physically unrecognisable as an 'Irish' city and, even to sympathetic observers such as the Halls, its character is 'peculiar' when seen in relation to Ireland as a whole. Indeed, for a subsequent visitor such as Sean O'Faolain, the blackouts of the Second World War turn this freakishness into a form of gothic horror:

> Those glimpses of light, the steadily tramping figures, two by two, looming up unexpectedly, the towering warehouses hardly seen, felt magnetically, the cavernous yards, the shrouded churches, more and more factory hulks, a

1 My thanks to Dr Colin Graham and Dr Eamonn Hughes, who offered invaluable advice and critical comment on early drafts of some of this material. I am grateful for the award of a DEL Research Studentship, which has made this research possible.   2 Neil Jarman, 'Intersecting Belfast', in Barbara Bender (ed.), *Landscape: politics and perspectives* (Oxford & Providence, 1993), p. 107.   3 Gerald Seymour, *Harry's game* (London, 1997), p. 50.   4 Mr and Mrs S.C. Hall, *Ireland: its scenery, character, &c*, iii (London, 1845), p. 52.   5 Ibid., p. 56.

sooty spire, all along that artery to the west, coalesced into the blackout of not only light but sweetness. One felt that nothing could, indeed, have possibly come of that nineteenth-century Sunday sleep, and all the red factories and the grey buildings, and the ruthlessness with which the whole general rash of this stinking city was permitted to spread along the waters of the lough but the bark of rifles and the hurtle of paving stones and the screams of opposing hates.[6]

Where the Halls see Belfast's early industrial expansion in the uncomplicated terms of advance and improvement, O'Faolain retrospectively condemns the same process as a 'rash' whose symptoms are evident in the contemporary disease of the city's sectarian conflicts. Indeed, Belfast here epitomizes the 'brutalization by the North of Southern softness'; it is Ireland infected and disfigured to such an extent that it is no longer recognisable as Irish.[7]

For all their differences then, both the Halls and O'Faolain share the sense that Belfast cannot be confidently labelled 'Irish', an uncertainty that forms a recurrent pattern in the impressions of visitors from a variety of foreign parts. Chevalier de Latocnaye, who visited the town in 1797, remarked that 'Belfast has almost entirely the look of a Scotch town, and the character of the inhabitants has considerable resemblance to that of the people of Glasgow'.[8] Another French visitor, Madame de Boret, found late Victorian Belfast 'commercial, Protestant and wealthy; that is to say, profoundly uninteresting', and this disinterest is clearly related to her conviction that it is 'the least Irish of Irish towns. One might fancy oneself in Glasgow or Bristol'.[9] Through much of the nineteenth century, however, Belfast's growing industrial character and fame led most frequently to comparisons with cities in the north of England: the Halls imagined Belfast 'a clean Manchester',[10] while A. Atkinson thought that the city 'may be justly denominated 'the Liverpool of Ulster'.[11] However, William Thackeray has something to say about this last title in his *Irish Sketch Book* (1843):

> They call Belfast the Irish Liverpool; if people are for calling names, it would be better to call it the Irish London at once – the chief city of the kingdom, at any rate. It looks hearty, thriving and prosperous, as if it had money in its pockets, and roast beef for dinner: it has no pretensions to fashion, but looks mayhap better in its broadcloth than some people in their shabby brocade.[12]

While this personification is clearly a case of an Englishman casting the city in his own image, Thackeray's dubbing of Belfast as 'the Irish London' neatly

6 Sean O'Faolain, *An Irish journey* (London, 1941), p. 243. 7 Ibid. 8 Chevalier de Latocnaye, *A Frenchman's walk through Ireland 1796–7*, trans. John Stevenson (Belfast, 1917), p. 222. 9 Madame de Boret, *Three months tour in Ireland*, trans. Mrs Arthur Walter (London, 1891), p. 302. 10 Halls, *Ireland*, p. 53. 11 A. Atkinson, *Ireland exhibited to England* (London, 1823), p. 39. 12 William Makepeace Thackeray, *The Irish sketch book* (London, 1857), p. 307.

catches the city's ambiguous identity in an oxymoron whose two chief terms constantly tug in opposite directions.

This proliferation of parallels suggests that Belfast produces a sense of disorientation in many of its visitors, and 'Southern' nationalists can often seem particularly lost. One such example is William Bulfin, who finds himself unsure as to whether he is in Ireland at all: 'Belfast impresses you as being a very rich and a very busy city. But somehow it repelled me. As I stood within it I asked myself was I in Ireland ... Around the foot of the mountain, between it and the sea, where is Ulster and where is Ireland?'[13] Bewilderment gives way here to 'repulsion', as Belfast is imaginatively cut adrift from Ireland, removed from the nation like a tumour and denied a place within its borders. Indeed, Belfast's cancerous nature is suggested in Bulfin's dismissal of the city as 'simply the creation or outgrowth of a state of things completely un-Irish',[14] while its 'foreign complexion' is, remarkably, deemed less Irish than that of some English cities.[15] Bulfin's rejection and repudiation of Belfast, implicitly wishing it across (or beneath?) the Irish Sea, exemplifies a recurrent trend in Irish nationalist attitudes towards the city,[16] underscoring the sense in which Belfast itself resists any firm positioning upon crudely 'national' maps. This spatial ambiguity is pervasive, for while all of the travellers I have cited found it easier to compare Belfast to Scottish or English cities than to Irish ones, they each equally found enough residual 'Irishness' there to feel justified in including it in books describing their impressions of Ireland. For much of the nineteenth century, therefore, Belfast was a cultural Isle of Man, oscillating in a state of indeterminacy between Ireland and Britain, yet awkwardly and incompletely occupying a position within the frameworks of each.

If, as I am arguing, Belfast's socio-cultural make-up grants the city a certain degree of spatial 'mobility' – at least in imaginative or representational terms – then we also need to relate this to another crucial 'movement'; that is, its progress through time. History becomes especially tangible in the city, which exists in a state of flux; it is constantly changing, moving through new incarnations and phases in its evolution. As Patrick Geddes has it, 'a city is more than a place in space, it is a drama in time'.[17] To place the city in space, therefore, we must also take note of its position upon the historical timeline. Belfast's 'drama in time' – from its origins as a ford on the river Lagan through garrison post and manufacturing town, to industrial and 'post-industrial' city – has been well documented by its historians and sociologists.[18] Alternatively, the imaginative geog-

13 William Bulfin, *Rambles in Eirinn: Part 1* (Dublin, 1927), p. 117, p. 119. 14 Ibid., p. 125. 15 Ibid. Bulfin refers to Liverpool and London in particular. That the metropolis of the British empire should be considered 'more Irish' than Belfast is a particularly telling index of the distrust and distaste with which some Irish Nationalists viewed the city. 16 Noting that Belfast often seems to fall into a bibliographical ellipsis in books about Ireland, Maurice Goldring observes that 'the more republican the point of view ... the more Belfast somehow disappears': *Belfast: from loyalty to rebellion* (London, 1991), p. 14. 17 Patrick Geddes, 'Civics as applied sociology', in Helen E. Meller (ed.), *The ideal city* (Leicester, 1979), p. 79. 18 See for example George Benn, *History of the town of*

raphy that I am attempting to sketch here is intended to show that Belfast's 'place in space' is subject to similar, and directly related, shifts and indeterminacies. As the city moves through the various stages of its history it can also be seen to undergo a concomitant process of relocation, as inhabitants and observers from various periods position it differently upon their mental and narrative maps. Eamonn Hughes also notes this phenomenon when he argues that 'Belfast itself is in play, not only historically, nor even yet only because of its unsure foundations. It is crucially in play even in its location.'[19]

This 'playfulness' has thus far been evident in broadly national terms through the city's refusal to accept finally either the Irish or British tags that writers attempt to hang upon it. It might be useful, therefore, to compare this playful, mobile Belfast with Colin Graham's recent theorisation of Irish culture in which Ireland becomes 'Ireland', a floating signifier that 'sails symbolically on the Gulf Stream, awaiting a docking with itself at some future (always future) moment'.[20] Like 'Ireland', Belfast is 'a place which, just as it is about to be placed, moves',[21] and both enjoy a sort of floating detachment that precludes any attempt to pin or tie them down. However, it must be remembered that Belfast's elusive mobility is largely due to the fact that it cannot be securely labelled 'Irish', and consequently both Ireland and 'Ireland' are places from which it is continually floating away. Furthermore, whereas 'Ireland' can be said to exist 'everywhere and nowhere'[22] as a perfected fantasy projected into a moment that is 'always future', Belfast can and must be located somewhere, even if that somewhere is both uncertain and provisional. 'Ireland' can never be a real place; Belfast can never be completely unreal. It seems clear, therefore that Graham's 'Ireland' and the 'floating' Belfast that I am positing here exemplify two different types of space, for while 'Ireland' is 'a utopia twice removed by deferral',[23] Belfast might usefully be thought of as an example of what Michel Foucault calls heterotopias, 'places that are outside all places, although they are actually localizable'.[24]

In his lecture, 'Different Spaces' ('*Des Espaces Autres*'), Foucault sets out to describe those different or 'other' spaces 'which are linked with all the others, and yet at variance somehow with all the other emplacements' that constitute normative or 'real' space.[25] These are divided roughly into two groups, utopias and heterotopias, and are distinguished by their relative relations to 'real' space. Utopias 'maintain a general relation of direct or inverse analogy with the real space of society' and are therefore 'spaces that are fundamentally and essentially

Belfast (Belfast, 1823); Jonathan Bardon, *Belfast: an illustrated history* (Belfast, 1983); W.A. Maguire, *Belfast* (Keele, 1993); Robert Johnstone, *Belfast: portraits of a city* (London, 1990); Emrys Jones, *A social geography of Belfast* (London, 1960); J.C. Beckett and R.E. Glasscock (eds), *Belfast: the origin and growth of an industrial city* (London, 1967); J.C. Beckett et al., *Belfast: the making of the city 1800–1914* (Belfast, 1983). 19 Eamonn Hughes, 'The urban dialectics of Belfast: cool breaths and flaming sewers', in *Cartography: the city: a catalyst arts project* (Belfast, 2000), p. 25. 20 Colin Graham, *Deconstructing Ireland: identity, theory, culture* (Edinburgh, 2001), p. 6. 21 Ibid., p. 4. 22 Ibid., p. 23. 23 Ibid., p. 7. 24 Michel Foucault, *Aesthetics, method, and epistemology*, ed. James D. Faubion (London, 2000), p. 178. 25 Ibid.

unreal'; while heterotopias are imagined to be 'sorts of actually realised utopias', an oxymoron that yokes the real to the unreal instead of simply opposing one to the other.[26] Furthermore, where utopias are absolutely different spaces in their unreal perfection, heterotopias are not only different or 'other' spaces: they are spaces *of* difference. In the third of six general principles, Foucault claims that 'the heterotopia has the ability to juxtapose in a single real place several emplacements that are incompatible in themselves'.[27] One of the examples he goes on to employ is that of the theatre stage, recalling Geddes' theatrical metaphor for the city in history, allowing for a consideration of Belfast as a heterotopian stage upon which what might crudely be termed 'Irish' and 'British' space are held in uneasy tension. This liminality is certainly a crucial aspect of the city's indeterminate, shifting location, yet to consider Belfast in relation only to Ireland and Britain is to lock it into a binary paradigm that unnecessarily limits the city's 'playfulness' by ignoring the larger European and global frameworks within which it may be considered. It is therefore worth returning to Foucault in order to borrow another heterotopian metaphor that may more accurately illustrate Belfast's ability to slip its moorings. 'The sailing vessel,' contends Foucault, 'is the heterotopia par excellence':

> [T]he ship is a piece of floating space, a placeless place, that lives by its own devices, that is self-enclosed and, at the same time, delivered over to the boundless expanse of the ocean, … from the sixteenth century up to our time, the ship has been at the same time not only the greatest instrument of economic development … but the greatest reservoir of imagination … In civilizations without ships the dreams dry up, espionage takes the place of adventure, and the police that of the corsairs.[28]

The ship is, of course, a particularly apt metaphor for Belfast because of its importance to the city's chief industries, not only as a product of its shipyards, but also as a vessel for imports and exports. Unsurprisingly then, this metaphor has been employed before and is perhaps elaborated upon most successfully in Ciarán Carson's poem, 'The Ballad of HMS *Belfast*,' which begins: 'On the first of April, *Belfast* disengaged her moorings, and sailed away/ From Old Belfast. Sealed orders held our destination, somewhere in the Briny Say'.[29] Carson significantly drops the troublesome 'HMS' of his title throughout the main body of the poem, having Belfast-as-ship sail away from its older incarnation towards 'the lands unascertained/ On maps'.[30] As so often in Carson's work, this idea combines the sense of movement across space with that of travelling through time, for, in forsaking the 'old Belfast' for one that promises to be new, the city-ship must symbolically leave one port in order to dock eventually in another. Importantly then, *Belfast* is a self-consciously heterotopian space of difference,

26 Ibid. 27 Ibid., p. 181. 28 Ibid., pp 184–5. 29 Ciarán Carson, *First language* (Loughcrew, 1993), p. 71. 30 Ibid., p. 72.

its motley crew being made up of 'Both Catestants and Protholics', while the ship itself is 'full-rigged like the Beagle, piston-driven like the Enterprise/ Express; each system was a back-up for the other, auxiliarizing verse with prose'[31] – much like Carson himself. This hybrid motif is further drawn out through the poem's preoccupation with metamorphoses and hallucinations, particularly those produced through intoxication. After one particularly drunken binge, the speaker and his fellow sailors 'felt neither fish nor flesh, but/ Breathed through gills of rum and brandy',[32] and the ship itself briefly becomes a 'bathyscope' trawling the 'vast and purple catacomb' of the deep for 'cloudy shipwrecks'.[33] Finally, the speaker deconstructs his fanciful tall tale, awakening the morning after the night before to find himself not in the 'urinous piazzas' of Vallambroso or Gibraltar, but in more familiar, but less salubrious, surroundings:

> And then the smell of docks and ropeworks. Horse-dung. The tolling of the
>   Albert clock.
> Its Pisan slant. The whirring of its ratchets. Then everything began to click:
> I lay in iron chains, alone, my aisling gone, my sentence passed.
> Grey Belfast dawn illuminated me, on boards the prison ship *Belfast*.[34]

Carson's *Belfast*, therefore, exhibits a similarly dialectical nature to Foucault's ship, functioning as both a fabulous schooner sailing on the currents of the imagination, and as a floating jail going nowhere in Belfast Lough. In this juxtaposition of adventure and incarceration Carson is illustrating one of the fundamental characteristics of the city, for as Burton Pike observes, 'the image of the city stands as the great reification of ambivalence, embodying a complex of contradictory foces in both the individual and the collective Western minds'.[35] The image of Belfast as prison is, as a number of critics have noted, a recurrent feature of fiction representations of the city.[36] Both Carson and Pike, however, insist that the city's dialectical complexity inevitably overspills such reductively one-dimensional representations. Belfast is neither only a place of purgatorial confinement, nor merely an 'instrument of economic development', but may also serve as, amongst other things, a 'reservoir of imagination'.

Importantly, there is a sense in which the Atlantic sailings of Carson's HMS *Belfast* parallel the actual city's progress through the 'Briny Says' of the late nineteenth and twentieth centuries. In this, Belfast's course was closely tied to its success within an increasingly international maritime economy. To this end, Christopher Harvie has argued that between 1880 and 1920 Belfast was one of a number of British ports that made up an arc of 'Atlantic cities',[37] which were

31 Ibid., p. 71. 32 Ibid., p. 72. 33 Ibid., p. 73. 34 Ibid., p. 74. 35 Burton Pike, *The image of the city in modern literature* (Princeton & London, 1981), p. 8. 36 See for example Eamonn Hughes, "Town of shadows': representations of Belfast in recent fiction', *Religion & Literature* 28:2–3 (Summer–Autumn 1996), 145, 149 and Laura Pelaschiar, 'Transforming Belfast: the evolving role of the city in Northern Irish fiction', *Irish University Review* 30:1 (Spring/Summer 2000), 122. 37 Christopher Harvie, 'From Garron Top to Caer Gybi: images of the inland sea', *Irish Review* 19

central to 'a capital-goods production economy' linking both sides of the
Atlantic.[38] These 'West British' Atlantic cities 'emerged as a sort of coastal federation of city-states bound more closely to one another by work and trade than
they were to their national hinterlands'.[39] Harvie notes, however, that this
Atlantic 'world' was a temporary phenomenon, 'contingent on a distinct technological and social intersection',[40] and as the global depression of the inter-war
years began to bite Belfast was forced to relocate again. From its position at the
forefront of the industrial world stage, Belfast receded into provincial obscurity
as work at its shipbuilding yards and linen factories dried up in the 1930s. W.
Black observes that after the First World War, 'the springs of expansion weakened dramatically',[41] circumstances largely unaltered when Belfast officially
became the capital of Northern Ireland in 1922.

In more recent times, Belfast has undergone several even more drastic and
high profile relocations. Since the latest outbreak of 'Troubles' in the late 1960s,
the city's image has gone from that of a dowdy middle-of-nowhere to an archetypal heart of darkness, the mythologized terrain upon which thriller plots
unfold. In such representations, argues Eamonn Hughes, 'Belfast is not Belfast
at all; it is simply a void, a blank space filled by novelists and film-makers with
stock properties',[42] and there is a related sense in which the city is no longer to
be found upon any maps of the 'civilised' world. For example, in pronouncing
Belfast 'one of the world's ugliest urban landscapes', Margaret Scanlan con-
signs Northern Ireland to the no-man's land of international politics: 'Since
1969, Northern Ireland ... is no longer a place where nothing happens. On the
contrary, it has lurched into the dubious company of Lebanon, Afghanistan,
and El Salvador as a place in which the frequency of violent events has rendered them inassimilable, incomprehensible.'[43] While keeping such 'dubious
company', however, Belfast can also be seen to have participated in a broader
experience of postmodern urbanity that stresses the connections, rather than
the disparities, that exist between it and other European and world cities. For
example, the group of thirty-something male friends in Robert McLiam
Wilson's *Eureka Street* (1996) exemplifies a new boomerang dimension to the
traditional Irish diaspora – 'They'd gone away, they'd come back' – that makes
it not entirely incongruous to mention Belfast in the same breath as Manchester,
Bayeaux, Bremen and Barcelona.[44] Remarking on this trend in Northern fiction, Laura Pelaschair argues that Belfast's image has undergone 'a dramatic
re-evaluation at the hands of a few young Northern novelists'[45] in the last fifteen years or so:

> [I]n the nineteen nineties Belfast has gradually become a new, fertile loca-
> tion, no longer a place from which escape is necessary, but rather a labora-

(Spring/Summer 1996), 45. 38 Ibid., p. 46. 39 Ibid., p. 49. 40 Ibid., p. 56. 41 W. Black, 'Industrial
change in the twentieth century', in Beckett and Glasscock (eds), *Belfast*, p. 163. 42 Hughes, '"Town
of shadows"' p. 141. 43 Margaret Scanlan, 'The unbearable present: Northern Ireland in four contemporary novels', *Etudes Irlandais* 10 (Dec. 1985), 145, 146. 44 Robert McLiam Wilson, *Eureka
Street* (London, 1997), p. 141. 45 Pelaschiar, 'Transforming Belfast' p. 122.

tory of opportunities, a post-modern place depicted as *the* only place where it is possible to build and articulate a (post)national conscience, the only location for any possible encyclopaedic, multivoiced and multi-ethnic development of Northern society.[46]

This is perhaps to overstate the case, and consequently to risk replacing one negative stereotype with another that is blithely positive. Yet it does assist in a further illustration of the city's peculiar urban dialectics if we recognize that Belfast's 'insular and historical 'dark side" is not simply supplanted by 'its European normalcy' *qua* Pelaschair,[47] but exists uneasily alongside it, as Wilson's novel admirably shows.

This contradictory amalgam of 'multivoiced and multi-ethnic' cosmopolitanism on the one hand, and the bleak vicissitudes of a seemingly intractable conflict on the other, is rendered strikingly in Albert Rechts' short but fascinating *Handbook to a Hypothetical City* (1986). Rechts' city is a doppelgänger for Belfast and his satirical weapon of choice is a sort of Swiftian parallelism, whereby Planters and Gaels are replaced by equally barbaric Mongols and Tartars, and the city's Christian sectarianisms are given an Islamic twist. In places, this tactic generates some very pungent humour, not least when the Rev. Ian Paisley is transfigured as the Ayatollah Omar, 'a most vociferous demagogue with a rousing and, sometimes, indelicate turn of phrase'.[48] Too often, however, Rechts seems merely to be recasting Belfast stereotypes in new and exotic forms, falling back on journalistic cliché and deterministic gloom more often than he delivers the welcome belly-laughs of which he is capable. A much more interesting, and genuinely radical, image of Belfast can be found, however, on the jacket sleeve of Rechts' book in the form of Hector McDonnell's pen and ink drawing of a transmogrified City Hall. McDonnell succeeds, with very little embellishment, in transforming the City Hall from a bastion of civic power and unionist pride into a splendid Eastern palace, adorned with slender towers and the distinctive reclining crescent moons of Islam. The familiar 'Ulster Says No' banner of the 1980s has been replaced by a message in Arabic, and a turbaned mullah with a paunch has usurped Queen Victoria's place on the marble plinth at the front of the building. A further touch of exotic 'colour' is added in the form of a few palm trees sprinkled around its base, whilst the whole image itself floats on a blank background beneath the bold-typed title. In this, there is a faint resemblance to Seán Hillen's 'paper collage', 'The Island of Newgrange, Co. Meath', which transports the Megalithic monument of its title to a tropical, palm-dotted island in front of which swirls a gaping whirlpool.[49] Indeed, like many of Hillen's images of 'Irelantis', McDonnell's City Hall 'undoes space

46 Ibid., p. 117. 47 Ibid., p. 122. 48 Albert Rechts, *Handbook to a hypothetical city* (Mullingar, 1986), p. 19. 49 See Seán Hillen and Fintan O'Toole, *Irelantis* (Dublin, 1999), or alternatively, http://www.irelantis.com. This image also appears on the front cover of Colin Graham's *Deconstructing Ireland*, implicitly representing the floating, utopian 'Ireland' discussed above.

and time' so that it 'exists outside sychronicity and diachronicity, but remembers both',[50] allowing Belfast to approach most closely the spatial condition of of Graham's 'Ireland', which paradoxically exists 'everywhere and nowhere'. There could perhaps be no greater contrast between this version of Belfast City Hall and Brian Moore's famous depiction of it as a 'designated centre' of Joycean paralysis in *The Lonely Passion of Judith Hearne* (1955).[51] Eamonn Hughes has argued that Moore's distaste 'is not for the city qua city but for the way in which this 'designated centre' stills and orders its potential',[52] and McDonnell's City Hall exhibits a similar dread of inertia, effectively decentring the city in order to highlight its mobile unpredictability. McDonnell's image, therefore, seems to capture the zenith of Belfast's locational indeterminacy, its slippery and evasive sense of place.

To accept such decentrings uncritically is to risk complicity with the rise of the late-capitalist 'everycity', where banal anonymity is passed off as 'cosmopolitanism'. That is one dead end we urgently need to avoid. On the contrary, this paper has sought to provide a deconstructive polemic against the fatalistic rhetoric of immutability that continues to pertain both in and about Belfast, and to affirm in its stead the dialectic of materialisation and etherealisation that Lewis Mumford regards as fundamental to the city in history: '[B]oth etherialization and materialization are indispensable to progressive human development ... Both stability and constant creativity are needed, and that combination was the supreme gift of the city.'[53]

Glenn Patterson and Ciaran Carson: the new Northern Irish literature

FRANCESCA BOVONE, TRINITY COLLEGE, DUBLIN

Literature has always given a very static image of Northern Ireland, in particular of its capital city. Belfast has been depicted not only as violent, but also as provincial, bigoted, backward and unprogressive. Novelists have used Belfast as the set for gloomy stories of crime, while poets have tended to recover an epic and rural past in order to oppose it to the disappointing present.

It is undeniable, though, that starting from the Seventies, the cultural changes that have characterized many European cities have reached Belfast as well, incit-

50 Graham, *Deconstructing Ireland*, p. 25. 51 Brian Moore, *The lonely passion of Judith Hearne* (London, 1994), p. 103. 52 Hughes, "'Town of shadows,'" p. 150. 53 Lewis Mumford, *The city in history: its origins, its transformations, and its prospects* (London, 1961), p. 113.

ing the most receptive authors to look for novel images and techniques to depict the new Northern Irish reality.

Amongst these writers it is obligatory to include Glenn Patterson and Ciaran Carson. These authors, each in his own extremely original and innovative manner, have altered both the vision of the Northern Irish writer as limited by specific themes and structures, and that of their nation as a static place. Patterson and Carson have descried another reading of their city, pointing out change as its real constant. Belfast is no longer solely the site of sectarian violence, bombings and destruction. It is also, and maybe first of all, a modern city, an ever-growing shape-shifter that is trying to recast itself in order to face the new economic and architectural development, as is very well symbolized by the theme of land reclamation, which, as we will see, is central to the work of both authors.

Belfast changes quickly, but its transformations take place in the context of a total respect for the past, for the history of the city. Carson and Patterson are both deeply aware of the fact that the only way to move on is to acknowledge, understand, remember and accept the past. They no longer see it as opposed, but as aligned to the present and, thus, to the future. The new light they cast upon Belfast induces a spontaneous similitude with other urban realities. In this sense it can be said that Patterson's and Carson's innovations manage to cross borders, to take literature beyond regional limits. Indeed, this paper aims at demonstrating that these writers do not write for an exclusively Northern Irish audience, and that the only way to understand the importance of their work is by grasping the authors' will to relate the Belfast experience to that of other urban environments.

The idea of the effacing of borders pervades with insistence all the works of Glenn Patterson. 'I do not believe in original states', he has declared, 'The history of the world actually is just one of people moving all the time … The closer you get to the border, the less necessary a border is.'[1] So, in *Fat Lad*, Granny Linden 'had lived in two different countries without ever moving more than three doors from the house where she was born'.[2] Clive White, owner of the International Hotel, in *The International*, 'developed a special fondness for border towns and border people. He admired the pragmatism that could wish the boundary away'.[3] Patterson likes cities because they are able to contain differences: 'They are places of mixture as opposed to countries and borders which are exclusive.'[4]

Black Night at Big Thunder Mountain is the novel in which mixture, movement, the crossing of borders, both physical and ideal, are more evident. The characters come from three different nations: Sam is from the United States, Ray is from Belfast and Ilse is from Stuttgart, even though she has lived in Berlin

1 Elke D'Hohker & Hedwig Schwall, 'Interview with Glenn Patterson', *Études Irlandaises* 25:1 (Spring 2000), 93, 94. 2 Glenn Patterson, *Fat lad* (London, 1993), p. 141. 3 Glenn Patterson, *The International* (London, 2000), p. 122. 4 D'Hohker and Schwall, 'Interview with Glenn Patterson', p. 95.

in the past few years. Their three histories, 'flare at random',[5] but are united in the virtual city that is Euro Disney. They are exiles and they love cities for their variety and their ability to change and to make diversities mingle. Sam, the American, is an absolute worshipper of Walt Disney's philosophy, according to which the animated world has no boundaries. To Sam, Disney's 'pleasure cities were films you could inhabit, ringed around with a railroad, laced with lesser tracks, like subplots, with a wienie, as Disney liked to say, at the end of every street to keep this whole thing moving'.[6] Ray left Belfast seven years before, but recalls it with extreme affection. 'It was instinctive in him, a city of shortcuts and sudden turns learnt as a child.'[7] His city could 'accommodate so much life' and he could remember 'a story for each street or landmark'.[8] He loves his city for its variety and generosity. On the day that he was born, 'Belfast was offered to him complete; it brimmed, but somehow made room for him. He swam in it and felt it flood him.'[9] However, Ray doesn't overlook war and violence (Patterson never does). He recounts that by 1967 Belfast was coming down around him and days were punctuated by the bombings. He experienced violence, racism and destruction first hand; he even let himself get involved in a racist reprisal, for which he was sent to prison. When he was released, he was astonished at how much his city had changed in only ten months. But, while Belfast was 'attempting at a more benign aspect, its parades had become more blood-curdling and overt'.[10] Ilse isn't foreign to bombings, violence and sectarianism either. When World War II was over, though, she was only four, so she mostly witnessed Stuttgart's effort to rebuild itself and fill in the gaps left by the bombs. Berlin was the city where she directly experienced the effects of intestine divisions. She could see the Wall from her house, and every time she looked at it, she wished some day there would be a mixture between East and West. But, when the Wall came down, she did not witness communion, as she had hoped, but only escape. Nonetheless, she loved Berlin 'for its incompleteness. There was such a desire to make use, to build from this jumble something altogether new. Everything was experiment.'[11]

It is puzzling that, even after the publication of *Black Night at Big Thunder Mountain* and of *The International,* journalists keep on asking Glenn Patterson if he writes for a *specifically* Northern Irish audience. Reading his novels, one senses that the author is implicitly dialoguing with his own country's audience. However, he doesn't write *specifically* for a Northern Irish audience. He never has. First of all, it must be pointed out that Irish literature has had no influence on him as a writer. In fact, the novel that most inspired him and that made his decision to turn to Northern Ireland for his subject matter effective, to 're-imagine' it, was Salman Rushdie's *Midnight Children*, where countries become collective fictions. The will to align the Belfast experience to that of other cities is absolutely clear since the very beginning of his career and it witnesses the author's

5 Glenn Patterson, *Black night at big thunder mountain* (London, 1996), p. 62. 6 Ibid., p. 70. 7 Ibid., p. 52. 8 Ibid., p. 92. 9 Ibid., p. 52. 10 Ibid., p. 141. 11 Ibid., 118.

intention to address an audience that goes beyond his home-country's borders. When he wrote *Burning Your Own*, Glenn Patterson was living in Norwich. It was the mid 1980s, the miners' strike was just over, leaving behind it the effects of violent riots and a marked polarisation between different communities. By looking at England, he hoped to find new perspectives from which to view what had happened in Northern Ireland, in particular the way in which small communities react to oppressive social pressures.[12]

It is due to this implicit similarity between Belfast and other European urban realities that Patterson feels the need to update the fictional map of Belfast. He thinks that 'the fictional representations of Northern Ireland got stuck about 1972, and it doesn't look like that anymore'.[13] The theme of land reclamation is central to *Fat Lad* and it is used as a metaphor for the ever-changing city striving to update itself. At the very beginning of the novel, on the bus from the airport to Belfast city centre, Drew, the protagonist, talks to a man who, thinking he's not a native, tells him how Belfast's soil was 'all underwater'.[14] 'The city centre was entirely built on mudflats, exposed by the retreating lough, ... sleech, ... or slobland.'[15] The concept of land reclamation stresses the continual demolition and rebuilding of the city. This process is very well explained by Carson in *Belfast Confetti*'s 'Brick': as the city was demolished by the war 'the tall chimneys and the catacomb-like kilns of the brickworks crumbled back into the earth, the very city recycled itself, and disassembled buildings were poured into the sleech of the lough-shore to make new land; vast armies of binmen or waste-disposal experts laboured through the years, transforming countless tons of brock into *terra firma*'.[16] This whole process of deconstruction and revision, as Patterson defines it, is to be seen as the sign that 'the city is constantly redefining itself',[17] and that change is the only constant of urban environment anywhere. Continual transformations, especially at the rate they have been happening in Belfast, are, of course, destabilising, both socially and psychologically. But, at the same time, they confer a liberating potential on the city: they 'resist the closure of traditional interpretations in which one unchanging territory is endlessly contested by two mutually exclusive tribes: the old politics of one thing or the other. Identity becomes dynamic, rather than birth-given and static. Concepts like flux and exchange replace the language of original states.'[18] Only by removing Patterson's works from traditional interpretations will it be possible to understand their potential to the full.

Transformations, dynamism and differences are very well represented by the countless individual stories the city is composed of. This is most clear in *The International*, where Patterson shows how the universal resides in details. In his

12 See Niall McGrath, 'Glenn Patterson', *Edinburgh Review* 93 (Spring 1995), 42–3. 13 Ibid., p. 50. 14 Patterson, *Fat lad*, p. 6. 15 Ibid., p. 18. 16 Ciaran Carson, *Belfast confetti* (Loughcrew, 1991), p. 73. 17 McGrath, 'Glenn Patterson', p. 47. 18 Glenn Patterson, 'I am a Northern Irish novelist', in Ian A. Bell (ed.), *Peripheral visions: images of nationhood in contemporary British fiction* (Cardiff, 1995), p. 151.

essay 'I am a Northern Irish Novelist', he states that 'The act of reading is the making of connections, the negotiation of the space between the particular and the general.'[19] This novel is, indeed, extraordinarily detailed. So, even if, like *Fat Lad*, it is set in a very precise moment in history, that is the day before the Civil Rights Association met in January 1967, and in a very precise place, the International Hotel, we cannot help but notice that Patterson avoids pointing out the political or religious preferences of the characters. Danny, the protagonist, says of his parents that 'in this most God-obsessed of cities, they had lost their religion … One had been born Catholic, the other Protestant [but] in the absence of grandparents I was never quite sure which was which.'[20] The details that Patterson underlines are especially those that make his characters more human, and consequently universal.

The relationship between the particular and the general is just as close as that between past and present. In fact, even highlighting changes and development, Patterson never discards the past. It is always there for the reader to read and for his characters to remember. It is especially in *Fat Lad* , set in 1990, that the author proves how, in order to move on, both a country (or a city) and its people must understand, remember and accept the past. Coming back after many years spent in England, Drew expects a backward and provincial Belfast. He can't tolerate his home-city because he associates it with public and private violence, as his father used to hit him. Drew has forgiven neither his father nor his city. But the Belfast he finds on his return is very different from the one he expected: it is a city going through a modernising process.

This idea of the past coexisting and mingling with the present permeates the whole novel in very different respects. It is introduced in the description of Bookstore, which has taken the place of a shop that had been in Belfast since the 1930s, but has kept the beautiful mosaic pavements; the new big Mall that is about to be built in the city centre will have a glassy façade, but its sides and back will be made of the old, inevitable Belfast brick. The idea Drew has for a commercial for his shop springs to his mind while he is looking through a book of old photographs of the city. His slogan will rely on the feeling of trust the past can bring about, associating the recently opened shop, set in Castle Place, with the old Belfast Castle, the very symbol of the history of the city. In Belfast the past coexists with the present also in the perceiving of the typical city sounds: the shooting in the distance and the noise of helicopters that have underpinned city life for the past twenty years are suffocated by the sounds of modernisation, the music coming from cars and shops and, more importantly, the noise of machines at work in the numerous building sites.

While he witnesses the changes taking place in Belfast, Drew's feelings start changing as well: the city slowly grows on him, until he literally loves it; this process goes hand in hand with Drew's forgiveness of his father's past behav-

19 Ibid., p. 152. 20 Patterson, *The International*, p. 41.

iour. By the end of the novel, he has managed to come to terms with his father, his city and his own identity. He is ready to leave Belfast to seek job advancements in other European cities. But this time he will not be fleeing, as he feels that he is leaving something very important and indissoluble behind him.

Ciaran Carson is another eloquent example of an author who has decided to operate outside given conventions, both in terms of metre and of contents. Opening his collections *The Irish for No* and *Belfast Confetti* one immediately notices the shape of the poems on the page. They are made of very long lines (up to twenty-two syllables) that go against the standard iambic line and facilitate the reproduction of a speaking voice telling a story to which other stories keep on adding, making it impossible to discern a beginning or an end. Carson denies the reconcilability offered by conventional forms:

> Poetry is about the urge to invent a story. To me, poems emerge out of a story structure … At the end of the day [my poems could be] a song or a tune or a reel. [Formally] I would describe them as being based on the structure of a reel, for instance the line is based on the length of four bars of a reel, or it is the long line of the Irish song. The line has to sing, in some way. It is very important to get a flow in the line … you do not want absolutely stock line.[21]

Like Patterson, Carson describes a city made up of individual stories where the particular becomes universal. The Belfast Carson fashions is a fragmented city. Belfast is composed of brands, street names, maps, local stories, national history and personal memories. It is a collage of innumerable little fragments, so that it is impossible to conceive it as a whole. In *The Star Factory* the author writes: 'Now that I can see the city's microscopic bits … I wonder how I might assemble them …; I must write it.'[22] But the need to write down a fragmented reality implies the use of a fragmented language, symbolized in the by now famous image we find in the poem 'Belfast Confetti', where violence has caused the explosion of language itself:

> Suddenly, as the riot squad moved in, it was raining
>   Exclamation marks,
>   Nuts, bolts, nails, car-keys. A fount of broken type. And the
>   explosion
> Itself – an asterisk on the map …
>
>   I was trying to complete a sentence in my head, but it kept
> Stuttering
> All the alleyways and side-streets blocked with stops and
> Colons.[23]

21 McGrath, 'Ciaran Carson', p. 63. 22 Ciaran Carson, 'The model shop', *The star factory* (London, 1997), p. 15. 23 Ciaran Carson, 'Belfast Confetti', *The Irish for no* (Loughcrew, 1994). p. 31.

The images of mental mapping and the labyrinth underpin all Carson's poetry. The author needs to map the city in his mind, for maps of Belfast cannot be trusted: 'There is a map of the city that shows the bridge that was never built, a map which shows the bridge that collapsed; the streets that never existed. Today's plan is already yesterday's, the streets that were there are gone.'[24] Again, in 'Question Time': 'Maps and street directories are suspect. No, don't trust maps, for they avoid the moment ... I know this place like the back of my hand, except, who knows how many hairs there are, how many freckles?'[25] Sectarian violence has turned Belfast into a shape shifter. 'The odds change, the borders move', he says in 'Barfly'.[26] Everything is provisional; everything needs to be continuously revised. And, in 'Revised Version', the speaking character realizes that maps can only exist in his imagination. He himself is the map of a city that is being 'improved, wiped out, began again, imagined, changed'.[27] And changes in the map of Belfast are so sudden, that the actual city can be the only map of itself.

Carson often describes these abrupt alterations in the configuration of the city's topography through metonymic images, the most striking appearing in the poem 'Smithfield Market', describing the old Victorian market after the bombing of 1974:

Sidelong to the arcade, the glassed-in April cloud ...
Gets lost in shadowed aisles and inlets, branching into
    Passages, into cul-de-sacs,
Stalls, compartments, alcoves. Everything unstitched,
    Unravelled – mouldy fabric,
Rusted heaps of nuts and bolts, electrical spare parts: the
    ammunition dump
In miniature ...

Since everything went up in smoke, no entrances, no exits.
...   I glimpsed a
    map of Belfast
I the ruins: obliterated streets, the faint impression of a key.
Something many-toothed, elaborate, stirred briefly in the
    Labyrinth.[28]

The image of the city as a labyrinth is certainly not a novelty, but here there is an explicit reference to the Minotaur, its original monstrous inhabitant. The mythical labyrinth, the one Minos had built, was in the bowels of the earth, and the remains of the market are in the deep hole left by the explosion. The labyrinth was a dismally silent place; the only noises were the sporadic screams of the victims designated to feed the monster. The silence and desolation that

24 Ciaran Carson, 'Turn again', *Belfast confetti*, p. 11. 25 Ibid., p. 57. 26 Ibid., p. 55. 27 Ibid., p. 68.
28 Carson, *The Irish for no*, p. 52.

follow the explosion of a bomb are just as spectral. And bombs, like the half-man, half-bull monster, devour human beings. A key is evoked, but there is only a 'faint impression' of it. There is no Ariadne thread here; no key can provide a way out. On the contrary, if there is a thread, it seems to lead only deeper and deeper to the centre of the labyrinth, making it impossible to ever exit it.

Associated with the image of the labyrinth is that of the spiral, which appears very early in Carson's poetry, in 'The Insular Celts', included in his first collection, *The New Estate*: 'In the spirals of their brooches is seen the flight of one thing into the other'.[29] This shape is also evoked in the 'loops and spirals of Irish dancing',[30] or in the 'spiral stairwell'[31] Mr Hyde runs down to escape from Dr Jekyll in 'Jawbox', just to make a few examples. The maps of the first labyrinths ever built, in their circularity leading to a centre, are reminiscent of the shape of a spiral. The first thing that springs to mind when thinking about spirals is the nautilus, whose fascination resides in the fact that it retains the past in a fossilized present, even being, at the same time, a shape in formation.[32] Just like the spires of a shell, Carson's Belfast contains its past: it is written on every street, on every building, on corners, walls and roofs. Like the Belfast described by both Patterson and Carson, a shell is built on successive strata. Belfast is a spiral city in that it keeps its memories. Both authors stress the importance of remembrance. In *The International*, at the end of the novel, Daniel states: 'We're powerful people for remembering here, I hope that is one thing we don't forget.'[33] The city remembers and contains its past not only in its buildings, but especially in its inhabitants' memories. Through them, past and present coexist in harmony, in a continual mutual exchange that keeps the city alive.

There is only one instance in which it seems possible to perceive the city as a whole and that is when it is seen from above, either by the poet from the top of a mountain, or by the eye of the military helicopters flying over the city. In 'Question Time' Carson writes: 'if there is an ideal map, which shows the city as it is, it may exist in the eye of the helicopter ratcheting overhead, its search-light fingering and scanning the micro-chip deviations ...'[34]

In 'Patchwork'[35] Carson remembers climbing a mountain with his father. Once on the summit, his dad would point out the landmarks of the city and, in *The Star Factory*: 'Come Spring, I knew my father and I would climb Black Mountain ... When we'd attained the celestial summit, we'd sit down on the undulating heather, and he'd light up a Park Drive cigarette and point it towards the various details of the urban map spread out below.'[36] Sometimes, the poet seems to feel the need to distance himself from Belfast in order to understand it better: viewing the city from above is the only way to avoid getting lost in its labyrinth.

29 Ciaran Carson, *The new estate and other poems* (Ireland, 1988), p. 12. 30 Carson, *The Irish for no*, p. 37. 31 Carson, *Belfast Confetti*, p. 94. 32 Cf. Maddalena Mazzocut-Mis, *La città e la conchiglia: Suggestioni a partire dalla morfologia di Calvino*, www.filolinux.dipafilo.unimi.it/itinera. 33 Patterson, *The International*, p. 318. 34 Carson, *Belfast confetti*, p. 58. 35 Carson, *The Irish for no*, p. 59. 36 Carson, *The star factory*, p. 166.

Carson's idea that the city is fully understandable only if viewed from above is reminiscent of the concept expressed by Calvino in the description of the carpet of Eudoxia, one of his *Invisible Cities*: 'In Eudoxia, ... a carpet is preserved in which you can observe the city's true form.'[37] Each part of the carpet represents a specific place of the city. It seems impossible to discern an order in Eudoxia, but the carpet proves that even if from inside the city you can only grasp an incomplete perspective of it, a spot exists from which the city shows its real proportions, its precise geometrical scheme. 'It is easy to get lost in Eudoxia, but when you stare at the carpet you recognize the street you were seeking' in one of its threads.[38] 'Every inhabitant of Eudoxia compares the carpet's immobile order with his own image of the city ... and each can find, concealed among the arabesques, an answer, the story of his life, the twists of fate.'[39] The carpet of Eudoxia is exactly like the map of Belfast as Carson sees it from the top of the mountain: it is an ideal map. Moreover, the carpet can be assimilated to the patchwork quilt Carson mentions so often in his works. It is first introduced at the end of *The New Estate*, in 'The Patchwork Quilt' written in the shape of a monologue by his Grandma, who stitched the quilt together:

> I think at first I had a pattern
> In my head, though I think now
> It changed. For when I look at it, it's hard
> To see where I begun, or where I ended.
> Then I recognise a bit of print, Janie's blouse
> The day she fell in the river. But then again, it looks
> Like something else. There are so many
> Lines, so many checks.[40]

Like Belfast, the quilt is made of mendings, stitchings and unravels. Like the city, it holds together the pieces of the past, but recalls them in a labyrinthine way. Similarly, in 'Patchwork', the last poem of *The Irish for No*, the author remembers bits and pieces of his own past and that of his whole family, finding, in the end, a suitable image for his mind's proceedings in that of his Grandma's quilt.

In her beautiful essay 'The Aesthetic and the Territorial',[41] Edna Longley talks about a 'territorial imperative' for Irish poetry, thus defining its strong attachment to the land of origin. Carson's poems definitely respond to this imperative, but not in the traditional sense Longley refers to. Carson demonstrates that it can concern not only the country, but also the city. Moreover, he manages to align Belfast to other European cities: violence is not only a characteristic of Belfast, and sectarianism and racism, as he describes them, are a constant in

37 Italo Calvino, *Invisible cities* (London, 1997), p. 96. 38 Ibid., p. 96. 39 Ibid., p. 97. 40 Carson, *The new estate*, p. 12. 41 *Contemporary Irish poetry. a collection of critical essays* (London, 1993), pp 63–84.

modern cities, due either to immigration or to historical oppositions, religious or political, that were never solved. The intestine divisions and wars compel the city to continually revise and rebuild itself and change, as we have seen, is the constant of every modern city. With his novels, Patterson moves one step forward, perceiving change as a liberating force.

Neither author proposes a solution for their city, nor do they try to establish responsibilities or to explain why certain things happen. They simply describe Belfast according to the way they perceive and see it and to the affection they feel for it. They tell stories of Belfast people, but the readers they have in mind certainly also live over the frontier of their nation. It is up to us to be sensitive enough to understand that they are writing for an audience that goes beyond Northern Irish borders. Otherwise we will get stuck in the traditional schemes of interpretation the authors themselves are willing to escape, and in our eyes Belfast will always be the static, hopeless city that is just not there anymore.

Camping in Utopia: Frank McGuinness' Carthaginians and the queer aesthetic

DAVID CREGAN, TRINITY COLLEGE, DUBLIN

In her book *Foucault and Queer Theory* Tasmin Spargo argues that queer theories serve as strategic tools for analysing representational techniques. She claims that 'queer' describes a diverse range of critical practices and priorities: readings of the representation of same sex desire in literary texts, films, music, images; analyses of the political power relations of sexuality; critiques of the sex-gender system; studies of transsexual and transgender identification, of sadomasochism and of transgressive desires.[1]

Embarking upon a 'queer' analysis of the contemporary Irish dramatist Frank McGuinness' dramatic body of work is not a project aimed at uncovering an alternative reading of his plays, but is rather an articulation of a complex range of queer topics which appear consistently in his work, and, as I argue, exist as intrinsic to his artistic vision.[2] In other words, reading McGuinness' texts and

[1] Tasmin Spargo, *Foucault and queer theory* (Cambridge, 1999), p. 9. [2] Throughout the paper I will refer to the word 'queer' in much the same way that queer theorists do: it is a term used to destabilize essentialist notions of the categories of gay, straight and bisexual. It is a term which, consequently, permits fluidity and cannot or should not only be associated solely with homosexuality. In other words, you do not need to be gay to write 'queer', nor are all gay writers 'queer'. Not all aspects of homosexual subjectivity are 'queer', but some aspects of heterosexual subjectivity are. This being said, it is a term which emerges out of the experience of dissident subjectivities and certainly includes

analysing performances of his plays through a queer theoretical lens is not to project onto the work an analysis which wishfully desires to justify queer elements within the writing, but is, however, the illumination of the queer space which these plays fundamentally inhabit. The queer space in which his writing exists lives within the greater canonical context of the Irish dramatic tradition, regardless of its popular or critical recognition. Consequently, a queer reading is not simply an academic or ideological aspiration, but is rather an archaeological-type uncovering of a hidden, lost or subverted aspect of Irish culture.

In his play *Carthaginians*, McGuinness contributes to clearing away the dust which for generations has covered over this often anomalous culture of queer physical positions and alternative ideological visions.3 This play focuses on a diverse gathering of citizens of the city of Derry in Northern Ireland, camping out in a cemetery on the outskirts of town, waiting for the resurrection of the dead. All of the characters are dealing, in one way or another, with the effects of the historical event of Bloody Sunday on themselves and their city. On 30 January 1972 several unarmed men, participating in a civil rights march through the city of Derry in Northern Ireland, were shot and killed by the Parachute Regiment of the British Army on what has come to be known as Bloody Sunday. In *Bloody Sunday in Derry: What Really Happened* Eamonn McCann describes the government response to the events of that day: 'Two days after Bloody Sunday, on 1 February, Prime Minister Edward Heath announced in the House of Commons that the Lord Chief Justice, Lord Widgery, had been appointed to inquire into the deaths in Derry'.4 The British establishment and media saw the appointment of Widgery as a sign of how seriously the government were taking the fatal events of that afternoon. And yet, there was a degree of anxiety from the Catholic neighbourhoods of Bogside and Creggan as to whether he could be trusted to reveal the truth. Widgery's eventual conclusion was that the British soldiers had acted justifiably in defence against IRA attack. His report was filled with 'inconsistencies, illogicalities, and untruths'.5 Lord Widgery was accused of viewing the events 'through a prism of class and national prejudice' which rendered a distorted impression of reality.6 It is this unfathomable sense of betrayal and confusion experienced by the people of Bogside and Creggan that McGuinness engages in his play *Carthaginians*.

The title of the play implies a connection with Virgil's *The Aeneid*. Where historical and political comparisons of space and time bear the weight of similarities in imperialist oppression and domination, my analysis seeks to unearth a far less serious, although equally politically ambitious, connection contained within McGuinness' reference to the classical text. I believe that a queer reading of McGuinness' *Carthaginians* reveals a much more playful engagement with this epic of antiquity as he weaves it into a series of iconic references by

or even highlights the homo and bi-sexual theoretical positions. 3 Frank McGuinness, *Carthaginians* in *Frank McGuinness: Plays 1* (London, 1996). 4 Eamonn McCann, *Bloody Sunday in Derry: what really happened* (Dingle, 2000), p. 91. 5 Ibid. 6 Ibid.

the implementation of what is described by queer theorists interested in the theory and practice of gay camp as a 'queer aesthetic'.

In her seminal text on the subject of camp, 'Notes on Camp,' Susan Sontag describes camp as 'sensibility – unmistakably modern, a variant of sophistication … esoteric – something of a private code, a badge of identity' and as a 'taste [that] tends to develop very unevenly'.[7] It is a quality that is discernable within a person, a style of behaviour, or an object. Camp people or things usually reside on the margins of the mainstream, and are always playful in relation to the persons or objects that capture its fancy. Sontag also classifies camp as 'a certain mode of aestheticism. It is one way of seeing the world as an aesthetic phenomenon. That way, the way of Camp, is not in terms of beauty but in terms of the degree of artifice, of stylisation.'[8] Although camp is not exclusively a homosexual aesthetic, historically it has become associated largely with, if not entirely co-opted by, the gay community. 'Camp taste turns its back on the good-bad axis of ordinary aesthetic judgement. Camp doesn't reverse things. It doesn't argue that the good is bad, or the bad is good. What it does is to offer for art (and life) a different – a supplementary – set of standards.'[9]

This 'queer aesthetic,' which *Carthaginians* embodies, is rooted in these very notions and practices of camp. The *Webster's II New College Dictionary* defines camp as 'A place where a group of people, as soldiers, are temporarily billeted in makeshift shelters, as tents or huts' or as 'A group of persons, parties, or states favourable to a common cause,' and finally as 'An affectation or appreciation of manners and tastes usually considered outlandish, vulgar or banal; banality, vulgarity, or artificiality when appreciated for its humour.'[10] These rudimentary definitions of camp indicate the word's illusiveness in relation to a single definitional categorisation, while simultaneously indicating its elasticity as a noun, inclusively denoting person, place and thing.

This trifold definition of camp allows for a queer analysis of *Carthaginians* which includes a closer look at the public geographical space which McGuinness' citizens inhabit, the particular subjective positions which these characters represent, and finally a common aesthetic which binds this peculiar Derry subculture together. The characters of this play represent an oddly exclusive gathering of seemingly disjunctive personalities, united with one another in their experience of personal or social alienation. In the combination of place, person, and aesthetic in this play McGuinness brings together the political, the dramatic, and, above all, the excessive characteristics of gay camp in order to artistically revisit the tragic events of Bloody Sunday; an event which provides the disheartening historical and emotional backdrop for *Carthaginians*.

The camp aesthetic is not, however, a completely unproblematic means of representation for McGuinness to employ in relation to a memory that contin-

---

7 Susan Sontag, 'Notes on "camp"' in Fabio Cleto (ed.), *Camp: queer aesthetics and the performing subject* (Ann Arbor, 2002), pp 53–4. 8 Ibid. 9 Ibid., p. 61. 10 *Webster's new college dictionary* (Boston, 1995), p. 160.

ues to serve as a depository for such deep and complex feelings of injustice in Northern Ireland. 'Taken for granted to be apolitical', camp's frivolity and comedy can, at first, appear to mock a serious and sensitive subject.[11] However, I argue that McGuinness employs camp as a type of cultural resistance that challenges meaning and reality in much the same way as his treatment of history does. Instead of rejecting the mythical status of the often times static historical memories which support and uphold versions of national identity, McGuinness employs them in order to point out their fictional instability. *Carthaginians* works within the crippling collective disappointment, confusion, and sense of loss in Derry in order to represent the ongoing complexity of people's relationship to this dangerously sensitive and highly charged political experience. In *Saint=Foucault*, David Halperin attempts to further define camp by describing its ability to work from within social or political systems of meaning:

> Camp, after all, is a form of cultural resistance that is entirely predicated on a shared consciousness of being inescapably situated within a powerful system of social and sexual meanings. Camp resists the power of that system from within by means of parody, exaggeration, amplification, theatricalisation, and literalisation tacit codes of conduct – codes whose very authority derives from their privilege of never having to be explicitly articulated, and thus from their customary immunity to critique.[12]

McGuinness makes use of camp in an effort to resolve feelings about Bloody Sunday. For McGuinness, camp functions as a queer prism through which the inconsistencies and untruths of Bloody Sunday are revealed, and work towards reconciliation can begin.

The complexity of both the categorisation and definition of the word camp creates a sort of 'discursive resistance, a semiotic excess, which translates directly into the exuberant, virtually inexhaustible camp corpus of reference. Representational excess, heterogeneity, and *gratuitousness* of reference, in constituting a major *raison d'être* of camp's fun and exclusiveness, both signal and contribute to an overall resistance to definition.'[13] The mobility and inconclusiveness of the term makes it a particularly strong analytical tool in any queer study that fundamentally seeks to disrupt essentialist categories. 'Tentatively approached as *sensibility, taste,* or *style,* reconceptualized as *aesthetic* or *cultural economy,* and later asserted/reclaimed as *(queer) discourse,*' camp offers a multivalent lens through which to interpret something as complex and layered as dramatic representation.[14] *Carthaginians* is so peculiar in setting, so diverse in character, and so completely excessive in representation and reference, that it requires this type of broad interpretive tool to match its dramaturgical breadth.

11 Moe Meyer (ed.), *The politics and poetics of camp* (London, 1994), p. 6.   12 David Halperin, *Saint=Foucault: towards a gay hagiography* (New York, 1995), p. 9.   13 Cleto, 'Introduction: queering the camp' in *Camp*, p. 3.   14 Ibid., p. 2.

In 'Campe-Toi! On the Origins and Definitions of Camp', Mark Booth emphasizes the marginality of the subject who chooses camp as a mode of political self-representation:

> To be camp is to present oneself as being committed to the marginal with a commitment greater than the marginal merits ... Camp self-parody presents the self as being wilfully irresponsible and immature, the artificial nature of the self-presentation making it a sort of off-stage theatricality, the shameless insincerity of which may be provocative, but also forestalls criticism by its ambivalence.[15]

Dido, McGuinness' gay, drag-queen protagonist in *Carthaginians*, is this type of character; an individual involved in the same project of self-representation and identification with the margins. It is interesting to examine how McGuinness introduces the character of Dido, whom, I would suggest, is the representational embodiment of the 'queer aesthetic' that permeates this production. Into the melancholia of the cemetery enters a creature clad in a colourful suit with trousers cut about six inches above the shoe, revealing a garish pair of striped socks and a pair of blue leather boots; an outfit which defies any attempt at complying with the norms of fashion. Under his suit he wears a T-shirt that reads 'Arm the Unemployed.' He enters pushing a child's pram and irreverently singing 'Danny Boy.' McGuinness uses the character of Dido as a means of dramatic anarchy, as he dispels the gloom and darkness, the sadness and anguish, of both the graveyard and its residents with the frivolity, the humour, and the sexually charged subversive language of camp.

In scene four of *Carthaginians* Dido writes a play titled *The Burning Balaclava*, allotting new 'roles' to each member of the cast. This play-within-a-play serves as a parody of life in Derry since the beginning of the troubles as it literally 'theatricalises' the violence of sectarian divisions in the North. Towards the end of *The Burning Balaclava* Dido calls out stage directions after arming all his new characters with water-pistols:

> DIDO: Our scene shifts to a Derry Street. Quick, everybody, pistols and balaclavas. Not you.
> HARK: You're in the middle of an ambush. Run through it with the Sacred Heart. Don't worry, he'll protect you. Right, everybody. Ready. Run, Hark, run. Squirt, everybody, squirt. Get that Sacred Heart. Stop the fight. Our scene changes to a Derry kitchen. A Derry mother nurses her Sacred Heart.
> MAELA: Ma, ma, has there been an ambush?
> HARK: There's been an ambush, son. Look, look.
> MAELA: Ma, your Sacred Heart.

15 Mark Booth, 'Campe-Toi! On the origins and definitions of camp' in Cleto (ed.) *Camp*, p. 69.

HARK: My Sacred Heart, son. My Sacred Heart. Son, son, where were you when my Sacred Heart was riddled with bullets? Where were you?[16]

McGuinness uses this dramatic technique to disrupt the unity of the linear plot previously established. *The Burning Balaclava*, working in line with the camp aesthetic of the play itself, becomes a queer moment that challenges and confuses the audience's perception of reality. Although McGuinness' play-within-a-play is highly exaggerated in its campiness the audience is nonetheless easily transported from one plot to the other, making transparent a central objective in queer theory: the disruption and disturbance of dominant narratives, and the subsequent replacement of them with alternative (albeit occasionally extravagant) versions of reality.

This device advances the 'queer aesthetic' of the play by creating a platform to exhibit multiple realities. The play-within-a-play advances the queer poststructuralist agenda of deconstructing reality by making it even more obvious that what the audience has been accepting as the 'reality' of the structure and narrative of the play is easily adapted to the expectations introduced by a new queer plot. Suddenly the gaze of the audience is overtly diverted by the camp character, and McGuinness offers a new plot; this time the story is based clearly and solely on the vision of the queer. In this moment of narrative revolution Dido takes control of the story, and he decides who plays what roles in the world he creates. The audience is led into his world of sexual and gender anarchy as Dido assigns men women's role and women men's roles. *The Burning Balaclava* allows McGuinness to not only subvert traditional gender roles, but even more significantly, to playfully engage volatile icons of Northern Irish cultural/political life such as flags, balaclavas and guns, which protect sectarian division. Dido's play allows a privileged moment where incongruity *is* the story, giving a queerly humorous interpretation of otherwise horrific realities.

In my final consideration I would like to return to the definition of camp, which describes it as 'a place where a group of people, as soldiers, are temporarily billeted in makeshift shelters, as tents or huts.' This final attempt to engage camp as a place, or a location, is a similarly fantastic venture of employing the excessive camp aesthetic to *Carthaginians*, given that McGuinness takes advantage of many of the same techniques of extravagance and artifice in setting as he does in iconography and personality. The alternative reality, which McGuinness has created with gender reversals, camp references, and cross-dressing intersects with the dramatic setting of the play that is located in the civic site of bereavement and loss: the cemetery. In this play McGuinness creates a marginal place *and* space for his group of characters; a geographical site to camp in and a common ground for those bound together in the collective experience and perspective of trauma and disenfranchisement to act out their alienated situations.

16 Frank McGuinness, *Carthaginians* in *Frank McGuinness: plays 1* (London, 1996), p. 342. Subsequent quotations taken from this edition.

McGuinness' camp is a place where oppositions are challenged and practices are changed: a very queer place that seeks to offset the sacrosanct space which houses the altar of normativity, which in Northern Ireland means strict sectarianism. Michel Foucault theorizes cultural space, and provides insight into post-Bloody Sunday anxieties surrounding the geographical place of the city of Derry and McGuinness' use of a graveyard in addressing the unresolved tensions of that horrible day. In *Aesthetics, Method and Epistemology* Foucault associates spatial and aesthetic realities in a similar fashion to McGuinness in *Carthaginians*. He highlights the ideological space of *utopias*, which he describes as 'emplacements having no real place ... that maintain a general relation or direct inverse analogy with the real space of society'.[17] But he also asserts that there are real places and actual spaces, 'places that are designed into the very institution of society, which are sorts of actually realized utopias.'[18] Foucault calls these places *heterotopias* and defines them as 'sorts of places that are outside all places, although they are actually localisable'.[19] These heterotopias are specific to a culture, but always signify difference within the social economy. Foucault identifies the cemetery as this unique type of social space, one that infers both difference from and sameness as all other cultural places and thus provides a spatial correlation for camp's engagement with and rejection of social icons employed by McGuinness in his setting in *Carthaginians*.

The graveyard is juxtaposed with the city in a relationship similar to that of the dead and the living. Location, objects and persons create a paradoxical camp in which diversity and reversals are a virtue, a heterotopia that flamboyantly thrives on the fundamental incongruence of 'reality.' McGuinness' dramatic project aligns itself spatially and ideologically with Foucault's conceptualisation of the heterotopia in relation to what this unique, and yet ordinary, space does to the remaining social spaces in which it is contained: 'the heterotopias have the role of creating a space of illusion that denounces all real space, all real emplacements within which human life is partitioned off, as being even more illusory'.[20] McGuinness' camp space in *Carthaginians* shares the expository characteristic of the heterotopia in revealing fault-lines in the artificial unity of culture in Northern Ireland, an exposition that seeks to renegotiate all kinds of political and cultural borders and boundaries.

The contradictions, alienations and segregations that McGuinness engages in this drama reflect the same series of experiences that trouble the actual events of Bloody Sunday, 30 January 1972.[21] What started off as a civil rights march 'when thirteen civilians were shot dead by paratroopers',[22] turned into an event which led to countless sectarian acts of violence. Issues of civil rights collided with ideas of political authority, and lost. The established relationship of animosity between Catholics and Protestants was upheld by the event, and made

17 Michel Foucault, *Aesthetics, method, and epistemology*, ed James D. Faubion (London, 1998), p. 177. 18 Ibid. 19 Ibid. 20 Foucault, *Aesthetics*, p. 184. 21 For more information see: R.F. Foster, *Modern Ireland, 1600–1972* (London, 1989), p. 591. 22 Ibid.

martyrs of the thirteen killed. But the killings only served to officially endorse the reality that social and cultural constructions of established identity were the governing standard in Northern Ireland.[23] Bloody Sunday was a day that had the potential to bring about understanding, and shift the balance of power away from segregation and towards integration; instead it launched an era that forced identity politics into their respective camps, and stimulated a defensive entrenchment of differences. Each party claimed to have the centre of truth, thus eliminating the in-between space, a common ground for reconciling difference.

McGuinness has engaged these identity camps by violating the borders that limit the possibilities for subjective identities, as well as by trespassing on spatial boundaries, which rely on the categorisations of what it means to be living or dead. In so doing, he has created his own theatrical heterotopia, which seeks to form a utopian camp of personal and political possibilities for modern Ireland.

At the end of the play, the character of Dido expresses the confusion and pain of life in Derry, opting in the end to give up on the possibility of change. Unlike Virgil's Dido, McGuinness' queen refuses to be consigned either to silence or living amongst the dead. She is too queer for that. Subtly she creates a space for transvestic thinking, but moves on to find a new city when her gender-bending, irreverent preaching fails to bring about change. McGuinness transforms his Dido as she rejects the traditional immovable narrative, and chooses, instead, to write her own future:

> DIDO: What happened? Everything happened, nothing happened, whatever you want to believe, I suppose. What do I believe? I believe it is time to leave Derry. Love it and leave it. Why am I talking to myself in a graveyard? Because everyone in Derry talks to themselves. Everybody in the world talks to themselves. What's the world? Shipquay Street and Ferryquay Street and William Street and the Strand and Great James Street. While I walk the earth, I walk through you the streets of Derry. If I meet one who knows you and they ask, how's Dido? Surviving. How's Derry? Surviving. Carthage has not been destroyed. Watch yourself.[24]

The story is changed, the narrative rewritten, and this queen goes off to find a new place to camp.

23 'Twenty-eight years after Bloody Sunday, relatives of those killed, and the survivors among the wounded, were able to attend the opening of the Saville Tribunal on 27 March 2000, and hear Christopher QC, Counsel for the Tribunal, say that this time, "the truth, the truth plain and simple," would be unearthed and laid out for all to see. It had taken a long struggle to reach this day, and for many it was a time of mixed emotion: sadness for the loss of loved ones; anger compounded by the frustration of the long wait; of relief and pleasure that there was now some prospect of a great wrong being, not righted, but at least recognized; and a sense of achievement, too, that the indomitable of ordinary Derry people had, in the end, compelled a recalcitrant British government, for the first time in legal or political history, to repudiate the findings of an official inquiry and to institute a new inquiry to look again at the facts of the Derry massacre': McCann, p. 255. 24 McGuinness, *Carthaginians*, p. 379.

De/re/construction work: female performances of Northern Irish nationalism in the works of Anne Devlin and Christina Reid

LAURA KANE, GEORGETOWN UNIVERSITY,
WASHINGTON, DC

From its very beginnings, Northern Ireland was an explicitly constructed state. With no intrinsic or pre-fabricated national properties to embrace or define themselves in relation to, it has been up to the citizens of Northern Ireland to build their nation, to determine who should have political power and rights, what it might mean to be a Northern Irish citizen, and to create a Northern Irish story for consumption by the world at large. This task has been complicated by the fact that Northern Ireland was from the start, and remains today, a contested state: though the Anglo-Irish Protestants have maintained political control of the state, they have thus far been unable to establish a supreme narrative of Northern Irish identity that would provide a model for the peaceful future life of the state. The Catholic minority has continually resisted, sometimes violently, the Anglo-Irish vision, and has offered alternative visions for the nation's future. The nation-building project in Northern Ireland cannot, therefore, be seen as logical and linear; instead, a continual fashioning and refashioning of images, a dialogic process of dismantling and rearranging the nation has characterized it.

The disputant Catholic and Protestant factions both situate their visions for Northern Ireland within the rhetoric of nationalism. As I understand it, nationalism is the story of a people and their characteristics created by proponents of, and promulgated in the service of, some political ideology. As Irish theatre scholar Vic Merriman puts it, 'One of nationalism's principle cultural goals is to communicate to its own people their homogeneity.'[1] Though the term 'nationalism' usually denotes the republican nationalism of southern Catholics in the Irish context, the term has been used somewhat differently in Northern Ireland. As author and theorist Seamus Deane indicates, '[Nationalism] is not, in the Irish context, an exclusively Irish phenomenon, for the island has now, particularly in the North, and has had for at least two hundred years, British nationalism as a predominant political and cultural influence'.[2] Each of these nationalisms creates images of what a proper citizen of Northern Ireland does and believes through speeches, parades, posters, militant action, political party ral-

---

1 Vic Merriman, 'Settling for more: excess and success in contemporary Irish drama' in Dermot Bolger (ed.), *Druids, dudes, and beauty queens: the changing face of Irish theatre* (Dublin, 2001), p. 56.
2 Seamus Deane, Introduction in Terry Eagleton, Fredric Jameson, and Edward W. Said (eds), *Nationalism, colonialism, and literature* (Minneapolis, 1990), p. 7.

lies and literature, symbols, theatre and other forms of cultural expression. Successful nationalist movements gain adherents who participate in the iterative construction of a particular worldview and eventually secure the political power to enforce it.

That Northern Ireland is contested means that the nation is currently constituted by this struggle between various nationalisms. There is no clear model for Northern Irish citizenship in a general sense; instead, the residents of Northern Ireland must enact citizenship and seize political agency by identifying with and performing some version of nationalism. To enact Northern Irish citizenship is thus to take sides, and at many moments in history, then, to enact citizenship has been to put oneself at risk of abuse, injury, or even death. To refuse to take sides has been at times no less dangerous, and involves an effective loss of political agency. And, in a country where so many have self-identified, it is unclear whether it is even possible for an individual to remain neutral. This is why scholars like Seamus Deane have wondered whether 'the nation' might be bankrupt as a form for organizing human society. Deane believes that it is time to work toward 'a new discourse for a new relationship between our idea of the human subject and our idea of human communities' in order to envision and secure a liveable future for Northern Ireland's inhabitants.[3]

In recent years, Northern Ireland's literary theatre has been one important site where the critique of nationalism that would permit such a re-envisioning of human communities has occurred. This, however, has not always been the case: for instance, during the 1970s, years that witnessed waves of unprecedented sectarian violence, the theatre essentially maintained the status quo. Theatre historians like Anna McMullan note that, 'because of the political sensitivity of the situation, it was some years before dramatists were prepared or allowed to overtly explore "The Troubles" in the theatre'.[4] Plays staged in Northern Ireland during the 1970s tended to image the Troubles as simply a part of the Northern Irish landscape, an intractable problem. Lionel Pilkington explains the failings of the theatre as an instrument of nationalism or its critique in the 1970s : 'As well as absolving the theatre spectator of all political responsibility, this portrayal of the conflict in terms of an irresolvable social pathology tends to foreclose the possibility of its political resolution.'[5] As the violence abated in the early 1980s, however, dramatists – some of whom gained their authorial voices as positive products of the civil and women's rights movements of the 1970s – began to write and produce plays that turned a critical eye on the events of the recent past.

Anne Devlin and Christina Reid were two of these new voices. Both born in Belfast, they emerged as playwrights on the major Northern Irish and English

3 Ibid., p. 3.   4 Anna McMullan, 'Irish women playwrights since 1958', in Trevor Griffiths and Margaret Llewellyn-Jones (eds), *British and Irish women dramatists since 1958: a critical handbook* (Buckingham, 1993), p. 112.   5 Lionel Pilkington, *Theatre and state in twentieth-century Ireland: cultivating the people* (London, 2001), p. 209.

stages during the 1980s. Both dramatists have taken the Troubles as a primary theme in their work, and both foreground the experiences of women who lived through the period of intense sectarian violence in the late 1960s and the 1970s. The feminist lens Devlin and Reid employ in examining the Troubles allows them to anticipate Seamus Deane's questioning of the nation as the proper organizing principle for human communities. Even as they posit alternative social formations, Devlin and Reid critique nationalism, exposing the mechanism of its awesome power, and laying significant groundwork for those who still seek to answer Deane's well-publicized call to reconsider the concept of the nation. In order to better understand the nature of this critique and its value, I will briefly examine the lives and bodies of female characters in the plays of Devlin and Reid, paying particular attention to the ways the women position themselves, or are positioned by others, with regard to the competing nationalisms described above.

The two plays I will discuss – Devlin's *Ourselves Alone* and Reid's *The Belle of the Belfast City* – are set primarily in Belfast during the 1980s. Devlin has tended to focus on presenting the stories of Catholic women and families, while Reid's main subjects are Protestants. But for all of the women of these plays, affiliation with one brand of nationalism or another begins at home, as a fact of family life. Nowhere is this clearer than at the outset of *Ourselves Alone*. The play's title is taken from the slogan of Sinn Féin, the political party linked to the Irish Republican Army. The Gaelic phrase 'Sinn Féin' translates to 'Ourselves Alone,' and has been used to signify the party's goal of establishing a 32-county Irish republic independent of Britain or any other foreign power. As we will see, however, Devlin's play offers another possible signified for this highly charged phrase: *Ourselves Alone* follows a group of three women, sisters Josie and Frieda McCoy and their sister-in-law (via common law marriage) Donna through eight months in the mid-1980s. Devlin stages several scenes throughout the play that position the three women alone within the walls of Donna's house. Donna, Frieda, and Josie sit in the living room or kitchen discussing their daily challenges, arguing with each other, and suggesting possible solutions. The three women come to constitute for each other a community of possibility – the only such community in their lives. Though we observe scenes from the individual lives of each of the women, the female community is the play's nexus. *Ourselves Alone* asks whether such a community might serve as an alternative social grouping to the nation.

As the play begins, we see Frieda singing a traditional nationalist ballad, as her pianist puts it, 'a Republican classic,' in a pub that is, according to Devlin's stage directions, the 'centre of Republican activity, both political and social, in West Belfast'.[6] As Frieda sings, the audience has the chance to gaze upon her and recognize the performance as another instance of a familiar trope in Irish

6 Anne Devlin, *Ourselves alone with The long march and A woman calling* (London, 1986), p. 13.

and Northern Irish drama: the woman as object of inspiration for men engaged
in the sectarian struggle. The audience's gaze is interrupted, and the familiar
romantic trope overturned almost immediately, however, when Frieda throws
down her song sheet and states:

> FRIEDA: *(Sings.)*Armoured cars and tanks and guns
> came to take away our sons
> every man should stand beside
> the men behind the wire.
> *(Throws the paper down.)*
> I don't want to sing this anymore! ...
> DANNY: *(Stops playing.)* Why not?
> FRIEDA: Because it's about a man.
> DANNY: The song's about Internment, Frieda!
> FRIEDA: I'm fed up with songs where the women are doormats! ... I want
>   to sing one of my own songs.[7]

Even in this first scene, we can see that Frieda is moved more by what the
nationalist rhetoric excludes – the narratives of women and the products of her
own creative activity – than by its political and cultural message. In an effort to
tell her own story, Frieda attempts to resist identification with the Republican
nationalism embraced by her family. This effort is complicated, however, by the
fact that Frieda's access to the stage comes only through the nationalism she
wants to transcend: her family connections to the Republican club give her the
forum where she can begin to realize her dream of becoming a professional
singer/songwriter, but she is immediately restricted to performing Republican-
sanctioned material.

   For Frieda, then, the choice is between artistic integrity in obscurity and a
public voice that is not her own. Throughout the play, Frieda blames nationalism for backing her into this corner. She views nationalism as an impediment
to self-definition and individual achievement: 'Nationalism is always the last
resort of people who've failed to achieve anything else.'[8] Frieda continually
attempts to resist affiliation with the nationalism that she feels has defined and
consumed her family by changing her body, her political affiliation, and even
her geographical location. For example, she dyes her hair, supposedly in an effort
to look like Marlene Dietrich for her act, but her sister Josie wonders why she
always wants to be someone else. Frieda responds: 'When did I ever have a
chance to be myself? My father was interned before I was born. My brother's
in the Kesh for bank robbery. You mention the name McCoy in this neighbor-
hood and people start walking away from you.'[9]

   In addition to changing her body, she tries to erase the Republican identity
inscribed upon her at birth by re-identifying with the Workers' Party. When

7 Ibid.   8 Ibid., p. 33.   9 Ibid., p. 21.

her father suspects that she has taken up with John McDermot, a Workers' Party member, he beats her. Soon after this incident, Frieda tells her lover that she'd like to join the party, reasoning that she never stayed with anyone who beat her, and that she needed money and shelter. Here, Frieda formalizes her relationship with her lover by taking on his political identity, his particular affiliation within the nationalist spectrum. In this moment of crisis, she effectively trades her identity for food, shelter, and companionship. The Workers' Party has gained a soul, but Frieda has lost hers. In the end, Frieda realizes that she is unwilling to make this compromise and breaks off the relationship with McDermot. In the play's final scene, Frieda makes plans to live in England, initially explaining to Donna that she and McDermot simply have different priorities; she has her singing career, and he his politics. Eventually, though, she admits, 'Oh, it's not him; it is Ireland I am leaving'.[10] Frieda's experience highlights the simultaneously all-consuming and exclusionary nature of the battle of nationalisms in Northern Ireland. For instance, one cannot simply be a singer; one must be a Republican or Loyalist singer. For Frieda, having rejected the politics of both father and lover, there is no shelter in Ireland. Furthermore, her economic opportunities are so few that it would be impossible for her to carve out a life outside the system of nationalisms and the protection of men.

But in the play's final scene, Frieda remains in Donna's house, frustrated with both her experiences in Ireland and her plans to live in England. Ultimately, despite fairly radical and independent action, Frieda cannot perform what she feels to be her own identity in Belfast because she is constantly forced to perform some version of nationalism. Devlin's construction of Frieda explores and rejects one possible subject position in Northern Ireland – that of the neutral individual. Frieda's struggles indicate that for at least some individuals, and perhaps for many women of her time, agency is limited to picking one's poison. Frieda can choose to take on a lover's political affiliation, but she must select a sponsor capable of providing for her, otherwise she will be forced to revert to the default position of being claimed by her father for the Republicans.

Where Frieda chooses to reject her republican nationalist roots, her sister Josie chooses to embrace hers, at least initially. At the beginning of *Ourselves Alone*, Josie not only argues the nationalist position during the three women's debates about politics, but acts as a courier for her father in the service of the Republican cause. Rather than hoping to somehow escape the political conflict, Josie seems to be making a play for power and agency *within* the system of competing nationalisms that she sees as intractable. Josie positions herself not against an idealized, individual self like Frieda, but against a mother whose relationships with men consisted mostly of fearful watching and waiting. Josie, like her mother before her, clearly desires a romantic relationship with a man, but she cannot envision herself in the passive position that women are typically offered within the nationalist struggle. Still, from the very beginning, Josie *is* passively

10 Ibid., p. 90.

'waiting on a man.' She is in love with and carrying on an affair with Cathal O'Donnell, a fellow Republican party worker and a very married man:

> JOSIE: I can't live like this any more. I sit here night after night wondering
> will he come tonight.
> DONNA: We're all waiting on men, Josie.
> JOSIE: If he has to go away for any reason but [his wife] I can stand it. [11]

Despite her belief in the republican principles she works for, Josie's life is still incomplete. Though Josie's status as an insider in the struggle of nationalisms helps her partially escape her mother's fate – she has an active role in the political action, rather than simply waiting at home – it does nothing to fulfill her desire for a healthy, loving relationship.

In fact, through her performance of nationalism, Josie often seems to take on male roles, postures, and ways of speaking in an attempt to sublimate her seemingly impossible and traditionally 'female' desire for a romantic relationship with a man, in favour of the surrogate of homoerotic friendship within the bonds of the nationalist tribe. In describing her relationship with Cathal to Donna, Josie says, 'Sometimes when we make love I pretend … I'm not even a woman. Sometimes I'm a man – his warrior lover, fighting side by side to the death.'[12] It is only later in the play when she has begun a relationship and conceived a child with the Englishman and recent Republican recruit Joe Conran that Josie begins to consider the possibility of giving up her work in the service of nationalism:

> I'm tired. Tired of this endless night watch. I've been manning the barricades since 'sixty-nine. I'd like to stop for a while, look around me, plant a garden, listen for other sounds; the breathing of a child somewhere outside Andersonstown … I'm so afraid of losing it. It's like a beginning within me. For the first time the possibility of being happy. So I'm going to tell O'Donnell that I won't accept this or any other assignment.[13]

Before Josie can put her new plan into action, Joe is found to be a traitor to the cause, and Josie's body – and her potential new beginning – is threatened by her brother Liam, who wants her to abort the baby. Josie is only saved from harm when her father, Malachy, claims the child for himself, and presumably for the Republicans. Through Josie, Devlin presents a character that supposedly chooses to affiliate with a particular brand of nationalism. Josie's story indicates, however, that this 'choice' may be little more than choosing to reaffirm, rather than fight, the nationalist identity that was inscribed upon her at birth. Josie remains subject to problems including sexual and emotional dissatisfaction and domestic abuse, and ultimately cannot choose to leave the Republican fold. Her physical safety and that of her unborn child depend upon being claimed by her father.

11 Ibid., pp 15–16. 12 Ibid., p. 17. 13 Ibid., p. 77.

Taken together, the performances of the McCoy sisters serve to deconstruct the rhetoric of universality and homogeneity that characterizes all forms of nationalism. Neither Frieda nor Josie (nor Donna, for that matter) can achieve happiness by answering the call to citizenship that Republican nationalism issues, because this call fails to acknowledge or provide for the significant needs and wants – individuality and a new way of relating to men among them – of these particular Northern Irish women. Nor can they achieve their goals outside of nationalism, because for Josie, Frieda and Donna, there is no such thing as 'outside nationalism'. The ultimate signal of the impossibility of self-definition for these women is the failure to sustain the alternative community they establish when they are alone in Donna's house. The women are never really 'themselves alone': they are always interrupted by the arrival of men – fathers, lovers, policemen – who break up the community by forcing the women to somehow serve their needs.

Christina Reid's *The Belle of the Belfast City* presents another, older pair of sisters, Rose and Vi, and another potential alternative to the nation – this time, the family. Vi, the older sister, runs the family shop and takes care of their aging mother Dolly. Rose left Belfast at seventeen to pursue a career as a photojournalist in England. Vi's character allows Reid to demonstrate the positives and pitfalls of simply swallowing the version of nationalism one has inherited, while Rose, like Frieda of Devlin's *Ourselves Alone*, interrogates the possibilities of escape from nationalism. The play opens as Rose returns to Northern Ireland with her 18-year-old daughter Belle. Rose and Vi want to show Belle the sights, sounds and tastes of her Northern Irish heritage, but the visit is disturbed by politics as Vi is forced to consider whether to be bullied into closing the shop in support of a radical Protestant protest against the Anglo-Irish agreement that would give Dublin some say in the governance of Northern Ireland. Eventually, Vi is also asked to sell the shop to radical Protestants looking for a new meeting house. As the sisters debate these decisions, they reveal their own relationships to the moderate Protestant nationalism they inherited from their parents and are forced to reconsider their personal politics.

Vi, while condemning the actions of Protestant paramilitarists, says she supports their politics entirely. From her position as a complete outsider, having long ago removed herself from Northern Ireland, Rose is able to speak out against the violence and intimidation tactics of both Protestant and Catholic paramilitary groups, and argues that power-sharing may be the only hope to break the deadlock of nationalisms that has produced turmoil in Northern Ireland: 'Sooner or later, Protestant or Catholic, we all have to take that risk.'[14] Vi's character underscores, both verbally and through performances of nationalism such as paying Protestant radicals under the table to protect the shop from harm, that it is only this distance on the problem that allows Rose to maintain

14 Christina Reid, *The belle of the Belfast city and Did you hear the one about the Irishman …? Two plays by Christina Reid* (London, 1989), p. 38.

such neutrality: 'We? That's easy to say when you don't live in the middle of it. When there's no risk of losin' your nationality, your religion, everything you've lived your life by and believed in.'¹⁵ While Rose has cut quotidian ties with her family and Northern Ireland, Vi still lives among the people invested in the nation and involved in the struggle. For Vi, the conflict between nationalisms retains human dimensions; it is not yet a mere battle of ideologies. The people Vi knows and loves are all inscribed with Protestant, Unionist identities. To buck the dominant system could mean endangering or losing her life or those of the people she loves.

While Vi is correct that Rose risks relatively little in taking a stand against both sides of the nationalist struggle, the intergenerational nature of the play, along with its constant shifting back and forth between the past and present, allows us to see that Rose still has a stake in the Northern Irish conflict, and in some ways still identifies as Northern Irish. What Rose stands to lose through her exile is her past, her personal narrative of origin. By living in England, implicitly renouncing both nationalisms, Rose gains a measure of security and sanity, but for that she must give up, both for herself and for her child, access to the landscape, both social and physical, that she loves. This loss is voiced by Rose's daughter Belle in a confessional speech that is directed toward the audience and stands apart from the main narrative:

> Before I came here, I had two images of Belfast. A magical one conjured by my grandmother's songs and stories and recitations, and a disturbing one of the marches and banners and bands on the six o'clock news ... They are both true, but not the whole truth of this bizarre and beautiful city. Belfast is surrounded by soft green hills. All its inhabitants live within walking distance of the countryside, and like village people, they are inquisitive, friendly, hospitable. Belfast must be the best kept social secret in the British Isles ... ¹⁶

While Rose and Belle, unlike Vi and many other in Northern Ireland, are able to consider the possibilities of an arrangement like power-sharing with hope, they often lack perspective on the small daily triumphs and tragedies of the conflict. Visiting Vi reminds them that Northern Ireland is more than political turmoil and violence, and that certain solutions that sound simple from afar may not work until social conditions that affect daily life of the nation's citizens improve.

On the other hand, Rose's perspective challenges Vi's as well. When it becomes clear Jack Horner, Rose and Vi's cousin who wields some power among the Protestant radicals, is allied with members of the racist National Front, Vi decides to keep the shop open during the protest, come what may. She cannot abide oblique threats against mixed-race Belle, and decides that she must, in her own way, protest what she sees as immoral and shameful behavior on the part of Protestant nationalists:

15 Ibid. 16 Devlin, p. 30.

I'm in support of the protest, but I'm getting' out of the corner they boxed us into. 'Close your shop an' take to the streets if you don't support The Agreement.' I will never support that agreement, never. But neither will I be a part of what they've gotten us involved in. Civil disobedience aided and abetted by thugs. Them's I.R.A. tactics, an' I'll have no part of it … I'm British, an' that's what I'll fight to stay as long as there's breath in my body. But I'll do it respectably and with dignity. I won't be associated with the dictates of criminals.[17]

Through her interaction and debate with Rose, Vi's initial blind faith in and vague discomfort with 'the devil [she] know[s]' has transformed into a critical stance toward the methods of Protestant nationalism: 'I'm in support of the protest, but I'm gettin' out of the corner they boxed us into. Civil disobedience aided and abetted by thugs. Them's IRA tactics, an' I'll have no part of it.'[18] Vi chooses to push back, to try to re-shape nationalism itself through her individual actions. This gradual and subtle shift in Vi's politics, precipitated and achieved through the dialectic exchange with Rose, demonstrates the positive potential of the family unit as an alternative to the nation. The key to Vi and Rose's productive dialogue was their recognition that they had valuable common ground in Belle, Dolly, and other relatives. At the end of the play, they still don't agree on politics, but they have each made some concessions, and have renewed respect for each other's ideas and lifestyles. Furthermore, they each have the knowledge that protecting the family is each other's first priority.

Reid will not, however, leave us with this optimism. In the play's final scenes, despite her best efforts, Vi is implicated in sectarian violence as she unwittingly sells the family store to a Protestant mole. The store, the seat of family life for Vi, Rose, Belle, Dolly, and Jack's sister Janet, has been turned into a paramilitary meeting house through Jack's trickery. In the end, Vi is confronted with the proof that Jack feels more loyalty toward his version of nationalism than toward the family, and with the fact that her attempts to effect change within the Unionist movement have been futile. The family community in *The Bell of the Belfast City*, then, is broken up in much the same way as the female community in *Ourselves Alone*. Similarly, *The Belle of the Belfast City* reminds us that, at least for these women, the decision to alter one's position on the nationalist continuum may not be enough to effect the change: Jack won't let Vi make her protest against paramilitary violence, even if he has to deceive her to prevent it.

Though *Ourselves Alone* focuses primarily on young, Catholic and Republican-affiliated women and *The Belle of the Belfast City* presents middle-aged, Protestant and Unionist-affiliated females, the plays ultimately approach the same conclusions – and they are conclusions that complicate the notion of getting beyond nation. First, despite the progress of the women's rights movement there remains more work to be done, as some women in Belfast still suffer

17 Devlin, pp 49–50. 18 Ibid.

from a lack of material opportunity that prevents them from articulating their own identities and performing their own citizenships. Second, the system of nationalism is so entrenched in Northern Irish society that it is not simply a personal or individual matter; rather, at best, it is a product of the individual's desires and those of the people around them.

In these plays, Reid and Devlin began a process of envisioning a future where questions of nationhood are not the paramount concern for human communities. That the characters they construct cannot ultimately transcend nationalism should not be viewed as a failure. Rather, Reid and Devlin have succeeded in identifying stumbling blocks to be cleared on the way to creating post-nation communities and encourage us, through the play's open endings, to grapple with the issues of lingering misogyny and entrenched nationalism. In other words, the playwrights model the necessary deconstruction of nationalism itself that must precede the reconstruction of any human – and more humane – form of community that would supersede the nation.

Skirting around sexuality?: The plurality of the gay identity in Frank McGuinness' drama

KENNETH NALLY, NUI, GALWAY

Frank McGuinness' dramatic works utilize such varied settings as Renaissance Rome, Beirut in the 1980s, and the trenches of the Great War. His plays probe the margins of society illuminating varied social and cultural issues such as the coercive restraints of the family, the Protestant identity, homelessness, the role of the artist within society, imprisonment and international terrorism. Notwithstanding such diversity, the locus of this work is contemporary Ireland, in particular those aspects which modern Irish society has sought to ignore. This paper considers how McGuinness' work in the 1980s explored homosexuality at a time in which 'barbarous law and comfortable prejudice' comfortably co-existed in Ireland.[1] To date, assessments of his work have generally ignored its many engagements with queer issues. Moreover, studies of McGuinness that comment on queer issues see such concerns as being important only in so far as they facilitate a decentring of the traditional elements of the Irish identity. For instance, in 1988, Fintan O'Toole observed that McGuinness used 'the condition of homosexuality itself, as opposed to the situation of individual homosexuals ... as a physical metaphor for states of national consciousness'.[2] Though

1 Ailbhe Smyth, Foreword, in David Marcus (ed.), *Alternative loves* (Dublin, 1994), pp 3–6. 2 Fintan

McGuinness himself has pointed out that 'there are more divisions to disturb and obscure than between North and South', the weight of such pronouncements has limited perceptions of the depth of McGuinness' work.[3] This paper argues therefore that there is a need to retrieve McGuinness from the political debate about the Irish identity, in order to engage with other equally important aspects of his work.

McGuinness is perhaps best known for *Observe the Sons of Ulster Marching towards the Somme* (1985).[4] This play deals with the experiences of eight Ulster Loyalists at the battle of the Somme in 1916. Articulating the belief that Irishness could be something other than Catholic and Nationalist, its first performance was seized upon by academics and politicians as a key cultural text, revising our constructs of the national identity. That this play was staged just before the signing of the Anglo-Irish Agreement concreted such an assessment. The symbolic significance of *Sons of Ulster* is apparent. A play by a then self-professed Catholic Republican, it won praise for its 'profound identification with an alien point of view'.[5] First performed at the Abbey Theatre in 1985, it was subsequently revived in 1994 to coincide with the Northern Ceasefire, when it was lauded as a model of cultural inclusiveness, with its opening night being attended by politicians from north and south of the border.

However, the significance of McGuinness' intervention is less straightforward than such politically motivated appropriation suggests. For one, the approach to unionism is ambiguous, and indeed critical while elsewhere McGuinness has spoken of his unease with 'the neglect of diversities other than the Catholic-Protestant/Nationalist-Unionist ones' and pointed to the importance of the 'diversities between the needs of men and the needs of women, between the needs not simply of the rich and poor, but within the middle class, and of the homosexual and the heterosexual'.[6]

In 1985, in a hotly disputed review, David Nowlan, of the *Irish Times*, read the play as an 'attack on the trappings and tribalism of Ulster Protestantism'.[7] At the core of the debate lies the role of the play's central character, Kenneth Pyper, a failed artist who claims he has signed up to die. As the play develops, Pyper's dissidence gradually forces the other members of his company to question their loyalties. In the end the men, dressed in their sashes, go over the top together in an ambiguous gesture of solidarity and futility. Only Pyper survives to return to Ulster where he seeks through his actions to give meaning to the sacrifices of the others.

When the play is analysed, Pyper's homosexuality is judged to give him a somewhat privileged position from which to assess and critique Ulster union-

O'Toole, 'Island of saints and silicon', in Micheal Keneally (ed.), *Cultural contexts and literary idioms in contemporary Irish literature* (Totowa, 1988), pp 11–35, 32. 3 See Frank McGuinness, 'A sense of Irish identity', *Guardian* (5 October 1994), p. 10. 4 Frank McGuinness, *Observe the sons of Ulster marching towards the Somme*, in *Frank McGuinness: plays 1* (London, 1996). 5 Christopher Murray, *Modern Irish drama: mirror up to the nation* (Manchester, 1997), p. 206. 6 Ibid., p. 65. 7 David Nowlan, '*Observe the sons of Ulster marching towards the Somme* at the Peacock', *Irish Times* (19 February 1985), p. 11.

ism. Homosexuality is thus seen to provide, as Helen Lojek first noted, 'a useful perspective – a distance from which events, philosophies, social and moral issues may be evaluated'.[8] This reading of the play has provided the template for many critical assessments of McGuinness' body of work. Anne F. Kelly-O'Reilly, Hiroko Mikami and Des O'Rawe have all detailed how a range of McGuinness' works utilize the 'outsider' perspective of the homosexual to critique society from the margins.[9] The problem with such analysis is that homosexuality is seen as a perspective, but not as a thematic concern, reflective of a wider reluctance to examine McGuinness' exploration of queer issues.

In general, readings of McGuinness that treat homosexuality as perspective note that his plays investigate nationalism through gender play, and the signifiers of sexual transgression. For instance, Ann F. Kelly O'Reilly suggests that in *Carthaginians*, a play first staged at the Peacock Theatre in 1988, 'the outsider position of the homosexual questions perceived assumptions'.[10] This play is often seen as a companion play to *Sons of Ulster* in that it explores the Catholic nationalist perspective of the Troubles. Set in Derry's Creggan graveyard, the play focuses on a group of people who are trying to come to terms with the aftermath of Bloody Sunday. Its central character, Dido Martin, is a cross-dressing gay man who shares much with Pyper in *Sons of Ulster*. Queer theorists such as Judith Butler suggest that, 'in imitating gender, drag implicitly reveals the imitative structure of gender itself – as well as it contingency';[11] and in recognising that Pyper and Dido each issue a series of challenges to notions of fixed gender and tribal identities, Anthony Roche suggests that McGuinness' work critiques dominant ideologies through gender trouble, to contest the truth of gender itself.

Such analysis fits with Dido's arrival in the graveyard in the opening scene of *Carthaginians* for he immediately offers a challenge to the conventional demarcation of martyr and mother. Dressed in drag and pushing a pram he tells how he fought his 'way to the graveyard through three army checkpoints.' More unusually, he details how his 'ambition in life is to corrupt every member of Her Majesty's forces serving in Northern Ireland'.[12] It is here that we encounter a certain reticence on the part of many commentators. Despite the professed sexual intentions of the 'war effort of Dido Martin, patriot and poof', readings have 'skirted around' the issue of Dido's sexuality to focus instead on the subversive possibilities of his campness.[13] This considered with the significance of *The Burning Balaclava*, the play-within-a-play that cross-casts the graveyard's trau-

8 Helen Lojek, 'Difference without indifference: the drama of Frank McGuinness and Anne Devlin', *Éire-Ireland.* 25.2 (1990), 56–68, 58. 9 See, for example: Anne F. Kelly-O'Reilly, 'Carthaginians: narratives of death and resurrection in a Derry graveyard' in Helen Lojek (ed.), *The theatre of Frank McGuinness: stages of mutability* (Dublin, 2002), pp 92–107; Hiroko Mikami, *Frank McGuinness and his theatre of paradox* (Ulster Editions and Monographs, 2002); Des O' Rawe, 'Dissidence and desire in Frank McGuinness' *Observe the sons of Ulster marching towards the Somme* and *Carthaginians'* in P.J. Mathews (ed.), *New voices in Irish criticism*, i (Dublin: Four Courts Press, 2000), pp 155–62. 10 Kelly-O'Reilly, 'Carthaginians', pp 92–107, p. 95. 11 Judith Butler, *Gender trouble: feminism and the subversion of identity* (New York, 1990), pp 137 8. 12 McGuinness, *Frank McGuinness: Plays 1*, p. 302. 13 Ibid.

matized characters leads to the conclusion that, as Riana O'Dwyer notes, 'the exchange of gender roles in the play-within-a-play allows a sense of resolution to develop that has political, more than gender, implications'.[14]

For me, the focus on gender play and trouble in *Carthaginians* and *Sons of Ulster* has meant that the sexuality of these characters has rarely been considered in its own terms. Alternatively, when critics have discussed the representation of homosexual desire, it is conflated with national allegories such as that which O'Toole suggests. Such readings leave the relations between individual gay men unexamined and few critics have looked at the significance of McGuinness' consistent forefronting of male same-sex desire in relation to public assumptions regarding homosexuality. There is, I believe, a need to develop the significance of homosexuality as a theme rather than as a perspective, an allegory, or an aspect of gender-crossing. After all, such interpretative readings suggest that the significance of homosexuality in these plays lies only in facilitating the investigation of something else – usually some element of the national identity. Commonly, such readings leave the relations of individual gay men to the national identity unexamined and ignore queer issues. Contrary to such prevailing trends, I believe that the degree to which plays such as *Carthaginians*, which are generally seen to explore national politics may also be seen to deal with queer issues, merits further consideration.

I suggest therefore that we reverse the analytical process somewhat and read some of McGuinness' plays and their reflections on the national identity in terms of what they say about homosexuality. For instance, a footnote to Eamonn Jordan's consideration of the blood imagery within the *Sons of Ulster* tells that 'McGuinness has suggested that his awareness of the AIDS epidemic informs the play to some extent'.[15] A look at other McGuinness plays validates such a queer reading. In *Dolly West's Kitchen* (1999), *The Bread Man* (1991), and *Baglady* (1985), the colour red has also been used to indicate elemental concerns suggesting themes of blood and violence. In such plays red also connects the issue to the rituals and symbolism of Catholicism, a deliberate ploy designed to focus on the Church's teachings regarding homosexuality.

Thankfully, it is not always necessary to read between the lines in this way, and symbolic readings can be as occlusive of queer issues as their nationalist counterparts. Often queer issues are forefronted quite deliberately in McGuinness' drama; and just as often ignored. Take, for example, *Carthaginians*. In attending to the play's hybridising tendencies, little attention has been paid to Dido's situation as a gay man in Northern Ireland during the Troubles. Northern Ireland is not known for its tolerance of homosexuality, one issue on which the two major church faiths agree. It is a place that is highly politicized, and gay rights have often been perceived as a minor concern in the light of

14 Riana O'Dwyer, 'Dancing in the borderlands: the plays of Frank McGuinness', in Greet Lernout (ed.), *The crows behind the plough* (Amsterdam, 1991), pp 99–115, p. 101.   15 Eamonn Jordan, *The feast of famine: the plays of Frank McGuinness* (Bern, 1997), p. 38.

grander narratives. Moreover, the privileging of mothers and motherhood with nationalisms can, as McGuinness' plays acknowledge, operate to exclude alternative sexualities. This has resulted not only in the suppression of a number of counter discourses, such as the homoerotic, but also in outright homophobia – a prejudice which was perhaps most succinctly encapsulated by the 1977 Democratic Unionist Party's 'Save Ulster from Sodomy' campaign.[16]

Despite the fact that *Carthaginians* touches upon the oppression of gay men, within nationalism as well as outside, this matter has been overlooked in many assessments, buried beneath a myriad of theorisations about the play's pronouncements on ideologies. For example, towards the end of Scene two we see Dido confronted by Hark, an ex-IRA man. Drawing on the tension between public and private lives, this scene revolves around the dual meaning of the term 'picked up' as it conflates a sexual encounter with arrest by the security forces.

> HARK: Are you alright, Dido?
> DIDO: No.
> HARK: … Have you ever been picked up, Dido? Picked up, by the army or police? Will I pick you up? …(*Hark touches Dido on the face.*) This is how, Dido. And after that, Dido, do you know what they do? Answer me. Tell me the truth. Tell me who you are involved with.
> DIDO: Hark.
> HARK: Who's Hark. Tell me, who's Hark? Is he your boyfriend? Do you love him? Is he a married man? Would his wife like to hear about it? Would his girlfriend? Who's she? Tell me. Tell me. I'll let you go if you tell me.[17]

Here, though Anne F. Kelly-O'Reilly notes that 'Hark's abhorrence of the sexuality of the gay man is as abhorrent as the imagined soldier's image of the united Ireland', there is generally a certain reluctance to see the wood for the allegorical trees.[18] What is often overlooked is that this scene looks upon the particularities of homophobia within the political context of Derry in the 1980s. Space was, and is, highly politicized in Northern Ireland, a place where sectarian divides are marked by barriers and murals, and where disputes over rights of way can lead to community conflict. *Carthaginians* emphasizes that in Derry in the 1980s transition was dangerous, particularly for a gay man. Sean Cahill in an article written just after the declaration of 1994 cease-fire claimed: 'closeted gay men cruising along Derry's Foyle River are picked up by police or soldiers, and are threatened with outing to their friends and family if they don't become informants'.[19] In such a context homosexuality is a perceived vulnera-

16 A campaign organized as 'a response to recommendations from the European Court of Human Rights that the 1967 liberalization of British laws on homosexuality be extended to Northern Ireland' Kathryn Conrad, 'Women troubles, queer troubles: gender, sexuality and the politics of selfhood in the construction of the Northern Irish state', in Marilyn Cohen & Nancy J. Curtin (eds), *Reclaiming gender: transgressive identities in modern Ireland* (New York, 1999), pp 53–68; p. 55.   17 McGuinness, *Frank McGuinness: Plays 1*, p. 314.   18 Kelly-O'Reilly, 'Carthaginians', pp 98–9.   19 Quoted in Conrad,

bility and a source of blackmail. McGuinness' response is instructive. Dido responds to Hark:

> I know my kind, Hark. Do you want me to name them? Well there's me. That's all … Some people here fuck with a bullet and the rest fuck with a Bible, but I belong to neither.[20]

Here we see that the play is a rebuke to cultures that force gay men to remain closeted, and simultaneously oppress them because they do. Indeed, in neglecting to focus on the practise of homosexuality in these plays, many critics are occluding such issues in a way that is similar to the nationalisms they critique with reference to the homosexual perspective.

In focussing on homosexuality as a theme, one becomes aware that readings that concentrate primarily on gender trouble suggest that McGuinness' work is compromised somewhat by having characters such as Pyper and Dido, who after all, essentially adhere to the traditional stage stereotypes of gay men in their effeminacy. Indeed, a problem with gender trouble readings is that they collude with society's acceptance of homosexuality as long as it is presented in conjunction with effeminacy. What is suggested is that the effeminate homosexual can be seen as a transgendered, 'pretend' woman, allowing the association of homosexuality with gender more than with sexual acts. McGuinness' play *Mutabilitie,* premiered at London's Royal National Theatre in 1997. In part, it examines the introduction of theatre to Ireland. As one character describes it, theatre is a place where men 'can be kings or queens or men or women … they call it playing a woman.'[21] In such a view the effeminate man is not considered a deviant sexual type. The association of homosexuality with effeminacy dates back to Victorian times. Alan Sinfield, in charting the patterns that shape modern understandings of homosexual desire, argues that effeminacy only became recognisably queer after 1895 and points out that 'up to the Wilde trials … far later than is widely supposed – it is unsafe to interpret effeminacy, as defining of, or a signal of, same sex passion'.[22] This association is also the reason why I believe that *Innocence* – a play often neglected due to the commonly held belief that it does not explore the Irish identity – should hold a more central position in assessments of the achievements of McGuinness' drama.

Innocence, a play about the Italian renaissance painter Caravaggio, was first performed at Dublin Gate Theatre on the 7 October 1986. This expressionist play forefronts the themes of homosexuality and artistry. Significantly these are the elements of *Sons of Ulster* that were overlooked in most assessments of the 1985/86 productions when reviews tended to focus on the political significance and the play's revising of the national identity. In contrast to the Abbey's 1985

'Women troubles, pp 53–68. 20 McGuinness, *Frank McGuinness: Plays 1*, p. 315. 21 Frank McGuinness, *Mutabilitie* (London, 1999), p. 25. 22 Alan Sinfield, *The Wilde century: effeminacy, Oscar Wilde and the queer moment* (London, 1994), p. 27.

production of *Sons of Ulster*, the Gate Theatre's production of *Innocence* in 1986 presented and recounted the play's homosexual acts. Despite belated acknowledgement of the importance of Pyper's sexuality to the concerns of *Sons of Ulster*, *Innocence* stands as the first of McGuinness' plays to confront an Irish audience with an explicit representation of a queer sensibility.

The play is divided into two acts: 'Life' and 'Death', both of which are compressed into one day and which seek to evoke the sensibility of the painter. It does not examine what is conceived of as the actuality of history but focuses instead on the imaginative possibility of what 'could have happened'. All its action takes place on the day Caravaggio kills Raduccio Tomassio, an act McGuinness attributes to homophobic abuse and, specifically, the association of homosexuality with effeminacy, though there is no historical evidence of such a motive.

> WHORE: Who is dead?
> CARAVAGGIO: A Man
> LUCIO: It was a clean fight. Caravaggio was brilliant. Absolutely fucking magic, honest to Jesus. And the guy who got it had it coming to him.
> LENA: What did he do?
> LUCIO: He called us names
> WHORE: What?
> LUCIO: He called us girls. He picked the wrong man to insult.[23]

Why did McGuinness choose to reshape the events of Caravaggio's life in such a way? In part, justification for his construction may be deduced from a comparison of Pyper and Caravaggio in which he pointed out: 'both men court death, both are killers, and both are homosexual. I add the last detail in the light that recent productions of *Sons of Ulster* censored Pyper's relationship with Craig, and Renaissance art scholars more willingly accept that Caravaggio was a murderer than that he was gay.'[24] Interestingly, Caravaggio is best known for a style of painting that rejected idealism in favour of realism. Using models and painting from life, he created an enfranchising religious vision and popular accounts tell us that when Caravaggio needed a Virgin, a local whore posed for him and similarly how his saints and apostles were humble men illumined by their faith. The radical nature of *Innocence* broke with Irish theatrical tradition almost as much as Caravaggio broke with traditional forms of representation. In *Innocence*, McGuinness seems to have relished the chance to pointedly challenge the association of effeminacy with homosexuality.

McGuinness' Caravaggio was not the stage-homosexual found in previous Irish plays. Far from being meek, or comically effeminate, he was violent and

23 McGuinness, *Frank McGuinness: Plays 1*, p. 262.   24 Frank McGuinness, 'An Irishman's theatre', in Jacqueline Genet and Elizabeth Hellegourac'h (eds), *Studies on the contemporary Irish theatre* (Caen, 1991), p. 62.

virulently masculine. It was a creation that had its origins in historical accounts, both of Caravaggio and of Renaissance Italy. The existence of social networks involving male-male eroticism has been particularly well documented for Renaissance Italy. In his historical account of same sex categorisations, David F. Greenberg points out that 'between 1432 and 1502, approximately 25 percent of the male population of Florence – by modern standards a remarkably high percentage – was arrested on sodomy charges'.[25] Drawing on such a historical reality, *Innocence* presented audiences with an explicitly homosexual content, one made all the more shocking when presented in a religious context by a Caravaggio who loudly proclaimed the fact that he had 'been up the arses of more priests' than he cared to remember.[26]

Irish audiences did not easily accept McGuinness' deviation from the earlier stage stereotypes and walkouts occurred at the Gate Theatre's production of *Innocence*. While some of the Gate protestors identified *Innocence* as being sacrilegious, it is my belief that the disquiet of the audiences runs deeper. In many ways *Innocence* stood as a criticism and a challenge to a less than liberal Irish society. At the time Lynda Henderson noted that the production 'caused quite a flutter ... among audiences, for reasons which Yeats, Synge and O'Casey would find quite familiar – the hypocritical sensitivities of an insecure culture'.[27] This after all was a culture where the 1994 Dail Debate on Equality saw Paul McGrath TD protest that he was 'concerned about the possible effects on Irish society. Will we now see exhibitions in public by homosexuals holding hands, kissing, cuddling, etc.?'[28] Ten years after the first performance of *Innocence* McGuinness looked back, noting that: 'attitudes have changed an awful lot since then ... I don't know if people knew what hit them.' He points out that while 'there had been plays about homosexuality or with homosexuals in them before in Ireland [none of these had] ... ever flashed so potently'.[29]

Much of the disquiet following *Innocence* may be attributed to the virulent masculinity of the gay Caravaggio. What was particularly hard to accept for the audiences of the Gate Theatre in 1986 was that a violent, masculine, and religious man could also be homosexual. They saw that the violent masculinity of Caravaggio contrasted with the effeminate serenity of Wilde's aestheticism or the traditional arch campness of Pyper and Dido. For those who viewed and objected to the Gate's production of *Innocence* the threat presented by homosexual desire is not its difference, but its sameness. For Irish theatre, the importance of the play is that in it McGuinness severed the traditional link between homosexuality and effeminacy. In relation to the perceptions of Irish society

25 David F. Greenberg, 'Transformations of homosexuality-based classifications', in Roger N. Lancaster & Micaela di Leonardo (eds), *The gender/sexuality reader: culture, history, political economy* (New York, 1997), pp 179–93, p. 184. 26 McGuinness, *Frank McGuinness: Plays 1*, p. 247. 27 Lynda Henderson, 'Innocence and experience', *Fortnight*, 240 (1986), p. 24. 28 Lance Pettit, 'Pigs and provos, prostitutes and prejudice: gay representation in Irish film, 1984–1995', in Éibhear Walshe (ed.), *Sex nation and dissent in Irish writing* (Cork, 1997), pp 252–84, p. 252. 29 Jacqueline Hurtley, *Ireland in writing: interviews with writers and academics* (Amsterdam, 1998), pp 51–70, p. 62.

this is perhaps the key achievement of McGuinness' work. Radically for Irish theatre, McGuinness' plays present homosexuality as a spectrum of tempera-ments, as varied as those of heterosexuality. While Dido could 'be the queen of Derry', Caravaggio could also be 'the butcher boy of Rome'.³⁰ These plays sug-gest that homosexuality allows for a plurality of identities.

Perhaps most significantly for Irish drama, *Innocence* represented a move-ment away from both Ireland and the Irish identity. Despite this, it is perhaps the play which said most about homosexuality in Ireland. The world shown on the Gate stage would be a mirror for Ireland, and *Innocence,* by means of show-ing the world of Renaissance Rome to Ireland, was also to show Ireland to itself. McGuinness acknowledges: 'it is rooted in the reality of Renaissance times' and explains that in writing the play he 'used the city of Derry as ... [the] model for the Rome' of Caravaggio's time, drawing on Derry to construct Renaissance Italy in much the same way as Caravaggio used the poor of his locality to re-imagine biblical scenes.³¹ That the Gate's production of *Innocence* was not designed as a purely historical work is evident from the stage design and its designer, Joe Vanek, has noted that the play was distinguished 'by a refusal to be frozen in anachronism – *Innocence* did not belong to a specific period'. The design 'incorporated Victorian Fires, fifties chairs and a lot of modern junk' into an 'obstensibly Renaissance setting, thus ensuring that the play was not merely seen as a museum piece'.³² Furthermore, the Gate's production used Irish accents under the direction of Patrick Mason, to emphasize a context that found easy parallel with that of Ireland. In its graphic representation of homosexuality in relation to 'Irish themes' of Catholicism, land and the family, *Innocence* forced the audiences of 'Catholic Ireland' to confront the issue of homosexuality. In 1986, Ireland was a far from liberal state and seven years had yet to elapse before that homosexuality was decriminalized in Ireland. Set in Renaissance Italy but exploring Catholicism, land and the family, *Innocence* forced the audiences of 'Catholic Ireland' to confront the issue of homosexuality while detaching it from considerations of the national identity. The result was a radical reassessment, one that was as fundamental to Irish concepts of homosexuality as *Sons of Ulster* was to the revising of concepts of Irishness.

In concluding we should consider how McGuinness' life of Caravaggio is a subjective account, an interpretation where McGuinness 'pieced together a fic-tion of [Caravaggio's] life based on a reading of clues', which he imagined Caravaggio had 'left in his paintings'.³³ In this, Caravaggio's *The Martyrdom of St Matthew* was a key influence. McGuinness tells how the painting:

> hangs in a tiny chapel, without windows. Stand long enough looking at it in darkness and the strength and order of its events, even its power of colour,

30 Frank McGuinness, Interview with Colm Ó Briain, 'Personal Concerns.' Dir. Louise Lentin. Dublin: Cresendo/RTE, 1991. Videocassette. 31 McGuinness, *Frank McGuinness: Plays 1*, p. x. 32 Derek West, 'Riches to spare: interview with Joe Vanek', *Theatre Ireland* 29 (1992), 24–8, 26. 33 McGuinness, 'Personal Concerns'.

start to make their force felt, even in negative. Both inside the painting and inside yourself, even in darkness, something is happening, black and frightening and of great violence. Christ knows what conditions Caravaggio had established, but they're there, and then you can either panic or dance in the
- dark, for the observer is within the control of a great artist, who has ... told his story simultaneously and subversively.[34]

Innocence is a play that dances in this dark. The story it tells simultaneously and subversively is the reality of homosexuality, within Ireland, but also within the wider world. Thirteen years before *Innocence* was produced, the Gate Theatre presented Micheál MacLiammóir's *Prelude on Kasbeck Street,* a play that explored same-sex desire. At the time, its director, Hilton Edwards wrote: 'there is a tendency to fear the theme and to dance off into comedy which is inclined to make the comedy obtrusive'.[35] Today, in relation to assessments of McGuinness' work, we may substitute here questions of national identity for comedy as criticism; tending to fear the queer theme has all too often danced off into post-colonial concerns. To an extent, the neglect of *Innocence* in many studies of McGuinness' drama is a consequence of McGuinness displacing his usual explorations from Derry to Renaissance Rome. It is a significant omission from any consideration of McGuinness, for, in terms of queer politics, it is I believe the key text. The most important realization of McGuinness' drama is not the revising of the national identity through the use of homosexual perspectives, allegories or gender associations. Nor is it the revising of a homosexual identity. It is instead the fact that by representing the many facets of the homosexual temperament, McGuinness has consistently demonstrated that same-sex sex acts allow for a multiplicity of identities.

McGuinness' body of work has continually explored queer issues, both directly and indirectly, and contrary to most critical assessments, it is in *Innocence* that I believe McGuinness' most significant realizations lie. However its achievement reaches beyond McGuinness' work. The 1980s were dark times for Ireland's gay and lesbian communities. In her foreword to *Alternative Loves,* Ailbhe Smyth quotes Mary Dorcey's statement regarding gay men and women in 1980s Ireland, 'it is not in the light we lived but in spaces in between – in the darkness'.[36] The final part of *Innocence* sees the stage directions stipulate that 'light rises from Caravaggio's raised hands'.[37] This moment is often taken to symbolize the redemptive qualities of the painter's creativity. However, to labour a metaphor, it may be seen to symbolize the degree to which the first production forefronted male same-sex desire at a time when it was usually deliberately obscured. Its production ensured that there was a space that could be inhabited by later plays where homosexuality would finally be treated as a matter of course. Confirming

34 McGuinness et al., *The arts and ideology,* p. 68.   35 Christopher FitzSimons, *The Boys* (Dublin, 1994), p. 295.   36 Smyth, Foreword, in Marcus (ed.), *Alternative loves,* pp 3–6, p. 6.   37 McGuinness, *Frank McGuinness: Plays 1,* p. 279.

that McGuinness' work engages queer issues, the case of *Innocence* suggests that we need to look more closely at works such as *Sons of Ulster* and *Carthaginians* if we are to assess the significant contributions of these works to queer politics. Moreover, in that it illuminated the general unease in that cultural darkness of prejudice and homophobia, it is time that *Innocence* is seen as a landmark production, not just within McGuinness' body of work, but also within Irish theatre history. In terms of mainstream representations of homosexuality the Gate's production of *Innocence* should be seen as the most important production within Irish theatre history.

Writing the Irish Republic

JUDITH PRYOR, CARDIFF UNIVERSITY

A founding document constitutes a nation in a performative manner by calling that nation into being. As Jacques Derrida has noted, this act of constitution interpellates 'the people' that it creates as subjects. In order to exist, 'the people' must found themselves. Textually, the signature of 'the people' retroactively authorizes itself to sign.[1] The need to formally set down in writing a rupture from a sovereign power, in the form of declarations of independence, treaties, and constitutions, signals an erasure of the ties binding an existing community together. These texts in turn help constitute a new nation and establish a new narrative of origin or history for that nation. This collective subject – the nation – is constituted by texts which write its identity into being in a performative manner. Furthermore, such texts establish the ideal underpinnings of the new state, which interpellates the subjectivity of its citizens in such a way that their own identity is dependent on, and defined by, the dominant ideology in which they live.

A foundational text will continue to signify in the absence of its signatories, as a representation of the founding moment of the nation. As this originary moment is commemorated in the text, it is also separated from that moment and both requires and creates an archive to preserve the Event by which the new entity is established. The text witnesses the Event after the fact, the instant of constitution is fleeting and past. Yet, at the same time, it remains always to-come, containing a promise of the newly constituted nation in the future-to-come.[2] Thus, the signature is haunted from both the past and the future, archiving the origin of the nation and heralding a new entity yet to come beyond its name.

1 Jacques Derrida, 'Declarations of independence' in *New Political Science* 15 (1986), 7–15. 2 The phrase 'future-to-come' derives from a translation of the French *l'avenir / à venir*. Derrida uses the

At the beginning of the twentieth century, the nation 'Ireland', ventrilo-
quized in the 1916 Proclamation and performatively called into being by its
authors, was to take the form of a republic. The republican vision of the 1916
rebels implicitly equated the concept of the nation with an ethnic definition of
'Irishness' whilst simultaneously addressing itself to the 'people of Ireland'; this
new vision of the nation would be 'the property of the people', although who
exactly these people were remained somewhat more ambiguous. Disagreements
over this republican definition of the nation led to the establishment in law of
a partitioned island constituting the Irish Free State (later the Republic of
Ireland) and Northern Ireland.

As Joe Cleary has noted, the partition of the island did not, and does not,
solve conflicting questions of national definition and national sovereignty, rather
it has the effect of exacerbating them. Furthermore, partition could not be
accomplished 'without extraordinary communal violence. The violence does not
end with the act of partition: violence is not incidental to but constitutive of the
new state arrangements thus produced.'[3] I will argue that this violence is both
foundational, in the sense that Cleary identifies, and, as a consequence, conservative; the dominant position that is founded needs to be constantly (re-)iter-
ated in order to preserve and conserve it. Thus, the violent Event, which set in
motion the process that led to the establishment of Northern Ireland and the
Irish Free State, is commemorated as a foundational event in the Republic of
Ireland. That it is the 'glorious rebellion' of Easter 1916 that is commemorated
rather than the Civil War of the early 1920s indicates that it is this more unified vision of the Irish republic that the state wished to preserve as its foundational moment rather than the more divisive later conflict which, in more practical terms, led to the foundation of the Free State. I argue that it is this particular
text that founded an idea of the nation-to-come that haunts subsequent texts
that have attempted to define the Republic along more conservative lines.
Although the state is now called the Republic, following legal confirmation by
the Republic of Ireland Act of 1949, the nation-as-republic remains, rather, an
imagined Irish community. Although it strives for the functional unity promised
in the Proclamation, this unified entity remains always in the future-to-come.

Despite the impossibility of the unity for which it strives, the Proclamation
can be described as a foundational text. Foundational is not the same as being
original. It implies a more active constitutional role in the shaping of hegemonic
cultural and political narratives than a text that may have chronologically preceded it. The Proclamation thus forms a textual substratum, which both writes

neologism 'l'à-venir' which comprehends both the noun l'avenir (the future) and the infinitive of
the verb à venir (to come) thus indicating that the future is always in the process of becoming. The
use of the ordinary noun for future, however, also has this sense of coming or advent. This usage
recurs throughout Derrida's work – see, for example, Derrida, Spectres of Marx: the state of the debt,
the work of mourning and the new international, trans. Peggy Kamuf (London and New York, 1994),
p. xvix and translator's note, p. 177. 3 Joe Cleary, Literature, partition and the nation state: culture and
conflict in Ireland, Israel and Palestine (Cambridge, 2002), p. 11.

and supports the nation it is calling into being. Moreover, it is the Proclamation, and the actual violence of Easter week with which it went in tandem, that is commemorated as foundational by the state that it helped constitute and legitimate. As part of this commemorative drive, the material remnants of this text, preserved in its original appearance, are made into sacred historical objects and also consumable tourist souvenirs.

The question of what is 'foundational', rather than merely 'original', relates to the question of legitimacy. 'Foundational' texts such as the Easter Proclamation play a crucial role in this process of legitimation, preserving the originary Event in both legal and popular discourse, and subsequently forming a textual precedent for the constitutional texts which come after it.

In 'Force of Law', Derrida argues that the two types of violence identified by Walter Benjamin – the foundational and the conservative[4] – cannot be kept apart, but are instead caught in an intractable double bind. Each needs the other in order to legitimate the new entity that they call into being. Indeed, just as the signature appended to a declaration of independence authorizes its signer to sign retroactively, foundational violence likewise legitimates what it has produced in hindsight. Thus the violence of Easter week is foundational in terms of leading to the setting up of the Free State; once the Free State was established and internationally recognized, it retrospectively conferred legitimacy on both the Rising and the Proclamation. The Easter Rising and, more particularly, the moment when the Proclamation was read out, thus legitimating the action, is instituted as a point of origin to which the collective subject of the nation can trace its line of descent.

As a result of this process of legitimation, the foundational moment is seen as an irruption into history that sweeps all previous colonial institutions before it, making new laws and institutions. However, in order to contain the threat of further possible 'law-making' irruptions, this revolutionary moment must be domesticated by valorising and commemorating it as a point of national origin. The 'new entity' distances itself from the violence of the foundational moment as, aware of the lawmaking potential of this force, it perceives the threat that non-sanctioned violence could have to its stability. As the individual is divested of the agency that is valourized in the figures of Pearse and others, so this violence is conferred onto the state and recuperated as legitimate force. Because this foundational violence becomes institutional, for example, as a national police force, the new state still remains aware of the threat simultaneously instituted. This law is both 'threatening and threatened by itself'.[5] Therefore, the 'original' foundational violence is venerated and commemorated while other violence,

---

4 Benjamin refers to them as 'lawmaking' and 'law preserving'. Walter Benjamin, 'The critique of violence' in Marcus Bullock and Michael W. Jennings (eds), *Selected writings, Volume 1, 1913–1926* (London and Cambridge, MA, 1997), pp 236–52. 5 Jacques Derrida, 'Force of law: The "mystical foundation of authority"' in Drucilla Cornell, Michel Rosenfeld, and David Gray Carlson (eds), *Deconstruction and the possibility of justice* (London and New York, 1992), p. 41.

such as in this case, sectarian violence, which threatens to undermine the state it once played a part in creating, is outlawed.

So how is this foundational moment and simultaneous constitution of a collective subject represented within the Proclamation?

In this text, the rebels called for the shedding of nationalist blood, 'pledging our lives and the lives of our comrades-in-arms' in the cause of 'sacrifice ... for the common good'.[6] It is this blood, both literal and metaphorical, which links the individual subject to the collective subject of the nation. The word 'nation' is etymologically linked to the Latin verb *nascor* meaning 'to be born' and the noun *natio* meaning 'breed, stock, race, nation.'[7] This etymology invokes the corporeal and genealogical origins of national communities, traces that are often represented as blood-ties firmly linking the 'people' as individual subjects to the collective subject of the 'nation', thus giving a materiality to the imagined community. This blood is being called upon to be spilled, not just for the good of the nation but also for the good of the family.

The idea of blood sacrifice was very much in the air in the early part of the twentieth century. Writers such as Alvin Jackson[8] and Edna Longley[9] have shown that nationalists and unionists alike subscribed to the ideals of blood sacrifice circulating at the time of the First World War. The rebels appropriated the ideals espoused by British war propaganda and turned them to their own ends, calling for sacrifice in the name of the Irish nation rather than Great Britain. Drawing on this rhetoric of blood sacrifice, the rebels refer to the planned uprising as something akin to Christ's sacrifice and resurrection, a link the Easter date readily offers. Indeed, it was with this imagery that one of the earliest revisionists of the Rising, Jesuit priest Father Francis Shaw, took issue, effectively critiquing the use of the idea of blood sacrifice to valorize and legitimate the state.[10]

This reference to blood opens the triumphalist text of the Proclamation to a reading of the foundational violence it also engenders. Blood, which Julia Kristeva has characterized as abject matter,[11] is expelled from the inside of the

6 *The Proclamation of poblacht na h Eireann the provisional government of the Irish republic to the people of Ireland* at http://www.ma.utexas.edu/users/fodea/aprn/graphics/resources/proc.jpg accessed 11 June 2002. Subsequent references to the Proclamation will be given in the text. 7 Definition of 'nation' from *The Oxford English dictionary online* at www.oed.com accessed 9 September 2002. 8 Alvin Jackson, 'Unionist history' in Ciaran Brady (ed.), *Interpreting Irish history: the debate on historical revisionism 1938–1994* (Dublin, 1994), pp 253–68. Jackson asserts that '[c]elebrating the loyalist tradition in Ireland also, inevitably, meant celebrating the contribution of Irish soldiers to the British war effort in the years 1914–1918 ... 1916 came to represent a different sort of 'magic number' to different types of Irishman, even if Protestants and Catholics were fighting and dying together on the Western Front. The War, the Somme in particular, dominated Unionist history-writing in the 1920s, when the Irish Free State was being supplied with a revolutionary mythology and hagiography by its scholarly and polemical defenders', p. 257. 9 Edna Longley, 'The rising, the Somme and Irish memory' in Maírín Ní Dhonnchadha and Theo Dorgan (eds)., *Revising the rising* (Derry, 1991), pp 29–49. Longley links Pearse's rhetoric to that of Rupert Brooke, especially 'the association of self-sacrifice with a 'cleansing' [and] ... the vision of a noble death as redeeming collective shame', p. 40. 10 Francis Shaw, 'The Canon of Irish History – A Challenge' *Studies: An Irish Quarterly* (Summer 1972), 117–53. 11 Julia Kristeva, *Powers of horror: an essay in abjection*, trans. Leon S. Roudiez

body, transgressing the boundaries between 'inside' and 'outside'. In an analogous way, the newly created state of Northern Ireland was 'sacrificed' in order for the Irish Free State to establish itself as a legal subject. The abject, or 'in-between', state of Northern Ireland continues to form part of the self-image of the nation, Ireland – a self not yet realized in the state formation of the Republic of Ireland. In the case of the republic, the blood of a succession of martyrs anchors them to a genealogy of resistance to colonial rule and incorporates them into the imagined body of the nation. Blood is therefore what links the people of the Republic to the imaginary community of the nation.

The two entities – the 'nation' and the 'republic' – are, however, held apart within the text. In the Proclamation, the Irish 'republic' at first appears to be used almost in loco parentis for the feminized Irish 'nation'. In the first two paragraphs of the text, the geo-political entity of Ireland is symbolized as a woman, more particularly, a mother calling her children to arms. This maternal image recalls figures such as Cathleen Ní Houlihan and other female representations of the Irish nation used covertly in poetry and plays to criticize the British occupation of Ireland. Yeats' play *Cathleen Ní Houlihan*, often thought to be a revolutionary catalyst, recasts Cathleen as a revolutionary figure who 'expects the tragic ending. She demands sacrifice and offers nothing in return but the promise that the names of the patriots will never be forgotten'.[12] While this reading fits in well with the ideal of blood sacrifice espoused in the Proclamation and elsewhere, I argue that the text of the Proclamation undermines this traditional idea of the woman-as-nation, supplanting it instead with the child that it has nourished: the gender neutral 'republic' whose identity continues to be written.

The shift in the roles of the nation and republic in constituting a collective subject can be seen in the usage of pronouns in the text. The pronouns 'she' and 'her' occur repeatedly throughout the first two paragraphs as Ireland as the mother-nation rallies her children to the nationalist cause. This invocation of kinship ties, 'children', ancestors and mothers, rather than citizens, signifies that the Irishmen and Irishwomen addressed at the beginning of the text share blood ties with each other which the 'alien' occupiers do not. However, as the text progresses, Ireland as Mother-nation becomes an Irish Republic referred to using the pronoun 'it'. Ireland, as the mother-nation, has nourished her children and now their representatives, with her sanction, are calling a new kind of nation into being, that of the republic. This republic is 'the property of the people'.[13] That is, it not only belongs to them, it is what is proper to them and is thus a defining characteristic of who they are.

(New York, 1982) 12 Rosalind Clark, *The great queens: Irish goddesses from the Morrigan to Cathleen Ní Houlihan* (Gerrards Cross, Bucks., 1991), p. 178. 13 Definition of 'republic' from Cicero, *De Republica* cited in Richard Kearney, *Postnationalist Ireland: politics, culture, philosophy* (London and New York, 1997), p. 40.

Just as the child must distinguish itself from the mother so the child-republic strives to separate itself from the mother-nation in order to provide the foundations for a state with stable legal and political institutions. The child-republic that the Proclamation calls into being finally supersedes the mother-nation, separating itself from the maternal body, urging the people to rally to this new entity in its closing call to arms: 'the Irish nation must, by *its* valour and discipline and by the readiness of *its* children to sacrifice themselves for the common good, prove *itself* worthy of the august destiny to which *it* is called (my emphasis).'

Indeed, the mother-nation becomes other to the child-republic as this child separates itself from the figure that has nurtured it and constituted its primary object of desire, in a bid to establish its own, discrete subjectivity. The idea of the republic, which will subsequently shape a new state formation, must repudiate this object which has hitherto been constitutive of its vision of self in order to found itself as a subject. The mother-nation must be supplanted, becoming an object of fear, a devouring mother who, like Cathleen Ní Houlihan, demands the sacrifice of her children.

However, the imaginary unified nation, in the form of a maternal body, remains a site of fascination for the child-republic. The perceived unity of the maternal body is what the child desires, yet it must separate itself from this body. This separation is not total, however. Although it constitutes the child-republic's subjectivity, the republic's new self image is threatened by the repudiation of what has brought it into being – the idea of the mother-nation. The child-republic thus depends on an idea of the mother-nation in order to found itself as a collective subject and legitimate a new state. Furthermore, the fear of the mother's generative power ties in to the threat of the law-making function of violence; the mother-nation must be domesticated and conserved within the new state formation that is established in the name of the child-republic so she does not keep calling her children to violent rebellion in her name.

This foundational split, in which the collective subject desires the perceived unity of the mother-nation yet fears the sacrifice and law-making violence that she demands, demonstrates the contradictory impulses that constitute the desire for subjectivity. The collective subject fears the disintegration of its body as it tries and fails to achieve the unity it has earlier perceived. The rebels' call for blood sacrifice, then, is at once both destructive and generative. The abject matter of blood becomes symbolic of this contradictory drive towards subjectivity. This blood firmly links the rebels, through blood sacrifice, and the people of Ireland, through blood-ties, to the new political entity established in the name of the child-republic, thus conferring legitimacy on the new state.

I have argued that Ireland, in the form of the mother-nation and the 'Irish Republic', are used interchangeably throughout the text of the Proclamation but do not represent the same answer to the question 'what is a nation?' A similar tension is at work in the imagining of the Republic. Is Ireland as 'the property of the people' to be 'the Republic of Ireland' or an 'Irish Republic'? The text ambiguously uses both appellations to herald the new state; indeed, both are used in the title of the document. The translation of the Irish *Poblacht na hÉire-ann* as 'Republic of Ireland' is in a tense double movement with the succeeding 'Irish Republic'. Both titles refer to the new republic that has supplanted the mother-nation. However, there is a subtle, but important, difference between the 'Republic of Ireland' and the 'Irish Republic' revealing an ambivalence about how to answer the question of 'what the nation is' within this text.

The 'Irish Republic' can be said to be that constituted by the Irish people, that is, a people who share a common ethnic and cultural background, which includes the diaspora of 'her exiled children in America', while the 'Republic of Ireland' signifies an attachment to place marked out by the geo-political borders of the island of Ireland and comprehends all inhabitants of the island regardless of creed or ethnicity. Likewise, the 'Irish nation' that takes the form of this republic is one constituted 'in the name of the people' rather than 'in the name of God and of the dead generations', drawing its ideological force from an ethnic definition of the nation. These differing views of 'what a nation is' – as either an ethnic, religious or geographical bond – are contained within the same text making the question undecidable. This undecidability informs the process of constructing a history for the new nation.

As the republic is constituted, the Proclamation simultaneously creates its historical raison d'être, thus constituting it as a conceptual object. The history of the nation then, as the selective and interpreted record of its collective past, is the story and process by which the collective subject's identification of self becomes inscribed. The 'history' of, or, rather, historiographic writing about, 1916 does not solely come after those events in the form of scholarly interpretation and analysis. By invoking the 'dead generations' and previous failed rebellions, Pearse et al also performed a historiographic gloss on Ireland's past, which is at once romantic and mythic. The invoking of a tradition of resistance, in which the 1916 rebels could place themselves, provides both an authorisation of action and a legitimation of their particular suitability to act as the natural successors to Tone, Emmet and others. At the same time, this romanticized view of previous glorious failures, to which and for which they will succeed, has an eye to the future or the destiny of the nation. The imagined future-to-come of Ireland after the 'alien government' had been expelled would look back to the pre-colonial Gaelic past, one not marked by capitalism and individualism but rather tribal communalism. In doing so, it would 'guarantee … religious and civil liberty, equal rights and equal opportunities for all its citizens' and would furthermore 'pursue the happiness and prosperity of the whole nation and of all of its parts, cherishing all the children of the nation equally, and oblivious of all the differences carefully fostered by an alien government'. This egalitarian rhetoric, referring intertextually to phrases from the American Declaration of Independence, suggests that the Republic that is being called into being will be one that is founded on more communitarian principles than that of its occupier. It is because the Proclamation provides an elastic vision of a 'glorious future in the transfigured past', without actually outlining in practical terms what that might be, that I would suggest the Irish state looks back to this text and venerates it as foundational. This more mythic vision of community also pre-dates the partition of the island, therefore providing a more unified self-image for the collective subject. The Constitution, on the other hand, implicitly legitimated the partition of the island in order to found a workable legal and political framework for the new Irish Free State.

That the text of the Proclamation actively played a part in constituting the Republic as a conceptual object is evidenced by its performativity. In the act of reading out this Proclamation, Pearse performatively called the Irish Republic into being. In order to bring the new Republic into existence it was necessary for this text to be read out or performed rather than merely circulated, thus ritually conferring its new national status. Drawing on speech-act theory, Jean François Lyotard has defined a performative utterance as one in which:

> its effect upon the referent coincides with its enunciation … That this is so is not subject to discussion or verification on the part of the addressee, who is immediately placed within the new context created by the utterance. As for the sender, he must be invested with the authority to make such a statement.[14]

The act of proclaiming the new republic did not have the immediate effect of constituting a new state formation. It did, however, have the effect of altering the nation as a conceptual object, constructing it as a collective subject in the form of a republic. The immediate addressee of the performative utterance was not, then, the 'alien government' but, rather, the 'Irishmen and Irishwomen' who would define the new republic. The text not only created a newly emancipated nation, 'the Irish Republic', but also entrusted its provisional government to the leaders and actors of the Rising, a government which again the text 'hereby constituted'. Retroactively, the new state accepted the authority the rebels and their Proclamation claimed and used it to confer legitimacy upon itself.

Conflicting answers to the question 'what is a nation?' in turn inform the writing of the nation both in the sense of foundational texts, including the Easter Proclamation, and historiographic commemorations of past events, such as the Easter Rising. This writing of the nation conserves and commemorates the revolutionary instant that simultaneously founds and legitimates the new state formation. By re-reading one of the Republic's foundational texts, I have sought to show how the constructed self-image of the collective subject plays an ideological role in the constitution of both a new state formation and individual subjectivity.

14 Jean-François Lyotard, *The Postmodern condition: a report on knowledge*, trans. Geoff Bennington and Brian Massumi (Manchester, 1984), p. 9.

'The Ireland which we dreamed of':[1] the significance of the 1937 Irish Constitution

JOHN-PAUL MC CARTHY, NUI, CORK

This paper examines the significance of the 1937 Irish Constitution from an historical and legal perspective.[2] Though initially focusing on the genesis and prescriptions of the Irish Constitution when first adopted, it touches on some of the more modern elements in Irish constitutional history as well. The paper is broken into four parts. The first part offers some general thoughts on the importance of the historical methodology in a general sense. The second part describes the contents of the basic law and the complex process by which the document was produced between 1935 and 1937. The third section discusses *Bunreacht na h-Éireann*'s merits vis-à-vis civil and political rights, whilst the final section suggests some ways in which this complex document reflected the worldview of the generation who produced it.

HISTORICAL METHODOLOGY

Since this volume contains a series of papers from a variety of disciplines, it invites its contributors to make explicit their particular angles of approach. This paper uses an historical perspective and suggests some reasons why this is useful. The historical mind is distinguished by its contention that all ideas exist in some context. Historians argue that texts or statements or events should be related to the environment from which they originated if they are to be fully appreciated. Historians distrust abstractions in general, arguing instead that intellectual endeavour should never fully separate the subject matter from the environment in which it operates. This is a particularly important task when discussing the intellectual life of a particular era.

Constitutions aspire to moral status and as such, they should be approached from an ethical point of view. Historians are well placed to give a meaningful insight into the dynamic nature of moral life. Historians are sensitive to the circumstances in which moral judgements are made. This approach shows the extent to which circumstance tempers the interpretation of seemingly universal moral categories. It also shows the extent to which circumstances determine how each generation implements these very same moral categories.[3]

1 A phrase from Taoiseach Eamon de Valera's famous St Patrick's Day 'dream speech', 17 March, 1943. For the full speech see, Maurice Moynihan (ed.), *Speeches and statements by Eamon de Valera: 1917–73* (Dublin, New York, 1980), pp 466–9. 2 The author would like to acknowledge the invaluable assistance of the Irish Research Council for the Humanities and Social Sciences in researching this work. 3 Discussing the seminal role played by the idea of liberty in the modern American

[59]

In discussing the nature of moral judgements, historians have taken a variety of positions on this controversial issue. There are two poles that animate these debates. Some scholars have suggested that moral categories are the specific product of the era in which they are applied. Here it is argued that morality is a creation of historical time. If this is accepted, then each historical epoch can only be understood in its own terms.[4] Other scholars have argued that certain moral categories are of a universal nature and capable of transhistorical manifestation.[5] This insight is compatible with universal historical judgements.[6] This paper suggests that moral judgement in all historical epochs involves the specific application of a series of moral categories that, at their most basic, are capable of universal recognition.[7] The exigencies of that specific application often result in a particular aspect of a moral ideal getting stressed more than others. This process allows the historian to note differences in the moral vision of successive epochs.

A close scrutiny of an historical problem or a political strategy helps inoculate against dogmatism or a tendency towards facile moral prescriptions. The

historical experience, one scholar argued that the history of this idea is 'a tale of debates, disagreements, and struggles rather than a set of timeless categories or an evolutionary narrative towards a preordained goal' (p. xiv). He also argued that 'no overarching definition or single set of categories can capture the elusive meaning of freedom. American understandings of freedoms have changed many times' (p. xvii). See Eric Foner, *The story of American freedom* (New York, 1998). 4 This interpretation of moral categories is the basis of two scholars' sophisticated critique of the campaign in Britain for the pardoning of 306 soldiers of the British Army who were executed by their own colleagues for a variety of reasons during the Great War. Their rejection of both a blanket pardon for all concerned and their unenthusiastic response to calls for a statutory review of individual cases is based, in part, on the contention that 'the majority of those executed for military crimes in the First World War were guilty of the charges laid against them and, by the standards of their time, their sentence was not regarded as inappropriate.' See Cathryn Corns and John Hughes-Wilson, *Blindfold and alone: British military executions in the great war* (London, 2001), p. 460. 5 William Ewart Gladstone, classical scholar and four times British prime minister between 1868 and 1894, held this view with an Evangelical passion. In a paper written for an American scholarly journal in 1887 entitled *Universitas Hominum, or, The Unity of History*, Gladstone testified to his belief in man's universal goodness, a characteristic that gave history a universal, benevolent unity. He traced this pervasive unity from the trials of the ancient Jews and Greeks, through Dante Alighieri and Renaissance Italy to the modern world. This is discussed in D.W. Bebbington, *William Ewart Gladstone: faith and politics in Victorian Britain* (Grand Rapids, Michigan, 1993), pp 237–8. 6 Even Leopold von Ranke could be accused of incoherence on this subject given the fact that he seemed to have applied both sets of views in his historical writings. Arguing on the one hand that each generation should be approached as a thing unto itself, he also made universal value judgements. On this tension in his writings see Leonard Krieger, *Ranke: the meaning of history* (Chicago, 1977), pp 14–19, pp 153–6. 7 This perspective takes cognisance of Professor Collingwood's analysis of Benedetto's Croce's mature claim that 'a universal truth is true only as realized in a particular instance: the universal must, as he puts it, be incarnate as the individual.' See R.G. Collingwood, in Jan Van Der Dussen (ed.), *The idea of history: revised edition with lectures 1926–1928* (Oxford and New York, 1994), p. 194. Ranke made a similar point throughout his work. For discussion of this idea and various interpretations on it see Krieger, *Ranke*, p. 17. Here, he notes that 'it can be argued that Ranke's commitment to 'eternal ideas', 'moral laws' and 'universal history' confirmed rather than abridged the sovereign particularity and individuality of historical events, since, for him, general ideas and laws were unknowable in themselves and were knowable only as functions of the particular data and individual agents in which they were exclusively manifested.'

historical approach illustrates the complexities of moral life, given the fact that it analyses both the process by which the universal ideal is enunciated (be it equality, freedom or whatever category is in question) as well as the difficulties that arise in its application in the actual world.[8] In political terms, the historical imagination can help us conceptualize present day problems, if only through an appreciation of past approaches in analogous situations.[9]

As regards the topic of this paper, the 1937 Constitution, few other subjects illustrate the gulf that can often open up between historians and other disciplines. Depending on the methodology one adopts for its examination, *Bunreacht na h-Éireann* can be seen as a rather sinister testament to chauvinism or a sophisticated attempt to bring international precedent to bear on peculiarly Irish concerns. This paper proceeds from assumptions that are illustrated in the following quotations. These concern themselves with the relationship between ideas and context, particularly political context. Louis Menand's study of the history of American scepticism illustrated a peculiarly American belief that:

> ideas are not out there waiting to be discovered, but are tools – like forks and knives and microchips – that people devise to cope with the world in which they find themselves. They (the four intellectuals he discusses) believed that ideas are produced not by individuals, but by groups of individuals – that ideas are social. They believed that ideas do not develop according to some inner logic of their own, but are entirely dependent, like germs, on their human carriers and the environment. And they believed that since ideas are provisional responses to particular and unreproducible circumstances, their survival depends not on their immutability, but on their adaptability.[10]

A very young R.H.S. Crossman spoke of the need to integrate the historical imagination with our yearning for moral clarity. Citing the inherent limitations of abstract thought, the future Government minister argued that political theory could never reach final conclusions:

> because the environment in which we live is constantly being changed, partly by uncontrolled natural processes, partly by human effort. It cannot think out and lay down once and for all how men should live, and how states should be organised. You cannot remove a little slice of life called politics or a slab of organisation called the state from the intricate structure of human society and hope to understand it. We have got to see politics as one aspect of the life of an epoch, and political theory as one aspect of the thought of

---

8 For a moving example of this discerning approach see William Lee Miller, *Lincoln's virtues: an ethical biography* (New York, 2002).   9 The utility of historical thought is discussed in these terms in Martin Mansergh, 'The freedom to achieve freedom? the political ideas of Collins and de Valera' in Dermot Keogh, Gabriel Doherty (eds), *Michael Collins and the making of the Irish state* (Cork, 1998), p. 155; Henry A. Kissinger, *A world restored: Metternich, Castlereagh and the problems of peace* (Boston, 1957).   10 Louis Menand, *The metaphysical club* (New York, 2002), pp xi–xii.

an epoch. Right and wrong, good and bad gain meaning for us first from reflection on our own problems: we cannot reflect them back into the past until we have discovered in what ways the problems of our epoch are analogous to those of past ages.[11]

GENESIS AND PRESCRIPTIONS

The 1937 Constitution may have had only one father, but it boasts many midwives.[12] Eamon de Valera, then President of the Executive Council of the Irish Free State, supervised and directed the drafting of the constitution from start to finish.[13] He relied heavily though on the insight and wisdom of an elite group of senior civil servants. The two most important officials in this complex process were John Hearne,[14] Legal Advisor in the Department of External Affairs and Maurice Moynihan,[15] de Valera's closest advisor for almost three decades. President de Valera provided the policy instruction, and then Hearne translated it into legal language, whilst Moynihan helped infuse the text with a basic liberalism and structural coherence, particularly as regards the religious provision, the nation-state equation and the directives for legislative guidance.

The heart of the new constitution was provided by the so-called 1934 Constitution Committee, a conclave of senior civil servants who were asked to isolate those elements in the existing Free State Constitution that should be rendered immune from ordinary legislative amendment. This committee identified those fundamental rights and freedoms that were duly entrenched in Bunreacht na h-Éireann, whilst also proposing innovations as regards emergency powers and reporting informally on an amending formula for the new document.[16] The formal decision to begin the drafting of a new basic law for Ireland was taken quite late by de Valera – this came in the form of an oral instruction to John Hearne to draw up the heads of a new constitution in 1935.[17]

11 R.H.S. Crossman, *Government and the governed: a history of political ideas and political practice* (London, 1939), pp 3–4. After a brilliant academic career in Oxford, Crossman went on to serve in successive Labour Cabinets in Britain, 1964–70, as Minister for Housing & Local Government, Leader of the House of Commons and Secretary of State for Social Services. 12 Dermot Keogh, 'The Irish constitutional revolution: an analysis of the making of the Constitution' in Frank Litton (ed.), *Administration: the constitution of Ireland, 1937–87* (Dublin, 1988), 35:4. 13 Basil Chubb, *The politics of the Irish constitution* (Dublin, 1991), p. 20. 14 John J. Hearne (1893–63). Described by Maurice Moynihan as 'lively, vivacious and very articulate ... a highly intelligent man and widely read'. See Brian Kennedy, 'The special position of John Hearne' in *Irish Times*, 8 April 1987. 15 Maurice Gerard Moynihan (1902–1999). Commonly acknowledged by historians as having been one of the most influential members of the Public Service during his career; Hearne edited de Valera's papers after his death, producing *Speeches and statements by Eamon de Valera, 1917–1973* in 1980. 16 Gerard Hogan, 'The constitution review committee of 1934', in Fionán Ó Muircheartaigh (ed.), *Ireland in the coming times: essays in honour of T.K. Whitaker's 80 years* (Dublin, 1997), pp 342–69. 17 Earl of Longford & T.P. O' Neill, *Eamon de Valera* (Dublin, 1970), p. 290; J. Faughnan, 'The Jesuits and the drafting of the Irish constitution of 1937' in *Irish Historical Studies* 26:101 (May, 1988), 79–80.

The 1934 committee provided the framework in which the detailed drafting of the new document took place during the summer of 1936. The polished text of the constitution came out of the penultimate official committee, chaired by Maurice Moynihan, which worked throughout the spring and summer of 1937.[18] The final document had much in common with the old Free State Constitution, but also contained some important innovations.[19] The most important addition came in the form of the decision to entrench a bill of rights in the text and to give the courts the task of protecting these rights by appeal to the doctrine of repugnance. This affected a legal revolution in Ireland, making the country almost unique in Western Europe in its constitutional structures.[20] *Bunreacht na h-Éireann* replaced the ethic of parliamentary supremacy with a new commitment to judicial activism and a rights based constitutionalism. The new constitution created the offices of President of Ireland and Taoiseach, recognized the existence in the State of a variety of religious congregations and committed the Oireachtas to a series of Basic Directives of Social Policy.[21] Articles 2 and 3 asserted traditional nationalist demands for territorial unity. It reflects a trinity of influences, namely, the 1916 Proclamation, Enlightenment liberalism and Catholic social thought.[22]

BUNREACHT NA H-ÉIREANN & CIVIL RIGHTS

The report in May 1996 of the Constitution Review Group paid tribute to the document it was instructed to amend. Though the report of the Review Group contained many important proposals for amending the basic law in light of historical experience and international best practice, its lawyers recognized the general sophistication of the thinking that informed the 1937 draft.[23] They distinguished between the form of the constitution – which they applauded – and its content – which contained inevitable traces of the 1930s *Weltanschauung*. They saw particular difficulties as regards the inconsistent qualification of the fundamental rights in Articles 40–44, that is to say, those covering equality and discrimination,[24] personal freedoms such as the right to association and expres-

18 National Archives, Department of the Taoiseach papers, S. 8946 (henceforth, NA, D/T). 19 On the similarities between the 1922 and 1937 Constitutions, see Tom Garvin, *1922: The birth of Irish democracy* (Dublin, 1996), p. 178; Garret FitzGerald, *Reflections on the Irish state* (Dublin, 2003), 41–6; Tim Murphy (ed.), *Ireland's evolving constitution: collected essays* (Oxford, 1998). 20 Hogan, '1934', p. 361; see also *Report of the Constitution review group* (Dublin, 1996), p. 214 (henceforth *CRG*). 21 For a summary of the 1937 Constitution's most important provisions see J.J. Lee, *Ireland: politics and society, 1912–85* (Cambridge, 1989), pp 201–11; R.F. Foster, *Modern Ireland: 1600–1972* (London, 1988), pp 543–5; Brian Farrell (ed.), *De Valera's constitution and ours* (Dublin, 1988); FitzGerald, *Reflections*, pp 39–46. 22 For an analysis of these sometime contradictory influences and others that are in evidence in the 1937 Constitution, see D.M. Clarke, 'The concept of the common good in Irish constitutional law', in *Northern Ireland Legal Quarterly* 30:4 (Winter, 1979). 23 The Review Group described the 1937 Constitution as a 'far-reaching attempt to improve the method of protecting fundamental rights.' See *CRG*, 216. 24 Here the Review Group recommended changing this article

sion,[25] the family,[26] education,[27] and property rights.[28] They also remarked on some gaps in the Irish bill of rights, namely, the right to travel, the right to remain free from torture or not to be enslaved.

They pointed out the fact that very few countries in the 1930s had provided for the protection of fundamental rights and freedoms through an entrenched bill of rights. They acknowledged the far-sighted attempt by the draftsmen here to provide a mechanism to insulate the citizens' rights from executive or parliamentary abuse.[29] One member of the group also remarked with some surprise on the quality of the thinking that produced the 1934 Committee's report, particularly that part of its conclusion that discussed the establishment of a special Constitutional Court to specifically assess alleged infringements of fundamental rights. This was seen as an especially advanced idea for its time.[30] Since the passing of the UK Human Rights Act in 1998, the Scottish political landscape has been coming to terms with this new idea of judicial declarations of invalidity as regards legislation passed by the new Assembly. Though the courts in Scotland and the UK in general only have the power to issue findings of incompatibility rather than whole scale invalidity like Ireland, they have shown appreciation of the advantages conferred by the ECHR. The Review Group responded vigorously to those who called for the whole scale deletion of Articles 40–44 and their replacement by another rights instrument such as the European Convention on Human Rights. They argued that such was the relative sophistication of Irish case law as based on the articles produced in 1937 that whole scale incorporation of the ECHR would actually create gaps in the level of pro-

to outlaw discrimination according to a specific set of criteria, pp 458–60. This issue is discussed in J.M. Kelly, 'Equality before the law in three European jurisdictions', in *Irish Jurist* 18:2 (Winter, 1983,), 259–88. The Review Group also suggested inclusion of a comprehensive list of all fundamental rights invoked or recognized by the courts up to the present along with a qualifying clause modelled on the European Convention on Human Rights. Protecting new rights such as the right to life, freedom from torture and slavery guarantees might require special attention. See CRG, 458–60. 25 On the freedom of expression guarantee, the Review Group was particularly robust in its criticism of the present wording. They recommended the complete revision of this article in order to bring it into line with the Article 10 of the ECHR, thus deleting the references to blasphemy and sedition. The Review Group also made similar suggestions to strengthen the guarantee covering the right to assembly, viz., modelling their recommended qualifying formula on Article 11(2) of the ECHR. As regards association, the Review Group suggested a similar change to the present wording, pp 461–3. 26 Here the Review Group recommended changing this article to take account of non-traditional family structures and to provide for the right of the State to safeguard the welfare of children. They suggested deleting the phrases taken specifically from the Catholic natural law canon, viz., 'inalienable' &c., the alteration of the gender specific section 2, subsection 1 and a reworked guarantee of child protection modelled on Article 8(2) of the ECHR, pp 464–5. 27 Here the Review Group recommended changes to this article so as to eliminate those adjectives drawn from the Natural Law canon as above and suggested extending the education provision pledge to second as well as primary level, pp 465–6. 28 Here the Review Group recommended merging the two separate references to private property rights contained in the fundamental freedoms section, viz., Article 40 and 43. They also recommended retention in principle of that section that qualified the right to private property *in lieu* of the State's duties as regulator of the common good. These could be done by judicious application of Article 1 of the First Protocol of the ECHR to the 1937 provision, pp 466–7. 29 *CRG*, p. 216, p. 458. 30 Hogan, '1934', p. 356, pp 364–5.

tection that the Irish courts could offer citizens.[31] In this sense the 1937 Constitution's protection of personal rights, the right to trial by jury, the right to own private property and the guarantee of non-endowment is superior to that offered by the ECHR.[32] The Report suggested that the eventual incorporation of the ECHR would have to be executed on a selective basis. As such, in a formal manner, *Bunreacht na h-Éireann* showed a clear commitment to individual rights and suggests that its draftsmen understood the perpetuation of individual freedoms to be a laudable goal of social organisation.

INTERNATIONAL PERSPECTIVE

The sophistication of *Bunreacht na h-Éireann* can also be appreciated by tracking the extent to which its creators modelled their endeavours on best international practice as understood in the 1930s. In this regard, the 1934 Committee looked at all written constitutions in Western Europe, focusing on their treatment of fundamental rights and their proportional qualification.[33] This included the constitutions of Estonia, Poland, Finland, Germany, Mexico and the United States. In this context, *Bunreacht na h-Éireann*'s ban on state honours came from the 1917 Mexican Constitution,[34] its recognition of the special position of the Catholic Church as well as its commitment to religious freedom in part from the 1921 Polish Constitution,[35] whilst its Preamble and the form of the presi-

---

31 *CRG*, p. 218. On the incorporation of the ECHR into Irish law, the various ways this might be done and the problems of incorporation by replacement, constitutional amendment or via sub con stitutional legislation see Gerard Hogan, 'One Method of Incorporation: The Impact of the Convention on Irish Law', a paper delivered at the Law Society of Ireland Conference on the Incorporation of the European Convention on Human Rights into Irish Law, Saturday 14 October 2000. The full text of proceedings is available at www.lawsociety.ie/ECHR.htm. See also Ivana Bacik, 'A Human Rights Culture in Ireland?' in Ivana Bacik and Stephen Livingstone, *Towards a human rights culture in Ireland* (Cork in association with the Centre for Cross Border Studies, Armagh, 2001), pp 10–29. Both papers highlight the superior protections offered by the Irish Constitution in the area of jury trial (entrenched in Irish law) and as regards the strict criteria that must be met before the Supreme Court will allow preventative detention. 32 *CRG*, p. 218. 33 Hogan, '1934', pp 353–4. 34 See 'Observations on the 1st revise of the draft constitution, 23rd March, 1936': a paper by Michael McDunphy, Assistant Secretary, Department of the President of the Executive Council, member of Maurice Moynihan's drafting committee. McDunphy notes the Mexican parallel. This paper comes from the archives of the UCC Department of History's project on the drafting of the 1937 Constitution, *The Irish constitutional tradition*. Henceforth *ICT*. 35 The relevant article (114) in the 1921 'March Constitution' of Poland contains an initial assertion of theological dogma and a subsequent qualification providing for a freedom of conscience guarantee, viz., 'The Roman Catholic religion, being the religion of the majority of the people, has a supreme authority in the State among other religions which enjoy *equal* treatment. The Roman Catholic Church is governed by its own laws. The relation between the Church and State shall be determined on the basis of a concordat.' This is further qualified by a previous article outlining the right of all Polish citizens not to be discriminated against on the basis of 'birth, class, aristocracy, *religion, conscience*, press ...'. Quoted in Bozena Cierlik, 'A comparative analysis of some aspects of political life in Ireland and Poland: 1918–39' (unpublished PhD thesis, University College, Cork, 1997), p. 102. This article is also noted by Faughnan, 'Jesuits', p. 99.

dency show similarities to the American Constitution.[36] One scholar sees the roots of Ireland's guarantee of equality *before the* law (rather than *at law*) as coming more from the 1791 Declaration of the Rights of Man than from any specifically Catholic source.[37]

The original Articles 2 and 3 reflect a pre-Yalta determination that states should be structured along largely majoritarian grounds, an understanding de Valera gleaned from the life's work of his great hero, the twenty-eighth President of the United States, Woodrow Wilson.[38] In modern times, the Irish Government has maintained this honourable commitment to constitutional kleptomania. During the recent Peace Process, the Irish Government's understanding of how self-determination should operate in partitioned areas was based on a detailed appreciation of how this ideal has been implemented in relevant international scenarios. Of the half dozen or so countries partitioned in the twentieth century, Ireland has an interest in developments in Germany, Cyprus, Yemen (united concurrently in 1990 after British partition), China and Korea (effectively partitioned by Soviet Union after liberation from Japanese in 1945).[39] This sensitivity to developments in international law has led to an appreciation that self-determination must be based on a democratic concurrence of wills rather than on a simple majority vote in either of the partitioned territories.[40]

This new understanding is based on developments at the United Nations in particular and a refining of its Charter's support for the self-determination of peoples. Self-determination now focused on internal reform within partitioned states, giving rise to a number of novel approaches to conflict resolution, particularly ones that stressed power-sharing, individual rights, mutual vetoes and concurrent majorities in parliament. This can be contrasted with the more traditional Wilsonian model that contemplated border changes along ethno-linguistic lines. This modern approach reflected a new stress on Article 2 of the UN Charter, the 1960 UN General-Assembly Declaration on Decolonisation, the dictates of the 1975 Helsinki Final Act and the 1993 Vienna Declaration on Self-Determination and Human Rights. All of these instruments stress the destructiveness of boundary change without clear agreement and argue for an under-

36 This is a recurring theme in Owen Dudley Edwards, *Eamon de Valera* (Cardiff, 1987). In the Irish Constitution, the President is sworn in to office, is given a qualified power of pardon, a veto of sorts over legislation and is made commander-in-chief of the Defence Forces.   37 J.M. Kelly, 'Equality', p. 261.   38 On Wilson's enduring significance see Henry Kissinger, *Diplomacy* (New York, 1994); On the de Valera–Wilson relationship see Edwards, *de Valera*: on Wilson's ethnocentric model of self-determination see Derek Heater, *National self-determination: Woodrow Wilson and his legacy* (New York, 1994). For a description of the revized understanding of how self-determination must operate in the modern world, see Asbjørn Eide, *A review and analysis of constructive approaches to group accommodation and minority protection in divided or multicultural societies* (Forum for Peace and Reconciliation Consultancy Study, No. 3, Dublin, 1996).   39 For the definitive statement of Irish Government's revised policy on self-determination, see a speech delivered by the then Taoiseach, Albert Reynolds, *Self-Determination in the Joint Declaration for Peace*, at the Cearbhall Ó Dálaigh Dinner, Law Society of Ireland, January, 1994. For further analysis see Kevin Rafter, *Martin Mansergh: a biography* (Dublin, 2002), p. 65, pp 154–5.   40 Reynolds, *Joint Declaration*.

standing of self-determination based on democratic reform *within already existing territories*. By Article 29 of the 1937 Constitution, Ireland is automatically committed to these new developments and as such, this moderate Article has helped dilute some of the dangers inherent in the pre-1998 Articles 2 and 3.[41]

MIMICRY

Mimicry is the highest form of flattery, a phenomenon that is very apparent in constitutional law. Ireland's unique constitutionalism has been admired by many other states that have found themselves grappling with similar challenges to those that confronted de Valera in the 1930s. In the attempt to bring some form of democratic quasi-federal order to a chaotic post-partition scenario, the 1947 Constitution of the Union of Burma saw much to admire in *Bunreacht na h-Éireann*. They approached their own problem of sectarian divisions by using almost *verbatim* the special position formula of our own Article 44.[42] Their Preamble and their articles relating to the Burmese Presidency show a close scrutiny of the Irish model. The independent Constitution of the Federal Republic of India contains a presidential model very similar to the Irish office. Here the Indian President takes precedence over all others in the State, though remains under the control of the democratic executive.[43] Konrad Adenauer may well have read the Irish Constitution very closely when the drafting of the West German *Bundgerecht* was underway in 1948–9. In the West German policy of non-recognition of the East and its claim that German unity had never legally been sundered, we can see clear echoes of Ireland's Article 2 and the declaratory first clause of Article 3.[44] Article 15.2.2 of Bunreacht na h-Éireann may also have been brought to the attention of the post-war German elite, since they included a very similar provision in their *Bundgerecht*. Their Article 23 allowed the West German Parliament to recognize subordinate legislatures, an article revoked on the day before unity in 1990.[45]

Like de Valera, Dr Adenauer spent many months poring over papal encyclicals from Popes Leo and Pius during his wilderness years at the Benedictine Maria Laach Monastery in the early 1930s.[46] Scholars have also noted the impor-

41 Artickes 2 and 3 have been the subject of different interpretations since their adoption in 1937. For an example of conflicting interpretations of the significance of Article 3 as regards the powers of the Irish Government to seat MPs for Northern Ireland in the Oireachtas, compare the conclusions of the then Attorney General, Cecil Laverty, to those of Maurice Moynihan in 1949 at NA, D/T. S6390. Moynihan put forward a conservative interpretation of this article, arguing, *contra* the Attorney-General, that it specifically precluded the Oireachtas from seating or granting a right of audience to elected representatives from another legal jurisdiction. Moynihan's view ultimately prevailed.   42 This is noted in Longford O'Neill, *de Valera*, p. 297. The relevant sections of the Burmese Constitution from 1947 can be seen at www.shanland.org/SHAN/publications/constitution of the union of bur.htm.   43 These sections of the 1947 Constitution of India can be seen at www.alfa.nic.in/const/a1.html.   44 This is noted by Reynolds, *Joint Declaration*.   45 Ibid.   46 Charles Williams, *Adenauer: father of the new Germany* (London, 2000), pp 221–4.

tant similarities in wording and intent in the German, Italian and Irish constitutional guarantees of equality before the law and their related stricture that discrimination between citizens must be based on relevant differences.[47] Article 29 of the Irish Constitution formalised de Valera's concept of 'External Association', a concept that reconciled the form of neo-imperial association with the content of republican sovereignty.[48] This formula was of some interest to the Labour Government in Britain in their approach to impending Indian independence. Professor Nicholas Mansergh made sure that Whitehall was well briefed on the nature of de Valera's formula.[49]

The charge of confessionalism has been frequently levelled at the 1937 Constitution with good cause.[50] Though it is eminently possible to interpret the natural law principles in the Constitution in a non-theistic manner[51] and though the special position of the Catholic Church in Article 44 is based on a numerical calculation rather than a normative assertion,[52] there is a more compelling factor in querying this general appellation. The amending formula chosen by de Valera was a popular referendum.[53] He showed strong determination during the drafting process to entrench the referendum provision. As such, he vested control of the basic law in the citizenry. Even the most cursory glance at authoritative Catholic pronouncements on the nature of authority and the State during the late nineteenth and early twentieth centuries show that popular sovereignty as envisaged by the Preamble and Articles 6, 46 and 47 of the Constitution are incompatible with Catholic social and political thought. This argued that all rights came not from the people, but from God who empowered the people in a general sense to designate rather than legitimize the civil authority.[54] In his desire to make amends for his appalling civil war argument to the effect that 'the majority had no right to do wrong' de Valera entertained no opposition to his populist amending formula in 1937.[55] This appears to throw an interesting light on the confessional charge, at least at a philosophical level.[56]

---

47 Kelly, 'Equality', p. 262. 48 On the constitutional aspects of this idea see Diana Mansergh (ed.), *Nationalism and independence: selected Irish papers of Nicholas Mansergh* (Cork 1999), pp 114–15; J.M. Regan, *The Irish counter-revolution: treaty-ite politics and settlement in Ireland, 1922–36* (Dublin, 1999), p. 5; here Regan describes external association as de Valera's 'brilliant, if unpolished constitutional diamond'. 49 J.J. Lee, 'Foreword', in Mansergh, *Irish papers*, p. xvi. 50 *Seven ages: the history of the Irish state* (Dublin, RTE, 1999); Garret FitzGerald, *Towards a new Ireland* (London, 1972); Conor Cruise O'Brien, *States of Ireland* (London, 1972). 51 *CRG*, pp 250–1. 52 Lee, *Ireland*, p. 203. 53 Garvin, *1922*, p. 180. 54 This idea noted in the Quebec context in Pierre Elliott Trudeau, *Federalism and the French Canadians* (New York, 1968), p. 11; more generally in M.J. Schuck, *That they be one: the social teachings of the papal encyclicals, 1740–1989* (Washington, 1991). 55 Article 6 reads 'All powers of government, legislative, executive and judicial, derive, under God, from the people, whose right it is to designate the rulers of the State and, *in final appeal, to decide all questions of national policy, according to the requirements of the common good.*' 56 It is true that Article 6 of the Irish Constitution does use the 'under God' formulation in its affirmation of popular sovereignty. This no more detracts from the essential liberal pedigree of the amending procedure than does the similar mention of God in the Canadian Charter of Fundamental Rights and Freedoms or in the American oath of presidential office.

THE SIGNIFICANCE OF THE 1937 IRISH CONSTITUTION

This paper concludes by suggesting some general ways in which this document is historically significant. In the first instance it offers a vivid illustration of the applicability of Conor Cruise O' Brien's depiction of the post-Parnellite generation, a generation that swept the Home Rule elite aside. This document shows signs of that 'unusual degree of mental activity' that O'Brien identified in the first generation of cultural nationalists.[57] In many ways this generation was, intellectually speaking, hyper-stimulated. The tendency to draw on diverse sources of philosophical inspiration is in large measure the cause of tension and contradictions in the text.[58] These gaps are peculiar to that generation who were influenced simultaneously by traditional nationalism, Enlightenment liberalism and a potentially radical corpus of Catholic social thought.[59] Each of these intellectual movements had differing interpretations of human nature, fundamental freedoms and political economy. To take the example of personal rights, both nineteenth-century Irish nationalism and Catholic social thought tended towards a communal understanding of rights. Both argued that in certain circumstances (especially in the area of sexual morality and cultural expression) the rights of the individual should be subordinated to the perceived needs of the majority. The liberal element in the Irish political heritage had a very different interpretation of personal freedoms. As was seen during the work of the Constitutional Committee of 1934, the principal draftsmen of Bunreacht na h-Éireann were concerned to ensure the creation of a democratic and tolerant society where the rights of the individual would be protected.[60] The final text tried to knit these contradictory influences together.

The Constitution also bears witness to the cosmopolitanism of that generation.[61] As indicated, they put the final text together by drawing greedily on constitutional ideas from all around the world. The American influence is particularly striking in the area of the presidency, the entrenchment of a bill of rights, and the provision for judicial review.

The complex drafting process during the years 1935–7 show one thing very clearly. They illustrate the awesome power inherent in the modern Westminster-style premiership:[62] de Valera drew up the document on his own terms and

57 O'Brien's ideas here are discussed in D.P. Whelan, 'Conor Cruise O'Brien and nationalism' (unpublished PhD, University College Cork, 1998), p. 122. 58 Clarke, 'Common Good', p. 340. 59 This radicalism is a recurring theme in Finola Kennedy, *Cottage to crèche: family change in Ireland* (Dublin, 2001); Finín O'Driscoll, 'The search for the Christian state: an analysis of Irish social Catholicism: 1913–39' (unpublished MA, University College Cork, 1994). 60 The Preamble to the Constitution stated that one of the ambitions of the new basic law was to ensure 'that the dignity and freedom of the individual may be assured.' 61 John Regan has extracts of Desmond FitzGerald's intense correspondence with Jacques Maritain among other major European intellectuals. See Regan, *Counter-revolution*, pp 280–2; Gerard Hogan notes the 1934 Committee's 'very sophisticated understanding of the dynamics of constitutional law'. See Hogan, '1934', p. 356. 62 On the Westminster style premiership see variously: Peter Hennessy, *The prime minister: the office and its holders since 1945* (London, 2001); Chris Wrigley (ed.), A.J.P. Taylor, *British prime ministers and others essays* (London,

according to his own time table, using a select team of civil servants rather than his ministers or even his attorney-general. He directed the proceedings with an unusual degree of detail and thoroughness.

In common with nearly all nationalisms, Irish nationalism had great expectations of 'the State', especially in social and economic matters.[63] Though enumerated in a non-substantive form, this faith in state-led action is seen in Article 45. This provision was much indebted to the papal encyclicals in the details.

It is also important to mention that the communal mindset that outlawed divorce, contraception and widespread sponsored censorship was based not so much on an anti-liberalism as on a repudiation of the notion of atomism. The generation that wrote *Bunreacht na h-Éireann* did not reject individual rights. They did however reject the idea that these same individual rights could be understood in a social or economic vacuum. These measures were based on the contention the individual cannot be understood except in the context of the group that gives his/her life meaning. As such, this mindset argued that the State should give positive recognition in law to the collective ethos of the territory. [64] As the modern crisis in Canadian federalism has illustrated, these contentions are not peculiar to de Valera's Ireland. [65] Even the excoriated Article 44 and its 'special position' formula, when looked at in the context of 1930s Europe, exudes an admirable confidence and generosity particularly as regards the Jewish congregations.[66]

CONCLUSION

Bunreacht na h-Éireann is significant insofar as it attempted to give specific life to a series of peculiarly Irish preoccupations. As such, it shows that ideas about rights and justice cannot exist in the abstract and will always bear the stamp of the society that ponders them. By including a popular amending formula, de Valera seemed to recognize that a constitution must have an in-built capacity to change according to the needs of succeeding generations. In his devoted pop-

1999); Michael Bliss, *Right honourable men: the descent of Canadian politics from Macdonald to Mulroney* (Toronto, 1999); Howard Cody, 'MMP meets Westminster: early lessons from mixed member proportionality in New Zealand's Westminster politics' (private paper of author examining, in part, the New Zealand premiership); P. Weller, H. Bakvis, R.A.W. Rhodes (eds), *The hollow crown: countervailing trends in core executives* (Basingstoke, New York, 1997); Katherine Frank, *Indira: a biography of Indira Gandhi* (London, 2000). 63 M.E. Daly, 'The state in independent Ireland' in Richard English, Charles Townshend (eds), *The state: historical and political dimensions* (London, New York, 1999), p. 77. 64 For a philosophical discussion of the relationship between personal identity and the external world, see Charles Taylor, *Multiculturalism and the politics of recognition: an essay* (Princeton, 1992). 65 For more on the communal characteristics of Quebec, especially in the area of linguistic and educational policy, see Lorraine Eisenstat Weinrib, 'Trudeau and the Canadian charter of rights and freedoms: a question of constitutional maturation' in J.L. Granatstein and Andrew Cohen (eds), *Trudeau's shadow: the life and legacy of Pierre Elliott Trudeau* (Toronto, 1998), pp 278–9; Philip Resnick, *Letters to a Quebecois friend* (Montreal, 1990). 66 J.J. Lee, *Ireland*, p. 203: generally see also Dermot Keogh, *Jews in 20th Century Ireland: refugees, anti-semitism and the Holocaust* (Cork, 1998).

ulism, he recognized clearly that constitutions exist for citizens rather than *vice versa*. With its principled rejection of some of the key tenets of the Westminster constitutional ideal, one can argue that this generation gave vivid life to those radical maxims that spawned the Irish revolution. Doing things 'our way' was, after all, what the *Sinn Féin* project was supposed to be about. As such, *Bunreacht na h-Éireann* marked the high point in the one generation's search for 'an independence rooted in individual and national self-esteem', a search that sought 'in the exercise of political autonomy on the part of Irish people the communal embodiment in civil society of an indigenous version of the 'good life', which an oppressive and exploitative colonial/imperial connection with our British island neighbours had hitherto made impossible'.[67] The fact that their prescriptions may be out of kilter with the needs of their children should not be allowed to cloud appreciation of the significance of their achievement.

External associations: Ireland and postcolonial studies

EOIN FLANNERY, MIC, UNIVERSITY OF LIMERICK

In the Monty Python film, *The Life of Brian* there is a scene in which an 'anti-imperial', Judean resistance cell furiously affirm their title as the 'People's Front of Judea' and emphatically not as the 'Judean People's Front' or the 'People's Popular Front of Judea.' Without wanting to reduce the gravity of current academic debates within Irish and postcolonial studies to such inane levels, the tenor and nature of certain aspects of contemporary cultural theory, specifically postcolonialism, seem to generate similar superficial and frankly circuitous dialogue. At bottom, there is a marked willingness within many critical analyses towards persistent deferral and disavowal; too often the security of abstraction and conceptual circuitousness disabuses theory of its practical potential, and indeed relevance. Nevertheless, with a degree of vigilance, I plan to delineate some of the most instructive interventions in current Irish postcolonial studies. The impact of theory, or specifically the advent of an Irish franchise of postcolonial studies, has produced a contentious as well as progressive commerce of ideas and theoretical paradigms within the broader discourse of Irish Studies. Despite the poststructuralist murkiness, paradigmatic vanity, and indulgent verbosity of some international postcolonial theory, I would contend that the ongoing work of Declan Kiberd, Luke Gibbons, Richard Kirkland, and Colin

---

67 Gearóid Ó Crualaoich, 'Responding to the Rising', in Máirín Ní Dhonnchadha and Theo Dorgan (eds), *Revising the Rising* (Derry, 1991), pp 50–70.

Graham provides signally enabling mechanisms for Irish cultural inquiry. These critics are emblematic of the most perceptive facets of Irish, and indeed international postcolonial criticism, and are constituents of a lateral economy of ideas: what might be seen as a postcolonial cathexis within Irish studies.

In the editorial of a recent, specially commissioned issue of the *Journal of Commonwealth and Postcolonial Studies: Ireland as Postcolonial*, Caitríona Moloney and Helen Thompson dispatched a manifesto for prospective interventions in Irish cultural studies:

> [i]n order for Ireland to be considered part of the postcolonial paradigm, the paradigm itself must change. And conversely, Irish studies must do away with its isolationism … in order to see itself relationally with other cultures and nations.[1]

I have chosen this particular editorial clarion-call to initiate my discussion, not because it heralds any revolutionary theoretical strategy or seismic methodological innovation, but simply because it pithily, and at times unwittingly, alludes to and simultaneously embodies what has, is and needs to be addressed within the broader discourse of Irish postcolonial studies. The overriding assumption of the editorial is that Ireland does indeed seek to be part of the postcolonial paradigm. The presumptions of the editors consequently elide two inherent problems of their manifesto. Firstly, there is an unequivocal aspiration to locate Ireland *successfully* within a nexus of postcolonial cultures. More troubling, however, is the inference of an undifferentiated postcolonial paradigm. The project of Irish postcolonial studies is emphatically not to formulate serviceable theoretical archetypes, typologies, or vocabularies; its usefulness is adumbrated clearly by Colin Graham and Richard Kirkland in their own editorial introduction to *Ireland and Cultural Theory: The Mechanics of Authenticity*:

> [a] cultural theory informed by postcolonial criticism … locates moments of transience, instability and inauthenticity; a process designed not so much to buttress the existence of a new state but rather to question the frame in which the ideas of the state are articulated.[2]

POSTCOLONIAL ARCHAEOLOGY

Luke Gibbons embraces cultural materialism in his dialectical relation to both modernisation theory and revisionist historiography. Culture is no longer benign

1 Caitriona Moloney and Helen Thompson, 'Introduction: "Border traffic"', *Journal of Commonwealth and Postcolonial Studies: Special Issue: Ireland as Postcolonial* 7:1 (Spring 2000), 4. 2 Colin Graham and Richard Kirkland (eds), *Ireland and cultural theory: the mechanics of authenticity* (Basingstoke, 1999), p. 4.

and ethereal; it is of course profoundly political. His critical project is targeted at preventing the deflection of creative energies into a rarefied aesthetic or 'imaginary' realm entirely removed from the exigencies of everyday life.[3] The cultural critic is charged with the task of recovering marginal or 'unrepresentable' politico-cultural formations and narratives that can serve to problematise the modernising certitude of official discourse. Homogenized 'official knowledge' operates in an institutionalized and self-perpetuating manner and engenders a form of discursive certainty. Modernisation theory and its advocates unequivocally celebrate the *telos* of progress with its effacement of the dead weights of recalcitrant traditional discourses. Consequently, Gibbons envisages a materialist contextualisation of literary and historical texts that does not simply represent but is representative; that is not simply formative but is formed within and by the material conditions of their provenance. He asserts:

> the placing of texts in wider generic and historical settings releases their manifold interpretations, reminding us, in the process that there is no one way of mapping out an experience, even if some ways are more appropriate in specific contexts than others.[4]

In his 1995 article 'Unapproved Roads: Ireland and Postcolonial Identity',[5] Gibbons offers a tentative, and potentially subversive, theoretical alternative to the normative 'vertical mobility from periphery to center.'[6] Postcolonial theory has undeniably 'travelled', usually from a Western sanctioned centre to peripheral contexts. By invoking the *Distant Relations* art exhibition, Gibbons gestures to the possibility of 'lateral mobility.' Through this cultural exchange, he identifies the germ for a cross-periphery solidarity, in which postcolonial cultures can interact in mutually edifying cultural exchanges. Indeed, the pursuit of such 'unapproved roads' can be extended to include not just artistic exchange, but equally to encompass the formulation of radical theoretical innovation. Gibbons' more recent publication, 'The Global Cure? History, Therapy and the Celtic Tiger',[7] goes some way towards crystallising a definite theoretical trajectory for such a trans-geographical project. He encourages a constructive trans-geographical engagement with memory and tradition as a means of forging 'new solidarities in the present'.[8] These 'new solidarities' extend from his previous advocation of a laterally mobile postcolonial criticism. Ireland's 'Third World memory' should therefore operate within a polyvocal discourse of egalitarian

3 Luke Gibbons, *Transformations in Irish culture* (Cork, 1996), p. 8. 4 Ibid., p. 22. 5 'Unapproved roads: Ireland and post-colonial identity' was originally published in: Trisha Ziff (ed.), *Distant relations: Chicano/Irish/Mexican art and critical writing* (New York, 1995). It was later collected in Gibbons' publication *Transformations in Irish culture* (Cork, 1996) to which all subsequent references will be made. 6 Gibbons, *Transformations*, p. 180. 7 See Peadar Kirby, Luke Gibbons and Michael Cronin (eds), *Reinventing Ireland: culture, society and the global economy: history, theory, practice* (London, 2002), pp 89–106. 8 Kirby et al. (eds), 'The global cure? history, therapy, and the celtic tiger', in *Reinventing Ireland*, p.105.

'historically grounded cosmopolitanism'.[9] Critical authority must be reconstituted in marginal postcolonial contexts rather than administered from the ivory towers of western academia.

Gibbons' employment of the literary trope of allegory is justified on the grounds that it constitutes an indirect and figurative discourse through which recalcitrant or previously unrepresented areas of experience can be rehabilitated and become formative elements in a re-figured Irish identity. By engaging with the trope of allegory in terms of a cultural historicist methodology, Gibbons locates allegory within the politics of the unverbalized in which it becomes a figural practice that infiltrates everyday experience, giving rise to 'aesthetics of the actual'.[10] Art, specifically poetic forms, is in constant interface with the material, as the demarcation of text and context recedes. The certainty of identity is replaced by figural ambiguity as, to echo Seamus Deane, the real and the phantasmal coincide.[11] There is instability of reference and contestation of meaning to the point where it may not be at all clear 'where the figural ends and the literal begins'.[12]

Gibbons' mobilisation of allegory within a postcolonial theoretical paradigm emphatically politicizes an ostensibly literary trope. As justification for such a manoeuvre, he claims that:

> [a]ll culture is, of course, political, but in Ireland historically it acquired a particularly abrasive power, preventing the deflection of creative energies into a rarefied aesthetic or 'imaginary' realm entirely removed from the exigencies of everyday life.[13]

Allegory is not canvassed as a textual device, but further diagnoses the ritualistic or theatrical fabric of allegory; allegory as dramatisation of marginalized cultural discourses. Linking Gibbons, Kiberd, Seamus Deane and David Lloyd is the sense that narrative discontinuity is a fundamental, if not *the* fundamental, Irish condition. Most explicitly, Gibbons attempts to trace politico-cultural accretions that fail to register or that are wilfully excluded from legitimate narrative representation. These critical inquiries that focus on concepts such as allegory, lateral mobility, solidarity, adulteration, postcolonial melancholy survivals are not simply textual ruses or postmodern, theoretical sleights of hand, but constitute radical efforts to intervene in a modernising teleology, a teleology that too frequently diminishes subaltern or peripheral politico-cultural constituencies. Theory is not a form of academic therapy, and what Gibbons canvasses is an attention to the rituals of anti-colonial cultural representation in all its forms. Identity, then, is not 'a conscious, psychic choice, but developed as and through

9 Ibid., p. 100. 10 Gibbons, *Transformations*, p. 20. 11 Seamus Deane, 'Different strokes: politically charged fiction from Northern Ireland; a biography of an eccentric British expatriate', Interview with Seamus Deane by Nicholas Patterson, *Boston Phoenix* (June 1998), 4–11. 12 Gibbons, *Transformations*, p. 20. 13 Ibid., p.8.

a series of acts', and equally through what might be termed 'an apprenticeship of communal activities'.[14] For critics like Gibbons, then, Irish history and polyvalent nationalism represent a variegation of possibility.

Thus the oppressive colonial conditions that obtained in Ireland inflame cultural discourses with a rabid political import and intractable urgency. Allegory, then, enables Gibbons to trace 'the oblique and recondite' socio-cultural formations which have been categorically elided from officially sanctioned, nationalist narratives, both during the processes of anti-colonial resistance and in the post-Independence period.[15] By definition, narratives are as markedly exclusive as they are inclusive; the mechanics of selectivity and elision underwrite all narration at all levels, whether in terms of the individual, the local community, or the nation-state. This insuperable problematic is transfused with a caustic political temper within, and indeed because of, Irish postcolonial studies; access to verbal representation is synonymous with political representation.

In his capacity as director of the Yeats Summer School, 1985–7, Declan Kiberd can claim a share of responsibility for the direct importation of postcolonial criticism into Irish cultural studies, and indeed Irish academia. By inviting the so-called 'godfather' of global postcolonial studies, Edward W. Said, to deliver what transpired to become a seminal/controversial paper on 'Yeats and Decolonization',[16] Kiberd literally opened the door of Irish literary studies to the critical methodologies of postcolonialism. Postcolonial criticism had 'travelled' to Irish shores by the mid-eighties, yet still retains a profoundly contested valency, having never been unilaterally sanctioned within Irish academic or intellectual discourses. Kiberd exhibits an unequivocal commitment to a broadly comparative perspective; he embraces a theoretical vista that straddles diverse crucibles of anti-colonial struggle and postcolonial re-constitution. Ireland's status as the first English-speaking postcolonial society is assumed; indeed it is a fundamental precept of Kiberd's entire diagnosis that, 'the example of the Irish renaissance has been followed across the post-colonial world'.[17]

This pre-eminence within the field has been employed, and deployed, as a vehicle for much politicized commentary; Kiberd's cultural politics are consistently assailed as those of unrepentant nationalist dogma. The intention of Kiberd's criticism is to achieve an equilibrium between the aesthetic and the political; to probe the points of intersection and to identify the latent, mutually beneficial elements of artistic creativity and socio-political enterprise. Primary among Kiberd's critical targets is the crystallisation of a 'bogus unity' in the form of 'reactionary state apparatus'; central to this, then, are his critiques of nation-

---

14 Gibbons, 'Therapy on the ropes: *The quiet man* and the myth of the west.' Lecture delivered at MA in Culture and Colonialism seminar, NUI Galway, 25 October 2002. 15 Gibbons, *Transformations*, p. 16. 16 Edward W. Said's 'Yeats and Decolonization' was subsequently published in: Seamus Deane (ed.), *Nationalism, colonialism, and literature* (Minneapolis, 1990), pp 69–95. This publication is part of the Field Day pamphlet series. 17 Kiberd, Declan, 'Translating tradition: an interview with Declan Kiberd' in Susan Shaw Sailer, *Jouvert: A Journal of Postcolonial Studies* 4:1 (1999).

alism and conservative statism in terms of both colonial discourse analysis and postcolonial theory. The idea of exploding tendentious unities or monochromatic cultural discourses is at the core of Kiberd's discursive interventions, and central to this matrix is the invocation of a distinctly comforting fabric of Irishness: the patchwork quilt.

Kiberd's postcolonial criticism has, and is, characterized by his analysis of literature in terms of its social context, but equally he deems literary criticism as the foundation for participating in a critical social discourse. He has embraced a particular distillation of anti-colonial discourse, a tendency that is manifest in his consistent default to the work of Said, Fanon and Memmi. By invoking such a discursive heritage, Kiberd strives to execute a strategic political sidestep; Fanon, in particular, does not emphatically disavow the long-term legitimacy of nationalist postcolonial projects. His politico-philosophical teleology registers the limitations of intractable oppositional or 'mimic' nationalisms, while never explicitly jettisoning the radical potential of the popular discourse of nationalism and its conceptual archetype: 'the nation.'

Underlying Kiberd's Fanonian inflection of twentieth-century Irish literature is the conviction that the post-independence state did not answer the cultural and therefore political needs of a newly liberated nation. The state structure that crystallized in the 1921–2 period straitjacketed the critical and creative dynamism of the erstwhile literary renaissance. Accordingly, Fanon's tri-partite modulation of the decolonising dialectic was hamstrung by a 'state apparatus [that] remained unmodified since British days and condemned many citizens (as it was designed to do) to live like an underground movement in their own country'.[18] This insularity was reflected in the broad economic temper of de Valera's state and equally in the 'moral minesweepers' of his Ireland: the Catholic Church. Kiberd's critical logic, then, germinates in the fact that a decolonising phase, wherein bilateral engagement between cultural and economic discourses, has yet to actualize in Ireland. Indeed, Kiberd signals, in an Irish context, what Benita Parry has diagnosed in a broader theoretical context: 'the need to renew or reactivate memories [which] is distinct from the uncritical attempt to conserve tradition'.[19]

Such programmatic sentiments lead directly to Kiberd's most recent demand for an Irish 'national philosophy'.[20] Reiterating his unrestrained admiration for the cultural self-confidence that occasioned the Irish literary revival, Kiberd suggests that if such cultural assurance could be married to the prevailing economic success in Ireland, then a more representative and genuinely *postcolonial* Irish identity would emerge. He discerns the existence of a discursive hiatus between

18 Declan Kiberd, 'Reinventing Ireland'. Lecture delivered to members of the Danish Association of Teachers of English, Dublin, 9 September 1998.   19 Benita Parry, 'Resistance theory/theorising resistance or two cheers for nativism', in Francis Barker et al., *Colonial discourse/postcolonial theory* (Manchester, 1993), p.74.   20 Kiberd, 'Current cultural debate in Ireland', *Moving on: the Irish research seminar,* St Patrick's College, Drumcondra, Dublin, 13–14 April 2002.

economic modalities and the creative impulses of the cultural sphere. His contemporary modulation is for a new cultural self-belief to emerge in order to complement the overwhelming sense of economic assurance that has manifested in Ireland during the 'Celtic Tiger' period. Again, Kiberd's discourse is draped in the tropes of a distinctly materialist postcolonial analysis: culture is the active agent in the broader social context. Fundamentally, then, Kiberd sings from the same postcolonial 'hymn-sheet' as both Gibbons and Lloyd in attempting to re-present those 'minority groups who didn't form part of the main script [and were] edited out'.[21]

In canvassing such a radical imbrication of discourses, Kiberd's work neatly intersects with Gibbons' recent co-edited publication, *Reinventing Ireland: Culture, Society and the Global Economy*.[22] The advent of an economistically biased public sphere in Ireland has, according to the editors, circumscribed the potential for radical social thought in this country, and the logic of the collection is guided by a fundamental desire to re-infuse cultural discourse with a socially transformative aspect. The title of the edition, together with both the tropes and conclusions included, are overt critical 'curtsies' to Kiberd's *Inventing Ireland*. Gibbons and his fellow editors diagnose the convergence of culture and economic forces, a trend that has 'diminished [the] public sphere, and [silenced] an uncritical Academy'.[23] However, given the emergent imbrication of culture and economy, the critical potential of cultural discourses has effectively increased. As culture is assimilated and wedded to economic forces and becomes a constituent of the market economy, a sense of destabilising intimacy is amplified.

(RE)-INVENTING THEORY

While the tropes and paradigms of postcolonial theory as politico-cultural resource are gaining currency, concurrently there is a burgeoning concern, evidenced in recent interventions, with respect to the structural lexicon or theoretical idiom of the discipline. Specifically, critics such as Kirkland and Graham, among others, have initiated a self-reflective dialectic within Irish postcolonial studies. In effect, there has been a proliferation of intrinsic and extrinsic disciplinary postcolonialism; there is an identifiable expansion from a concerted discursis of the micro-details of theoretical inquiry to the elucidation of a meta-critique of the macrostructural paradigms of postcolonial analysis. Gerry Smyth outlines, at length, the charges laid against post-colonial theory: 'its elision of history, its textual fetishism, its exorbitant prose, its inability to register outside the institution, and its lack of self-consciousness with regard to its own function within wider politico-economic temporalities'.[24]

21 Kiberd, 'Translating tradition: an interview with Declan Kiberd', 1999. 22 Kirby et al. (eds). *Reinventing Ireland.* 23 Ibid., p. 17. 24 Gerry Smyth, 'Irish studies, postcolonial theory and the 'new' essentialism', *Irish Studies Review* 7:2 (August, 1999), 212–214.

Principal among Colin Graham's critical targets is David Lloyd's alternative to hegemonous nationalism, wherein 'he [Lloyd] re-inscribes nationalism as a subversive force in cultural theory'.[25] Lloyd's critique of nationalism is centred on the concepts of 'adulteration' and 'melancholy survivals', both of which are restless and residual manifestations of marginalised discourses. Lloyd, like Graham, is committed to problematising the homogenising *telos* of the nation-state; he does not believe that the teleology of nationalist struggle is necessarily enshrined in the formation of the state. However, as Graham points out, Lloyd fails to sanction any *telos* other than perpetual discontinuity and fragmentation, indeed 'Lloyd's understanding [of] nationalism [is] as always insurgent but never hegemonous'; as Graham correctly diagnoses, Lloyd's reading 'contorts the ideology of nationalism by separating it from and fetishising the concept of the state'.[26] Equally, Lloyd constructs a corollary fetish of the subaltern itself by 'ethically endowing' the notion of subalternity. Lloyd's interpretation is limited by his assertion of the presumed naturalness of the subaltern class and its fetishisation as an ethically pure formation. Graham's re-situation of the subaltern as a conceptual tool of postcolonial critique provides prescient elaborations on previous theoretical interventions. Graham's admonition is a *caveat* for postcolonial criticism as a whole; he concludes '[i]f nationalism is subaltern only when it is unsuccessful (still insurgent, rather than in the process of forming the state), then there is a serious intellectual danger of celebrating the subalternity of subaltern groups'.[27]

Graham diagnoses a peculiarly troubling facility in Ireland's proximate relationship with Britain; as both colonial victim and perpetrator, Ireland is signally a most fertile context in which to read Bhabha's subversive cultural politics. Concepts such as 'the fetish', mimicry, and hybridity acquire singular valency within the Irish context. Therefore it is on these bases that postcolonial analyses should proceed, not simply in terms of empirical, ethnic, or geographical qualifiers or disqualifiers. Graham is indicative of a deepening of postcolonial theorisation vis-à-vis Ireland and its Anglo-Irish relations. He argues:

> [o]n a metacritical level the question is: how does criticism of Irish writing proceed beyond the justificatory argument for the value of postcolonial paradigms and begin to deploy the strategies of such theories in ways which are sensitive to the contours of Irish particularities.[28]

Criticism, therefore, needs to evolve beyond the defensive postures of 'positions' and towards a realisation that postcolonial theory is not, and never was, as insidious a political stratagem as has been widely canvassed. Instead, it is time to

25 Colin Graham, 'Subalternity and gender: problems of post-colonial Irishness', *Journal of Gender Studies: Special Issue: Gender and Post-Colonialism* 5:3 (1996), 367. 26 Ibid., p. 368. 27 Ibid. 28 Colin Graham, 'A diseased propensity: fetish and liminality in the Irish 'colonial' text', in Colin Graham and Glenn Hooper (eds), *Irish and postcolonial writing: history, theory, practice* (Basingstoke, 2002), pp 32–3.

consider the potentially illuminative theoretical mechanisms within which one can read transcolonial analogies as well as illuminate, as Graham notes 'the contours of Irish particularities.' Simply, it is the ability to identify 'transcultural movements and interactions'[29] which marks postcolonial theory as a potentially productive intervention in Irish culture, and that has seen postcolonial theory emerge, as Joe Cleary contends, 'as an attempt to dislodge the certainties of modernisation theory.'[30]

Richard Kirkland asserts:

> [p]ostcolonial theoretical terminology has become normative within Irish Studies ... [for] many critics what is troubling in such a development is not merely the ethical or teleological imperatives of postcolonial theory but the fact that despite Ireland's status as one of the first nations to decolonize, the incomplete nature of this project has, until recently, inhibited the development of what can be considered an indigenous mode of postcolonial thinking.[31]

As we have seen, one of the primary indictments of postcolonial theorisation is its easy transferability, within which the concrete, material circumstances of postcolonial societies are elided or remain undifferentiated. Kirkland offers a suitably metacritical counsel for Irish postcolonial discourse, urging, 'that the postcolonial can be perceived through Ireland rather than, crucially, Ireland being perceived through the postcolonial'.[32] While accepting the employment of broadly comparative theoretical models, Kirkland does so only in so far as the integral specificities of (post) colonial contexts are differentiated. Indeed, in deference to the materiality of postcolonial analyses, Kirkland resurrects Fanonian anti-colonial discourse. However his inflection of Fanon's discourse differs sharply from Kiberd's strictly modular version; such a modulated 'transfer' is anathema to the specificity of place and sensitivity toward divergent material conditions canvassed by Kirkland.

Alternatively, he enlists Fanon's work in terms of its commitment to, and resolute belief in, 'the total liberation [which] concerns all sectors of the personality'.[33] The postcolonial imperative is sanctioned to the extent that it addresses the diversity and particularities of given historical, colonial contexts. Postcolonial perspectives enable specific historical readings of specific colonial conditions, and postcolonial theory provides a battery of discursive resources with which to address these issues. Kirkland echoes Smyth in his overt conviction that postcolonial theory has compromised its integral, and founding, relation with 'decolonising practice'.[34]

29 Colin Graham, 'Liminal spaces: post-colonial theories and Irish culture', *Irish Review* 16 (Autumn/Winter, 1994), 41. 30 Joe Cleary, 'Irish colonial/postcolonial studies', in *Moving on: the Irish research seminar*, St Patrick's College, Drumcondra, Dublin, 13–14 April 2002. 31 Richard Kirkland, 'Frantz Fanon, Roger Casement and colonial commitment', in Colin Graham and Glenn Hooper (eds), *Irish and postcolonial writing*, p. 53. 32 Ibid. 33 Ibid., p. 55. 34 Ibid., p. 62.

Following Graham's disavowal of an 'ethically endowed' subaltern, Kirkland broaches another lexical postcolonial condition or typology: hybridity. By invoking the concept of hybridity, Kirkland firstly interrogates a key trope within postcolonial and cultural studies, and crucially examines its deployment at the level of institutional or academic discourse. What is at stake for Kirkland, then, is not only the radical deconstruction of hybridity as a viable critical trope, but equally the active forms it assumes within Irish postcolonial studies. The development of an effective meta-critique of postcolonial theory is at least partly predicated on the policing of both its terminological politics, and its specific and comparative applications. Thus, Kirkland's explication of hybridity, and its functions, is part of a larger critical constituency that is designed to foreclose the facile domestication and/or partial 'celebration' of postcolonial idioms. By encasing hybridity in a form of apolitical and celebratory pluralism, postcolonial critics endow artists with 'a prophetic function ... one which operates at a level remote from "practical politics"'.[35] Again, we return to the notion of discursive fetishisation that canvasses the idealized margins or the purified peripheries. Essentially, it is an effort to destabilize the prevailing normativity of postcolonial theoretical tropes within Irish literary and cultural studies, a process of normalisation that disabuses criticism of its interventionist responsibilities.

Hybridity is canvassed as a potentially enabling, and subversive, discursive and political location within postcolonial studies. Its syncretic fabric is demarcated as a site of 'slippage' and cross-pollinated potency in both colonial and postcolonial societies. The indistinct or hybrid identity, then, operates within a Saidian or Foucauldian continuum in which naming or identity recognition constitutes a form of oppressive or controlling hegemony. The instability of reference thus enshrined in hybrid identities or cultures is perceived as a means of liberatory cultural politics. However, in an astute appraisal of such a discursive programme, Kirkland identifies serious elisions in what is ostensibly a liberating conceptualisation. Kirkland adumbrates the proximity of hybridity and institutional self-propagation. He notes, 'the danger remains that in evoking the subaltern category within Irish cultural studies we merely buttress the prevailing academic discourse against its other by restricting the play of the hybrid to a *containing metaphor* [my italics]'.[36]

Just as Graham registers the limitations of Lloyd's fetishised subaltern, Kirkland notes just such an operation in both Gibbons' *Transformations in Irish Culture* and Kiberd's *Inventing Ireland*. Through a methodology grounded in cultural historicism, both critics point to the possibility of creative, and by extension political, liberation above and beyond both the rhetoric of traditional nationalist expression and liberal modernisation. Kirkland's intervention, then, is motivated by the need to transcend any simple *recognition* of cultural hybridity. By merely registering the subversive potential of allegory, or adumbrating

35 Richard Kirkland, 'Questioning the frame: hybridity, Ireland, and the institution' in Graham and Kirkland (eds), *Ireland and cultural theory*, p. 223. 36 Ibid., p. 220.

the Fanonian architecture of 'the literature of the modern nation', neither Gibbons nor Kiberd 'allow the recognition of the hybridized identity to question the frame of the relationships between subaltern, institution and nation'.[37] The hybrid is not an applied or generic term or state, but an unpredictable, ambivalent series of differentiated instances, processes, and utterances. Significantly then, Kirkland questions the sociality of the hybrid as operative within postcolonial theory, he concludes, '[f]rom an institutional perspective the postcolonial framework of the hybrid as it is emerging often appears totalising and contextually insensitive due to an inability to recognize the full epistemological instability it engenders'.[38]

The danger, as diagnosed by Kirkland, is that the 'exorbitant prose' of postcolonial theory is becoming more sequestered within a containing lexicon of its own making. Through the creation of an attenuated theoretical idiom of concepts and paradigms, the gap between postcolonial and decolonising practice, and postcolonial theorisation is widening. Consequently, the very real instability and heterogeneity of 'the local space' is compromised. Kirkland's express scepticism concerning the deployment of a truly subversive hybridity, coupled with Graham's wariness about the ethically endowed subaltern, brings into focus one of the principal problematics of contemporary Irish, and international, postcolonial criticism. A taxonomy of postcolonial concepts has developed wherein the theoretical tropes have become signifiers for diverse socio-political groups. The facility to cast oneself as 'subaltern', 'hybrid', or 'marginalised' has become a *sine qua non* of postcolonial respectability; it is a situation in which 'terminology-as-type' is operative.

'PADDY' AND THE POSTCOLONIAL

Postcolonial theory's remit is not to ensure that 'its application assumes and underwrites the triumph of the independent post-colonial nation'.[39] An effective cultural theory radically interrogates the contemporary structures of both nation and state, as well as the mechanics of its liberation and/or foundation. Graham continues, '[t]he increasing institutionalisation of the practices of Irish Studies seems likely to cement rather than diffuse the critical assumptions through which Ireland has been understood until now'.[40] The roles of political and cultural representation, then, remain the crucial issues at stake within postcolonial analysis. Clearly, then, intellectuals become tenured within institutionalized formations; at a 'macro' level we note the specialisation of academic labour, and increasing alienation and/or suspicion within and between academic disciplines. Simultaneously, there is a definite institutionalisation of critical tropes and methodologies, as political affiliations and investments impede the gestation and application of competing cultural theories.

37 Ibid., p. 222. 38 Ibid., pp 225–6. 39 Graham, *Ireland and cultural theory*, pp 3–4. 40 Ibid., p. 3.

The institutionalisation of Irish Studies, within which postcolonial criticism is operative, manufactures homologies of *legitimate* discourse. A familiar vocabulary of intellectual practice evolves through sanctioned academics, approved journals, and hermetic conferencing. As Kirkland diagnoses critical theory frequently operates with its own interests in mind, the 'containing metaphors' of academic nomenclature, in this pessimistic view, promise little more than attenuated and conditional identities. The task, then, as articulated in an Irish context by Kirkland, Graham, and latterly Claire Connolly, is to re-present the tropes and paradigms of postcolonial criticism in less trammelled and politically ineffectual guises. In effect, 'an awareness of the hybrid, the heterogeneous and the anomalous should not be the catalyst for celebration'[41] but should produce a criticism that reneges such containing fiats in favour of a more participatory cultural politics.

The hegemony of the paratext:
An tOileánach *and* The Islandman

DAVID O'SHAUGHNESSY, NUI, GALWAY

In Gerard Genette's book *Palimpsests* (1982), he discusses his most recent neologism 'transtextuality'. He defines it as 'all that sets the text in a relationship, whether obvious and concealed, with other texts'.[1] He then proceeds to illustrate five different types of transtextuality, three of which are of interest to this analysis.

The first is *paratextuality*, or, the title, subtitle, intertitles, prefaces, postfaces, forewords, illustrations, footnotes, authorial biography etc. Genette argues that these marginalia provide a book with 'a setting, sometimes a commentary … and cannot be disregarded, in terms of shaping a reading, as easily as some readers would like'.[2] The second is *metatextuality*, most often labelled 'commentary.' This 'unites a given text to another without necessarily citing it'.[3] The final type of transtextuality that I will be concerned with is that denominated as '*hypertextuality*'. Genette writes 'by hypertextuality I mean any relationship uniting a text B (which I shall call the hypertext) to an earlier text A (hypotext), upon which it is grafted in a manner that is not of commentary'.[4] He gives two examples of different categories of hypertextuality: the relationship between a hypotext such as *The Odyssey* to two hypertexts: *Ulysses* and *The Aeneid*. *Ulysses*, he argues, is a simple transformation of *The Odyssey* – the action is transposed to

41 Kirkland, 'Questioning the frame', pp 225–6.
1 Gerard Genette, *Palimpsests: literature in the second degree*, trans. Newman et al. (Lincoln & London, 1997), p. 1. 2 Ibid., p. 3. 3 Ibid., p. 4. 4 Ibid., p. 5.

modern Dublin. *The Aeneid* is a little more sophisticated, in terms of hypertextuality, as Virgil draws on a model established by Homer and also imitates his style – there are no direct allusions to *The Odyssey* but, crucially, *The Aeneid* couldn't have existed without the *The Odyssey*. A final point on these different types of transtextuality is that they are not, Genette tells us, 'separate and absolute categories without any reciprocal contact or overlapping'.[5]

The argument of this paper will be that the original edition of Tomás Ó Criomhthainn's *An tOileánach* operates under different intertextual relationships with Robin Flower's English translation *The Islandman* and Pádraig Ua Maoileoin's reissue, in Irish, of *An tOileánach*. Flower's text has a metatextual and paratextual correlation with the original whereas Ua Maoileoin's has a hypertextual relationship. I hope to demonstrate that this reading has significant implications for how we should reappraise the three texts.

An tOileánach was first published in 1929. It is the story of a Blasket Island life, not only of Tomás Ó Criomhthainn, the eponymous *oileánach* of the tale but as Sean Ó Tuama noted 'the biography of an entire community'.[6] The narrative, edited by *An Seabhac*, recounts the trials and tribulations of the native islanders as they struggled with their Spartan existence, and communicates the stoicism with which they dealt with the inevitable tragedies that came hand-in-hand with their precarious existence. The island attracted a number of European scholars who came to study what E.M. Forster called a 'Stone-Age' society[7] and Professor George Thomson, another eminent Blasket scholar, described as a 'contemporary version of Homer's Ithaca'.[8] The most famous of these scholars was an Oxford don by the name of Robin Flower. Known to the islanders as *Blaithín*, he spent many hours with Ó Criomhthainn learning the Blasket dialect and culture. He fell in love with the place, and between 1910 and 1930, Flower spent a considerable amount of time living amongst the one hundred and fifty inhabitants of the Blaskets. Eventually, he translated *An tOileánach* and it was first published in English by Talbot Press in 1937 and subsequently went through thirteen reissues between 1951 and 1979 by Oxford University Press. The original version of *An tOileánach* was written in a Gaelic script, an orthography which is difficult to read for modern readers, so, in 1973, another Kerry man of letters, Pádraig Ua Maoileoin re-edited the text and reissued *An tOileánach* for modern readers.[9]

Robin Flower's translation has come in for strong criticism from modern scholars of the language and literature of the Gaeltacht. The precise subject of their vilification is his brief preface to the text – the primary example of the paratext in *The Islandman*. Flower claims that: 'the great value of this book is that it is a description of this vanishing mode of life by one who has known no

5 Ibid., p. 7. 6 Sean Ó Tuama, 'The other tradition: some highlights of modern fiction in Irish', Patrick Rafoidi & Maurice Harmon (eds), *The Irish novel in our time* (Université de Lille III, 1975/76), p. 39. 7 Patrick Sims-Williams, 'The medieval world of Robin Flower' in Mícheál de Mórdha (ed.), *Bláithín: flower* (An Daingean, 1998), p. 78. 8 John Dew, 'The contribution of English scholars', in de Mórdha (ed.), *Bláithín,* p. 11. 9 Throughout this essay, I have modernized the orthography of Ó Criomhthainn's text to facilitate the reader.

other, and tells his tale with perfect frankness, serving no theory and aiming at *no literary effect*' (my italics).[10] Flower uses this perception of authorial intention and combines it with his belief that the Irish literary written dialect fails to convey the 'colloquial simplicity of the original' to justify the omission, in his translation, of the more 'sophisticated forms of literary English'.[11] It is readily apparent how this ideology – the positioning of the *gaeilgeoir* as simple, honest and direct and juxtaposing this stereotype with the sophistication of the English language – would be inflammatory to Irish scholars. Louis de Paor argues that his '"plain straightforward English" gives no sense of the perfectly wrought tight-lipped classicism of Ó Criomhthainn's Irish'.[12] The fear is that the paratext has the power to displace meaning from the narrative and create a certain type of reading strategy before one comes into contact with the actual text.

Further paratextual evidence lends credence to de Paor's concerns. There are two photographs of Ó Criomhthainn in the Oxford edition. The first appears before the title page, the foreword, the table of contents and the actual text. It shows a side profile of Ó Criomhthainn by himself, staring into space and clutching a copy of his book. The second appears in the middle of the text and it is, structurally, the central photograph – there are three pages of photos before and three after. This photo shows the author and translator engrossed in conversation. An aggressive reading of this pictorial contrast would lead one to be highly suspicious of the implicit hierarchy demonstrated – the author cannot appear within the text without being in the company of the translator. It is the translator who enables the literariness and the publication of the novel and it is his judicious translation of the non-literary language into English that allows this. Without the translator the author would remain aloof and unread, outside the privileging site of literature, staring stoically into space.

Pádraig Ua Maoileoin was born in Dunquin, the village on the mainland which figures largest in Ó Criomhthainn's tale. His achievements in the cultivation of the Irish language in many spheres are widely acknowledged to be outstanding. He has been one of the major voices in both lexicography and creative writing for over forty years in Ireland.

Ua Maoileoin's agenda was to introduce a seminal text in the development of *litríocht na Gaeilge* to a new generation of readers. However, it will be my contention that he allows other agendas to corrupt the integrity of his editorial process and he allows his edition to become hypertextual, rather than purely metatextual, which I would contend is what a re-edition, under Genette's taxonomy, should be. While one may think that a re-edition should not come under the umbrella of any of the categories of transtextuality, as it is supposed to be a mirror image of the original, the re-edition's paratext (e.g. introduction) will invariably comment on the original, thus transforming it into a metatext.

10 Tomas Ó'Criomhthainn, *The Islandman,* trans. Robin Flower (Dublin, 1937), p. vii.   11 Ibid., p. x.   12 Louis de Paor, 'Disappearing language: translations from the Irish', in David Pierse (ed.), *Irish writing in the twentieth century: a reader* (Cork, 2000), p. 1104.

However, Ua Maoileoin goes beyond the metatextual and by significantly altering the original text enters the realm of hypertextuality. This slide into hypertextuality means that Ua Maoileoin's work is a new literary production, rather than a faithful facsimile of the old. I hasten to add that this is not necessarily a negative phenomenon but that it would be disingenuous of Ua Maoileoin to claim to be transposing directly the authentic voice of Ó Criomhthainn.[13]

I want to discuss briefly four significant variations between Ó Criomhthainn's text and that of Ua Maoileoin's in the hope that they will demonstrate what Ua Maoileoin's objectives were and how they differed from Ó Criomhthainn's.

The first is an excellent example of the paratext. Ó Criomhthainn's text is divided up into chapters as is Ua Maoileoin's. Ó Criomhthainn not only titles each of his chapters but subdivides the chapters again, and gives titles to sections of the chapter. For example, chapter sixteen is divided as follows:

An Inro, 1878

Cleamhnaistí agus póstaí agus cóisírí, i gcás idir dhá chomhairle, cleamhnais, mé pósta, an cúram, an obair, an chlann agus an mí-ádh[14]

However, Ua Maoileoin does not use chapter titles and subtitles. I suggest that this is the first step in the construction of Ó Criomhthainn's author-function as an authentic pastoral voice of Gaeltacht lyricism for the modern reader. Ua Maoileoin does not want us to perceive the author as undergoing a logical, prosaic and laborious writing experience such as the construction of a narrative from the building blocks of autobiographical memory. He wants to minimize the perception of the book as autobiography and invest it with literary qualities. The absence of chapter titles and subtitles gives a greater impression of spontaneous recital, a greater impression of the oral culture the tale comes from. This is only the first step of Ua Maoileoin's subtle regenrification of *An tOileánach*. There are many minor editorial changes made by Ua Maoileoin which contribute to this reworking or distortion, depending on your sympathies: an excellent example is the omission of the first line of Ó Criomhthainn's narrative 'Là San Tomás, sa mbliain 1856, 'seadh rugadh me.' This line roots us firmly in the world of fact, we know from the outset what period of history we're in, we know that we are about to read an autobiographical text, we know how the author got his name. In Ua Maoileoin's edition, the first line is 'Is cuimhin liom mé a bheith ar bhrollach mo mháthair' – a much more poetic image of an anonymous child suckling at the breast of his mother at no fixed point in his-

13 Whether the initial edition in 1929 can be considered to be Ó'Criomhthainn's authentic voice is debatable, given that An Seabhac edited the text. However, it will be this paper's position that it is certainly the closest we can get to it with the exception of going to the original manuscript. If we are to speak of 'literature' and the 'text' in a public arena with any hope of speaking about the same bibliographic entity, the reality is that we speak of editions, as access to manuscripts is not feasible for the general reading public. 14 Translated by Flower as: 'Shrovetide, 1878. Matches and Wedding Feasts, A Quandary, My Marriage, Responsibility, Work, Children and Trouble'.

tory: a timeless, natural image. And this is not the only example of Ua Maoileoin deleting a date from the text. Another good example is found again in chapter sixteen, a central chapter as it records the wedding of Tomás. Again, the date is not only in the chapter title 'Shrovetide, 1878' but in the first line of the chapter. Naturally, both are missing from Ua Maoileoin's version. This chapter is also important for another reason, the second variation I would like to highlight.

If we consider the chapter title and subtitles discussed above, we can see the division of topics that we are to be introduced to. Tomás, in his inimitable style, impassively recounts the celebration of his wedding, the responsibilities that it brings, the various depressing deaths of the majority of his ten children – be it falling from a cliff, measles or drowning, the emigration of another child and the death of his wife, one after the other. We are left in no doubt as to the bleakness of life on the island and the tenuous hold on life and happiness the islanders had.

Ua Maoileoin cannot have these morbid tales of misery infecting his narrative. He deletes all mention of deaths from this chapter, deletes approximately eight hundred of Tomás' words to leave the chapter solely as a testament of happiness and celebration, an evocation of idyllic pastoral. In Ua Maoileoin's version, the chapter ends with the recital of a song 'Caisleán Uí Neill', a celebration of love and marriage with none of the attendant responsibilities and hardships that come with it, such as those Tomás described. Thus the virility of the poet's productive powers and sustainability of his way of life are not challenged, as they are by the recording of the deaths of his children. He also removes the reference to emigration, the idea that descendants of this quasi-mythical Blasket poet would voluntarily depart this rural paradise, its pre-capitalist way of life and the cultural wealth it offers.

The third significant passage that Ua Maoileoin omits is contained in chapter twenty-four. In it Ó Criomhthainn describes the functionality of the islanders' Catholicism: the difficulty they have in going to mass and confession, the correct way to address a priest and recounts the only visit a bishop made to the island in his memory. It is a curious omission as the text to this point has made it clear that the island is very much a theistic society, one where God intervenes and interacts with their daily lives. Tomás is fond of rationalising the tragedies that affect him and his people by putting them down to God's will. Ua Maoileoin is attempting to minimize the connection between the Blasket community and the extraneous apparatus of church dogma; he does not wish to draw attention to any notion that these people are subservient to mainland ideologies and tries to create the notion of a deistic society where God and orthodox religion are subsumed into proverbial clichés and where they only have the smallest of cameo roles in the islanders' ceremonies. This is more in keeping with his trope of utopian pastoral.

The final and most significant, to my mind, of Ua Maoileoin's editorial deletions I wish to comment on is concerned with Ó Criomhthainn's relationship with *file an oileán* – the island poet. Up to this point in Ó Criomhthainn's text, the poet has been a character that has been the subject of ambivalent opinions by Tomás: while he enjoys the poet's stories, he, in one episode, gets annoyed at the interruption to his day's work a conversation with the poet entails. Nonetheless, after a brief exchange of dialogue by the two, Ó Criomhthainn is moved to write 'Since I'm talking of the poet, I may as well have something to say of him here'.[15] There follows an assessment of the poet's character which is far from ambivalent: Ó Criomhthainn describes him as 'having a great character'; he had 'great stuff and spirit in him'; and finally, 'nobody had the least thing against him, he was always a merry man'.[16] This section also takes note of the poet's death and Ua Maoileoin eliminates this reference lest there is a chance that the reader will find this suggestive of Tomás only being able to ascend to poetic and literary eminence in the absence of the poet.[17]

It is also pertinent that this is the only occasion that Tomás names the poet – Sean Dunlevy. Ua Maoileoin, I suggest, views this name as a reification of the poet which solidifies him from the ephemeral figure he has been in the text to someone who can possibly challenge Ó Criomhthainn's claim for the title of the Blasket poet and man of letters. This thesis gains currency when we realize that other missing material from Ua Maoileoin's version includes Ó Criomhthainn's footnote citing a satirical poem that Dunlevy wrote, 'The Blackfaced Sheep.' Again, there can be no challenge from external works which may threaten *An tOileánach*'s claim to sole authority. Finally, and tellingly, in this extract Ó Criomhthainn writes of Dunlevy:

> It was in the Island he died, after being ill for some time. He had had enough of life in this world. As he said himself, *'Of all miseries told 'tis the worst to grow old / With no man to heed or respect you.*'[18]

This is unacceptable to Ua Maoileoin's project as it shows Tomás having recourse to another's words to elucidate a state of being. Only Tomás can have a creative voice in this text, albeit one that is shaped and controlled by Ua Maoileoin.

This paper is not intended as an assault on Ua Maoileoin's scholarship. What it is intended to do is to offer a reappraisal of how we contextualize its objectives and achievements and argue that what he essentially does is attempt to regenrefy the original text of *An tOileánach* from an autobiographical or biographical work to a literary production. It is a case of hypertextuality, literature in the second degree. Indeed, one could argue that given that Ó Criomhthainn's culture is primarily one of oral narrative, Ua Maoileoin is well within his rights to do so. Jan Vansina in her book *Oral Tradition* argues: 'All such anonymous oral traditions have to some degree or other the common characteristic of being transmitted from one person to another and consequently the original form may be distorted'.[19] Ua Maoileoin himself explicitly says in his foreword that this is what he set out to do:

15 Ó'Criomhthainn, *The Islandman*, p. 215. 16 Ibid., p. 216. 17 A distinction between 'poetic' and 'literary' relates to the distinction between oral and written literatures. While Ua Maoileoin is keen to emphasize the traditional purity of Ó Criomhthainn's literary origins, his book also attempts to capture the transition from oral to written culture on the Blaskets. 18 Ó'Criomhthainn, *The Islandman*, p. 216. 19 Jan Vansina, *Oral tradition*, trans. H.M. Wright (London, 1969), p. 125.

Mar a dúirt cheana, is leabhar do léitheoirí an lae inniu a chuireas romham a sholáthar. Ní do scoláirí a bheartaíos é – b'fhusa dom é sin a dhéanamh ná é seo ach an lámhscríbhinn a leanúint go dlúth idir litriúchan agus uile – ach ní mheasaim gur saothar litríochta a bheadh ansin again ach obair shuaitheantasach ná beadh suim ach ag fíorbheagán daoine ann.[20]

Rather than view Ua Maoileoin's work as a distortion, I suggest we read it as a re-imagining of the text, one that lends the Gaeltacht's literary heritage an important milestone in the shift from oral to written narrative. It is my view that this is a shift that Ó Criomhthainn would have supported as can be seen from an encounter with *file an oileán* alluded to above. In this passage, Tomás is cutting turf and the poet interrupts him by recounting a tale. Tomás complains: 'I wasn't too happy then; and no wonder: a man who had a sensible bit of work on hand in the morning, and now it was laid aside for a pointless job!' On one level, this is Ó Criomhthainn explicitly stating that the value and importance of culture will always be subservient to the demands of economic activity in this subsistence society. On a more fundamental level though, I suggest that the author is questioning the value of an oral culture, in a pre-Derridean fashion, which sits with his overall project of recording the life of a dying society in the immutability of written literature. A written literature can be consumed at leisure without interrupting the labour of life unlike an oral narration which must be engaged with immediately.

In his essay 'What is an Author?', Foucault outlines how a discourse inevitably returns to its discursive origin to advance itself, the process that Ua Maoileoin is carrying out. He writes:

> This return, which is part of the discursive field itself, never stops modifying it. The return is not a historical supplement which would be added to the discursivity, or merely an ornament; on the contrary, it constitutes an effective and necessary task of transforming the discursive practice itself.[21]

What this paper has also implicitly demonstrated is that a reappraisal of Ua Maoileoin's work implies a simultaneous reappraisal of both Flower's and Ó Criomhthainn's productions. If Flower's text appears to fail to transmit the literary quality of Ó Criomhthainn's text, it is, I suggest, because the original *An tOileánach* is not an outstanding work of literature: the ability to recount a biography through the medium of pithy, ironic, humorous aphorisms does not constitute a literary text, despite being cloaked with what Genette would call the *factual* paratext – the author being re-imagined as a figure of literature by Irish

20 Tomas Ó'Criomhthainn, *An tOileánach* (ed.) Padraig Ua Maoileoin (Dublin, 1973), p. 9. Translated it reads as follows: 'As I have said previously, I intended to produce a book for the reader of today. It's not for academics – it would have been easier for me to do that as it would have just involved transcribing the manuscripts – but I don't think it would be a work of literature then; it would have been rather an esoteric work, of interest to very few.' 21 Michel Foucault, 'What is an author?', in David Lodge (ed.), *Modern criticism and theory: a reader* (London & New York, 1988), p. 208.

language scholarship, or being published by Oxford under the category of 'Literature.' Ó Criomhthainn's *An tOileánach* is a fascinating read – but from the perspective of anthropology and sociology. Sean Ó Tuama, for example, a prominent Irish language author and scholar, believed that 'the most lasting achievement of Irish literature in the 1920s and 1930s was not in the field of storytelling but in autobiography' and categorized *An tOileánach* as a 'majestic *sociological* document' (my italics).[22] It is the hypertext of Ua Maoileoin's construction that constitutes the literary work. Ua Maoileoin and other Irish scholars have moulded the author-function that Ó Criomhthainn's name is to give modern currency to their ideological reimagining of Gaeltacht pastoral oral narrative. Foucault gives a précis of this inevitable, not insidious, process:

> A characteristic of the author-function is that it does not develop spontaneously as the attribution of a discourse to an individual. It is, rather, the result of a complex operation which constructs a certain rational being that we call 'author.' Critics doubtless try to give this intelligible being a realistic status, by discerning, in the individual, a 'deep' motive, a 'creative' power, or a 'design', the milieu in which writing originates. Nevertheless, these aspects of an individual which we designate as making him an author are only a projection, in more or less psychologizing terms of the operations that we force texts to undergo, the connections we make, the traits that we establish as pertinent, the continuities that we recognize, or *the exclusions that we practise* (my italics).[23]

The Irish tenor: metaphor and its voice in Irish criticism

MICHAEL O'SULLIVAN, NUI, CORK

'But though the Irish are eloquent, a revolution is not made from human breath.'[1]
[James Joyce]

'What writing itself in its non-phonetic moment betrays is life. It menaces at once the breath, the spirit, and history as the spirit's relationship with itself.'[2]
[Jacques Derrida]

How revealing is it of Irish criticism's approach to language and semiotics that it refers to its younger critics as *new voices*, as somewhat disembodied and self-

22 Ó Tuama, 'The other tradition: some highlights of modern fiction in Irish', p. 39. 23 Foucault, 'What is an author?', p. 201. 1 Kevin Barry (ed.), *James Joyce: occasional, critical, and political writing* (Oxford, 2000), p. 126. 2 Jacques Derrida, *Of grammatology*, trans. G.C. Spivak (Baltimore, 1998), p. 26.

estranged? Are we denied a certain materiality, or is there something in the materiality of the language used, the title employed, that connotes a distinct understanding of metaphor, an understanding implicit in the prevailing Irish critical idiom, namely, the postcolonial? Is such criticism so accepting of a culturally-assumed, subaltern lust for the lyrical, of a heretofore repressed sense of 'Irishness', that it fails to interrogate how language can ever wholly represent a cultural identity not to mention one that regards itself as heretofore repressed? The postcolonial discourse frequently works to a historical thematic that neglects a careful analysis of post-structuralism's placing of signification under an institutional contingency already marking us as 'new hyperlinks' or 'new trademarks'. Does a critical tradition that can refer to its younger critics as new voices', all too readily ascribe an empirical stratum to the function of analysis? In employing voice unproblematically as a metaphor for consciousness and for a lineage or 'type' of criticism it invests in a sense of metaphor debunked most effectively in the early texts of post-structuralism and deconstruction. One must also question how a voice indeed can be new. Intertextuality's recently acquired intra and inter-textual critical baggage may rather imply that we are 'echo chambers' for a generation of older critics never having the opportunity to write as 'New Voices'. The paper therefore questions the place of the postcolonial as the prevailing mode of Irish criticism not solely because of the programmatic historicist readings it makes of literature, but also because in prioritising a historical episteme as formative of styles of interpretation it neglects how reading literature may primarily 'voice' phenomenological and aesthetic motivations. Does the prevailing Irish criticism ever allow itself the critical space, the introspective state, of even a Beckettian Krapp, so that we might suffer something akin to the shock of experiencing our own voice on a spooling tape-recorder: 'Hard to believe I was ever that young whelp. *The voice*! Jesus! And the aspirations [my emphasis]?'[3] Beckett's play destabilizes any direct correlation of the voice with consciousness. The voice for Beckett, enmeshed in a complex representation of its recording and mechanisation, becomes something that unsettles rather than proclaims semantic and subjective identity.

Irish criticism occupies an innocuous location alongside the Anglo-American and Continental critical hegemony, reluctantly received into the post-colonialist debate, and never wholly able to examine the structuralist or tropological potential of its own critical language. This paper will examine its institutional and critical standing, its structuralist tenor, working through some of the implications of the metaphor of *voice* for an Irish criticism. Unlike its Anglo-American and Continental counterparts, Irish criticism never institutionally embraced a structuralist school, or a 'linguistic turn'. Our critics have wrestled with an elaboration of Irishness predominantly by way of a historical thematics and a critical idealism, leaving the philosophical and figurative analysis of writing very

3 Samuel Beckett, *Krapp's last tape*, in *Samuel Beckett: the complete dramatic works* (London, 1990), p. 218.

often to the artists themselves. As early as 1907, at the age of 25, Joyce was bemoaning the Romantic Movement by way of what he described as its 'insensible figures'.[4] Beckett, also at 25, informs us in his college dissertation that for Proust 'the *quality of language* [my italics] is more important than any system of ethics or aesthetics'.[5] And yet our critics seem intent on neglecting any such engaged analysis of language's pre-eminence, disdaining any suggested 'rupture in the lines of communication' (to employ what might already be a dead metaphor) between a tradition of literature and its shadowing history. Irish criticism never housed a structuralist school or embraced a 'linguistic turn,' thereby never interiorising or gaining comfortable parlance of post-structuralism's processual account of the conditions of signification. Its explication of the post-colonial always suggests a historical shadow for the reading of literature; Seamus Deane writes in the preface to *A Short History of Irish Literature* that Irish 'literature has been inescapably allied with historical interpretation and with political allegiance'. David Lloyd also gives a postcolonial reading of the field, speaking of a rather refreshing sense of 'self-estrangement' within the text while yet regarding this state as only being 'encouraged' by either 'official nationalism or colonial powers'.[6] Declan Kiberd has spoken recently of the 'turn to geography' in criticism as an 'attempt to shift the grounds of Irish identity from race to locality and to make a virtue of ambivalence', yet it is an ambivalence grounded in the physical geography of place rather than of the text. Gerry Smyth's *Decolonisation and Criticism* while noting that Irish studies for the most part is 'locked within conservative modes of analysis',[7] and while recognising the importance of Homi Bhabha's 'Third space', or the condition of language, as marking the moment between reality and representation, still never wholly addresses the linguistic potentiality of this space for the reading of literature.

It is necessary to inspect the space between the interplay of critical discourses and to take account of how earlier critics of Irish literature have regarded the field. As a graduate student and teacher of English at University College Dublin Denis Donoghue published an essay entitled 'Notes towards a Critical Method'. In this essay Donoghue seeks to question a prevailing tendency in criticism. He seeks to describe rather than define the poetic, regarding poems as 'gestures of defiance against the tendency of ordinary living to be wayward'.[8] He notes a failure in critical studies to distinguish between ideas and their poetic transformations, and makes the point that 'historical studies of literature have too often been undertaken in a spirit of almost complete detachment from any consideration of literature *as* literature'.[9] In response to Donoghue's article Vivien Mercier wrote an essay entitled 'An Irish School of Criticism?' while Donald Davie responded with 'Reflections of an English Writer in Ireland'. Despite certain

4 Barry (ed.), *James Joyce*, p. 53. 5 Samuel Beckett, *Proust and three dialogues with Georges Duthuit* (London,1999), p. 88. 6 Seamus Deane, *A short history of Irish literature* (London, 1986), p. 1 7 Gerry Smyth, *Decolonisation and criticism: the construction of Irish literature* (London, 1998), p. ix. 8 Denis Donoghue, 'Notes toward a critical method' *Studies* 44 (1955), 181. 9 Ibid., p. 187.

differences of opinion their debate raises interesting questions and comments in relation to the state of an Irish criticism. Mercier replies that the 'gulf between scholarship and criticism seems ever wider and deeper in Ireland than it normally is in other countries'[10] and Davie suggests that there 'has never been any Irish critical tradition at all'.[11] Almost fifty years later, at a period in Irish criticism when Irish Studies is considered synonymous with postcolonial criticism (as a plenary speaker recently informed Ireland's new voices), Donoghue's and Mercier's questions are more pertinent than ever.

The successful critic must take some heed of cultural heritage in formulating a message for the groups or classes she addresses. The objective conditions determining the material and symbolic interests of those groups predispose them to attend to certain discourses over others. However, when an institutionally prescribed account of identity, formulated at some remove from the specific context and site of its occurrence, is then regarded as essential for a reading of literature it impedes tropological accounts of reading. The Irish critic is expected to either re-inscribe the Irish canon for the American academy, or to resurrect some subaltern voice from the demesne of neglected Irish writers. The scarcity of figurative analysis and critical theory in the Irish critical canon is indicative of a recalcitrant institutional and its hierarchical allocation of critical discourses. One might align this with Foucault's notion of 'intelligibility', 'intelligibility' being an aggressive practice, a practice that does not make *the* world intelligible, but excludes other worlds.[12] By such a model the purpose of critical analysis should be to question, not solely reiterate, existing structures of intelligibility, a purpose somewhat stymied by the postcolonial when it reads some repressed, 'unvoiced' notion of identity as being directly mediated by unexamined conditions of signification.

And yet the Irish School should not be so disheartened. Schools such as the French and the Yale schools were pan-nationalist groups that merely adopted the name of their institution of tenure. They may not have created a discourse and 'way' of reading, but rather set in place an interpretive strategy which required institutional reification. Critical theories require certain codes and culturally accepted models of reading before they are canonized. The teaching of American and French schools of critical and post-structuralist theory only serves to map on the discursive level, albeit wholly allusive in its rhetoric, a pre-existing institutional stratification. The want of an Irish appraisal of a figurative and stylistic discourse, running concurrent with the postcolonial, might either imply that Irish colleges have nothing to say in relation to post-structuralism and critical theory, or rather display its contentment with an allocated critical register.

10 Vivian Mercier, 'An Irish school of criticism?' *Studies* 45 (1956), 84. 11 Donald Davie, 'Reflections of an English writer in Ireland', *Studies* 44 (1955), 441. 12 Michael J. Shapiro, 'The ethics of encounter', in David Campbell and Michael J. Shapiro (eds), *Moral spaces: rethinking ethics and world politics* (Minneapolis, 1999), p. 59; Paul Ricoeur, *Interpretation theory: discourse and the surplus of meaning* (Fort Worth, 1976), p. 49.

It is therefore distinctly important to question how the institutionally carried notion of a Yale school, or a French school, of literary theory segue into accounts regarding certain 'ways' of reading and writing as nationally bound or implicated. Are the 'Locations of Culture' elsewhere for the Irish student, in that the interpretive models and discursive strategies we attach our thematic analyses to, must be consistently imported and imitated? And if so how does analysis whether it be, comparative, intertextual, or historical posit a form of discourse that does not read its literature, as the postcolonial might frequently suggest, as a direct expression of a repressed identity?

John Guillory's *Cultural Capital* constructs an intriguing model for the analysis of canonicity, a model furthering the investigation of the relationships between critical discourses. Just as the canonicity debate allowed certain texts to be *taught* as non-canonical, reifying the inclusion/exclusion dichotomy at the institutional level of the academy, so did this institutionalisation of canonicity allow 'the social referents of inclusion and exclusion, the dominant and subordinate groups respectively, to be represented in the discourse of canon formation by two groups of authors and texts'.[13] One might consider whether such a model displaying the affects of canonicity might be transposed from the level of the curriculum debate onto the level of discourses within literary criticism. Does a critical tradition's practice of certain discourses over others serve merely to reify that tradition's institutional possibilities, prowess, and ultimate unwillingness to confront this reification? The positing of a canon of critical discourses, accounting for how one should interpret is more problematic than a canon of primary texts. Creating a canon of styles of interpretation already prioritizes the model of one of these styles, namely canonicity. The question is important for the reading of an Irish critical tradition. Can we ever indeed speak as *new voices* in criticism when our words are always inserted into interpretive models we unproblematically translate? The Irish tradition's prevalent acceptance of the post-colonialist discourse, its tentative allusion to post-structuralist neologisms, and its neglect of critical theory, serves merely to construct a palimpsest of critical terminology rather than any integrated interpretative system. This brings us back to a fundamental weakness in Irish criticism, namely, its naive engagement with systems of signification. Irish criticism too often evokes ahead of time what 'language' and 'linguistic' mean, as though the reference of these words were stable and knowable, as though, in short, the 'referent of 'language' and 'linguistic' could be phenomenalised, could appear, as an object of consciousnes.[14] The employment of the metaphor 'voice' for consciousness borrows from such a naïve epistemology.

Chantal Mouffe regards 'metaphorical totalization' as creating 'purely analogical relations that fully saturate the social space of the text', a situation that

13 John Guillory, *Cultural capital* (Chicago, 1999), p. 9. 14 Andrzej Warminski, '"As the poets do it": on the material sublime', in Tom Cohen et al. (eds), *Material events: Paul de Man and the afterlife of theory* (Minneapolis, 2001), p. 23.

marks any cultural text that does not examine its conditions of signification.[15] Metaphor here is employed in the sense Paul Ricoeur assigns to ancient rhetoric where the metaphor does not 'represent a semantic innovation' or 'furnish any new information about reality'.[16] The movement of an Irish critical tradition all too often becomes a metaphor for the texts that have for so long sought a kind of cultural redemption or 'redemptive poetics'. Yet redemption of any kind requires an appeal, a cry for help, a voice in the wilderness. Irish criticism very often becomes invested with a distinct teleology and the figure most apt, most autotelic in such a plight, may be the metaphor, one that works off resemblance rather than invention. Jacques Derrida enables us to question the 'new voice's' connoting of the originary metaphor of voice for pure self-expression or consciousness through his early work 'The Voice That Keeps Silence'.

The proposal of a certain kind of figuration, of a metaphoric mediation, as a distinctly Irish critical interpretive model, a model open to certain ideological persuasions, also distances the Irish critical canon from the discourse of deconstruction. Derrida's work initially brought to light the essential difference between orality and writing, voice and *écriture*. Working through an investigation of the *voice* (what we are referred to in this text by our 'critical precursors') his early writings enable us to investigate the 'ground' of all metaphors, of all semantic transformations, namely, that between voice and self-presence. For Derrida *écriture*, or writing, does not directly mediate or represent what is spoken, or what might be spoken, both to oneself and to others. Writing does not solely relay some inner sanctum of self-expression. Derrida has much to say on voice, and we must ask whether Irish criticism is listening to his words. Derrida's essay 'The Voice That Keeps Silence' questions Husserl's easy conjoining of thought and voice, and asks why 'using words get[s] mixed up with the determination of being in general as presence, or why the epoch of the *phonè* [is] also the epoch of being in the form of presence [or ideality]?'[17] Husserl speaks of a notion of 'pure expression' which reflects 'the pre-expressive stratum of sense', a perfect expression which consists of the total restitution in the form of presence of a sense actually given to intuition'.[18] Derrida wishes to deconstruct here the 'unfailing complicity' between speech [*voix*] and idealization, an unfailing complicity that is rehearsed when in Irish criticism 'new voices' are regarded as unproblematically relaying an essential cultural tradition or idealisation. Derrida continues: if an ideal object is an object whose showing may be repeated indefinitely, an object that is indefinitely re-iterable precisely because it is freed from all 'mundane spatiality' then I can express without having to pass 'through the world'. Derrida goes on to state that, in Husserl's reading, the subject owning the voice does not have to pass forth beyond himself to be immediately affected by her expressive activity, 'My words are 'alive' because they seem not to leave me: not to fall outside me, outside my

15 Cohen et al., *Material events*, p. 239.   16 Ricoeur, *Interpretation theory: discourse and the surplus of meaning* (Fort Worth, 1976), p. 49.   17 Jacques Derrida, *Speech and phenomena and other essays on Husserl's theory of* signs, trans. David B. Allison (Evanston, 1973), p. 74.   18 Ibid., p. 75.

breath, at a visible distance; not to cease to belong to me, to be at my disposition'. Derrida contests this idealisation which is motivated once again by the guiding metaphor of voice for pure self-expression or consciousness. He reads Husserl as only privileging the voice and *phonè* through the limitation of language to a secondary stratum of experience.[19] If writing is to receive any regard in Husserl's model, it is only as 'phonetic writing,' a writing which inscribes an already prepared utterance.[20] Writing is therefore secondary, a palimpsest re-inscribing an original spoken word. Derrida also contests this notion of pure expression, 'the pure inwardness of phonic auto-affection' on its notion of time. 'The going-forth into the world' implies a concept of 'Time' hinged on notions of 'absolute subjectivity', an impossibility for Derrida as time cannot be conceived on the basis of a self-presence of a present being. Irish criticism's tenor of cultural redemption, its unwillingness to take a cue from a literary tradition foregrounding formal experimentation, may similarly seek to 'delay this going forth into the world' for the critic. As a voice such criticism becomes a metaphor for 'the regaining of language in its fullness without syntax', for 'a pure calling by name'.[21] Perhaps we are reluctant to inspect Derrida's unsettling of the *originary metaphor*, of the semantic transformation existing between voice and pure self-expression.

It is perhaps no coincidence then that when Derrida was asked to give the plenary at the Ninth International James Joyce Symposium in Frankfurt in 1984, his only paper presented on an Irish writer, the English title became 'Ulysses Gramophone: Hear say Yes in Joyce?' Derrida's attention to inspecting the inscribed voice of this self-exiled Irish writer, brought him to count the number of yeses in *Ulysses*. His essay, one might say, deconstructs Ireland's foremost literary export at the level of the voice, eliciting its strangeness and unfamiliarity, likening himself in a footnote, reading the Joycean text, to 'the visitor at an exhibition of electricity who cannot believe that the voice which the gramophone restores unaltered to life is not a voice spontaneously emitted by a human being'.[22] It appears then that we are back with Krapp. We have Krapp before his tape-recorder and Derrida vicariously before his gramophone, all the time seeking to disrupt the easy complicity of voice and self-presence, of the Irish voice and its recording. Their deliberations on, and representations of, the relationship between voice and self-expression, between expression and a recording of some cultural lineage, are ironic representations that consistently fold back on or displace any pre-ordained site of enunciation. The persistent self-reflexivity of their claims working through a rigorous assessment of the conditions and forms of signification, ultimately prioritizes the conditions of writing and the text. Such a move is difficult both for an Irish post-colonial redemption of repressed cultural identity and for a concurrent formal analysis pinned to a 'metaphoric totalization'. As Derrida suggests,

19 Ibid., p. 80. 20 Ibid., p. 81. 21 Jacques Derrida, 'White mythology: metaphor in the text of philosophy', *New Literary History* 6 (1974), 73. 22 Jacques Derrida, 'Ulysses gramophone: hear say yes in Joyce [*l'oui dire de Joyce*]' in Derek Attridge (ed.), *Acts of literature* (London, 1992), p. 259.

If there is something in literature which does not allow itself to be reduced to the voice, to epos or poetry, one cannot recapture it except by rigorously isolating the bond that links the *play of form* to the substance of graphic expression.[23]

And in respect to Beckett and Derrida, both critics of the Irish voice, it might be time to read 'as the poets do it', to take note of the post-structuralist and figurative accounting for any text's non-closure. Irish criticism must yet imbibe more from the literature which it invests with such thematic preponderance. Criticism must engage in a performative reading with tropological sensitivity.

A look at Joyce's *Ulysses* acts both as an instantiation of Joyce addressing questions raised thus far, and also raises the much larger question of whether Irish criticism has entirely dispensed with onto-theological notions of faith and belief uncomfortable with post-structuralist undecidability. Carl Schmitt informs us that the Irish have Catholicism to thank for a large part of their national strength of resistance,[24] and it must be questioned whether our critical resistance might yet, in the era of criticism's 'turn to theology', retain a Catholic interpretant. It is a topic that is merely broached here, requiring lengthier discussion, but one relevant to a reading of the Joycean oeuvre where aesthetic works are assigned religious terminology e.g. epiphany and epiclesis. Joyce's *Ulysses* questions metaphor and religious figures simultaneously. He names his own most sacred presence, the artwork, by way of the religious terminology he never assigns to its established context (I refer here to the notion of epiphany, epiclesis). Leopold Bloom's musings at church, consistently refer to the Eucharist as 'it', and he stumbles over its Latin phrasing, He muses:

> Then the next one: a small old woman. The priest bent down to put it into her mouth, murmuring all the time. Latin. The next one. Shut your eyes and open your mouth. What? *Corpus.* Body. Corpse. Good idea the Latin. Stupefies them first. Hospice for the dying. They don't seem to chew it; only swallow it down. Rum idea: why the cannibals cotton to it.[25]

We can read Joyce here as referencing metaphoricity, and his own method of applying religious figures to aesthetic paradigms, a 'Hospice' or *horsepiss* for the devout, stupefying us readers with grandiose artistic terminology such as epiphany and epiclesis, so that we will 'swallow it down' and never wholly analyse its etymology, or 'chew' over its formal linguistic capabilities. Joyce is aware of the tendency within scriptural and academic exegesis to lie bedazzled before exotic terminology. He indirectly asks us to 'chew' over his motivations for employing such terms as epiphany and epiclesis. Irish criticism's disregard for critical theory and for the conditions of signification similarly enacts a 'swal-

23 Jacques Derrida, *Of grammatology*, p. 59.   24 Carl Schmitt, *Roman Catholicism and political form*, trans. G.L. Ulmen (Westport, Conn., 1996), p. 6.   25 James Joyce, *Ulysses* (London, 1992), p. 99.

lowing down' of the rhetoric of signification and criticism, failing to 'chew' over its meaning so as to enrich potential readings. Bad faith just like bad criticism will always embrace certain recovered signs and annunciations within the history of a religious tradition only to overlook the methodologies employed for the analysis of such figures. Any such reading invests the religious figure or indeed the tropes of criticism with an autotelic quality, a self-revelatory function which is less figurative than sacramental. Joyce's 'play' with religious *ikons* wishes to locate some of the religious figure's *mana* in the artwork, only to reveal such 'annunciations' for what they are, linguistic tropes which only achieve an epiphanic prowess when they are so defamiliarized as to destabilise signification in a curious deconstruction or 'abnihilisation of the etym'.[26] Much recent Irish criticism dominated by the postcolonial, in seeking to 'continue the conversation', resembles a steady accumulation of figures rather than an analysis of such figures modes of being. A grasp of the writer's dexterous figurative play and rhetorical awareness, should enable us to confidently listen back, or even view the video-conferencing of future 'New Voices', once again like Krapp, shocked by our collective voice, 'Hard to believe I was ever that young whelp. The voice! Jesus! And the aspirations?'

'Each nebulous atom in between': reading liminality – Irish Studies, postmodern feminism and the poetry of Catherine Walsh

CLAIRE BRACKEN, UNIVERSITY COLLEGE DUBLIN[1]

Liminality is a prevalent term in contemporary Irish post-colonial theory, where it is used as part of theoretical debates attempting to move away from a nationalist ideology of identity politics. This article will consider the concept of liminality as it specifically relates to the field of Irish Studies, through an analysis of post-colonial theory, postmodern feminism and the poetry of Catherine Walsh.[2] I shall argue that current representations of the liminal in the field of

26 James Joyce, *Finnegans Wake* (London, 1992), p. 353. 1 When I gave this paper in February 2003 I had recently completed my Master's degree at University College Cork. This article is based on my Master's thesis which I submitted there. I would like to sincerely thank Professor Patricia Coughlan for her guidance and advice on this work. I would also like to thank Catherine Walsh for all her help in my research. Since September 2003 I have been a student at University College Dublin. I would like to acknowledge the Irish Research Council for the Humanities and Social Sciences for PhD scholarship funding. 2 The work of the contemporary Irish poet Catherine Walsh has received very little critical attention. Walsh has nine published works to date, four of which have

Irish Studies constitute a misreading of the concept itself and, as such, render obsolete the potentialities of the liminal space for Irish post-colonialism. Furthermore, I will argue that postmodern feminist theory provides the apparatus through which the essential constitution of liminality can be articulated. Drawing on the poetry of Catherine Walsh, I will suggest that it is through such apparatus that current debates about contemporary Ireland and liminality should be approached.

IRISH POST-COLONIAL THEORY: MISREADING LIMINALITY

Derived from the Latin word *limen*, meaning threshold, the liminal constitutes a space that features in terms of the boundary or margin. Due to this, the concept of liminality has been said to refer to an ambiguous in-between sphere of non-differentiation in which oppositional poles of difference cannot be maintained and in turn break down and deconstruct. The anthropologist Victor Turner puts such a view of the liminal forward. In his work *The Ritual Process*, Turner defines liminality as an 'ambiguous' state 'betwixt-and-between' and argues that it is a non-definable space of 'neither here nor there'.3 This neither/nor formula negates oppositional categories due to its inability to differentiate and distinguish. Such an inability points towards the connections and similarities between differences, differences that are then erased as a result. However, I believe that if we view the liminal as solely a space of non-differentiation, we enact a misreading of the space itself, because such a belief contains within it an implicit assumption that difference cannot be articulated from a position which figures connection and similarity. What is crucial in any examination of the liminal is to recognize that it constitutes a border area. While this border area is one in which differences mingle and mix, it also represents a space which differentiates and divides. Configurations of the liminal as an entity of non-differentiation function to reinforce the oppositional categories they seek to negate. The positing of the in-between as a space of connection and similarity locates it as antithetical to difference and distinction. It functions to misrepresent and misread the integral features of the liminal borderline space.

been published by hardPressed Poetry, a small press which she runs with her husband Billy Mills. All of Walsh's poetry has been issued through independent small presses. Her poetry, which makes use of the entire space of the page and does not conform to structured stanza form, consistently shifts registers of voice and place in a bid to figure a space of multiplicity and indeterminacy. Such poetic practice is relatively rare in terms of the Irish literary tradition. Her work can be (tentatively) aligned with other Irish contemporary experimental poets such as Trevor Joyce, Geoffrey Squires, Randolph Healy, Maurice Scully and Billy Mills. Works by Catherine Walsh: *The Ca Pater Pillar Thing and More Besides* (Dublin, 1986); *Macula* (Dublin, 1986); *Making Tents* (Dublin, 1987); *Short Stories* (Twickenham, 1989); *From Pitch* (London, 1993); *Pitch* (Durham, 1994); *Idir Eatortha and Making Tents* (London, 1996); *City West* (Limerick, 2000); *Pomepleat 1* (Limerick, 2002); and *Jacket Magazine* 22 (http://jacketmagazine.com/22/caddel-walsh.html). 3 Victor Turner, *The ritual process: structure and anti-structure* (New York, 1995), p. 95.

And yet it is this view of the liminal, as solely a space of non-differentiation, which is continually put forward in the field of contemporary Irish Studies. In recent years, Irish post-colonial theory has moved to challenge the philosophy of identity politics, hitherto so central to the post-colonial state. It recognizes that such a political formula, which operates within binary models of thinking whereby a stable and coherent sense of self is set in direct opposition to an undesirable and differentiated other, is as repressive as historical colonisation since it is through the self/other divide that colonialism maintains itself. Discussing the work of the Subaltern Studies Group in India, Colin Graham notes: 'no longer need the nation be regarded as the glorious achievement ... of an oppressed people; the post-colonial nation can now be figured as ... repeating and aping the colonial structures which it displaced'.4 Thus, contemporary Irish post-colonial theory is currently working to re-figure and re-negotiate its own theoretical structures and is interrogating key terms such as nationhood and identity.

The use of the concept of liminality in contemporary Irish Studies is an example of this shift in the post-colonial paradigm. However, I believe that what is evident in Irish post-colonial theory's engagement with the liminal is a positioning of the space in terms of connection and non-differentiation. In his article 'Breaking the 'cracked mirror': binary oppositions in the culture of contemporary Ireland', Shaun Richards traces the continuous inversions in Irish cultural theory and practice since the formation of the Free State. Drawing on Derrida, he argues that the subjugated pole of opposition gains precedence through a dislodgement of the dominant term from its elevated position. In terms of Irish history and culture these inversions have moved from the valuation of imperial rule to an idealisation of rural Gaelic Ireland and then on to a preference for modern urbanisation. Richards argues that the problem with such inversions is that a hierarchical structure is consistently retained, with one pole of the binary being subjugated to the other. So as to disrupt such a dualistic construction, Richards investigates an alternate space where 'the indigenous can be rescued, as the modern is redeemed, if a creative harmony can be established *between* them' (my emphasis).5 This 'creative harmony' locates the liminal ('between') as a connective space of similarity where difference is overcome and reconciled. That this alternate space is linked to liminality is evident in the word 'between'. This positioning of the in-between as a space of 'creative harmony' locates the liminal as a connective space of similarity where difference is overcome and reconciled.

Colin Graham's article '"Liminal spaces": post-colonial theories and Irish culture' locates the liminal space as a positive theoretical tool for Irish post-colonial theory. He argues for the need of the in-between space so as to focus 'on cross-cultural movements rather than on the simple cultural dichotomy of the

4 Colin Graham, *Deconstructing Ireland: identity, theory, culture* (Edinburgh, 2001), p. 83. 5 Shaun Richards, 'Breaking the "cracked mirror": binary oppositions in the culture of contemporary Ireland', in Colin Graham and Richard Kirkland (eds), *Ireland and cultural theory: the mechanics of authenticity* (Basingstoke, 1999), p. 118.

colonial situation' and to 'prioritise cultural interchange within a colonial structure'.[6] Graham also deals with the concept of liminality in his book
Deconstructing Ireland, where he argues that '[p]ostcolonialism's movement into
the 'liminal spaces' of colonial discourse needs to be superimposed over the
model which sees colonial structures purely in terms of division'.[7] However, in
this work he is more cautious with the concept of liminality, identifying that
the radical potentialities it holds may be lost due to the powerful force the idea
of nationhood still retains in the Irish psyche. However, what remains the same
in Graham's two texts is his definition of liminality itself. In both of these works
he terms 'liminal spaces' as 'marginal areas, where the ultimate opposition of
colonizer and colonized breaks down through irony, imitation and subversion'.[8]
In this way Graham posits the liminal as a space of non-differentiation where
'opposition' 'breaks down' and is eradicated.

   A valuation of the transitional site of liminality is also evident in the work
of Richard Kearney. Like Richards, he identifies a dichotomous tendency in
Irish culture either to 'revive the past' or else to 'repudiate it'. [9] The former he
locates as traditional revivalism and the latter as modernism. Kearney is seeking to figure an in-between, transitional place, whereby both past and future are
valued. In *Postnationalist Ireland: Politics, Culture, Philosophy*, he figures this transitional space as 'The Fifth Province' which operates 'as a network of relations
extending from local communities at home to migrant communities abroad ...'
Kearney asserts that '[t]he fifth province is to be found, if anywhere, at the swinging door which connects the "parish" ... with the cosmos'.[10] 'The Fifth Province'
is thus constructed in terms of the threshold, 'the swinging door'. That Kearney
equates liminality with non-differentiation is evident through his use of the
word 'connection', which he attributes to the in-between space of 'the swinging
door'. As a result difference does not figure in this articulation of the liminal,
but rather is located exterior and separate to it.

   While I agree with Irish post-colonial theory's call for a rejection of binary
and oppositional thinking, I take issue with its construction of the liminal space.
How can the diversity and complexity of present-day Ireland be articulated in
a space figured as devoid of difference? By presenting the liminal as a solely
non-differentiated sphere we run the risk of suffocating difference in a generalized totality. I would also question the extent such representations of the liminal succeed in discarding the restraints of binary thinking. Liminality, as a sphere
in which differentiation and non-differentiation exist simultaneously, stands
outside the bounds of a dichotomous mindset. This ambiguity is not achieved
in contemporary Irish versions of the space. The liminal is presented in terms
of connection and similarity, with elements of difference seemingly located out-

6 Colin Graham, '"Liminal spaces": post-colonial theories and Irish culture', *Irish Review* 16 (1994),
32, 41.   7 Graham, *Deconstructing Ireland*, p. 93.   8 Ibid., p. 86. Graham, '"Liminal Spaces"', p. 33.
9 Richard Kearney, *Transitions: narratives in modern Irish culture* (Dublin, 1988), p. 10.   10 Richard
Kearney, *Postnationalist Ireland: politics, culture, philosophy* (London, 1997), p. 100.

side it. This separation and segregation of difference and connection causes Irish post-colonial theory's engagement with liminality to remain within a representational system predicated on opposition.

Richard Kirkland's pioneering essay 'Questioning the frame: hybridity, Ireland and the institution' cautions against negligent representations of the liminal arguing that '[a]n awareness of the hybrid, the heterogeneous and the anomalous should not be a catalyst for celebration but rather should investigate a considered process of rereading to assess just how far the frames of representation themselves need to re-evaluated'.[11] I agree with this call for a 'process of rereading' as liminality, if read correctly, can provide an adequate articulation of the diversity and complexity of contemporary Irish life. The liminal has the ability to register such diversity due to its border constitution, which signifies difference itself, thus allowing an infinity of multiple differences to be addressed and articulated. However, that the liminal also refers to non-differentiation and similarity is crucial in the maintaining of this multiplicity. This is because moments of connective experiences within differences – a recognition of likeness or similarity – allows for an understanding, a shared empathy. This empathy diffuses antagonistic rivalries that can exist among differences, rivalries that would destroy a space of multiplicity in their bid to establish a supreme or ultimate victor. Thus it is in this way, due to its unique balance of difference and sameness, that the liminal facilitates a non-hierarchical articulation of multiplicity, difference and diversity. I believe the field of Irish Studies should reassess and re-read its representation of liminality so as to gain access to such an articulation. It is my opinion that this process of re-reading should involve an engagement with postmodern feminist thought, as this theory is capable of registering the ambiguity of the liminal in-between space.

POSTMODERN FEMINISM: ARTICULATING LIMINALITY

Postmodern feminist theory exemplifies the constitution of liminality in its ability to balance difference and sameness, connections and diversity. It pays attention to the multiple differences that exist among women, while simultaneously allowing space to forge temporary political ties. The postmodern nature of the theory highlights multiplicity and diversity, while the feminist viewpoint calls for collective political action. In her book *Nomadic Subjects*, Rosi Braidotti constructs an image of postmodern feminist consciousness through the figure of the nomad. Braidotti argues that 'the nomadic consciousness combines coherence with mobility ... [t]his form of consciousness combines features that are usually perceived as opposing, namely the possession of a sense of identity that rests not on fixity but on contingency'.[12] The nomad is posited a liminal figure

11 Richard Kirkland, 'Questioning the frame: hybridity, Ireland and the institution', in Graham and Kirkland (eds), *Ireland and cultural theory*, p. 226.   12 Rosi Braidotti, *Nomadic subjects: embodiment*

because of an association with the border. This association is due to the fact that
the nomad is located on the margins of societies because of a refusal to settle in
a fixed place. As such, nomadic wandering constitutes a dual process of both
roaming and resting. While the process of roaming refers to a space of non-differentiation and connection, the moments of rest allow for points of difference
to be registered and mapped. Braidotti uses this liminal existence as an emblem
of postmodern feminism, which has the ability to simultaneously articulate elements of diversity and connection.

    The nomad is thus read as a symbol of the liminal discourse of postmodern
feminism. Such a nomadic figuration permeates the poetry of Catherine Walsh's
1996 book *Idir Eatortha and Making Tents*.[13] The condition of being in-transit
is consistently presented in the work through images of skiing, sailing and hiking.
One section of poetry constructs an image of liminal wandering punctuated
with differentiation and non-differentiation:

> is it this way then?
>
> no
> yes
>
>   each nebulous atom inbetween
>
>
> what a break   rest now   ease aside   there's one there
>
> alright[14]

The speaker of this section asks 'is it this way then?' and receives the response
'no / yes / each nebulous atom inbetween'. The response to this question locates
the process of wandering in terms of non-differentiation. There is an inability
to distinguish between the opposites of 'yes' and 'no', so both are provided. This
'inbetween' space is described as being 'nebulous', a vague and formless sphere
where opposites collapse into each other. However, the word 'atom', inserted
between 'nebulous' and 'inbetween', refers to an element that is a fixed point.
Etymologically, the word 'atom' is derived from the Greek word for 'indivisable'.
This implies an irreducible element with a concrete position. Thus, the 'atom'
can be read as a differential resting point amidst the non-differentiated space
of wandering. However, the temporary nature of this resting point is indicated
through the paradoxical meaning of the word atom, because although it means
'indivisibility' it can in fact be split. Thus, the fixed point of resting which the

and sexual difference in contemporary feminist theory (New York, 1994), p. 31. 13 The first section of
this work, 'Idir Eatortha', is comprised of new material, while the second part, 'Making tents' constitutes poetry published as a pamphlet in 1987. 14 Walsh, *Idir eatortha and making tents*, p. 29.

'atom' represents is not a permanent one. The fact that it can be broken down indicates that this site is only temporary. This will eventually require the wanderer to reconstitute the roaming process.

The possibility of a differential point of reference amidst a space of indistinguishability is furthered in the subsequent lines: 'what a break rest now ease aside there's one there / alright'. The 'break' and 'rest' allow for a process of differentiation whereby a decision can be made. The phrase 'there's one there' refers to a choosing position from which a suitable resting-place is decided upon. The repetition of the word 'there' reinforces the notion that this is a definite and fixed location that is different from others. Walsh's poetry, however, does not negate the existence of these others. There is a recognition that other forms of difference ('resting places') exist since 'we all have our favourites'.[15] The passage cited above ends with the word 'alright', which infers an ending to this 'break' and a reconstitution of wandering. This reconstitution will facilitate a meeting with other forms of difference as other 'resting places' are approached and provisionally occupied.

The opening page of Walsh's *Idir Eatortha and Making Tents* contains an image of skiing whereby the speaker is 'tunnelling down the slope'. A 'neither here nor there' liminal formula succeeds this motif with the phrase '(but wasn't that somewhere else?'[16] The use of the word 'that', which implies a moment of specificity, is said to be located 'elsewhere' and not within the realm of non-differentiation. Similarly, it is important that the phrase is formulated as a question to which no answer is given. This retains the ambiguity of the space, as an answer would provide a binary yes/no reply. However, the refusal to close the parenthesis at the end of the sentence implies that there is more than non-differentiation to this liminal sphere. The structure of a parenthesis constitutes an in-between space. It is inserted into a sentence and is enclosed in brackets between the words of that sentence. Thus, the refusal to close this structure implies that there is more information concerning the in-between to come. The next few lines of this piece provide this extra information:

[horrified]

even snow near top of the hill/here
– weather
    – bumps

no coffee house along this cateyed road[17]

The liminal condition of skiing is presented as having differential moments. In the poem the 'snow' 'near' the 'top of the hill/here' is presented as 'even'. This

15 Ibid., p. 24. 16 Ibid., p. 7. 17 Ibid., p. 8.

line highlights a definitive 'here' position, from which the speaker can make assertions and judgements. That this is a position concerned with differentiation is made evident through the subsequent use of the word 'bumps', which contrasts and is different from 'even'. The final line of the piece succinctly illustrates the condition of this liminal sphere: 'no coffee house along this cateyed road'. The 'house' is a containing structure whose walls separate inside and outside, thus negating fluid interchange. In contradistinction, 'the cateyed road' constitutes a space of both sameness and difference. The cat's eyes are points of distinction set alongside the non-distinguishability of the travelling 'road'.

The nomadic tones of Walsh's *Idir Eatortha and Making Tents* construct a liminal space in which difference and sameness can co-exist. That liminality is a central concern of the work is reflected in the title itself, as *Idir Eatortha* is an Irish phrase which means 'between two worlds'. Walsh's figurative use of nomadic liminality allows her poetry to register a fluid space of heterogeneity and multiplicity. Location consistently shifts in the work ranging from places as diverse as Barcelona, Spain, the Irish countryside and the outskirts of Dublin city-centre. This rejection of a focus on a fixed Irish location constitutes a refusal on Walsh's part to engage in a mythical search for grounded Irish identity. The work also figures a multitude of speaking voices and diverse subjective experiences. Disparate material, such as the experience of the sick 'blind widow' who lives in a 'cold' and 'damp one room flat', the conversation of a pair of 'drunk' builders or the instructions of a teacher, consistently intersperse the poetry.[18] The fluidity of the non-differentiated element of liminality denies precedence to any one particular experience, thus allowing for a non-hierarchical treatment of different viewpoints and positions.

That this liminal border area is related to a postmodern feminist consciousness is implied in a short poetic section, which discusses various means of approaching difference:

>   abuse difference viewed as
>   problematic   role defined
>   threat
>
>   divisive
>
>   use difference is
>   evolvement   role defining
>   catalystic
>   necessary factor
>   part of a whole socio-linguistic pattern
>
>   our women's minds[19]

18 Ibid., p. 34, pp 36–42, p. 79.   19 Ibid., p. 48

The first section describes an improper usage or 'abuse' of 'difference' that is 'problematic' and a 'threat'. This second piece describes a more positive means of dealing with 'difference' ('use' as oppose to 'abuse'), one that is fluid and can make connections. In this space subjective positions are in a process of 'evolvement' and are thus inter-connective and linked. The multiplicity available from such a position of 'evolvement' is implied in the words 'role defining', which, opposed to the 'role defined' in the previous section, suggests a never-ending construction of different 'roles' or subjectivities. The multiplicities of this space are further reinforced in the penultimate line through the use of the word 'part'. The intricate 'pattern' of a new 'socio-linguistic' symbolic space is directly linked to the facility of 'our women's minds'. The word 'pattern' refers to the liminality of the new space. It provides an image of a complex structure of multiple and differential parts, which, while all being different, can also meet up and link. This liminal image is translated into the postmodern feminist statement 'our women's minds', a statement which simultaneously connects all women through the use of the word 'our', while also distinguishing between them through the use of plural nouns which register the differences of 'women's minds'.

However, it is important to recognize that this linking of the liminal with a postmodern feminist space in no way operates to feminize the concept of liminality itself. Rather, I believe that Walsh's poetry demonstrates a strong resistance to those theories that construct an ostensible feminisation of the liminal space. Such a form of feminisation is evident in the work of Jacques Derrida. Like Walsh, Derrida constructs a liminal space of both difference and sameness. Derrida's terms of 'undecidability', the most well-known being that of *différance*, refer to a space that is '[n]either/nor' and '*simultaneously* either or'.[20] This co-existence of sameness and difference is constructed within the word *différance* itself, which in French holds the double meaning 'to differ' and 'to defer'. Derrida uses these terms of undecidability to deconstruct the hierarchical, binary logic of Western philosophy and thought. However, his strategy has proved to be problematic for feminism. This is because, as Braidotti argues, for Derrida '[w]oman is the name for the precondition of thinking, it is *différance* insofar as it refers to an originary space beyond dualistic dichotomies, or before them'.[21] Derrida appropriates the image of the feminine as a deconstructive tool due to its representational absence from a symbolic order predicated on phallocentrism. To quote Braidotti again: 'For Derrida … the symbolic absence of the feminine is the source of its strength as a counter-strategy by which to destabilize the symbolic'.[22] Thus, Derrida explicitly feminizes his liminal concept of *différance* by equating it with the category 'woman'.

However, this feminisation of the liminal is problematic in that it functions to silence and repress the voices of women. Derrida's liminal space of *différance* allows for, albeit temporary, speaking sites. These sites constitute the points of

20 Jacques Derrida, *Positions*, trans. Alan Bass (Chicago, 1981), p. 43. 21 Rosi Braidotti, *Patterns of dissonance: a study of women in contemporary philosophy*, trans. Elizabeth Guild (Oxford, 1991), p. 101. 22 Ibid., p. 101.

difference that are interspersed in the fluidities of deferral. However, how is a woman to speak from these positions if she is said to constitute the matter of their production? The feminisation of the liminal locates 'woman' as a representative tool, as a vehicle, which facilitates the articulation of Derrida's *différance*. This use of 'woman' as a means of representation essentially functions to deny her agency and autonomy as she is subjected to a representative cause. Similarly, the multiplicity and heterogeneity of women is erased, conflated as it is under the feminine signifier. Therefore, 'woman' (women) is silenced in Derrida's *différance* and allowed no access to the speaking moments of difference registered in the liminal scheme.

In her study of the work of Luce Irigaray, Margaret Whitford argues that 'from an Irigarayan point of view, Derrida is colonizing women's potential space' due to his appropriation of the term 'woman'.[23] If 'woman', as the symbolic representative of *différance*, has no speaking position from it, then it follows that all voices (however temporary) are male. Whitford argues that Derrida's deconstructive strategies mask the patriarchy inherent to his theory:

> Because of the slippage between speaking 'like' and speaking 'as' a man or woman, Derrida is in the position where he can speak 'like' a woman (this is clearly very important to him) but, since he has deconstructed the opposition male/female, he can glide over the fact that he is speaking 'as a man'.[24]

By feminising the liminal space of *différance*, Derrida essentially denies women holding any meaningful speaking positions within it. Therefore what is presented as a feminine space is in fact a masculine one, predicated on the suppression of the female voice through the use of her body. Thus, while Derrida's theory of *différance* successfully articulates the constituents of liminality – a balance of difference and sameness – his apparently non-exclusionary system undermines itself in its gender inequality. Derrida's theory functions to uphold an age-old binary of male/female division, whereby woman is linked with body/matter and man with subjectivity.

Walsh's poetry attempts to move away from a position of hierarchical domination and construct a poetic space of non-mastery and heterogeneity. The features of the liminal can facilitate such a construction, depending on the mode of representation engaged with. It is evident from an analysis of Derrida's work that a feminisation of the liminal functions to silence and repress women's complex experiences, thus creating a binary space in terms of gender. In *Idir Eatortha and Making Tents* Walsh confronts such a problematical representation of the liminal:

    on the sea
    waves buoyant brought out resting

23 Margaret Whitford, *Luce Irigaray: philosophy in the feminine* (London, 1991), p. 128. 24 Ibid., p. 128.

places graves gulls gulls perhaps
tip understand

and metaphysical meaningnets with
joy jumping back out the holes[25]

In this piece an image of the sea is constructed in terms that illustrate the liminal space as one of both difference and sameness. The sea is a space of non-differentiation due to the fluid intermingling nature of its 'buoyant' 'waves'. This nature facilitates the production of points of difference, 'resting / places' that are 'brought out'. However, the subsequent lines indicate that exclusions are still perpetuated from this space: 'and metaphysical meaningnets with / joy jumping back out the holes'. Resting-places that have emerged are dragged back down again by 'metaphysical meaningnets' and are re-submerged into the ocean's depths. This subjugation can be related to a conventional symbolic representation of the sea as female. This gendered configuration results in a generalized representation of woman as matter and thus negates the possibility of an articulation of her differences. She cannot be included within a scheme of difference as it is her non-differentiation that produces differentiation itself: 'the *sea ... brought out* resting places' (my emphasis).

This image of the drowning and silencing of women in a symbolically feminized liminal space is also constructed through an image of gestation:

soaking. knees to chin.

thinking how much
more uncomfortable
                        you must have been
how loud the burbling
of the washing-machine
seems

during the siesta

conversation
drifts up the ventilation shaft
(there are 4 floors below)

snatched and strange

I understand nothing[26]

25 Walsh, *Idir Eatortha*, p. 22. 26 Ibid., p. 79

The foetal position depicted at the beginning of this piece ('soaking. knees to chin') implies that the speaker is positioned in the womb. The womb constitutes a liminal space of differentiation and non-differentiation, as child and mother are simultaneously linked by the umbilical cord ('ventilation shaft') yet are also separated ('(there are four floors below)'). The speaker of the piece is given an implied female position through her identification with the pregnant gestating body: 'thinking how / much more uncomfortable / you must have been'. This body, which is used to symbolize liminality, is constructed as drowning the female subject who is said to be 'soaking'. She cannot formulate a speaking voice from this position, as everything is 'snatched and strange' and she can 'understand nothing'.

However, simultaneously, the final lines of this piece also indicate a resistance on the part of the female subject to being constructed as a symbol of liminality. The speaker's final declaration indicates a refusal to be subjugated ('I under[-]stand nothing'). The result of such refusal is realized through the nomadic figure that permeates *Idir Eatortha and Making Tents*. This figuration of nomadic wandering can sustain the multiplicity of women's experiences due to its non-gendered position. While links are constructed between the nomad and a postmodern feminist conciousness, this space is not explicitly feminized or posited in terms of the female body. It is important to recognize that when Walsh creates a link between women and liminality she does so in terms which highlight female subjectivity as opposed to objectivity: 'our women's *minds*'(my emphasis). Thus, Walsh's poetry, unlike Derrida's theory, allows for speaking positions for women within the liminal space. However, these positions are always temporary, facilitating the articulation of many different subjective voices across a range of many different spatial settings.

SPATIAL REPRESENTATION AND LIMINAL NOMADISM

In her article 'A desire of one's own: psychoanalytic feminism and intersubjective space', Jessica Benjamin argues that the symbolic mode of representation is inappropriate for the articulation of female desire as it is 'organised and dominated by the phallus [which] keeps the female body in place as object'. [27] Thus, she argues that in order for female desire(s) to be expressed an alternative spatial mode is required. Such a spatial mode of representation is evident in Walsh's construction of liminality, the nomad. It is a figure, not a concrete symbol, which moves fleetingly through the work refusing to be pinned down or contained. This non-gendered spatial figuration allows for different feminine experiences to be registered such as the 'blind widow', the 'Dutch' woman and the 'Russian … girl'. [28] However, this ability to articulate difference is not exclusive to the

27 Jessica Benjamin, 'A desire of one's own: psychoanalytic feminism and intersubjective space', in Teresa de Lauretis (ed.), *Feminist studies/critical studies* (Bloomington, 1986), p. 92. 28 Walsh, *Idir eatortha*, p. 34, p. 32, p. 43.

representation of women's lives. I agree with Billy Mills' assertion that 'Walsh ... engage[s] with what might be called "women's issues", while not ceding other areas of the world to "men's issues"'.²⁹ Thus, while the non-gendered position of nomadic figuration enables an articulation of the feminine voice, it also allows for assertions of masculinity: '*he* draws heart trees sun / trees people trees' (my emphasis).³⁰ The simultaneously differentiated and non-differentiated space of liminal nomadism facilitates such a non-separatist scheme. It is a space of continuous movement that enables multiple points of difference to be consistently addressed. That this space is derived from a postmodern feminist consciousness highlights the crucial importance such a consciousness holds when considering the complex nature of contemporary life and experience.

Thus to conclude, it is crucial that prevalent constructions of the liminal be re-assessed, re-read. This is because it currently stands in Irish post-colonial theory as solely a space of non-differentiation and, as such, is restrictive. I believe it reinforces oppositional positions and would question its ability, at this level, to disrupt a philosophy of identity politics. Therefore, it is crucial to return to the meaning of what is liminal, recognize its border state and realize that it allows for moments of both separation and connection. It is here that postmodern feminism becomes essential, due to its ability to register this ambiguity. For this reason, I would suggest that the field of Irish Studies engage with this theory when formulating discussions of 'Irishness', Irish identity and liminality. I believe the poetry of Catherine Walsh succinctly illustrates the advantages such an engagement can bring.

The woman, the body and The Bell: *the female voice in* The Bell's *short fiction by women, 1940–1954*

KALENE NIX-KENEFICK, NUI, CORK

> And vowed that I would learn to loose the sap
> Locked in my roots beneath the mind's stout stone.
> 'Tombed in Spring'¹

The Bell magazine series comprises an eclectic collection of short fiction, novel extracts, poetry, interviews and book reviews as well as articles on politics, social

29 Billy Mills, 'Other places: 4 Irish poets', in Harry Gilonis (ed.), *For the birds: proceedings of the first Cork conference on new and experimental Irish poetry*, April 1997, U. College Cork (Dublin, 1998), p. 35. 30 Walsh, *Idir Eatortha*, p. 45. 1 Freda Laughton, *The Bell*, July 1945

problems and cultural issues. Its contents have been well-documented and social historians and literary critics alike agree on its prominent role in the intellectual life of Irish society during the years of its publication, 1940 to 1954. There is also general agreement that this was a period of social and cultural transition in Ireland and many aspects of this transition are apparent in *The Bell*. A total of 131 issues were produced in the magazine's lifespan and it had a monthly print run of 3,000 copies, with a third of those sold abroad.

The name most closely associated with *The Bell* is that of Sean O'Faolain. He edited the magazine from its inaugural issue in October 1940 until April 1946 when Peadar O'Donnell took over. He held the editorial reins until its demise in December 1954. In his first editorial, O'Faolain directly addressed all the men and women of Ireland and identifying himself with them, he beseeched them to seek out 'some corner of life that nobody else can know', ' anything at all that has a hold on you' and to write about it since 'it is our job to have a flair, a nose, a hound's smell for the real thing, for the thing that is alive and kicking, as against the thing that is merely pretending to be alive. We have to go out nosing for bits of individual veracity, hidden in the dust-heaps of convention, imitation, timidity, traditionalism, wishful thinking'.[2] This essay will examine how several women writers responded to this challenge, this clarion call.

A quick perusal of the magazines' contents shows that a number of women, who were personally close to O'Faolain and other male writers in *The Bell*, were regular contributors to the publication. Elizabeth Bowen featured prominently in the first issue and contributed articles and reviews in later issues. O'Faolain's wife, Eileen, wrote two articles, one on hats and another on nylon stockings. Her own writings, children's stories, did not appear in *The Bell*. Frank O'Connor was the first Poetry Editor of the magazine. His wife, Evelyn Bowen, an English divorcée whom he married in an English registry office in 1937 much to the disapproval of the Irish establishment, wrote articles and reviews on the Dublin theatre for about a year. Lucy Glazebrook was *The Bell's* first and only film reviewer in April 1945. She was an American married to Vivian Mercier, whose critical writing career began in *The Bell*. Similarly, the artist Norah McGuinness featured in the earlier issues. She had been married to Geoffrey Taylor for four years in the 1920s, and it was he who assumed the post of Poetry Editor after Frank O'Connor. Margaret Barrington, who wrote four short stories and several articles and book reviews for the magazine under both editors, was married to Liam O'Flaherty (also a *Bell* contributor) for a short period in the late 1920s. Another of O'Faolain's love interests was the Englishwoman, Honor Tracy, who wrote two articles for the magazine and also reviewed a large number of books for many years.

The contemporary American writer, Adrienne Rich, has described how women's work and thinking have been made to appear discontinuous and erratic and extrapolates how this attitude has affected women's writing in particular. This she considers to be a serious cultural obstacle encountered by any feminist

2 Sean O'Faolain, 'This is our magazine', Editorial, *The Bell* (Oct. 1940), pp 5–9.

writer since 'each feminist work has tended to be received as if it emerged from nowhere; as if each of us had lived, thought, and worked without any historical past or contextual present'.[3] This 'emergence from nowhere' has blighted women's cultural achievements for centuries, not least in Ireland where David Marcus (a contributor to *The Bell*), who edited and wrote the introduction to a 1992 anthology of Irish short stories, expressed amazement not only that half of the influx of short story writers since the late 1960s was female but this fact was 'unforeseen' and that for the first time in the Irish short story 'the voice of women, unrestrained and in chorus, was heard loud and clear. Issues of social and sexual exploitation, previously unmentioned and unmentionable, constituted their main material ... the transmutation into literature of authentic experience from a hitherto hidden realm gave the Irish short story a new immediacy'.[4] In another anthology published in 1990, the editors refer in their introduction to the selected contemporary writers as women who 'explore themes that have never before been addressed in Irish literature ... [and] evolve female characters who challenge orthodoxy and characters who reflect strictly female experiences'.[5] These comments are invalidated retroactively in women's writings of *The Bell*, particularly in the short stories which address 'issues of social and sexual exploitation' and which portray unconventional characters and describe feelings and desires that are unique to women, young and old.

The Bell's short stories form the most cohesive, integrated grouping of writings by women. The other genres represented are novel extracts, three by Maura Laverty and one from Kate O'Brien's *That Lady*. In poetry, there were no less than ten poems by a woman called Freda Laughton who has disappeared from the literary landscape, and one each by Margaret Corrigan, Rhoda Coghill, Brenda Chamberlain and Blanaid Salkeld – a meagre representation of women poets over the 14-year period. There are also several autobiographical essays and numerous journalistic articles, many written anonymously. Women's names also feature prominently among the book reviewers. O'Faolain was generous in his advice to short story contributors, so it can be reasonably assumed that the female-authored short stories in the magazine met the strict aesthetic and technical standards that the editors (world-recognized masters of the short story) applied to the genre, thereby confirming their literary quality as well-written short stories.

The writer, Eilís Dillon (who was born in 1920), has written of O'Faolain's support and how her early writing career was influenced by *The Bell*. Acknowledging her good fortune to have been born in a house full of books, unlike many of her contemporaries, she explains how O'Faolain's radio programmes on the short story guided her in the craft of writing. She wrote:

> The radio series came to an end, inevitably, and once more I was left with no guide. But then, miraculously, *The Bell* began, and there it all was again;

3 Adrienne Rich, *On lies, secrets and silences: selected prose, 1966–1978* (New York, 1979), p. 11. 4 David Marcus (ed.), *State of the art: short stories by the new Irish writers* (London, 1992), p. 1. 5 Daniel J., and Linda M. Casey (eds), *Stories by contemporary Irish women* (Syracuse, 1990), p. 1.

editorials, comments on contributions, appeals for contributions with the required attributes – and, best of all, examples in the form of short stories and articles which all had to measure up to this standard. How I envied those wonderful people their skill and confidence! What I didn't know until much later was that Sean had a hand in almost every one of these pieces, tightening up, advising, directing, teaching his craft to anyone who had the wit to listen. Most of them had – it was all unmistakably good advice and generously given. But down the country, I was too overawed ever to send him anything. I felt naïve, primitive, conservative and traditional – shortcomings that I knew he was denouncing every month in *The Bell*.[6]

However, those women who felt sufficiently confident and courageous to submit their works to the magazine and had them accepted for publication left a literary legacy that constitutes a significant element in the history of Irish women's writing.

A close reading of the selected texts reveals that the writers focussed on the body, by describing the physical feelings, the pain and the sexual desire of their fictional characters, by literally writing about the body. The reader is immediately reminded of what feminist theorists call *écriture féminine* or feminine writing. One of its proponents is the French theorist, Hélène Cixous, who in 1975, beseeched women to write:

> Woman must write her self; must write about women and bring women to writing, from which they have been driven away as violently as from their bodies – for the same reasons, by the same law, with the same fatal goal. Woman must put herself into the text – as into the world and into history – by her own movement.[7]

Cixous' theory of *écriture féminine* has been criticized as overtly essentialist, which is considered unacceptable to many critics, who claim that this biological reductivism is a retrograde step in the development of female consciousness and female creativity. But Elizabeth Gross has proposed that the body is a necessary part of any discourse and that Cixous' colleagues in the psychoanalytical field of literary criticism, Julia Kristeva and Luce Irigaray, have shown 'that *some* concept of the body is essential to understanding social production, oppression and resistance; and that the body need not, indeed must not be considered merely a biological entity, but can be seen as a socially inscribed, historically marked, psychically and interpersonally significant product'.[8] That the body is present to a greater or lesser degree in all texts is a truism but the female body is overtly

6 Eilís Dillon, 'Seán O Faoláin and the young writer', *Irish University Review* 6:2 (1976), 37–44. 7 Hélène Cixous, 'The laugh of the Medusa', in Elizabeth Abel and Emily K. Abel (eds), trans. Keith Cohen and Paula Cohen, *The signs reader: women, gender and scholarship* (London, 1983), p. 279. 8 Elizabeth Gross, 'Philosophy, subjectivity and the body: Kristeva and Irigaray' in Carole Pateman and Elizabeth Gross (eds), *Feminist challenges: social and political theory* (Sydney, 1986), p. 140.

present in the texts studied in this essay. To understand the significance of this particular theme, it is necessary to examine the strictures placed on the female body in Irish society of the period.

Historians today agree that a strongly conservative, predominantly patriarchal ideology permeated every facet of Irish life during the first half of the twentieth century. For the most part, women of that period are portrayed as marginalized victims of a patriarchal society and subjects of a male-dominated political system. In his study of the Catholic Church in Ireland, Inglis focuses particular attention on the Irish mother and how the Church hierarchy, represented at a local level by priests, nuns and brothers, exercised such extraordinary authority over women:

> [I]t was the knowledge and control that priests and nuns had over sex which helped maintain their power and control over women. Women especially were made to feel ashamed of their bodies. They were interrogated about their sexual feelings, desires and activities in the confessional. Outside the confessional there was a deafening silence. Sex became the most abhorrent sin.[9]

Contrary to Marcus' assertion that 'previously unmentioned and unmentionable issues of social and sexual exploitation' were new to Irish women's writing in the 1960s, controversial topics are to the forefront in many of *The Bell's* stories, such as the social stigma of single motherhood ('The Rustle of Spring'; 'Theresa'), the exploitation of children ('Whinny Hill'; 'Strong and Perfect Christians'), domestic abuse ('The Bishop's Turkey'), religious bigotry ('The Balancing of the Clouds'; 'The Funeral'), same-sex desire ('Girls'; 'The Boy in the End Bed'; 'Lough Derg') and non-marital sex ('Greek Sandals'; 'Optimists'). Male figures are portrayed in a negative light with the emphasis on strong, authoritarian, dictatorial characters, while men with a more pleasant disposition are backgrounded. The reader is introduced to the uncouth ape-like peasant farmer, to the drunken selfish father who terrorizes his children and gives their Christmas turkey to his greyhound, the cruel, violent estranged father remembered without love, the authoritative unchristian priest who banishes two young boys and their dog from his church and the sadistic school teacher who taunts and humiliates two pupils in his classroom. The stories that focus on children's responses to difficult situations are particularly evocative and are exemplars of writing that bears some of the hallmarks of *écriture féminine*.

One such story is 'Whinny Hill' by Nora T. Watson.[10] This first-person narrative maintains a personal, childish, yet mature and poignant voice throughout the text, as the narrator, a girl, describes in simple graphic detail, her humiliation at the hands of a cruel schoolmaster. To punish her for prompting a young lad named Concannon, the teacher orders them to re-enact a reading extract which depicts a

9 Tom Inglis, *Moral monopoly: the rise and fall of the Catholic church in modern Ireland* (Dublin, 1998), p. 188. 10 Nora T. Watson, 'Whinny hill', *The Bell* (Mar. 1953), 612–15.

wife tying a kerchief around her husband's neck and kissing him heartily. The girl carries out the first gesture but as soon as she places her hands on Concannon's arms, he hits her. She is sent out to the pump to clean up and is comforted by an understanding neighbour. The teacher beats Concannon and the games planned by the girl, her brother and his friends for the evening never materialize.

The two-part structure of the dramatic sequence is replicated in the story's structure where the girl's internal response to the teacher's command is expressed starkly and simply: 'I wanted very much to die then'.[11] This immediately changes the personal voice and aptly describes her deep sense of shame and embarrassment in front of her classmates. The tension, combined with the other pupils' laughter, is conveyed by means of spare dialogue and sharp pithy sentences and is further heightened by the physical, concrete details. The child's inner voice is now silenced, her emotions stifled by the experience of being coerced into a public display of a physical act with sexual connotations from the adult world. What should have been a normal rite of passage for a young girl (her first kiss) is converted into a pointless, exploitative act of punishment by a teacher whose motives can only be guessed at: prurient curiosity, sexual frustration, voyeuristic desire.

This story, however, focuses solely on the child's feelings and her awareness of her own physical reality that the author juxtaposes with her natural psychic frailty. She can ignore the pain inflected by playing with the boys and by the teacher's strap but she is very aware of Concannon's physical presence, his smell and his arms. His physical reality is sexualized when she attempts to kiss him: 'I noticed the small red hairs on his wrists. I put my hands on Concannon's arms. They were warm and stiff through his jacket. I remember thinking it was the first time I had touched him ...'[12] The author's use of ellipsis conveys the young girl's sudden realisation of his closeness and his maleness. This impression is reinforced by her later reference to the wind that 'cut sideways and made you conscious of the separateness of body and clothing'.[13] After school, she and her brother ostensibly blame the weather for the cancelled games but underlying their disappointment is the realisation that a boundary has been irrevocably crossed; they have been forced to enter adulthood and the bonds of childhood have been irreparably broken. The psychological damage inflicted on the young girl by her particular experience is forcibly signalled by the prophetic, concluding sentence: 'Some days happen like that, and you always remember'.[14]

A child's fear of an authoritarian figure is also featured in a Maeve Barrington story entitled 'Strong and Perfect Christians'.[15] The protagonist here is a young girl of ten, Marie-Anne, who hates her father. Using the child's perspective reinforces her moral dilemma which centres on the fact that she is due to be confirmed the following day but the unconfessed and unforgiven paternal hatred has stamped 'the black stain of this mortal sin on her soul'.[16] The prospect of receiving Confirmation in such state fills her with fear but her hatred domi-

11 Ibid., p. 613.   12 Ibid., p. 614.   13 Ibid., p. 615.   14 Ibid., p. 615.   15 Maeve Barrington, 'Strong and perfect Christians', *The Bell* (Jan. 1954), 48–52.   16 Ibid., p. 49.

nates this fear. Having established the family's social professional milieu, the narrator uses the child's voice to describe the cause of her hatred. A year earlier, the buttons of Marie-Anne's frock got caught in her hair while undressing and she unknowingly appeared, partially naked, during her parents' dinner party.

The father's overtly kind admonishment does not hide the cruel sarcasm that underlies her description: 'Daddy said, in his witty, party voice: "Marie-Anne, elder daughter of mine, light of my eyes, you must learn to wear your pantees when you come into polite dining-rooms".'[17] He ignores her extreme distress, asks his wife to remove the weeping child from the room and nonchalantly returns to his guests. The child's humiliation is compounded next day when the incident is recounted around the school. The immediate response of the mother, depicted as obedient and submissive to her husband, is singularly lacking in understanding towards her young daughter. She simply advises her to put on her pyjama legs before she takes off her frock and hints at unknown future fears. The duty of sexual modesty in young girls (reinforced here by the mother's failure to explain her attitude) is succinctly portrayed here as a feature of Irish society. This story, like the previous one, is also a comment on male exploitation of young female bodies and could be viewed as a metonymical representation of child sexual abuse, a suppressed and horrific aspect of Irish society during the early decades of the twentieth century.

Psychosocial forces that impact on a young girl similar in age to Marie-Anne are depicted in Mary Lavin's story 'A Glimpse of Katey'.[18] This is a powerful narrative of a young girl's attempted transition from childhood to independence within the family milieu. When young Katey wakes during the night, she hears the laughter of her mother and sisters downstairs and feels impelled to join them. But her father, also disturbed by the laughter, meets her on the landing, confronts her and she 'pulls into the marginal boards at the side of the carpet-strip as a cyclist pulls in to the kerb when a superior vehicle approaches with a view to passing it out while proceeding in the same direction'.[19] Katey's body is thus stranded physically, 'marginalized' on the landing caught between male power based upstairs and, oblivious to her dilemma, the happy female group downstairs. Psychically, she is trapped between her father's patriarchal, misogynist, angry dominance and her own immobilising mute fear. However, under her father's relentless questioning, she placates his anger by lying and ostensibly agreeing with him. Her conflict is unresolved because she feels she has betrayed her mother and sisters and the prospect of meeting 'them all'[20] the next morning fills her with dread.

The future holds no pleasure either for the protagonist in the Elizabeth Connor story, 'The Apple'.[21] This story illustrates the loss of innocence and its disturbing consequences for a middle-aged nun, Mother Mary Aloysius. She is given permission, after thirty years' seclusion in her convent, to look through the windows of her childhood home. She has been blissfully happy in the ordered

17 Ibid., p. 51. 18 Mary Lavin, 'A glimpse of Katey', *The Bell* (Nov. 1947), 40–7. 19 Ibid., p. 44. 20 Ibid., p. 47. 21 Elizabeth Connor, 'The apple', *The Bell* (Oct. 1942), 35–41.

life of her community where '[e]very hour was mapped out for you'[22] and 'she had never used her mind for thinking, only for recording the thoughts of others'.[23] However, as she peers through the downstairs windows of her home and recalls effortlessly the simple details of her childhood, the temptation offered by the open back door to view 'her own sea' from 'her own bedroom' overwhelms her sense of guilt and, with full knowledge and full consent, she enters the house. Despite being aware of her transgression, the memory of this 'sin' is reified as a 'treasure' in her heart but the cost of this possession is incalculable. Her childish innocence is irrevocably lost with the realisation that her physical transgression has not caused the fearful consequences that were inculcated in her during her childhood and convent life. Even the palliative forgiveness offered by the confessional will not assuage her guilt. Connor, through the simple expediency of moving the woman's body over the threshold of her home, has created a moral dilemma that is unsolvable. She further highlights the blackness of the nun's transgression by juxtaposition with nature's beauty around her home, just as her guilt is contrasted with the happy memory resulting from that transgression. To resolve and to reconcile her Catholic morality with her personal experience of sin is the task facing this distressed nun 'and now she must strive for ever to refashion out of chaos the world of her own mind'.[24]

The restrictions of Catholic morality impose no barriers, physical or moral, for the young couple in the Eily O'Horan story entitled 'Optimists'.[25] The setting in this story is a Dublin tenement in wartime where her bed-ridden domineering mother and her reckless unemployed brother trap Róisin in a life of poverty and deprivation. When she meets up with Paddy, whom she has previously refused to marry for family reasons, the claustrophobic atmosphere of the tenement, the tension created by their personal situation and the ominous presence of death is eased by their mutual joy in seeing each other again and in finding physical pleasure in each other's arms. But the socio-political reality of life, via the narrative voice, intrudes on their happiness, by allusions to stark concrete details: an air-raid shelter, the pawn office, labour queues, the smell of rats and garbage, fifteen shillings for turning coats, the flicker of turf fire, the solitary armchair. Similarly, the geographical location is also succinctly established by the author in her use of Hiberno-English dialect, references to Dublin Quays, green buses, the old Georgian doorway and the Angelus bell at six o'clock, thereby creating a microcosm of working-class life during the Emergency. The intrusion of the narrative voice underlines the lack of freedom shared by the young couple, exacerbating the palpable tension between the two sets of protagonists, Róisin and Paddy on one side, her mother and brother on the other. However, the lovers succeed in escaping for a brief interlude to an old country house and in an almost desperate attempt to 'shut out war and separation, poverty and death' they consummate their relationship. Their sexual union is described

22 Ibid., p. 38. 23 Ibid., p. 35. 24 Ibid., p. 41. 25 Eily O'Horan, 'Optimists.' *The Bell* (Feb. 1944), 410–17.

obliquely through nature: 'The sun had a penetrating warmth, and it languorous quality impregnated the moving air with radiant life'.[26] But the incessant cawing of the black rooks overhead the young lovers ominously foretells the calamitous future that awaits them outside their secluded love nest. Despite the couple's attempts to envisage a life together, their future is unpredictable.

The future for the young couple in Margaret O'Leary's story 'Between Two Bridges' is equally uncertain and separation looms ahead for them. One of the first-female-authored short stories printed in *The Bell*, this narrative recounts how the female protagonist, Nellie, contrives a meeting with the unsuitable Peter, a garage mechanic, who believes their relationship is finished, because his mother has acquired for him 'a fine big strapping girl that would make six of [Nellie]'.[27] Considerable emphasis is placed throughout the text, both by the narrator and Peter, on Nellie's physical weakness and her indecision, which are contrasted with his verbal dominance and antagonism in their conversation. However as soon as Nellie begins to cry, the young man's resolve is weakened, he hands her his handkerchief and the narrative continues:

> She cried softly into it for a minute or two, comforted by its size, its slight warmth, and its smell. Then, catching her breath with little sniffs, she wiped her face dry with it, but streaked all over with its dirt. Then she slipped it back into his hand again. He put it immediately to his face, as if to inhale the warmth and moisture left on it by hers, and began blowing his nose violently and clearing his throat with little gulps.[28]

Thus, the physicality of the simple gesture is encoded with a strong sexual connotation as the bodily fluids of the boy and girl mingle in the handkerchief, symbolic of their sexual union that will probably never happen. In some societies, it is believed that bodily waste (excreta, tears, blood, hair, nail clippings) has magical and dangerous qualities. In its marginality, in the way in which it traverses the boundaries of the body, [the waste material] comes to represent particular threats and powers, which ultimately symbolize social boundaries, transgressions, and threats'.[29] The transgression of Peter and Nellie, represented by their symbolic consummation, has violated the social order as defined by their socially-conscious mothers and the story ends as they continue their walk, hand in hand, 'their faces smudged with each other's tears and dirt'.[30]

A subtle but alternative undermining of the social order is suggested in the Val Mulkerns story entitled 'Girls'.[31] This is one of the few stories with an urban setting and concerns a group of three working girls in a city apartment who are preparing a party. It is also the only story by a woman in *The Bell* that includes an oblique reference to lesbianism. Two of the flatmates, Sadie and Angela, are incompatible, partly due to their interest in the same man, and the third girl, Pat,

26 Ibid., p. 416. 27 Margaret O'Leary, 'Between two bridges', *The Bell* (June 1941), 25. 28 Ibid., p. 26. 29 Janet Wolff, *Feminine sentences: essays on women and culture* (Cambridge, 1990), p. 122. 30 Ibid., p. 27. 31 Val Mulkerns, 'Girls', *The Bell* (July 1947), 46–52.

is the peacemaker, particularly with Sadie, who is threatening to leave the flat. The physical description of Pat (the androgynous name is significant) is feminized by her nun-like preparation of the table and by her spinning like a ballerina. Her attention is caught by Sadie's black hair and black eyes and the narrative continues: 'She watched them for a moment almost as if she herself were a man: Girls, all girls, were beautiful. Their hair in the light was beautiful, and their gestures, and the way they laughed'.[32] Admitting her inability to host a party as she would 'pair off all the wrong people', she is the one who always sings 'The Bohemian Girl'. Like its heroine who spends twelve years living with gypsies under a false identity until she is recognized by a scar, Pat is a displaced individual whose 'scar' may or may not be eventually recognized. In this story she has no role to play during the party, except to suggest some dancing. Her isolation is further highlighted by the author's emphasis on heterosexual 'couples in contented isolation'[33] and the other two girls' contest over Jed. The party, however, alters the dynamic of the group's relationship when Sadie and Pat are united in their celebration of Sadie's romantic success while Angela becomes isolated. At the story's conclusion, Pat is content, secure in the knowledge that Sadie will stay in the flat. This narrative is urbane and sophisticated when compared with the other texts and is also an example of what one critic has called (in relation to another Mulkern's story) 'the creative force of understatement' in her handling of what he euphemistically calls 'this difficult theme'.[34] Many years would pass before this 'difficult' theme could be treated more openly in Irish fiction.

These stories appeared over many issues of *The Bell* and suggest that Irish women's texts share similar themes and concerns. The focus of this essay is the woman's body, the suffering it endures, the pleasure it feels and the transgressive impulses of that body. These texts are at variance with the sexual and emotional repression that was inculcated in young Irish Catholic girls during the first half of the 20th century and perhaps are symptomatic of that repression.

These short stories, therefore, are narratives of identity focusing on female bodies, both young and old. They portray a corporeal identity that appears to be incompatible with the prevailing ideology of women of the period. They also portray, not only the reality of these individual's own lives within restricted confines, both physical and psychical, but also the attempts they make to transgress these boundaries. These transgressions, almost always expressed in a physical, bodily gesture, result in individual psychological development or trauma, inner growth or an understanding of female suffering. A number of the children and young adolescents experience powerful physical sensations in their coming to sexual awareness. Others are caught up in a moral or psychological trauma as a result of humiliation at the hands of patriarchal figures. Female characters are firmly located within the private sphere of the home and family, but, despite these restrictions, the main female protagonist in each story takes a few physical steps, sometimes

32 Ibid., p. 47.   33 Ibid., p. 51.   34 John Jordan, 'The short story after the second World War', in Augustine Martin (ed.), *The genius of Irish prose* (Dublin, 1984), p. 140.

hesitant, sometimes deliberate, outside these boundaries, be they social, religious or gendered, and thereby asserts her own independence, or learns from the experience, in spite of the sanctions or repercussions that will inevitably follow.

The writers write of their experiences as legitimate literary material. The need to express their own ways of thinking and feeling becomes, in the words of Kathleen L. Komar, 'a privileged port of entry into a psychological development that often cannot take place in the society at large'.[35] Most of these writers would probably never read Hélène Cixous' *Laugh of the Medusa* but they may well have the last laugh (posthumously for some) and a merited sense of self-satisfaction if they were to read her words today:

> Write yourself. Your body must be heard. Only then will the immense resources of the unconscious spring forth. Our naphtha will spread, throughout the world, without dollars – black or gold – nonassessed values that will change the rules of the old game.[36]

Freud's fetishism and the mermaid

CATHERINE KILCOYNE, NUI, CORK

The mythical character, the mermaid has her place in Irish folk tales, and as such has provided a source of inspiration for two particular Irish poems: 'Maighdean Mara' by Seamus Heaney and 'An Mhaighdean Mhara' by Nuala Ní Dhomhnaill. Freud's theory of Fetishism has much to offer us as we consider how the respective poets use this motif.

FREUD'S THEORY OF FETISHISM REVISITED

Freud introduces the notion of fetishism first in his 'Three essays on sexuality' (1905). It forms part of the first essay entitled: 'The sexual aberrations' and more specifically the subsection called: 'Unsuitable substitutes for the sexual object – fetishism.' This early essay assumes the 'normal sexual object' to be female and the subject making the substitution to be male. In doing so, Freud objectifies female sexuality and denies female desire. Freud renegotiates this equation in his essay 'Femininity'(1933). He argues that femininity is not passivity itself but is 'giving preference to passive aims'.[1] Because, Freud admits, the female subject

35 Kathleen L. Komar, 'Feminist curves in contemporary literary space', in Mararet R. Higonnet and Joan Templeton (eds), *Reconfigured spheres: feminist explorations of literary space* (Amherst, 1994), p. 104. 36 Hélène Cixous, 'The laugh of the Medusa', in Abel and Abel (eds), *The signs reader*, p. 285. I wish to acknowledge the support of the IRCHSS. 1 Sigmund Freud, 'Femininity', in Rosalind

occasionally gives preference to active aims (masculinity), she exemplifies 'bisexuality.' Freud's differentiation between being marked by passivity and being marked by the preference for passivity is meagre and insufficient. He does not adequately sever the connection between women and passivity. Later, Joan Riviere developed the idea that 'femininity' is a masquerade or a disguise that the female assumes to disarm man's fear of her power. This suggests that the passivity aligned with femininity is a male projection. Efrat Tseelon, takes this idea and deduces that this masquerade works like fetishism.[2] It masks female power, '… a denial of and a defence against a threatening reality. The threatening reality is the "castration" of the woman in the case of fetishism and the power of the woman in the case of masquerade.'[3] The female/passive assumption forms the basis for Freud's later more detailed examination of fetishism, as well as all his minor references to the phenomenon. For Freud the fetishist is necessarily male and the fetish always replaces a female other. He gives a quotation from Goethe's *Faust* to illustrate the occurrence of fetishism in 'normal love': 'Get me a kerchief from her breast, a garter that her knee has pressed.' Again this example illustrates the aforementioned assumption. The man chooses his fetish (a kerchief or a garter) in substitution for a woman (the breast and the knee). His final explanation of the notion, as a reaction to the castration complex in boys, is reliant on these initial assumptions. The boy disavows the discovery that his mother does not have a penis and so guards himself from the fear of castration. This theory cannot be applied to girls as they do not possess a penis which they might fear losing. Therefore Freud's completed theory excludes any representation of a female choosing subject.

It is my argument that, without including women in a model of fetishism, Freud, in his lecture 'Femininity,' inadvertently describes women's development in terms of a fetishisation of the penis. Furthermore, the steps that Freud outlines in women's development, which I identify as fetishistic, are for Freud, necessary for normality. Benjamin's critique of penis envy through the notion of 'ideal love,' – 'a love in which the woman submits to and adores an other who is what she cannot be'[4] – illustrates this fetishism, more in terms of a fetishisation of phallic power, without ever using the term. Penis envy works, like castration complex, as a reason to develop a fetish. The attainment of a male partner, owning a part in a penis, is a result of the woman's realisation of her lack. In choosing the compromised situation of a heterosexual relationship, this 'normal woman' can relive the pre-Oedipal stage of her life, when she too was not aware that her mother lacked a penis.[5] In the words of Mitchell: 'No phallus, no power – except those winning ways of getting one'.[6] The adult relation-

Minsky (ed.), *Psychoanalysis and gender: an introductory reader* (London, 1996), p. 215. 2 Efrat Tseelon, *The masque of femininity: the presentation of woman in everyday life* (1995), p. 39. 3 Ibid., p. 39. 4 Jessica Benjamin, *The bonds of love: psychoanalysis, feminism, and the problem of domination* (London, 1990), p. 86. 5 Freud, in his lecture 'Femininity', argues that a heterosexual relationship is a compromise for the woman. It is a resignation to the fact that she has no penis and thus no phallic power. Her mere part ownership of a penis is symbolic of her relationship with the man. 6 Benjamin, *The bonds of love*, p. 93.

ship also allows her to remember the phallic mother of the pre-Oedipal stage. Freud creates a hierarchy of successes against penis envy. The path to normal womanhood demands the acquisition of a penis through heterosexual relations with a man. Thus in Freudian terms the development of a fetish staves homosexuality off for women, just as it does for men. The process of disavowal is just as prevalent in this theory as in Freud's male model of fetishism. The woman believes and disbelieves at the same time that she, and all women, owns a penis. She relives the blissful ignorance of the pre-Oedipal stage.

Freud does not adequately discuss the position of fetishism in relation to pathology. In the section of 'Three essays' that deals with fetishism it is posited under the title of an 'aberration' and the essay asserts that the condition 'borders on the pathological'.[7] Conversely, however, it also argues that it exists to a degree in any normal love.[8] Both normal and pathological fetishes are defined in similar terms. They are an overvaluation of the sexual object (woman) and all that surrounds it. According to Freud, the fetish is pathological only when it actually replaces the woman, becoming itself 'the sole sexual object'.[9] Yet he does not explain what motivates a normal fetish to become a pathological one, in fact he acknowledges: 'we frankly are not able to explain.' Freud's theory thus suggests that fetishism, the pathology, is merely an exaggeration of an otherwise normal sexual instinct.

His later essay 'Fetishism'(1927) readdresses these vague categories. It seeks to place fetishism within the scale of neurosis and psychosis, clarifying his theories and distinctions between both. But it remains problematic. By identifying fetishism as a neurosis rather than a psychosis, Freud allows somewhat for its existence in normality. The mechanism of disavowal further allows the neurotic to coincide with the normal. The meaning of neurosis/psychosis is dependent on the distinctions between disavowal and what Freud calls scotomization. Freud argues that the fetishist deals with his castration complex by denying the truth that his mother, and hence women, have no penis. This refusal to accept the truth is first named 'scotomization.' Freud adopts this term from Laforgue. To scotomize the fact is to wipe it from consciousness completely. Such an abandonment of the real would, however, relegate fetishism to the realm of the psychotic. Since Freud identifies with the situation – 'no male human being is spared the fright'[10] – he does not want this. Freud abandons this theory. Rather, he argues that the fetishist experiences a split in his consciousness that allows him to believe the truth and to disbelieve it at the same time. This schizoid process called 'disavowal' (*Verleugnung*) renders fetishism neurotic.

In the conflict between the weight of the unwelcome perception and the force of his counter wish, a compromise has been reached, as is only possible under the dominance of the unconscious laws of thought – the primary processes. Yes, in his mind, the woman has got a penis.[11]

7 Sigmund Freud, 'Three essays on sexuality', in James Strachey (ed.) *The standard edition of the complete psychological works of Sigmund Freud*, xxi (London, 1953), p. 153. 8 Ibid., p. 154. 9 Ibid. 10 Sigmund Freud, 'Fetishism', in Strachey (ed.), *The standard edition*, xxi, p. 154. 11 Ibid.

Disavowal is comparable to the normal function of fantasy. Slavoj Zizek draws on Sloterdijk for his version of fetishism, as a social process: 'The subject is aware of the distance between the ideological mask and the social reality, but he nonetheless insists upon the mask'.[12] Zizek recognizes fetishism as a fantasy, whereas Freud labels fetishism as neurotic. The difference is, Zizek argues, that the aberrant understands the process somewhat. Freud denies that the fetishist has this knowledge. But Freud, in his earlier essay 'The loss of reality in neurosis and psychosis' (1924) connects neuroses with 'phantasy'.[13] If fetishism is a neurosis and neuroses draw on fantasy then surely the relationship between fetishism and fantasy is stronger than Freud acknowledges. He illustrates disavowal by recounting two separate cases where boys fail to take cognisance of their fathers' death. 'It was only one current of their mental life that had not recognized their Father's death; there was another current which took full account of this fact'.[14] Freud does not explore the possibility that the boys are aware of what they are doing; that they choose to wear the 'mask.' An analysis of Freud's language, however, illustrates how his assertions are belied by his diction. While Freud assumes the deciding party to be male, he states that men are not entirely conscious or deliberate in their choices of a fetish. 'Accidental circumstances have contributed' to their choice of fetish.[15]

Yet Freud's use of the word 'contributed' dilutes the argument. It means that these accidental circumstances do not dictate the choice either. There is deliberateness involved. Again in a later line he states, 'the fetish is precisely designed to …'[16] which again implies intention and logic in the choice. Freud recalls the young male's horror at the threat of castration, and posits the boy's overvaluation of the penis as natural rather than constructed: 'And against that threat there rose in rebellion the portion of his narcissism which Nature has, as a precaution, attached to that particular organ.'[17] This quotation does not describe the threat as imagined and so the 'rebellion' appears justified against real attack. Bergler argues that castration fear leads a man to develop 'an unconscious, powerful portrait of himself.'[18] He calls this imagined self the 'He-Man.' Freud's treatment of male identity does precisely this; he creates a heroic role for men.

The quotation also defines the penis as the place of power. Freud's logic denies societal influences on the child as well as the biased perception of gender received by the child, due to the respective roles played out by mother and father. Freud asserts that fetishism 'saves men from becoming … homosexual' which, for Freud is advantageous. Freud constructs a hierarchy of responses to the dilemma: the highest most successful retaliation is to surmount it completely; the next best response is to develop a fetish to fend it off and a complete failure to tackle the problem results in homosexuality. One can see the similarity between this triad and the other referring to the development of 'normal fem-

12 Slavoj Zizek, *The sublime object of ideology* (London, 1989). 13 Sigmund Freud, 'The loss of reality in neurosis and psychosis' in Strachey (ed.), *The works of Freud*, xxi, p. 187. 14 Freud, 'Fetishism.' p. 156. 15 Ibid., p. 152. 16 Ibid. 17 Ibid., p. 153. 18 Tseelon, *The masque of femininity*, p. 26.

ininity'. Freud's promotion of the fetishistic fantasy culminates in his coercive description of its attractiveness:

> The meaning of the fetish is not known to other people, so the fetish is not withheld from him: it is easily accessible and he can readily obtain the sexual satisfaction attached to it. What other men have to woo and make exertions for can be had by the fetishist with no trouble at all.

I argue that Freud's theory itself fetishizes male heterosexual desire. The process repeats itself at a metalevel. In Freud's main essay on the topic, he argues that an aversion to female genitals is never absent in the fetishist. Therefore the fetishized woman (the woman who is substituted) is denied her very biological femaleness. Freud argues that the homosexual man is so as a reaction to the fear of castrated women. Fetishism 'saves the Fetishist from becoming a homosexual … by endowing women with the characteristic that makes them tolerable as sexual objects'.[19] Here, women are doubly denigrated. They are 'sexual objects' due to their 'lack' (of penis), and so, are defined in the negative (non-phallic). Yet even their object status is spurious; it is reliant on male imagination to 'endow' them with an imaginary penis. Their greatest fate thus is to be 'tolerable' sexual objects for men. Male heterosexual desire depends on disavowal, a split in consciousness, without which they would be homosexual. To desire women, men must imagine her as biologically male. This is another split in the male psyche that Freud has ignored.

I also argue that Freud's theory itself is a fetish. We can see how it functions as such, when we take into account Kaja Silverman's criticism of 'Fetishism' (1927). Silverman, through a different route, also deduces that the Freudian 'lack' is a male projection onto the female other.[20] The lack becomes distasteful to the male and he then covers it with a fetish. Freud's theory itself also does this. It explains male lack by projection onto a female other. It covers female lack but in doing so points to its existence. Silverman asserts that the 'normal male is constructed through the denial of his lack … what he disavows is his own insufficiency, and the mechanism of that disavowal is projection'.[21] This can be seen in Freud's words: 'The horror of castration has set up a memorial to itself in the creation of this substitute'.[22] Vision of this projected lack reminds one of one's own castrations (in Lacanian terms).

Silverman, drawing from Kristeva, argues that the male responds to his fear by 'insisting upon the absoluteness of the boundaries separating male from female'.[23] We can see also that Freud similarly polarizes male and female with his construction of 'Fetishism.' He divides male and female into subject and object. Their roles are rigid in his theory. Freud's theory bolsters male subjectivity and insists on female lack, by at once covering it and at the same time acknowledging it. Micheal Taussig, in his theory of state fetishism, describes this process in

19 Freud, 'Fetishism', p. 154. 20 Kaja Silverman, 'Lost objects and mistaken subjects: a prologue', in *The acoustic mirror: the female voice in psychoanalysis and cinema* (Bloomington, 1987), pp 1–43. 21 Ibid., p. 17. 22 Freud, 'Fetishism', p. 154. 23 Silverman, 'Lost objects and mistaken subjects', p. 17.

semiotic terms: 'The signifier depends upon yet erases its signification.'[24] Heather Findlay recognizes 'the uncanny way in which his theory doubles that of the little boy's'.[25] She argues that Freud 'erects a completed theoretical framework in the place of a lack: the 'disappointment' he fears he will 'certainly create' in his reader in the same way the boy erects a fetish in the place of female lack'.[26]

THE FETISH STARES BACK AT THE PHALLIC LENS: THE MERMAID SPEAKS

This part of the paper looks at how Seamus Heaney and Nuala Ní Dhomhnaill appropriate the mermaid/fetish motif in their respective poems of similar titles. Seamus Heaney's 'Maighdean Mara' forms part of his collection *Wintering Out* (1972). Nuala Ní Dhomhnaill's poem 'An Mhaighdean Mhara' is in her first collection *An Dealg Droighin* (1981). I wish to contrast the two poems on their disparate manipulations of the mermaid. Heaney, in his poem, occupies the position of the storyteller, the dreamer and, I shall argue, the fetishist. His poem, narrated from the point of view of the fetishist, delineates the very process of fetishism. Consequent to this perspective, the poem gives voice to the phallic perception.

In opposition to this, I wish to demonstrate Ní Dhomhnaill's successful problematising of Freud's fetishism through her use of the mermaid image (a product of fetishism). By giving the mermaid a voice, Ní Dhomhnaill enables her to deconstruct her own image. The mermaid of her poem disempowers the fetishist and contests Freud's *'fetischismus'*. Ní Dhomhnaill represents the meek mermaid from Andersen's tale (by allusion) as well as the more typical, victimized mermaid of the Irish tradition and she liberates them both through speech.

Heaney's 'Maighdean Mara' (1972) inverts the traditional, beginning-middle-end sequence of the Irish legend (the source of both poems). The mermaid of this poem, unlike Ní Dhomhnaill's mermaid, has no desire to live on land. In keeping with the original story, she is coercively forced to reside there and so the poem celebrates her return to the sea.[27] However, the mermaid's homecoming is marred by her experience on land; she cannot regain the contentment she enjoyed prior to her marriage. Likewise, the mermaid of Ní Dhomhnaill's poem expresses frustration at this in her last words: 'The tide also fails us / and a rat / gnaws at the very sun'.[28]

Heaney also extends the time frame of the myth: he includes a contemplation of the mermaid's eventual life at sea.[29] Traditionally the mermaid's return to sea ends the story, she is freed from captivity and escapes the phallic gaze.

24 Michael Taussig, *The nervous system* (New York, 1992), p. 118. 25 Heather Findlay, 'Freud's fetishism' and the lesbian dildo debates', in Jane Price and Margarit Shildrick (eds), *Feminist theory and the body: a reader* (Edinburgh, 1999), p. 453. 26 Ibid., p. 453. 27 Some versions of the tale state that the mermaid was very happy in her marriage and with her life on land but contradictorily she always seizes the opportunity to return to sea. 28 Nuala Ní Dhomhnaill, *Nuala Ní Dhomhnaill selected poems: rogha dánta*, trans. Michael Hartnett and Nuala Ní Dhomhnaill (Dublin, 2000), p. 50, line 20. 29 Seamus Heaney, 'Maighdean Mara', *Wintering out* (London, 1972), stanza 1.

Not only does Heaney continue the story beyond this point, however, he also continues to fetishize the mermaid. She does not escape subjugation. Her life at sea, contrary to expectation, is portrayed in terms of a continuation of her life on land. She remains voiceless and passive and the sea resumes the abuse that her husband begins. The narrator colludes with the sea-world and objectifies the mermaid. The very first word, 'she', sets up the perspective of the poem. It is told entirely in the third person. The inverted chronology of Heaney's poem means that the mermaid, rather than the man, is the first character to be introduced. This shift in emphasis empowers the speaker, enabling him to appropriate the female subject. While drawing attention to the plight of the female, the focus of the poem furthers the manipulation of her character.

The imagery of the first stanza depicts the mermaid as being mistreated by the sea: 'Her cold breasts / Dandled by undertow'.[30] The stanza contains a stark contrast between extreme activity in the form of invasion and extreme passivity in the form of torpidity. The mermaid is a passive entity who is acted upon by the sea and all that the sea contains ('seawracks,' 'wort' and 'Liens'). Thus the voice of the fetishist aligns activity with the ocean and passivity with the mermaid. The sea assumes the 'masculine'[31] role previously assigned to the mermaid's husband and the narrator acts as vehicle for the mermaid's fetishisation. 'She sleeps now, her cold breasts / Dandled by undertow'.[32] Here, the tidal movement of the sea fondles and manipulates the sea-maiden's breasts; it caresses the mermaid's body as she sleeps. The passive tense emphasizes the mermaid's lack of agency: 'Her hair *lifted* and *laid*.'[33] The passive image of the mermaid acknowledges the submission that she is forced into. Bo Almqvist suggests in an essay about the poem that the mermaid is in fact dead. However, I disagree with Almqvist that the passive mermaid is 'repulsive,'[34] rather she is statue-like; she remains beautiful (through fetishisation) though she is dead. Her portrayal is similar to those analysed by Elisabeth Bronfen in her essay 'Fatal conjunctions: gendering representations of death'.[35] In this essay Bronfen critiques Edgar Allan Poe's assertion that 'the death of a beautiful woman is unquestionably the most poetical topic'

Bronfen's analysis of this trope asks the question: 'the most poetic for whom?' In light of my argument that Heaney's poem enacts fetishism, this is interesting because if the answer to Bronfen's question is: 'it is the most poetic for a male audience' then it suggests that Heaney's use of the image also satisfies a male readership. As Bronfen explains 'the combination of beautiful and dead seems a contradiction in terms'.[36] But as fetishist, the narrator allows death and beauty to coincide, *disavowing* the reality that the former eradicates the latter.

30 Ibid., p. 56. 31 'Masculine' in the Freudian sense meaning 'active' both generally and with regard to fetishism. 32 Ní Dhomhnaill, *Nuala Ní Dhomhnaill selected poems*, line 1. 33 Ní Dhomhnaill, 'An Mhaighdean Mhara', *Nuala Ní Dhomhnaill selected poems*, p. 20. 34 Bo Almqvist, 'Of mermaids and marriages. Seamus Heaney's 'maighdean mara' and Nuala Ní Dhomhnaill's 'an mhaighdean mhara' in the light of folk tradition', *Béaloideas* 58 (1990), 35. 35 Elisabeth Bronfen, 'Fatal conjunctions: gendering representations of death', in Willy Apollon and Richard Feldstein (eds), *Lacan, politics, aesthetics* (New York, 1996), pp 237–60. 36 Ibid., p. 238.

The sea and the sea-vegetation sexually peruse the sedate mermaid and they eventually advance upon her: 'Cast about shin and thigh'.[37] The ocean penetrates the 'sleeping beauty' image: 'Liens catch, dislodge gently'.[38] As with Ní Dhomhnaill's poem, the tidal movement creates momentum, but here the rhythm horrifically sounds the rape of the mermaid by the sea. The provocative words: 'Catch, dislodge,' are echoed in the fourth line of the second verse: 'steeped and dishevelled,' linking the 'Land years' with the 'great first sleep / of homecoming'.[39] The supposed escape from captivity, the return to sea, simply facilitates a new form of torture. The transference of roles from the mermaid's husband to the sea illustrates the mermaid's altered psyche; as a result of her punishment on land she experiences life at sea differently.

The retrospective second part of the poem recalls the mermaid's aggressive seizure from the sea. The violent language, which forms a subtle undertone in the first part, is used more explicitly here: 'He stole … He hid … [He] charmed her'.[40] In contrast to his power, her futility is inferred by the words: 'follow / was all that she could do'.[41] The lecherous imagery of the first part of the poem lends the term 'man-love nightly,' connotations of rape.[42] Also, the words 'four walls, / Warm floor' give the entire third stanza a claustrophobic atmosphere.[43] The fourth stanza continues similarly: 'She suffered milk and birth − / She had no choice − conjured / Patterns of home and drained / The tidesong from her voice'.[44]

The third part of the poem begins with the mermaid's journey back to sea. She approaches it with relief, as one falling asleep: 'entering / Foam, she wrapped herself …'[45] Yet the next three lines tell of all the sore memories that surround her and will not allow her to rest comfortably: 'smoke-reeks,' 'Straw-musts and films of mildew.' Tragically the man will never be punished, his secret abuse of her is buried with the mermaid in the sea: 'She dipped his secret there'.[46] 'She sleeps now …' with all that she endured on land.

If Heaney's narrator enacts the phallic gaze then Ní Dhomhnaill's mermaid is the object of this stare. By giving the mermaid a voice, Ní Dhomhnaill allows her to gaze back at the phallic lens. Thus the mermaid commands agency. As an analysis of Freud's theory shows, fetishism demands that the female be passive, so that Ní Dhomhnaill's mobilisation of the mermaid, the fetish, liberates her from Freud's restrictive theory. A close reading of this poem reveals the mermaid's unrelenting rebellion against the passive position consigned to the female in Freud's theory. 'Ebbtide,' the opening word, denotes the low psychological state of the mermaid. Ebb tide is a regressive moment held fast by a strong, backward gravitational pull; yet ebb tide anticipates the floodtide. This sequence from regression towards progression reflects the aspirations of the poem. A microcosm of this sequence is seen in stanza two: 'Floodtide ebbtide / floodtide ebbtide / rise and fall / rise and fall / the same again'.[47] These lines create the

---

37 Heaney, 'Maighdean mara', *Wintering out*, line 5. 38 Ibid., line 7. 39 Ibid., lines 9 and 10. 40 Ibid., lines 14–18. 41 Ibid., line 16. 42 Ibid., line 19. 43 Ibid., line 19 and 20. 44 Ibid., line 21–4. 45 Heaney, 'Maighdean mara', *Wintering out,* line 28. 46 Ibid., line 32. 47 Ní Dhomhnaill, 'An

momentum of the poem, tying the rhythm of speech to the tidal movement. However, they also illustrate the powerful impetus of nature, which Ní Dhomhnaill and the mermaid have to work against. 'The tide will have to turn,' the mermaid says. The fetish rebels against her objectification (as subject matter of the poem and ' alternative sexual object[48] for the fetishist). The role that she is assigned by fetishism 'makes [her] nauseous'[49] and what better way to rebuff her subjugation than to compare it to 'lugworm's faeces?'[50]

Resistance to change is eloquently inferred in the strong hold of the 'limpets' to the 'rocks' and the psychological damage to the mermaid caused by her objectification is symbolized by the 'waste of sand,' and the 'wrack drying waterless.' As the ebb tide is followed by the abundant floodtide, similarly, the comparison between the dry wrack and the vellum[51] offers hope and reinterprets the bareness described in the third line as a tabula rasa on which to begin again. However, the despotic voice of the fetishist is pervasive: 'But "we have ways of making you talk."/ I hear in Gestapo accents'.[52] This line also refers to the mermaid story type that tells of a mermaid who refuses to talk while she is on land, but laughs three times during her stay. This particular version is referred to as 'The Three Laughs of the Mermaid Tale'.[53] Peig Sayers tells of such a mermaid. In Peig's story the mermaid's brother-in-law beats her until she speaks, at which point she eloquently refutes the accusations that are directed at her.[54]

Freud in his lecture 'Femininity'(1933) describes women's normal development in terms, I suggest, of a fetishisation of the penis. Jacques Lacan identifies it as such in *Feminine Sexuality*. He says: 'The organ actually invested with this signifying function takes on the value of a fetish'.[55] Jessica Benjamin reaches a similar conclusion, in her analysis of 'ideal love.' She discusses the perverseness of the obsessive self-denial that is penis envy and the nature of romantic relationships that it occasions. Though she acknowledges its existence she reasons, contrary to Freud, that social conditioning causes its occurrence rather than nature. Ní Dhomhnaill's poem is in agreement, the last two stanzas sympathize with women in such self-abnegating relationships. The mermaid image, in general, represents a woman who renounces her own interests in favour of the interests of another, whether by choice (as is the case in the Andersen story) or by compulsion (as with many of the Irish versions).

The Andersen tale is alluded to in the last stanza but one, where the mermaid describes the pain that she endures, similar to treading on sharp knives, in order to be on land. 'Not without pain / have I landed'.[56] This reference to *The Little Mermaid* aids Ní Dhomhnaill's argument well. Andersen's mermaid renounces her own subjectivity in exchange for the love of a man. She trans-

mhaighdean mhara', *Nuala Ní Dhomhnaill selected poems*, line 9. 48 Freud, 'Fetishism', p. 154. 49 Ní Dhomhnaill, 'An mhaighdean mhara', *Nuala Ní Dhomhnaill selected poems*, line 8. 50 Ibid., line 7. 51 Ibid., line 6. 52 Ibid., line 17. 53 Almqvist, 'Of mermaids and marriages', p. 29. 54 Ibid., p. 30. 55 Juliet Michell and Jacqueline Rose (eds), *Feminine sexuality: Jacques Lacan and the Ecole Freudienne*, trans. Jacqueline Rose (London, 1982), p. 84. 56 Ní Dhomhnaill, Nuala, 'An mhaighdean mhara', *Nuala Ní Dhomhnaill selected poems*, line 30.

poses her desires onto him and all that he engenders. Effectively she seeks happiness vicariously through another, the Other: the prince. The superimposition of the Andersen story onto the Irish myth in the poem is very clever. Both tales are used simultaneously to critique the self-effacing nature of 'ideal love.' 'Not without pain have I landed'.[57] This landing is indicative of an arrival at Freud's definition of normal femininity, having acknowledged one's own 'inferiority.' It is an arrival marked by the 'compromise' (as Freud deems it) of heterosexual love: a means to acquire phallic power, even if it is shared with another. The poem is in agreement with Benjamin that such submissive femininity is a social construct: 'I broke the natural law'.[58] The natural is corrupted by the social.

The compromise of Freudian femininity is symbolized in the mermaid's discomfort with walking. Ní Dhomhnaill likens the awkward first steps of the mermaid to that of the curlew, a bird with long legs whose steps are very pronounced and seem self-conscious. The mermaid regresses to infancy and must learn to walk. Ní Dhomnaill, in an interview, compares this to the imposition of the English language on native Irish speakers. Like the mermaid, they too had to relearn a skill originally acquired as a child, the skill of speaking.

The final stanza sees the return of the ebb tide. The incessant movement of the tide continues and the mermaid's last words are despondent in tone. She departs from the myth and confronts the man for whom she came ashore. 'You left / and took my magic cap. / It's not as easy to get back / in the roof's rafters / as it was in the fable'.[59] Ní Dhomhnaill explains this irresolution in an interview. Jokingly she says: 'There is no resolution because this mermaid knows all about mermaid stories'.[60] Bo Almqvist suggests that the central message of the tale is that you should marry 'one of your own kind, station and neighbourhood, the message expressed by the Irish proverb *pós ar an gcairn aoiligh.*'[61] Though the tale may accommodate such a reading, Almqvist ignores the fact that it is not difference that makes the marriage unsuccessful but rather, lack of consent from the female.

To conclude, both Heaney and Ní Dhomhnaill cleverly manipulate the Irish folk tale 'An Mhaighdean Mhara.' Heaney's poem rearranges the order of the story, casting extra focus on the mermaid and enabling the reader to sympathize more deeply with her plight. Yet Heaney's mermaid is figured in fetishistic terms, she is manipulated by the phallic perspective and objectified by the third person point of view. Ní Dhomhnaill's mermaid, empowered by speech, responds to her own objectification and fetishisation. Her resistance to subjugation is surmised in her frustration with the incessant movement of the waves: 'The tide will have to turn'.[62] Ní Dhomhnaill uses the 'An Mhaighdean Mhara' myth to allow female characters to gaze back at the phallic lens, to interrupt and deconstruct male fetishisation of the female as delineated by Freud in 'Fetischismus'(1927).

---

57 Ibid., line 30. 58 Ibid., line 32. 59 Ibid., line 41. 60 'Is í seo an mhaighdean mhara go bhfuil a fhios aici na scéalta mar gheall ar na maighdeanacha mara' (Almqvist, p. 43). 61 Almqvist, 'Of mermaids and marriages', p. 38. Literally 'Marry on the dunghill.' 62 Ní Dhomhnaill, 'An mhaighdean mhara', Nuala Ní Dhomhnaill selected poems, line 2.

The new woman and the boy in fin de siècle Irish fiction

TINA O'TOOLE, UNIVERSITY OF LIMERICK

Introducing the recent critical collection *Theorizing Ireland*, Claire Connolly addresses the question 'What is the subject matter of Irish studies?' and points out that 'not all of Irish culture arranges itself neatly under the heading "Irish". A great many things have happened and are happening on the island that are not primarily concerned with nationality and its discontents.'[1] She goes on to say:

> From the vantage point of feminism, it is possible to see how it is not only questions of national identity and definition that have motivated an Irish turn to theory. Sexual politics have played a key role in determining the shapes critical and cultural theory has taken on this island.[2]

In this essay, I examine a text derived from a political and cultural project that challenged hegemonies at the end of the nineteenth century in Ireland. In so doing, I touch on the work of a group of writers at the *fin de siècle* who exploded the binaries of Irish/British definition by exploring Scandinavian texts, and addressing revolutionary politics in Italy and Poland. The cultural project of these so-called 'New Woman' writers of the 1890s problematised gender dualism and opened up the construction of gender identities for discussion.

Much critical work has been done in recent years on the New Woman project, and on the work of Sarah Grand in particular.[3] However, scholars have tended to neglect the Irish dimension to this work. Interestingly, many of the key New Woman writers had Irish origins: Sarah Grand herself was born in Donaghadee, Co. Down, in 1854; George Egerton (1860–1945) was born in Australia, but was the daughter of an Irish Catholic army captain and spent her formative years in Dublin, going on to write her best-known work *Keynotes* (1893) while living in Millstreet, Co. Cork; 'Iota' (Kathleen Mannington Caffyn) (*fl.*1883– 1900) was born and grew up in Co. Tipperary; E.L. [Ethel Lillian]

---

1 Claire Connolly, *Theorizing Ireland* (London, 2003), p. 2.   2 Ibid., p. 3.   3 Such as Gail Cunningham, *The new woman and the Victorian novel* (London, 1978); Linda Dowling, *Language and decadence in the Victorian fin de siècle* (New Jersey, 1986); Sally Ledger, *The new woman: fiction and feminism at the fin de siècle* (Manchester, 1997); etc. Sarah Grand's work is considered in the following: Marilyn Bonnell, 'The legacy of Sarah Grand's *the heavenly twins*: a review essay' *English Literature in Transition* 36 (1995), 467–78; Susan Gorsky, 'The art of politics: the feminist fiction of Sarah Grand', *Journal of Women's Studies in Literature* 1 (1979), 286–300; John Kucich, 'Curious dualities: *the heavenly twins* (1893) and Sarah Grand's belated modernist aesthetics', in Harman and Meyer (eds), *The new nineteenth century: feminist readings of underread Victorian fiction* (New York, 1995), pp 195–204.; Teresa Lynn Mangum, *Married, middlebrow and militant: Sarah Grand and the new woman novel* (Ann Arbor, 1998); etc.

Voynich (1864–1960) was the Cork-born daughter of George Boole, Professor of Maths at Queen's College Cork; and L.T. [Elizabeth Thomasina] Meade (1844–1915), a pioneer of fiction for girls at the end of the nineteenth century, was from Nohoval, Co. Cork, but moved in adulthood to London. So, to reflect again on Connolly's assertion that 'not all of Irish culture arranges itself neatly under the heading "Irish"', it becomes clear that often writers such as these, whose childhood, influences, and sometimes even writing careers were squarely located in Ireland, tend to be ignored by scholars of Irish writing, and assimilated in studies of an English movement in letters. In relation to the material I focus on here, the effect of this is to deny a tradition of feminist writing which interrogates gender and sexualities, and exclude it from considerations of Irish literary history.

The New Woman project of the 1890s concentrated on 'difference', whether that of class, gender, or ethnic background. The interrogation of sexuality was a major project shared by the 'New Women' and the Aesthetes at the *fin de siècle*, but disrupting the heterosocial economy both by addressing women's rights, women's sexual expression, and the public discussion of syphilis were singular to the New Woman mission. I would like to begin by briefly situating the work of Sarah Grand in a matrix of social and cultural sites of contestation, and examining the impact made by her radical fiction at the end of the nineteenth century.

Grand was a key feminist activist in the 1880s and 1890s. Both in her writing and her life, she created a feminist figure who exploited the fissures between women's potential and the roles foisted upon them in a patriarchal society. Her narrative deployment of her childhood in Ireland, particularly in *The Beth Book* (1897), unsettles dominant cultural and ideological readings of both 'women' and 'Ireland'.[4] Throughout her work, Grand uses settings both in Ireland and England to reveal her protagonists' contradictory position in the colonial system. Born in the 1850s, Grand was familiar with Irish customs and traditional Irish narratives by virtue of her childhood spent in the west of Ireland where her nurses were all local women. Angela Bourke discusses the methods employed by Irish storytellers of the nineteenth century, whom she describes as 'the artists and intellectuals of a tradition that was not amenable to the rules of the logical and literate nineteenth and twentieth centuries'. She writes: 'They used vivid imagery and repetition to make facts, techniques and ideas memorable ... Their stories often hinge on what has come to be known as "lateral thinking", the solving of problems by indirect, or apparently illogical means.'[5] The use of similar lateral approaches to social problems by writers such as Grand, posing a direct challenge to the late nineteenth-century hegemony, could be said to have come from their engagement with dominant discourses from the position of cultural outsiders who grew up in the 'colonies'. Similar traits can be found in the work of Olive Schreiner, who was South African.

4 Sarah Grand, *The beth book* (1897 repr. Bristol, 1994). 5 Angela Bourke, *The burning of Bridget Cleary: a true story* (London, 1999), p. 60.

To exemplify this contention, I focus here on a reading of Grand's work based specifically on extracts from *The Heavenly Twins* (1893).[6] This was possibly Grand's best-known novel, a best-seller when it was published and one of the key texts in the advancement of the New Woman project to a mass audience.[7] I begin by revisiting some of the earlier episodes in *The Heavenly Twins* in order to provide a background to Grand's later use of the figure of the 'boy'. The central characters in this novel, the eponymous 'heavenly twins', Angelica and Diavolo Hamilton-Wells, are early examples of Grand's 'New Woman' and 'New Man', which she later developed in novels such as *Adnam's Orchard* (1912). Having introduced her interrogation of gender socialisation early in the novel, I then move on to examine a later extract, 'The Tenor and the Boy' from Book IV of *The Heavenly Twins*. This section marks a departure from the overall scheme of the text, leaving aside the social issues, which are Grand's stock-in-trade, or perhaps tackling them in a subtler way.[8] This section of the novel is the only point in Grand's work where her writing moves towards the contemporary Decadent movement.

The device of opposite-sex twins in *The Heavenly Twins* not only gave Grand the means to access a wider reading public (who read and further publicized the novel because of the humour value of the twins' antics, which soon became common currency in the 1890s, as is clear in reviews of the novel by contemporary critics such as Clementina Black) but also gave her the opportunity to compare the gender stereotyping of a boy and a girl who have shared the exact same gene pool and environment. Introducing the twins to the novel as babies enables Grand to foreground their social conditioning from the start. One of the first of the many pranks for which the novel became well-known in late Victorian society is the twins' gender-swap at a neighbour's wedding. Dressed as bridesmaid and page for the wedding, they switch clothes and hide the deed under large wraps in the carriage. Only when they enter the church, as a voice exclaims: 'What a sweet little boy, with his lovely dark curls!' does their mother, recognising the description of her dark-haired daughter, realize what her little darlings have been up to:

> There was nothing to be done then however; so Angelica obtained the coveted pleasure of acting as page to Evadne, and Diavolo escaped the trouble of having to hold up her train, and managed besides to have some fun with a small but amorous boy who … knowing nothing of the fraud which had been perpetrated, insisted on kissing the fair Diavolo, to that young gentleman's lasting delight.[9]

---

6 Sarah Grand, *The heavenly twins* (1892), (Ann Arbor, 1992).   7 The impact of the novel on the reading public, and as an influence upon other women writers of the period is legendary. To cite just one example, shortly after the publication of *The heavenly twins*, Edith Somerville noted in her diary: 'All here reading Heavenly Twins – much controversy' (*sic*). Gifford Lewis, *Somerville and Ross: the world of the Irish R.M.* (London, 1987), p. 6.   8 This section may have originally been written as a stand-alone piece, and Heinemann published it later as *The tenor and the boy* (1899).   9 Grand, *The heavenly twins*, p. 61.

The most obvious result of such a scene is humour, however, its attendant subversive potential is clear. Grand gives the lines: 'It is unnatural! It will bring bad luck' to the bride's mother, which serves to underline this potential. In fact, the assumption that their gendered games are harmless is one of the most subversive moments in this novel. Her successful introduction of 'gender trouble' in this way depends on late nineteenth-century ideology relating to childhood, which presumed young children to be without gender, and sexless. Using children to unsettle the gender and sexual stereotypes of her day is disruptive, all the more so given that other late nineteenth-century constructions of childhood tended to use prepubescent children as a way to escape the volatile world of adult roles and sexuality. In his survey of *fin de siècle* culture, Dijkstra discusses this, pointing out the investment in the cult of the child at this time:

> To escape the frighteningly physical, and emotional demands grown women tended to place on them, many men who had expected to find in the women of their own age group the same meek, nunlike qualities they had seen in their fathers' wives, began to yearn for the purity of the child they could not find in women.[10]

Many of Grand's readers clearly did not go beyond a reading of the children as a diversion to the darker aspects of the novel. However, located in the context of her indictment of the double standard and social roles in period, it becomes clear that she has deployed the twins to unsettle a patriarchal order which prescribes gendered roles and separate spheres.

This is further emphasized in passages relating to the twins' education: 'Mr Hamilton-Wells had old-fashioned ideas about the superior education of boys, and consequently, when the children had outgrown their nursery governess, he decided that Angelica should have another, more advanced; and had at the same time engaged a tutor for Diavolo.'[11] In the novel, Angelica is constructed as the brighter child who displays a genuine interest in academic learning, in comparison to Diavolo. Again, as with the wedding escapade, the twins conspire against their father, exaggerating their behaviour in order to plague their respective teachers – Angelica's brilliance destroys the governess' nerve and Diavolo appears to be an utter imbecile in front of his tutor. Keeping up this strategy for several days, the twins then once again swap places, Angelica stating categorically to Diavolo's tutor: 'Diavolo and I find that we were mixed somehow wrong, and I got his mind and he got mine … It's like this you see. I can't learn from a lady, and he can't learn from a man … You don't understand about twins I expect … the fact of the matter is that *I* am Diavolo and *he* is me'.[12] Like feminists of the period who struggled to gain access to education on an equal footing with their male peers, Angelica explains her predicament in terms of the

10 Bram Dijkstra, *Idols of perversity: fantasies of feminine evil in* fin de siècle *culture* (Oxford, 1986), p. 185. 11 Grand, *The heavenly twins*, p. 123. 12 Ibid., p. 124.

knowledge being withheld from her on the basis of her sex: 'it is beastly unfair
... to put me off with a squeaking governess and long division, when I ought to
be doing mathematics and Latin and Greek ... Men are always jeering at women
in books for not being able to reason, and I'm going to learn, if there's any help
in mathematics.'[13] Mr Hamilton-Wells capitulates and the children are subsequently educated together.

Having enjoyed gender equality within her own family as a child, Angelica
is well placed to disrupt patriarchal mores as an adult. However, in adolescence,
she begins to realize that her place in the Victorian social world will be carefully
policed and circumscribed. Angelica never quite recovers this prelapsarian existence following the death of her friend and neighbour, Edith Beale, at whose
wedding the twins had perpetuated their first gender disruption. Edith dies of
syphilis having given birth to a syphilitic child, and dies raging against her family,
her husband, and the social system which kills her, and will ultimately kill her
child. Grand's depiction of Edith's deathbed scene is a feminist call-to-arms,
rejecting the passive self-sacrifice of other heroines of melodrama. Armed with
the knowledge of the double standard from which her peers were protected, and
its terrible consequences, Angelica begins to understand what it is to be an adult
woman. In flight from the possibility of a fate such as Edith's, she meets Mr
Kilroy, an old family friend twenty years her senior, and proposes to him thus:
'Marry me, *and let me do as I like*' (sic).[14] Begun in this way, the relationship
between Kilroy and Angelica is chiefly one of friendship, and Grand conveniently
side-steps sexual desire as a component of adult relationships. Reference to sexual
desire in the novel using terms such as 'animalism', and the 'coarser pleasures',
links it with the feminist ideologies of the day, echoed in the suffragist catch-
cry: 'votes for women, chastity for men'. Dowling notes the New Woman's 'fierce
insistence on a renovation of the sexual relationship [which] becomes, in this
context, the very epitome of the *fin de siècle* desire to live beyond culture'.[15]

In Book IV, Grand opens the section named 'The Tenor and the Boy' with
Angelica's growing sense of isolation as a result of the distance between herself and the other people in her life. Her alienation is partly a result of her lack
of ease with her social role as an adult woman. Throughout much of this
period, activities such as taking a stroll in the city could not be undertaken by
a 'respectable' woman on her own. For a woman to be seen wandering the
streets was an indication of sexual availability, as Virginia Woolf commented
in *The Pargiters*: 'To be seen alone in Piccadilly was equivalent to walking up
Abercorn Terrace in a dressing gown carrying a sponge'.[16] Rejecting the
straight-jacket of feminine respectability, Angelica begins to roam about the
town by night. In order to gain free passage at such late hours, she cross-dresses
as a boy. Thus, Angelica transgresses gender and sexual boundaries, entering

13 Ibid., p. 125. 14 Ibid., p. 321. 15 Linda Dowling, 'The decadent and the new woman in the 1890s',
Nineteenth Century 33 (1979), 434–53, see 439. 16 Virginia Woolf, *The Pargiters*, Mitchell A. Leaska
(ed.) (London, 1978), p. 37.

spaces denied to her as an adult woman, just as she had done as a child in
appearing before her brother's tutor.

While out one evening wearing a boy's suit and a short wig over her dark
plaits, Angelica meets a newcomer to the town in the market square, with whom
she begins a relationship. Again, reflecting back to earlier passages in *The
Heavenly Twins*, Angelica once again adopts the role of her twin when in company with her new friend, who is a tenor in the local cathedral. By day, constructing herself in her feminine role as Mrs Kilroy, she goes regularly to the
cathedral to hear the Tenor sing.[17] The situation is compounded by the Tenor's
courtly love for this distant lady, which he shares 'man to man' with the 'the Boy'
during their evening meetings. Eventually of course the Tenor discovers the
truth about his Boy, during an accident while boating on the river, and, in saving
the Boy's life, he catches pneumonia and dies shortly afterwards.

My view on this episode is that Grand shows a definite awareness of the
effect of using cross-dressing and that she was absolutely in control of its effect,
which is to challenge the binary of sex and gender.[18] She made use of female
transvestism again in *The Beth Book*, which shows a persistent interest in this
subject in her work. Homing in on the area of dress, she details the exact method
Angelica uses in her gender-swap, from sending off measurements to a tailor[19]
to the way she hides her hands in order to distract attention from their diminu-
tive size. With statements such as: 'isn't it surprising the difference dress makes?
I should hardly have thought it possible to convert a substantial young woman
into such a slender, delicate-looking boy as I make. But it just shows you how
important dress is'.[20] Considering what she terms the 'resistance to the female-
to-male transsexual', Marjorie Garber suggests that this results from: 'a sneak-
ing feeling that it should not be so easy to 'construct' a man – which is to say, a
male body'.[21] Radclyffe Hall was famous for her transvestism,[22] and Vita
Sackville-West's 'Julian' walked openly about Mayfair with her female lover.[23]
Grand is clearly aware of this wider context, as she makes mention of George
Sand and James Barry during this section.[24] This sumptuary confusion broaches
a practice considered to be an outrage by many at the *fin de siècle*, fulfilling all
of the dire warnings against Rational Dress Movement made by *Punch*. As

17 The parallels with *Twelfth night* are clear here, and with later New Woman work by Lady Florence
Dixie and Katherine Cecil Thurston. 18 By contrast, in other aspects of her work the intended
effect is not always clear, particularly in relation to the question of imperialism as is obvious from
her second novel, *The Beth Book*. 19 This episode gives us a fascinating insight into male dress
during the period, down to the wearing of an 'ulster', or heavy overcoat, by men of the day. 20
Grand, *The heavenly twins*, p. 452. For further discussion of sumptuary laws in Britain see Anne
McClintock, *Imperial leather: race, gender and sexuality in the colonial contest* (London, 1995), p. 174.
21 Marjorie Garber, *Vested interests: cross-dressing and cultural anxiety* (London, 1992), p. 102. 22 See
Sally Cline, *Radclyffe hall: a woman called John* (London, 1997) 22. 23 See Nigel Nicholson, *Portrait
of a marriage* (London, 1973) 112. 24 For further discussion of this issue, see Wheelwright. Grand
was probably familiar with Ellen Clayton's treatment of the subject, which was used as an argument
in favour of suffrage: 'Female warriors', *Memorials of female valour and heroism from the mythological
ages to the present era*, i (London, 1895), p. 3.

Angelica protests: 'You cannot bear to see me decently dressed as a boy, but you would think nothing of it if you saw me half undressed for a ball, as I often am; yet, if the one can be done with a modest mind, and you must know that it can, so can the other, I suppose'.[25] Angelica wholeheartedly commits herself to a masculine role, and in fact Grand suggests that she is more at home in her body as a boy than as an adult woman. Simply examining the ways in which the narrative shows she could relax when in male attire, and the enjoyment she gets from physical activity in the outdoor world (e.g. occupations such as rowing which would otherwise have been closed to her) provides evidence of this.

Intensifying the debate about gender roles, Grand juxtaposes the Tenor's *desire* for Angelica, with his *attachment* to the Boy. The comparison in his affections between his lady and the Boy are rendered in terms of: 'the continual recurrence to his mind of some one or other of the Boy's observations … his thoughts being pretty equally divided between him and the lady whose brilliant glance had had such a magical effect on him the first time he encountered it'.[26] Reverting to a trope used effectively in the early sections of the novel, when Grand paralleled the education and expectations of Angelica and Diavolo, here it is Angelica and her other self, the Boy, who are contrasted. The Tenor anticipates a public career for his Boy, but his aspirations for the lady are merely that she will become his wife: 'He saw in the girl an ideal, and had found soul enough in the laughter-loving Boy to make him eager to befriend him'.[27] The hollowness of this ideal echoes throughout their later debate, when Angelica taxes him with the observation that: 'There is no room to move on a pedestal.'[28] She goes on to rail: 'You go and fall in love with a girl you have never spoken to in your life, you endow her gratuitously with all the virtues you admire without asking if she cares to possess them; and when you find she is not the peerless perfection you require her to be, you blame her!'[29]

Despite the fact that this representation of female transvestism enables Grand to transgress sexual boundaries in her fiction, the implications of this for this feminist reader are not always without their difficulties. Angelica claims that 'mentally and morally' she had crossed the gender divide, and this *apparent* gender identity of the Boy is where the problems begin: 'I was a genuine boy. I moved like a boy, I felt like a boy; I was my own brother in very truth. Mentally and morally I was exactly what you thought me, and there was little fear of your finding me out'.[30] In order to legitimate her claim to masculinity, Angelica takes on male privilege, and sheds her investment in feminism. The chief example of this comes when the Tenor and the Boy discuss relationships, and the Boy lauds: 'the calm, human fellowship, the brotherly love undisturbed by a single violent emotion, which is the perfection of social intercourse for me. I say the scene is hallowed, and I'll have no sex in my paradise.'[31] The (internalized) misogyny inherent in this statement is not diminished by the reader's knowledge of the 'true'

25 Grand, *The heavenly twins*, p. 454. 26 Ibid., p. 380. 27 Ibid., p. 385. 28 Ibid., p. 458. 29 Ibid., p. 459. 30 Ibid., p. 456. 31 Ibid., p. 423.

gender identity of the speaker. Dijkstra discusses the discomfort of nineteenth-century male intellectuals when faced with the reality of women's physical bodies and sexual desires, which they could not reconcile with their ideal of the perfect, asexual woman.[32] The assumptions underlying this reaction can also be perceived in the Boy's description of 'the calm, human fellowship', read as masculine, which could be disrupted by 'violent emotion', the domain of the feminine.

The critic Goodman makes the point that, in such a society, a woman's 'coming of age' depends upon her willingness to behave more like a child than heretofore, unlike her male counterparts. Discussing the male-female double *bildungsroman*, she writes that the female protagonist: 'is ontologically or radically alienated by gender-role norms from the very outset. Thus, although the authors attempt to accommodate their heroes' development to the general pattern of the genre, the disjunctions ... inevitably make of the woman's initiation less a self-determined progression toward maturity than a regression from full participation in adult life'.[33] This point is underscored by Angelica's assertion above: her maturity is that of a boy, her role can never be one of a fully-grown adult, no matter what her guise. As I have demonstrated, at puberty Angelica was forced to surrender her claim to a world where she was her brother's equal. She uses cross-dressing as a tool to facilitate her own unique way of trying to regain this prelapsarian experience. That in taking on this new role, she relinquishes any affinity to other women, or to her female self, is hardly surprising given her circumstances.

In the novel as a whole, as Angelica moves away from the period of being the Boy, the incidences of doubling in the text are not left behind. Having lived as a man, she understands all the more fully the restrictive effects of Victorian patriarchal ideology on women's lives and ambitions. Grand's later sketch of *Angelica* as the *angel* in the house, isolated, with no occupation, and only her servants for company is poignant.[34] Seeing and not-seeing herself in the portrait of herself hanging in her parents' home, and most obviously, in a mirror (a trope which is repeated), Angelica appears to be unable to reconcile the various aspects of her life, her 'feminine' and 'masculine' characteristics, in one whole and satisfied woman.

We could also consider the representation of Angelica and her disguise as an example of doubling, common to much nineteenth-century literature. Poovey discusses the doubling of characters in the period as:

> One of the distinguishing features of novels written by nineteenth-century women ... [giving novelists] an opportunity not only to dramatize the negative counterparts of the heroine's perfect qualities but also to play at different roles, to explore, often through the characters of servants or lower-class women, direct actions forbidden to the more proper lady.[35]

32 Dijkstra, *Idols of perversity*, pp 202–3. 33 Charlotte Goodman, 'The lost brother, the twin: male novelists and the male-female bildungsroman', *Novel* 17 (1983), 28–43, see 29. 34 See Grand, *The heavenly twins*, pp 494–5. 35 Mary Poovey, *The proper lady and the woman writer* (Chicago, 1984),

Grand takes on this doubling of characters in earlier novels in a more literal and dramatic way, as she doubles Angelica's 'feminine' identity with another, more vibrant and sensuous self in the character of the Boy. *Fin de siècle* 'doubling' tended to take on more diabolical features than that of the early century. There is a hint at this diabolical 'other' which Angelica has summoned up, in the feverish imaginings of the Tenor during his last illness: 'He had been enchanted, like Reymond of Lusignan in olden times, by a creature that was half a monster' (*sic*).[36] Her monstrous act – the assuming of a male guise – illustrates the extent to which selfhood is a role, not only for women, but also for men, given that the 'true' identity of the Tenor is not at all clear in the novel either. As Kucich points out, this episode involves 'two disguised and self-inventing characters (and) revolves around the malleability of sexual differences and sexual relationship'.[37] Well-known examples of *fin de siècle* uses of doubling such as *The Interesting Case of Dr Jekyll and Mr Hyde*, and *The Picture of Dorian Gray*, spring immediately to mind, although there are countless other incidences less well-known than these in minor literature of the day. Cross-dressing and disguise is used in a similar way in other New Woman novels, such as Lady Florence Dixie's *Gloriana; or the Revolution of 1900* (1890), and Katherine Cecil Thurston's *Max* (1910). In Olive Schreiner's *The Story of an African Farm* (1883), perhaps more unusually, it is a man who cross-dresses in order to claim female privilege.[38] Here, Gregory Rose takes on the role of a nurse in order to be at the heroine Lyndall's deathbed. Assuming female clothing confers a certain dignity on this rather pathetic character who certainly lacked such dignity as a man. As a woman, he takes on not only a new role, but also new characteristics, in much the same way as Angelica in the above passage. It seems as if, in an ideal world, these authors say, Angelica would make a much more able man and Gregory Rose a better woman.

The work of the New Woman project has been almost completely obscured by the writing of Irish literary history in the intervening century, but the contribution made by New Woman fiction to a feminist history of ideas, and to Irish literature should not be underestimated. Writers such as Sarah Grand created the intellectual and aesthetic space for early feminists to explore new ideological and theoretical perspectives, and to invest in themselves. As well as writing best-selling fiction, the work of these feminist writers was critically acclaimed at the end of the nineteenth century. The experimental projects carried out by New Woman writers influenced the work of many of their peers, and changed the face of writing in the pre-modernist period. Readdressing the work of the New Woman project from an Irish perspective enables us to construct new readings of this feminist fiction. More importantly, relocating this feminist fiction in an Irish context illuminates new paths for scholarship and understanding of late nineteenth-century writing in and about Ireland.

p. 43. 36 Grand, *The heavenly twins*, p. 504. 37 John Kucich, 'Curious Dualities: *The heavenly twins* (1893) and Sarah Grand's Belated Modernist Aesthetics' in Harman and Meyer (eds), *The new nineteenth century*, pp 195–204, see 198. 38 Olive Schreiner, *The story of an African farm* (London, 1883).

Imaginary characters: writing, talk and truth in Maria Edgeworth's Castle Rackrent[1]

CIARA HOGAN, UNIVERSITY COLLEGE, DUBLIN

Many of the interpretative problems that surround the writing and reception of Edgeworth's *Castle Rackrent* (1800) derive from an over-emphasis on the empirical reality behind the tale's study of the Irish manner of living and the Irish manner of speaking.[2] In the year of its publication, Richard Lovell Edgeworth records in correspondence the early response of King George III: 'he rubbed his hands & said what – I know something now of my Irish subjects'.[3] The context implies that what he saw was something of the Irish colonial stereotype, profligate after the usual manner and inimical to telling the plain truth. This is a stereotype that has resolved itself theoretically in the twentieth century in studies of the novel's style, as the vaunted social and psychological fecklessness of the Irish is said to be realized in an idiom that embodies 'amorality' and intellectual 'indiscipline'.[4] And yet, returning to source, the bemused tone of the author's father is proof that the relationship between idiom and morality, as between intellectual and cultural discipline, is not as transparent as the stereotype allows. Neither is the relationship between the text and 'truth' in *Rackrent*, as transparent as it seems.

This is largely due to *Rackrent*'s text's form and style. A dramatic text, it purports to record an oral narrative of the Rackrent clan as told by a steward on the family estate. Even taking this fictional framing narrative at face value, what we are faced with in *Rackrent* is a representation of a representation, a written record of an oral narrative. As such it is at least two narrative removes from the characters whose lives it claims to record. 'Truth' has been passed through two filters: first that of the narrator, Thady M'Quirk, then that of the anonymous amanuensis/editor, with all of the necessary epistemological instability that implies.

Of course *Rackrent* is not fact, but fiction – 'the characters all imaginary' as Edgeworth herself had it, though she admits that the tale's idiolect was inspired by the 'character' and 'dialect' of an old Edgeworthstown land steward, John Langan.[5] The fact that Langan has been identified as the source of the text suggests that he is also its prime referent, an Irish subject behind the representa-

1 I would like to acknowledge the IRHSS, whose Government of Ireland Research Scholarship in the Humanities and Social Sciences has facilitated my research. 2 Maria Edgeworth, Castle Rackrent: *an Hibernian tale taken from the facts and from the manners of the Irish squires before the year 1782*, in Marilyn Butler (ed.), Castle Rackrent *and* Ennui (1800, 1809) (London & New York, 1992). 3 Richard Lovell Edgeworth to Daniel Augustus Beaufort, 26 Apr. 1800. Cited in Marilyn Butler, *Maria Edgeworth: a literary biography* (Oxford, 1972), p. 359. 4 Joanne Altieri, 'Style and purpose in Maria Edgeworth's fiction', *Nineteenth Century Fiction* 23:3 (1968), 265–78. See 273; Brian Hollingworth, *Maria Edgeworth's Irish writing* (Houndsmills, England, and New York, 1997), p. 121. 5 Maria Edgeworth to Mrs Stark, 6 September 1834, cited in Butler, *Biography*, pp 240–1.

tion who is there to be known. In fact, this reading only holds good for the short opening section of the *Rackrent* memoir, and then only problematically. The problem reveals itself in the time lapse that occurred between the writing of this opening section and the 'Continuation', the narrative of Sir Condy, which was written some two years later. Of the former, completed sometime around 1794–5, Edgeworth could affirm 'the only character drawn from the life … is Thady himself, the teller of the story'. Yet by 1797, referring to the 'Continuation', she explicitly states that her material was 'not drawn from the life'.[6] Langan/Thady has transmuted into a structuring principle in Edgeworth's imagination, where he is used to guarantee aesthetic unity as the tale accumulates incident and progresses to a publishable length. The Irish subject has turned into an Irish style.

Readers are by now aware of the way *Rackrent* writes historical events in the Edgeworth family history into its fictional frame. In the main Edgeworth draws these from *The Black Book of Edgeworthstown*, a family memoir covering the period from the late sixteenth to the early nineteenth century.[7] But her own subjective and imaginative part in that history also features, including the historical moment that the aspirational writing style realized in *Rackrent* was engendered. The year 1782, encoded in the full title of published text, was the year Edgeworth returned from England to settle permanently on the Longford estate. We learn from a family *Memoir* of the author how deeply she was impressed by her 'new and extraordinary' environment, and how that first impression had a permanent effect on her literary imagination. It notes 'the delineations she long afterwards made of Irish character probably owe their life and truth to the impression made on her arrival at this time as a stranger'.[8] The phraseology is interesting, for the *Memoir*'s subtle distinction between 'life' and the 'truth' as they inform Edgeworth's fiction tallies with the author's own account of how inspiration and authenticity, imagination and empirical observation join together to form the style of the fictional memoir of the Rackrent family.

The same *Memoir* reprints Edgeworth's late account of how she met 'Thady himself, the teller of the tale' in that year. Again, the phraseology is telling:

> I heard him when first I came to Ireland, and his dialect struck me … and I became so acquainted with it that I could speak it without effort: so that when … I began to write a family history as Thady would tell it, he seemed to stand beside me and dictate and I wrote as fast as my pen could go.[9]

The emphasis here on ear, idiom, voice, and writing suggests that whatever factual significance Langan had was, from the beginning, excitedly sequestered to serve her future dramatic fiction. Indeed, even in this private letter, written after

6 Ibid., p. 241. 7 H.E. & H. J. Butler (eds), *The black book of Edgeworthstown and other Edgeworth memories, 1585–1817* (London, 1927). 8 Mrs Francis Edgeworth (ed.), *Memoir of Maria Edgeworth with a selection from her letters*, 3 vols (privately printed, 1867) i, p. 13. 9 Ibid., iii. p. 152, emphasis added.

an interval of thirty years, it is Thady, not Langan, that her mind remembers meeting. The 'life' her text drew from Langan, then, was its lively literary manner. She even names her narrator for this manner, giving him the surname M'Quirk – my quirk – a name which signifies individuality of manner, peculiarity of character, and, importantly, a signature writing style. For, as her sixteenth-century forebears in the *Black Book* would have understood it, the term 'quirk' signified a stylish flourish, just as one develops in one's handwriting.[10]

To allow for Edgeworth's artistic investment in the tale's idiolect is essential. For it puts us in a position to reconfigure the relationship between the dynamic textual energy of *Rackrent* and the documentary facts of the Irish scene to which it is said to refer. Doubtless those plot elements that chart the 'lives' of the Rackrent family are of historical and cultural interest. This much, we might say, is transparent, insofar as their history is the text's subject. But it is not the text's primary subject, which has the greatest claim to the reader's interest. This, as the Preface makes plain, is the character of the old land steward, Thady M'Quirk. And yet, as we have seen, the notion of Thady as a coherent Irish subject behind the text is highly unstable. And it is precisely this instability that reveals the genuine textual sophistication of Edgeworth's tale, for it foregrounds the language ascribed to him and so doing lays the text's system of representation open to analysis. For not only is *Rackrent* writing masquerading as speech, but 'Thady' is a writing style masquerading as a human subject. He is the vehicle for a peculiarly lively literary language, whose prime source of reference is itself.

To allow the text's intense self-referentiality is not to sever the text from the context and culture that inspired it. On the contrary, language and literature are a product of culture, and produce it in their turn. Hence, to subject the style to analysis is necessarily to analyse the culture that informs it. If *Rackrent* cannot be said to be documentary realism, it is a real cultural document nonetheless, and one published at a radical juncture in the history of the country in which it was written. 1800 was the eve of Ireland's political Union with Britain, a time when the country's national identity itself was subject to redefinition, by virtue of its relocation within the broader frame of the British Empire. Among the things Edgeworth, and consequently *Rackrent*, is conscious of is the scrutiny of a British audience. This scrutiny is all the more charged when we remember that we are dealing with Anglo-Irish relations in a post-revolutionary moment. *Rackrent* was published a mere two years after the peasant uprising of 1798, a time when prejudice against the native Catholic population ran high. And if Edgeworth's text is informed by this political climate, it is also informed by her private reflections on the causes and consequences of 1798, and the lessons the Union audience should learn from them.

The fact that the author's father had spoken out against the social and religious victimization of this group throughout the decade in which the novel was

10 Refer to the *Oxford English Dictionary*

written means any reading of the native voice in *Rackrent* must be informed by the Edgeworth family's sympathetic understanding of the social abuses against which the peasants reacted: the Rackrents' exaggerated abuse of drink, litigation, and the responsibilities of land management number among these. Unlike a novel such as Griffith's *Collegians* (1829), *Rackrent* does not plot the effect of corrupt landlordism on the tenantry, but it does dramatize its effect on their style of speaking. So doing, it engages directly, and before a Union audience, with the stereotyped gap between talk and truth in an Irish context. If the text is self-conscious about what can be said and how, it is because the Catholic masses are self-conscious about how speech and action are prejudiced by the power relations that inform any narrative and historical act. Edgeworth sympathy with the idiom is in part the sympathy of an ascendancy author impressed by the narrative power of a beleaguered native population. The Union audience reads a tale of power and repression that cuts deep into the question of how truth, subjectivity and national identity can be constructed in language.

The Preface to *Rackrent* makes clear, in fact, that when dealing with Thady's narrative we are dealing with a peculiar type of language, one that is different from the 'measured prose' of literary histories in the manner that it is invited to be read. Foremost is the notion that the narrative is 'incapable of translation', 'in plain English' not amenable to paraphrase, but rather a cognitive object in its own right. It is, moreover, like the world in which Thady moves, self-referential and self-contained. Thady's story of the Rackrent clan is composed 'in the full confidence that ... [their] affairs will be as interesting to all the world as they were to himself' and 'scarcely intelligible, or ... perfectly incredible' to those not of his world. Credibility is a function of context just as it is a function of style.[11] In fact, it is Thady's 'characteristic idiom' that guarantees 'the authenticity of his story'. The truth in *Rackrent*, therefore, is in the telling; the tale embodies truth, dramatically and idiomatically. As for intelligibility, this can only come from familiarity, a model of which is found in the formal fellowship of the narrator and editor in committing the tale to the page, a relationship which is itself a model of the sympathetic fellowship of the ascendancy author with the Hiberno-English medium, or perhaps the sympathy of an enlightened landowner with a beleaguered Catholic underclass.[12]

The best way to judge this sympathy in action is to examine how the editorial apparatus, typically associated with standard English, interacts with,

11 *Castle Rackrent*, pp 62–3. 12 For studies that work against old shibboleths of Edgeworth's ascendancy isolation to bring out her sympathy with the context and culture she shares with the native Irish population, see Marilyn Butler, 'Edgeworth's Ireland: history, popular culture, and secret codes', in *Novel: A Forum on Fiction* 34:2 (2001), 267–291; Declan Kiberd, *Native informants: Maria Edgeworth and* Castle Rackrent (Irish Classics London, 2000), pp 243–64; Mitzi Myers, 'Goring John Bull: Maria Edgeworth's Hibernian high jinks versus the imperialist imaginary', in James E. Gill (ed.), *Cutting edges: postmodern critical essays on eighteenth-century satire* (Knoxville, 1995), pp 267–94. Butler, Kiberd and Myers variously develop Edgeworth's sympathetic 'cross-dressing' and 'cross-writing' across the once fixed borders of gender, class, nationality and genre in her Irish writing. My reading of her sympathy with the Hiberno-English style is informed by the theoretical clearances of all three.

echoes and supports Thady, or Edgeworth's Hiberno-English style in action.[13]
The Glossary that accompanies Thady's narrative heightens the autonomy of
the idiomatic tale, assents to its organization and grammar, and confirms
Hiberno-English as the medium that best comprehends the power relations
that inform communication and interpretation in the Irish context. In the first
printing of *Rackrent*, this Glossary appeared at the front of the book, where it
anticipated and diffused any interpretative problems in the narrative that followed. Although shifted to the back of the book in subsequent printings, it is
significant Edgeworth's initial instinct was to preserve the linguistic integrity
of Thady's text, allowing it to proceed in its own manner and according to its
own internal logic.

Generally speaking, Glossary notes can be divided into two groups according to their length and purpose. Shorter notes 'translate' idiomatic phrases to
make them intelligible for English audiences. Thus 'kilt' is defined as 'not killed,
but much hurt'; 'Canting – … not … talking or writing hypocritical nonsense,
but selling substantially by auction'.[14] This tendency to explicitly define them
against standard usage in an English context is useful, but weak in comparison
to the effect achieved by reading them in the altogether more impressive context of Thady's narrative. Indeed, it is arguable that a literal definition is useful
only to demonstrate the intelligent and energetic movement of Thady's language itself. Take the term canting as it appears in the body text. In practice, it
is just one term in a phrase that depends for its force on the rhythmic accumulation of abuses the landlord exerts on his wretched tenants:

> … for let alone making English tenants of them, every soul, he [Sir Murtagh]
> was always driving and driving, and pounding and pounding, and canting
> and canting, and replevying and replevying, and he made a good living of
> trespassing cattle; there was always some tenant's pig, or horse, or cow, or
> calf, or goose, trespassing, which was so great a gain to Sir Murtagh, that he
> did not like to hear me talk of repairing fences.[15]

Here the meaning of Thady's words, in the fullest sense, is beyond the remit of
a mere definition. To grasp Thady's point one must attune the ear to the inexorable repetition and multiplication of terms that mimetically enact Sir
Murtagh's inexorable abuse of the landlord/tenant relationship. Such meaning
can only emerge if the text is realized without interruption.

It is here that the poetics of the idiomatic text open out onto the cultural
context that informs it. Thady's rhythmic speech dramatically affects a critique
of Sir Murtagh that he is reticent to voice too literally – a reticence figured in
miniature where his fear of Sir Murtagh prevents talk of repairing fences on the
estate. This wise reticence to speak out openly against the abuse of power is

---

13 I use 'Thady' throughout the following discussion as shorthand for this style of narration. 14
Edgeworth, *Castle Rackrent*, p. 138, p. 128. 15 Ibid., pp 69–70.

caught in what can best be described as the text's characteristic refrain, the 'I said nothing' that Thady substitutes for explicit critique.[16] Substitution, evasion, mystification and the deliberate confusion of grammatical subject are commonplaces in the text, and evidence of Edgeworth's sympathy with the Irish colonial subject's problematical access to narratable truths. That is to say, she sympathizes with the necessity of using language as both armour and shield. As, for instance, in the lines preceding those quoted above, where Thady's deliberately vague paratactical construction makes it possible to say that it is impossible to say whether the 'the poor wretches, … always breaking and running away' from Sir Murtagh are, in fact, chickens or tenants.[17]

If Thady shields himself with vagaries, he makes his point figuratively: the tenants are pounded and driven like beasts, and the beasts metonymically represent the extent and number of the tenants so pounded. Pig, horse, cow, calf, or goose: for Thady the devil is, of necessity, in the detail and minor gripes must suffice to illuminate the extent of the colonial problem. So much energetic evasion going on in the vicinity of the term canting, returns us to the complexity of the relationship between language and truth on this Irish estate. And this in turn returns us to the Glossary, which now comes to read as a sombre but supportive pun both on the social context and on the signifying practices of the body text. For the editor the devil is in the idiom, and the idiomatic use of the term canting brings hypocritical talk into radical juxtaposition with real socio-economic victimization. The juxtaposition suggests to the imagination what it denies in fact. As such, it offers a terse model of how speech acts in certain Irish contexts must seek to repress meaning and express meaning at one and the same time. In this way we can account for the dynamism and duplicity of Thady's narrative. Thady's whitewashing of the Rackrents' behaviour is determined by his economic reliance on them. And yet, the more he whitewashes, the worse their behaviour comes to appear. The partial cover-up, multiplied and extended in numerous instances across the text, converts in the act of reading, into a powerful critique, the critical imagination reactivated, and the critique intensified, with each 'I said nothing.'

The fact that the idiom embodies a truth about the Irish context that is difficult to articulate outright or otherwise is borne out by the nature of second type of editorial note found in *Rackrent*. Generally, these notes struggle to bring out the historical, cultural and sociological context from which the Hibernian tale is bred. As a consequence, the notes tend to be far longer, and again the material they struggle to encompass inspires a manner of narration that mimics Thady's own: for while they are largely intellectual in tone, they are anecdotal in manner and digressive in the extreme, one digression freely generating another within individual notes. If the authoritative editorial persona does indeed mimic Thady's narrative mode, it is to confirm that mode as the most apt means of narrating 'truth' in an Irish context. Elaborate narrative digressions are not a

16 See for example pp 68, 72, 74, 78, 115, and 121. 17 Ibid. p. 69

sign of intellectual indiscipline, but the only way the pen can go about recording the complex social and psychological structure of the Irish scene.

This fact can generate the impression that the editorial notes are supereroga-
tory. There is the sense that their Interventions could be multiplied at length,
and with it the impression that this body of notes is more tangential to the tale
then not. Indeed, notes on the 'whillaluh' or caoine, fairy mounts and Irish wakes
come at their object from such a variety of angles, sketch so many differing interpretations of their cultural uses and effects, that the 'truth' they are after seems
to blur in the telling.[18] Although these glosses ally themselves to the larger social
economy from which Thady's tale is drawn, they are, more properly, journey-
ings to and from a set of dynamic social objects they can never definitively grasp.
Ultimately, the moral and social economy of Thady's narrative remains the best
context in which to judge their functional meaning. Thus the real value of the
Glossary lies in the way it confirms this very fact.

The gloss on Thady's knowledge of legal entails, for example, extends across
four pages to take in comments on the general interest in the law visible among
the Irish peasantry, and records and analyses a typical peasant testimony in court,
to illuminate what is clear as day in the body text.[19] That this gloss concludes,
at last, with an anecdote about a justice of the peace who preferred to buy off
peasant disputants to hearing their lengthy testimonies, may seem ironic given
the useless lengths to which the editor has gone. But, such a squandering of editorial energy is justified if we notice how the note itself steadily dramatizes the
realization that the idiom is the final authoritative reference point for the social
relations the editor would describe.

For having dramatized the power of peasant disputants in action, the note
closes with a formal gesture to Hiberno-English rhetorical power. The closing
lines slide from standard editorial prose, first, into free indirect style, and, from
there, to quotation of the peasant voice:

> But he was soon cured of this method of buying off disputes, by the increas-
> ing multitude of those who, out of pure regard to his honour, came 'to get
> justice from him, because they would sooner come before him than before
> any man in all Ireland.'[20]

This resort to the peasant voice is clearly the editorial version of saying nothing and everything at one and the same time. He avoids further need to critique
this irresponsible method of social administration and its outcome by adopting
the rhetorical veil used by the Hiberno-English speakers themselves, in balance
with this justice, this truth.

Let it be clear, these peasant disputants are as artless as they are artful in
their compliance within his honour's administration of justice. As such they
offer a useful model of the relation between language and truth, text and truth,

18 Ibid., pp 124–7; 129–31; 137–8. 19 Ibid., pp 132–5; 86. 20 Ibid., p. 135, see pp 133–5.

in an Irish context. Their motivation is not impenetrable to the understanding, though it is impermeable to critique. Much the same is true of the Hiberno-English narrative that comprises *Rackrent* as a whole. For in spite of the casuistry we associate with the body text, the experiences that inform it, and the sheer rhetorical verve of the performance, puts it beyond the absolute moral judgement of the judicious reader.

Thus *Rackrent* is proof that readers must bring both sympathetic imagination and a sharp eye and ear to the stories told by the peasant populous. The cameo example of Justice of the Peace shows it is both administrative knavery and personal folly to 'rid [oneself] of the trouble of hearing their stories'.[21] The image the Preface provides of one Irishman constantly recording another Irishman constantly recounting so many stories offers a vigorous counter-example to this. Written into *Rackrent's* dramatic frame is the message that if only one had time, like Thady, to witness all of Irish history, and time, like the editor, to hear all the tales, then the truth expressed and the truth that elides expression would converge. Audiences would know something of the complex pressures operating on the Irish scene. As Thady massages the Rackrent history into a narratable form, the editor records the exercise in a manner that assents to the truth embodied in the telling. The text produced opens the way to understand how Irish subjects have been authorized by society to speak and act.

Nineteenth-century Ireland and the Orient: Tom Moore's Lalla Rookh

SHELLEY E. MEAGHER, ST HUGH'S COLLEGE, OXFORD

How did the Irish view the Orient during the Union era? One might expect the post-1800, pre-Famine Irish to draw analogies between Ireland and the Middle East and India, the East being the site of growing British imperial interest and Ireland being Britain's original colony. Debates about the ways in which nineteenth-century Ireland does or does not constitute a colony, and the pertinence to Union Ireland of postcolonial theory, play a prominent part in contemporary Irish Studies. The debate colours understandings of the nature of nineteenth-century Irishness. Literary critics, however, tend to disregard the participation in British imperialism by a large section of the Irish population. That participation does not correlate to one particular political stance toward the Union. If, as Edward Said argues, we only ever define ourselves by invoking an Other, then

21 Ibid.

in an investigation of Irish identity under the Union, it is worth exploring the extent to which the Irish shared what Said claims was then the dominant English concept of Otherness, the Orient.[1]

Thomas Moore's *Lalla Rookh, an Oriental Romance* was published in 1817, relatively soon after the Act of Union. The poem consists of four lays, knitted together through the tale of a Moghul princess, Lalla Rookh, who travels to Cashmere to marry the Prince of Bucharia.[2] During the evenings and siestas, a minstrel from Cashmere, Feramorz, entertains her by singing romances set in Persia, Syria, Egypt, Cashmere and India. Lalla Rookh falls in love with Feramorz, who, happily, turns out to be the prince in disguise.

Excepting Feramorz's third lay, critics tend to view Moore's oriental romance as exoticist escapism contrived to exploit a contemporary market. Moore indeed profited greatly from his poem's attractiveness to a readership fascinated by the Orient: his publishers regarded *Lalla Rookh* as 'the cream of copyright'.[3] Moore does not disguise his commodification of the Orient. He labels Feramorz's lays, for example, 'Stories of the East,' even though it is in Cashmere that Feramorz is famous while his stories mostly concern lands to Cashmere's west. For Moore's contemporary readers, among whom prevailed a taste for the *Arabian Nights' Entertainments* and eighteenth-century European versions of Eastern tales, the anomaly signposted an attractive product.

Lalla Rookh reflects the contemporary relationship between British imperialism, exoticism, and perceptions of wealth. By the early nineteenth century, European conceptions of the East as epitomising luxury had developed into a political desire to attain and control the East. As its repeated adaptations to opera and ballet in the nineteenth century indicate, Moore's poem evokes the Orient in terms of an exotic spectacle:

> The bazaars and baths were all covered with the richest tapestry; hundreds of gilded barges upon the Jumna floated with their banners shining in the water; while through the streets groups of beautiful children went strewing the most delicious flowers around, as in that Persian festival called the Scattering of the Roses; till every part of the city was as fragrant as if a caravan of musk from Khoten had passed through it.[4]

Such ornamental portraits as this evocation of the Moghul Empire celebrate a quintessential element of European imperialism up to 1815, the quest for Oriental luxuries and wealth. *Lalla Rookh's* opening and concluding scenes take place in or outside imperial palaces; the naming of an East India Company ship after the poem, and its extravagant production (the cast of 186 people included the future Tsar of Russia and his wife) as a German imperial court pageant in 1821, reflect that a theme of empire is central to this romance.

1 Edward Said, *Orientalism* (New York, 1978). 2 Bokhara, today a city and region in Uzbekhistan. 3 Letter to Longman, 23 Nov. 1837 in Wilfred S. Dowden (ed.), *The letters of Thomas Moore,* 2 vols (Oxford, 1964), ii, p. 821. 4 Thomas Moore, *Lalla Rookh* (London, 1817), p. 2.

Nonetheless, the reception of *Lalla Rookh* in the nineteenth century, with its attention to the poem's opulence and spectacular elements, averts attention from the text's latent, subversive polemic. Moore's relationship with British imperialism was ambivalent. At university, he was friends with Robert Emmett and wrote two inflammatory articles supporting the United Irishmen. Yet he emigrated to the imperial metropolis of London aged nineteen, in 1799, and from that time pursued a Grattan-inspired patriotism, endorsing Catholic emancipation but not Repeal. In England, the Whigs' advocacy of Catholic emancipation led him to seek their patronage. Not only did the Whigs support Moore's literary career; they provided him with openings to an imperial career. Lord Moira secured Moore a position as registrar of a naval prize court in Bermuda in 1803. Moore spent only a year away from England (and that largely in America and Canada), but he retained his Bermudan investments until 1819; their profits derived from and required ongoing regional war.[5]

Moira was on the verge of appointment as Lord Lieutenant of Ireland when the Prince of Wales attained the Regency in early 1811. Moore's contemporary letters confidently anticipate Moira will procure him a position in the Irish administration. But on attaining the Regency, George IV revoked support for Catholic emancipation and posted Moira, one of its most vocal advocates, far afield to India. Moira also owned a large collection of eighteenth and early nineteenth-century orientalist texts. The connection between Moira's orientalism and British imperialism must have been poignantly evident to Moore, who was left to bury his disappointment in extensive research for *Lalla Rookh* when Moira departed for India as governor-general in late 1811.[6]

Only in 1812 did Moore recognize that Moira would never procure him a colonial position, and that his income would have to derive from literary projects. The Lansdownes and Hollands, prominent Whigs, then became Moore's principle patrons. The Lansdownes were strongly interested in orientalism, pursuing the subject not only in their reading, but also by inviting eminent oriental enthusiasts to Lady Lansdowne's salon (the Whig alternative to the royal court). In the reactionary xenophobia prevailing in Britain towards the end of the Napoleonic Wars and immediately afterwards, many conservatives viewed the Lansdownes' cosmopolitanism as incompatible with loyalty to the English crown. The oriental interests of the Lansdowne circle, however, provided Moore with an immediate audience for his oriental romance.

The backdrop to *Lalla Rookh's* orientalism is therefore complex, reflecting on the one hand, deep opposition to Westminster, yet, on the other hand, a willingness to profit from Westminster's imperial power and wealth. Moore's satirical writings in the 1810s offer some insight into the complexities of this backdrop. Their settings parallel the substitution of the East for Ireland in his

---

5 Stephen Gwynn, *Thomas Moore* (London, 1905), p. 27. 6 For a list of the orientalist collection at Donington Park, see Thérèse Tessier, *La poésie lyrique de Thomas Moore (1779–1852)* (Paris, 1976), pp 274–6.

personal imperial ambitions. 'A Letter to the Roman Catholics of Dublin' (1810) criticizes public – above all Irish Roman Catholic – opposition to the notion of Catholic emancipation conditional on a Government power of veto on episcopal appointments. In *Twopenny Post* (1813), an epistle by a Persian visitor to London satirises British discrimination against Catholics, while a novel Moore began at the same time, set in Sunnite Baghdad, condemns political religious intolerance and persecution.7 The contents of his contemporary satirical writings, then, suggest that for Moore, the metamorphosis from Irish to Oriental settings also symbolizes the shattering of hopes for Catholic emancipation.

Lalla Rookh is linked to Moore's satires by its framing narrative, which recurrently parodies contemporary British culture, most obviously through the character of Fadladeen, the Chamberlain of the Harem and Lalla Rookh's chaperone:

> Toleration, indeed, was not among the weaknesses of Fadladeen: – he carried the same spirit into matters of poetry and of religion, and, though little versed in the beauties or sublimities of either, was a perfect master of the art of persecution in both. His zeal, too, was the same in either pursuit; whether the game before him was pagans or poetasters, – worshippers of cows, or writers of epics.8

Parallels between Moore, renowned for drawing-room performances of the *Irish Melodies* (1807–34), and Feramorz, famed for kitar-accompanied recitations of lays concerning the Lalla Rookh's cultural heritage, suggest that Feramorz's Islamic lays contain a polemic pertinent to Ireland. Feramorz remarks that the ruined tower which inspires his celebration of Persian resistance to Arab-Islamic imperialists in his third lay, 'The Fire Worshippers,' reminds him of his ancestors' persecution:

> as a native of Cashmere, of that fair and Holy Valley, which had in the same manner become the prey of strangers, and seen her ancient shrines and native princes swept away before the march of intolerant invaders, he felt a sympathy, he owned, with the sufferings of the persecuted Ghebers, which every monument like this before them but tended more powerfully to awaken.9

Moore's description of the tower as 'the ruins of a strange and awful-looking tower, which seemed old enough to have been the temple of some religion no longer known, and which spoke the voice of desolation in the midst of all that bloom and loveliness' recalls his treatment of an Irish medieval round tower as a symbol for Ireland's lost hopes of national glory in 'Let Erin Remember the Days of Old' in the *Irish Melodies*.10 The Irish towers were emblematic of Irish proto-nationalism at the time of *Lalla Rookh's* publication, as a consequence of claims by Irish antiquarians opposed to the British Establishment that the builders of

7 The Chapter of the Blanket (published posthumously in 1878). 8 Moore, *Lalla Rookh*, p. 164. 9 Ibid., p. 172. 10 Ibid.,p. 170.

the towers were Phoenician migrants from Persia.[11] Feramorz's introduction to
'The Fire-Worshippers' thus implies Moore means the tale to eulogize Irish
national independence and condemn the English, Protestant occupation:

> That venerable tower, he told them, was the remains of an ancient Fire-
> Temple, built by those Ghebers or Persians of the old religion, who, many
> hundred years since, had fled hither from their Arab conquerors, preferring
> liberty and their altars in a foreign land to the alternative of apostasy or per-
> secution in their own. It was impossible, he added, not to feel interested in
> the many glorious but unsuccessful struggles, which had been made by these
> original natives of Persia to cast off the yoke of their bigoted conquerors.[12]

Several critics remark that Feramorz's plot bears strong resemblances to the
history of Sarah Curran, daughter of a Protestant Dublin judge and lover of
Robert Emmett, executed leader of the 1803 Rising.[13] Indeed, Feramorz's lay
revizes the official histories of the failed Irish rebellions of 1798 and 1803 and
the brutal British reprisals that followed:

> Rebellion! Foul, dishonouring word,
> Whose wrongful blight so oft has stain'd
> The holiest cause that tongue or sword
> Of mortal ever lost or gain'd.[14]

The view of Daniel O'Connell, recalled in Charles Kickham's novel
Knocknagow (1879), quoting the verse above in support of Irish nationalism, prevails in criticism of 'The Fire-Worshippers.' But the first of Feramorz's tales,
'The Veiled Prophet of Khorassan', complicates O'Connell's interpretation of
Moore's poem. Also set in Persia, this lay condemns an eighth-century uprising against the imperial Islamic ruler, labelling the rebel leader, Mokanna, an
'Impostor' and depicting him as a fiend: 'well th'Impostor knew all lures and
arts,/That Lucifer e'er taught to tangle hearts'.[15] Moreover, the backbone of the
army which the tale censures, is formed by Persian Fire-Worshippers:

> none, of all who own'd the Chief's command,
> Rush'd to that battle-field with bolder hand,
> Or sterner hate than Iran's outlaw'd men,
> Her Worshippers of Fire – all panting then
> For vengeance on the' accursed Saracen.[16]

---

11 See Joep Leerssen, *Remembrance and imagination: patterns in the historical and literary representation of Ireland in the nineteenth century* (Cork, 1996), pp 109–10. 12 Moore, *Lalla Rookh*, pp 171–2.
13 Moore had already eulogized both Emmett and Curran in three of his Irish Melodies, 'Oh breath
not his name', 'When he who adores thee' and 'She is far from the land'. Indeed, at the time *Lalla
Rookh* was published, Emmett's renown as martyr to Irish freedom, and the legend of his love affair
with Curran, owed their currency and political potency to these poems. 14 Moore, *Lalla Rookh*, p.
203. 15 Ibid., p.105. 16 Ibid., p. 91.

Feramorz differentiates between the ignorance and fanaticism of those who have empowered Mokanna – 'There on that throne, to which the blind belief,/Of millions rais'd him, sat the Prophet-Chief' – and the political oppression which provokes those, like the Fire-Worshippers, who join Mokanna once his uprising begins: 'Many who felt, and more who fear'd to feel/The bloody Islamite's converting steel,/Flock'd to his banner'.[17] He condemns the former outright, describing them as 'blind,/Burning and headlong as the Samiel wind'.[18] In contrast, he elucidates the Fire-Worshippers' motive as 'Vengeance at last for their dear country spurn'd,/ Her throne usurp'd, and her bright shrines o'erturn'd'.[19] The implicit sympathy in this couplet anticipates his defence of the Fire-Worshippers in his third lay. However, in 'The Veiled Prophet' he allows those of Mokanna's forces motivated by political oppression no reprieve: all are annihilated by either war or Mokanna's poison. The message Feramorz seeks to convey, then, is not that imperial Islamic rule is invariably unjustifiable nor that nationalist resistance to imperial rule by a minority religious ethnic group is always appropriate. Extending the allegory of British rule in Ireland in Feramorz's third tale back to the Fire-Worshippers in 'The Veiled Prophet', *Lalla Rookh* insists neither that continued British rule of Ireland is unjustifiable nor that all forms of Irish Catholic resistance to Britain, at all times, necessarily have right on their side.

However, while the Caliph's victory affirms conservative and imperial power, this affirmation is only superficial. The tale presents no argument in favour of the Caliph's rule other than the fact that it is the pre-existing government; it focuses on its condemnation of Mokanna, yet gives compelling rhetorical force to Mokanna's expression of political cynicism:

> Come what may, let who will grasp the throne,
> Caliph or Prophet, Man alike shall groan;
> Let who will torture him, Priest – Caliph – King –
> Alike this loathsome world of his shall ring
> With victims' shrieks and howlings of the slave … [20]

The politics informing the poem are more complex than the Caliph's victory suggests. Mokanna in fact gains upon the Caliph until Azim's leadership of the Caliph's army turns the tide, yet Azim, like Mokanna's Fire-Worshippers, is driven by desire for vengeance: 'One sole desire, one passion now remains,/To keep life's fever still within his veins,/Vengeance!'[21] The vengeance Azim seeks is for his lover, Zelica, who was driven mad by grief during his absence fighting for the Caliph in Greece. Her madness allows her to become the dupe of Mokanna, who makes her his wife and chief priestess. A prisoner of war in Greece, Azim is inspired by that country's nationalist struggle; he escapes, and responds to the simplistic rhetoric of freedom and liberty that Mokanna employs.

17 Ibid., p. 9, p. 90. 18 Ibid. 19 Ibid., p. 91. 20 Ibid., p. 101. 21 Ibid., p. 97.

But before he is entirely committed to Mokanna's fight he encounters Zelica, who reveals her plight. The desire to kill Mokanna and avenge Zelica leads Azim to return to the Caliph's army – not any conviction of the justness of the Caliph's power. Moreover, only by renouncing the worldly glory he has earned and spending the rest of his days in isolation, praying for Zelica, does Azim finally attain her in heaven.

Feramorz's sympathetic yet critical portrait of the state of mind which causes Azim to join Mokanna suggests the reason for which he censures the Fire-Worshippers in this tale. On his return from Greece, Azim is politically naïve:

> Full of those dreams of good that, vainly grand,
> Haunt the young heart; – proud views of human-kind,
> Of men to Gods exalted and refin'd; –
> False views, like that horizon's fair deceit,
> Where earth and heav'n but *seem*, alas, to meet![22]

The Fire-Worshippers in 'The Veiled Prophet' are 'Careless for what or whom the blow was sped,/So vengeance triumph'd, and their tyrants bled!'; their parallels to Azim suggest Feramorz condemns them not because they seek vengeance, but because they express their desire for vengeance in a crude, irresponsible, simplistic, violent politics.[23]

'A Letter to the Roman Catholics of Dublin' further unravels Feramorz's conflicting portraits of imperial rule and religious-nationalist resistance – so much so that the two works seem integrally connected. The essence of the essay is a satiric attack on Irish Catholic and British conservative extremist opposition to the veto. It urges that mutually beneficial co-operation between Ireland and England, rather than independence, is the key to Irish liberty.[24] Religious intolerance is unjustifiable because it is irrational, Moore asserts. However, the proposed veto is reasonable; moreover, it would hinder the Pope from exerting political influence in the United Kingdom.

'The Veiled Prophet' illustrates the 'Letter's' argument that 'The power connected with creeds is always much more obnoxious than their errors.'[25] The Caliph and Mokanna represent their opposing causes as divinely sanctified, inciting their armies to use religious battle cries, but their motives are fundamentally political, as Feramorz's description of Mokanna's victories in his case reveals: 'the Orient World's imperial crown/Is just within his grasp'.[26] Moreover, although Mokanna's use of language is alluring, Feramorz associates Mokanna's campaign with the

22 Ibid., p.14. 23 Ibid., p. 92. 24 This view belongs to the tradition of Grattan's patriotism which, as Leerssen points out, aimed at parliamentary reform and for heteronomy rather than autonomy, invoking 'arguments of equity and just representation of interests rather than an essential, national difference between Ireland and England.' Leerssen, *Remembrance*, p. 20. 25 Thomas Moore, 'A letter to the Roman Catholics of Dublin (1810)', printed in Richard Herne Shepherd, *Prose and verse: humorous, satirical and sentimental by Thomas Moore* (London, 1878), p. 241. Hereafter, 'Letter'. 26 Moore, *Lalla Rookh*, p. 93.

uneducated and working-classes – 'Such was the wild and miscellaneous host,/That high in air their motley banners tost' – to ensure that the rebel's cause is never attractive to the reader.[27] Moore employs similar distancing precautions in the 'Letter': 'The bigots of both sects are equally detestable; but if I were compelled to choose between them, I should certainly prefer those who have the Constitution on their side'.[28] Feramorz's gothic depiction of Mokanna as a satanical fraudulent prophet incarnates the 'Letter's' condemnation of the leaders of Irish opposition to the veto as 'more wicked in their folly than that people of antiquity, who set a fly upon an altar, and sacrificed an ox to it!'[29]

In contrast, the loyalty of the Fire-Worshippers to their leader Hafed in Feramorz's third tale illustrates the 'Letter's' more discreet defence of seventeenth-century Irish Catholic resistance to British rule. The 'Letter' asserts that the Pope's power of episcopal appointment in Ireland stems from the Reformation:

> nothing could be more natural than that the members of a persecuted religion should turn for support, for counsel and consolation, to the visible head of that faith for which they were suffering … that, possessing no political rights which foreign interference could injure, they should unreservedly abandon their church to his guidance, and find a charm in this voluntary obedience to him which consoled them for their extorted submission to others.[30]

The same perspective informs Feramorz's portrait of the Fire-Worshippers who follow Hafed: where Mokanna's disciples are a blind, ignorant rabble, Hafed's co-religionists are noble chieftains.

Moore explores the foundations of justifiable religious solidarity in the 'Letter' in order to differentiate between Reformation and Union Ireland. During the Reformation, the 'Letter' argues, the conquest of the Irish nation entailed the overthrow of the Irish religion: war on the part of the Irish was justified. In Union Ireland, however, Roman Catholicism and the Irish nation are no longer one and the same political body; their positions should not be amalgamated. 'The Fire-Worshippers', then, illustrates a defence of national-religious warfare that Moore holds sound in principle, but invalid in the case of Union Ireland.

The second of Feramorz's tales, 'Paradise and the Peri', narrates a fallen angel's return to heaven. The Peri offers up the blood of a Hindu who dies defending his country against an Islamic invasion, a motif which recalls Moore's description of Irish Catholics during the Reformation in the 'Letter' and anticipates Hafed's role in the following tale. As though signalling the motif's inappropriateness to contemporary Ireland, however, Heaven rejects the offering. The Peri next offers up the dying breaths of an Egyptian girl who sacrifices her life by tending to her lover as he dies of plague. This episode stems from the 'Letter's' argument that by conceding the veto and becoming part of the legis-

27 Ibid., p. 92. 28 'Letter', p. 251. 29 Ibid., p. 229. 30 Ibid., p. 236.

lature, Irish Catholics will regain and protect their own political and ecclesiastical freedom, and, by broadening the legislature, enhance liberty throughout the United Kingdom.[31] Moore assures the Dublin Catholics, 'your courage will rival the gallantry of that youth who courted his mistress at the moment when she was dying of the plague, and "clasping the bright infection in his arms," restored her to health and beauty by his caresses.'[32] Moore's reversal of the simile's gender roles and conclusion in 'Paradise and the Peri' suggests a new cynicism about Ireland's future: instead of portraying the Irish as rescuing a damsel in distress, 'Paradise and the Peri' evokes Ireland as a devoted but foredoomed spouse, capable of sacrifice but not effective action.

Moore wrote 'Paradise and the Peri' after writing 'The Fire-Worshippers' and 'The Veiled Prophet.' Whereas the 'Letter' focuses on Irish Catholic opposition to the veto, the dramatic force Feramorz lends 'The Fire-Worshippers' over 'The Veiled Prophet' suggests that Moore set out to attack conservative British opposition in *Lalla Rookh*. Over the period he wrote the poem, domestic unrest in England increased, and criticism of the establishment became increasingly dangerous. Noticeably, the most socially conservative section of the work was the final part he composed. The poem's narratal frame, written from 1816 to mid 1817, closes down the political implications of Feramorz's tales. Fadladeen's reaction to 'The Fire-Worshippers' as a 'profane and seditious' tale satirises, by its absurdity, bigoted conservative British opposition to the veto. In the context of the analogies to Ireland in Feramorz's lays, Moore could have implied, via Fadladeen's suspicion of a threat to the seventeenth-century Moghul establishment in India in Feramorz's tales, that the case of Ireland poses a threat to the consolidating power in India in 1817, Britain. Instead, Fadladeen's reaction to 'The Fire-Worshippers' satirises conservative literary critics more markedly than conservative politicians (indeed, contemporary reviews of *Lalla Rookh* remarked on the former satire alone).[33]

Yet *Lalla Rookh* does not unambivalently endorse the British imperial presence in India. Fadladeen caricatures contemporary East India Company officials, seizing the opportunities Lalla Rookh's journey offers him to trade in Mazagong oranges and Chinese porcelain, and embodying the irate expatriate when his trade fails: 'to eat any mangoes but those of Mazagong was, of course, impossible … to all these grievances is added the obstinacy of the cooks, in putting the pepper of Canara into his dishes instead of the cinnamon of Serendib'.[34] If Moore's poem commodifies and exploits the Orient, it also, in its parodic account of Fadladeen's agitation at the failure of his Mazagong-orange and Chinese-porcelain trade, implicitly satirises such activities in an imperial context. Never fully emancipated as analogous to Ireland, Moore's Orient in *Lalla Rookh* resists becoming entirely Other in any simple way.

31 Ibid., p. 238, p. 248. 32 Ibid., p. 249. 33 Moore, *Lalla Rookh*, p. 247. 34 Ibid., pp 124–5.

Theatricality and The Irish R.M.: *comic county house dramatics versus Abbey Theatre ideology*

ANNE OAKMAN, QUEEN'S UNIVERSITY, BELFAST

THE CRITICS AND AN UNCANNY COUPLING

At the turn of the nineteenth century, in 1899, both the opening season of the Irish Literary Theatre in Dublin, and in London the first published book-form edition of E. Œ. Somerville and Martin Ross' *Some Experiences of an Irish R.M.*, appeared on the literary scene. Despite the congruent timing and, as this essay will go on to argue, literary material, most critics have largely viewed these different projects as taking place on two widely incompatible ideological and cultural plateaus. In his introduction to *Irish Books and Irish People* (1919) Stephen Gwynn decided that the only part of Irish literature in the last twenty years of the nineteenth century that was exempt from the influence of Irish Revivalists such as Yeats, Synge and Æ was 'the work of Edith Somerville and Martin Ross'.[1] The inimical saturation of this perspective in Irish studies has proved difficult to reverse and the resultant estranged parochialism of these two author-chatelaines of the Irish country house has persisted in various guises and with diverse effects. Multiple and shifting reasons cited as the cause of Somerville and Ross' arguably conscious isolation from the Irish Revival movement have made a rather haphazard and contradictory appearance in the work that has been written about them over the last half century. But this somewhat exiguous body of writing is also usefully suggestive of ways in which the relationship between Somerville and Ross and the Irish Revival involves a much more mutable and symbiotic scope of relations than has previously been averred.

At a Somerville and Ross Symposium held in Belfast in 1968 John Cronin argued that despite incidental common interests, Somerville and Ross' 'literary curiosity was to be different' from their Revivalist counterparts.[2] F.S.L. Lyons later decided in 1970 that it was rather class and politics that kept the two groups apart. Somerville and Ross' 'instinctive mistrust' of Yeats and Lady Gregory's nationalist sympathies, plus the fact that the two cousins 'had no wish to attach themselves to a group which seemed to them to have conspicuously few *gentlemen* in it', were at the root of the split he claimed.[3] In 1976 Conor Cruise O'Brien took a slightly different stance on the debate by suggesting that despite the duo's rebuttal of the movement it was, in fact, the Revivalists who were influenced by Somerville and Ross. He goes on to confidently assert that the R.M. tale,

1 Stephen Gwynn, *Irish books and Irish people* (Dublin, 1919), p. 4. 2 John Cronin, 'Somerville and Ross: a symposium' (Belfast, 1968), p. 11. 3 F.S.L. Lyons, 'The twilight of the big house' *Ariel* 1:3 (1970), 120–1.

'Lisheen Races, Second-hand', was at the back of Synge's mind when he wrote *The Playboy of the Western World*.[4]

Aided by the new wealth of available biographical information that appeared after 1985, namely Gifford Lewis' work in the field, Declan Kiberd's study of *The Real Charlotte* in *Inventing Ireland* and, more recently, *The Silver Fox* in *Irish Classics*, has been the most prominent attempt to tackle once again the relationship between Somerville and Ross and the Irish Revivalists. Relying on material reproduced in both Lewis' biography and her edition of selected letters, Kiberd posits Somerville and Ross' refusal to be recruited to the movement in *Inventing Ireland* as a result of their severe 'reservations about the representation of the peasantry in the dramas of the Abbey Theatre'.[5] He follows this up in *Irish Classics* by focussing on the authors' active anti-Englishness in *The Silver Fox*, asserting that despite their hostility to the Revivalists Somerville and Ross were nevertheless, 'ever so quietly, placing themselves in alignment with the cultural revival'.[6] Kiberd wonders whether Ross' 'furtive visit to the Irish Literary Theatre in 1901' represents a 'frustrated empire loyalist ... sent ... deep into enemy territory with the intent of seeing whether it might not be the right time to change sides.'[7]

As it turns out Somerville and Ross never did change sides and I want to suggest that it was never quite their intention to do so, and also that the boundaries between the two 'sides' were not as clear-cut as Kiberd and other critics would have them. As Somerville herself put it in 1906, their position on 'the outer skin' (or in 'the shades at the back' as Ross put it) of Ireland's Literary Renaissance was where they were more than happy to be.[8] In this essay I'm going to take a more detailed look at the biographical incidents that led to such a dizzying array of critical opinions and suggest that Somerville and Ross' position on the outer fringes of the movement was a cultivated and tactical step that offered them a useful position of surveillance over their artistic contemporaries. Moreover, I want to argue that this arrangement further enabled Somerville and Ross to combat a discourse of Irishness, largely emanating from the Abbey's stages, that they perceived as increasingly unable and unwilling to encompass the multifaceted hybridity of English-Irish identity. I will conclude by briefly looking at some of Somerville and Ross' short stories and Irish R.M. tales, written and published between 1898 and 1915, and attempt to show their deliberate arrangement within a metaphorical and stylistic framework of the theatre. Concurrent with Ireland's highly politicized period of theatrical reform, I want to argue that these stories both create and sustain a literary dialogue with their Revivalist and theatrical contemporaries. In order to fully contextualize this line of argument, however, a concise narrative of Somerville and Ross' rather

---

4 Conor Cruise O'Brien, *Writers and politics: essays and criticisms* (London, 1976), pp 146–7.   5 Declan Kiberd, *Inventing Ireland* (London, 1996), p. 70.   6 Declan Kiberd, *Irish classics* (London, 2000), p. 364.   7 Kiberd, *Irish classics*, p.365.   8 Edith Somerville, letter to Cameron Somerville, 31 January 1906, Edith Œnone Somerville Archive, Cork, ms. L.A.492.a.

neglected history of actual relations with revivalist figures – such as Yeats, Lady Gregory, Douglas Hyde and the Fay brothers – becomes a necessary prelude.

'IF THIS WAS THE LOFTY PURITY OF THE IRISH DRAMA I WAS INDEED MYSTIFIED ...'[9]

Somerville and Ross' connection with several of the Irish Revival's prominent activists seems to have gained some significance with the publication of their first novel, *An Irish Cousin*, in 1889. Ross asked her cousin, Lady Augusta Gregory, to advertize Somerville and Ross' shilling shocker to Gregory's social and literary circle of friends and, over the years, Ross continued to communicate intermittently with Gregory about her and Somerville's joint literary projects. Gregory and her husband largely applauded and encouraged Ross' artistic endeavours, predicting 'great fame and popularity' for both Somerville and Ross after reading *An Irish Cousin*.[10] Gregory also urged Ross to reap a 'fine harvest' by writing about her experiences of 'Dublin life' and, in turn, Gregory sought Ross' commentary on her own and her revival colleagues' works.[11] In 1905, for example, Gregory sent Ross a copy of Synge's *Well of the Saints* for her to read and criticize.[12] The letters between Ross and Gregory are far from frequent but they do maintain a consistency over several years in the late nineteenth and early twentieth centuries. Gregory's last letter to Ross was written in July 1915, just four months before Ross' death, and in it she divulges her's and Yeats' enjoyment of Somerville and Ross' latest and final instalment of the Irish R.M. tales, *In Mr Knox's Country*.[13]

Somerville's connection with Douglas Hyde came in 1897 when, as noted earlier, he approached her through a mutual acquaintance, Timothy Keating, to ask if she would be interested and willing to gather, translate and assemble local Irish folk tales from the South West Cork area. Hyde expands in his letter to Somerville on the cultural importance of collecting and, like his recently deceased friend Patrick O'Leary, publishing these Cork stories in an Irish-English bilingual edition.[14] Somerville's well-documented interest in Irish folklore and concentrated attempts at learning the Irish language were still not enough to persuade her of the merits of such a project and she politely but firmly declined the offer. Both Somerville and Ross also appear to have taken a keen interest in the

9 Martin Ross, letter to Edith Somerville, 28 October 1901, in Gifford Lewis (ed.), *The selected letters of Somerville and Ross* (London, 1989), p. 254, hereafter cited as *SL*. 10 William Gregory, letter to Mrs Ross, 21 October 1889, Queen's University, Belfast, ms. 17/920. 11 Augusta Gregory, letter to Martin Ross, *c*.1914, Queen's University, Belfast, ms. 17/920. 12 Martin Ross, letter to Augusta Gregory, 20 February 1905, quoted in Gifford Lewis, *Somerville and Ross: the world of the Irish R.M.* (London, 1985), p. 104. 13 Augusta Gregory, letter to Martin Ross, 8 July 1915, Queen's University, Belfast, ms. 17/920. 14 Douglas Hyde, letter to Edith Somerville, 24 January 1897, Edith Œnone Somerville Archive, Cork, ms. L.B.192.a-d; also see Hyde's earlier letter to Somerville which is closely related to the themes in this later letter: Douglas Hyde, 17 January 1897, Edith Œnone Somerville Archive, Cork, ms. L.B.193.a–b.

plays staged by the Abbey Theatre and Ross, in particular, attended several Abbey and other Revivalist productions between 1901 and 1905 (and then again in 1909 with Somerville) at the behest of Gregory. Previous to this Ross had briefly come into contact with Yeats in 1896 at the home of the Morrises, a neighbouring Galway family, and her first impressions betray some of Somerville's and Ross' characteristic ascendancy superciliousness:

> He [Yeats] is mad about his old legends and spirits, and if someone said 'Thims fine lobsters' or anything, he would begin 'There's a very curious tradition about lobsters' and then he was off. He is thinner than a lath – wears paltry little clothes wisped round his bones, and the prodigious and affected greenish tie. He is a little affected and knows it – he has a sense of humour and is a gentleman – hardly by birth I fancy – but by genius ... [15]

It wasn't until August 1901 that Ross was properly introduced to Yeats and found an occasion to engage in some 'high literary conversation' with him at Coole Park and, in the process, defend 'humour ... [as] a high art'.[16] The letters Ross wrote to Somerville between 1901 and 1905 from Coole and Dublin reveal both admiration for Yeats' and Gregory's work but also a distinct hostility to their overall project. Her particularly acerbic criticisms of the Abbey Theatre are markedly directed at both the theatre's early use of English actors and the literary premises of the plays themselves. Ross' highest and most delectable praise is reserved for the Abbey's two notorious actors and directors, Frank and Willy Fay.[17]

It is also worth mentioning that Ross witnessed performances of Irish plays by the Irish Literary Theatre both before and after the Fays and Yeats worked together in 1902. In 1901 Ross went to see Jack Yeats' exhibition of Irish sketches in Dublin and also saw the Irish Literary Theatre's production of Yeats and Moore's *Diarmuid and Grania* at Dublin's Gaiety Theatre, which made use of the Benson's touring group of English actors. Ross was thoroughly unimpressed by both the play and the performance, mocking Yeats and Moore's reinvention of Celtic legends as a not particularly successful 'mix of saga and modern French situations.'[18] Writing to Somerville, Ross despairingly exclaims that, 'if this was the lofty purity of the Irish drama I am indeed mystified.'[19] The English actors fare little better as Ross picks at the Irish witch's conversational English accent, scathingly adding that: 'a more unattractive hero than Mr. B[enson]. I have seldom seen. In his love making he moaned over Mrs B[enson]'s face like a cat when a dog comes into the room. I could have thrown up.'[20] After digesting the same performance and obviously coming to a similar conclusion, Frank Fay, then writing as drama critic for the *United Irishman*, asked the following ques-

---

15 Martin Ross, letter to Edith Somerville [incomplete], *c.*1896, *SL*, p. 240.   16 Martin Ross, letter to Edith Somerville, 8 August 1901, *SL*, pp 251–2.   17 See *SL* p. 240; pp 251–6; pp 271–4; p. 276, and Edith Somerville, letter to Cameron Somerville, 31 January 1906, Edith Œnone Somerville Archive, Cork, ms. L.A.492.a–d.   18 Martin Ross, letter to Edith Somerville, 28 October 1901, *SL*, p. 254. 19 Ibid. 20 Ibid.

tion of Yeats' Irish Literary Theatre: 'why [is it that] the conductors of the Irish Literary Theatre who pooh-pooh the ordinary commercial theatre cannot entrust the performance of their plays dealing with Irish subjects to a company of Irish actors [?]'[21] Having founded his own group of Irish amateur actors seven years before Yeats and Gregory turned their attention towards the stage, Frank Fay knew that the potential existed for the plays of the Irish Literary Theatre successfully to be produced and performed by Irish directors and actors. The distinct change in Ross' opinion of the Abbey Theatre's productions noticeably coincides with the Fays' involvement. Her appreciation and admiration in 1905 for Yeats' *The King's Threshold* and Gregory's *Kincora* is distinctively influenced by what she observes as the interesting and artistic staging, as well as the characteristic acting techniques the Fay brothers introduced at the Abbey.[22]

It was earlier in this same year that Gregory had sent Ross Synge's *Well of the Saints* to read and Ross' criticisms largely focus on the use of dialect which she feared was so lacking in fire and spontaneity that it left the characters 'artificial and unreal.'[23] Some months after this Ross wrote to Somerville to tell her that Gregory was absolutely 'rampant' that she write a play for the Abbey Street Theatre.[24] Despite Gregory's enthusiasm and repeated entreaties to consider the idea further and get Somerville involved, both authors firmly turned the offer down. Ross' letters suggest that not only were she and Somerville very wary of what they perceived as an attempt by Gregory to 'rope in the upper classes and … drop politics', but that they were also dubious about the strictures Gregory hints would be placed upon their writing in her offer to choose for them a suitable plot and characters from their novels.[25] In January 1906 Somerville attended the closing performance of Synge's *Riders to the Sea* at the Abbey and the comic play, *The Eloquent Dempsey*, both of which she thoroughly praised, particularly Frank Fay's performance. It was during this trip that Somerville also ventured out to Dundrum to observe first-hand the Irish carpet making and bookbinding business started by the Yeats sisters, explaining in a letter to her brother Cameron that 'it will be interesting to see what they are doing'.[26] In June of the same year Somerville and Ross attended a celebratory dinner for the Irish Literary Renaissance in London and also commissioned Frank Fay to read two of their short stories, 'Poisson D'Avril' from the R.M. tales and 'A Patrick's Day Hunt', at the New Country Club in London. According to Somerville the dinner was somewhat plagued by internal divisions and the "Irish Literary Renaissance' wh[ich] the dinner was supposed to celebrate was hardly mentioned!' and 'Lady Gregory and the Yeats', and all that crowd, were ignored'.[27] Somerville concludes that there must have been 'trade

21 Frank Fay, 'The Irish literary theatre', *United Irishman* (May 1901), p. 8. 22 Martin Ross, letter to Edith Somerville, 30 April 1905, *SL*, pp 271–2. 23 Martin Ross, letter to Augusta Gregory, 20 February 1905, quoted in Lewis *Somerville and Ross*, p. 104. 24 Martin Ross, letter to Edith Somerville, 30 April 1905, *SL*, pp 273–4. 25 Ibid. 26 Edith Somerville, letter to Cameron Somerville, 31 January 1906, Edith Œnone Somerville Archive, Cork, ms. L.A.492.a. 27 Edith Somerville,

jealousies at the heart of things that we (thank heaven), are too much on the outer skin to know anything about'.[28]

Despite, then, their attendance at a dinner that is purportedly a salutation to the achievements of the Irish Revival movement, Somerville and Ross still manage to distance themselves from the revivals' public group of influentials, clearly seeing themselves as apart from Gregory and the Yeatses and 'all that crowd.' It was only on rare occasions that Somerville and Ross publicly attached their names to their Revivalist counterparts. In May 1910 Somerville and Ross attended a congratulatory dinner for Irish women writers at Dublin's (usually all male) Corinthian Club and the event was duly publicized and reported on in the *Irish Times* the following day.[29] Despite being clearly embarrassed by the honorific and specifically Irish Revival premise of the dinner Somerville and Ross felt that they ought to attend and there is a sense that they do so out of a desire to promote and celebrate women's writing in general rather than just Irish Revival women's writing.[30] Among others, Douglas Hyde and George Moore attended the dinner, the latter 'very entertaining & discomposing & alarming'.[31] Somerville and Ross also took in a performance of *The Shaughraun* at the Gaiety, which was, they afterwards decided, 'abominably done' and 'vilely acted'.[32] The only other time that the duo publicly and literally signed their names alongside the names of other Irish writers was in 1904. The two authors signed a letter to the *Irish Times* instigated by George W. Russell which asked for financial help to keep in Ireland an 'extraordinary collection of pictures by ... chiefly modern French artists'.[33] The letter was signed by 'Jane Barlow, Augusta Gregory, S.H. Butcher, Douglas Hyde, Edith Œ. Somerville, Martin Ross, Emily Lawless, George W. Russell ("AE")'.[34] When Somerville eventually met Russell in August 1919 during a stay in Dublin with Sir Horace Plunkett, she found him to be 'very much 'the hairy fairy', cum pantomime ogre, but delightful to be talked to by (one does not talk oneself).'[35]

Finally, in the summer of 1909, Somerville and Ross went together to see several performances at the Abbey Theatre with Somerville's cousin and wife of G. B. Shaw, Charlotte. This included seeing *The Playboy of the Western World*,

letter to Cameron Somerville, 6 June 1906, Edith Œnone Somerville Archive, Cork, ms. L.A.509.a–c. 28 Ibid.   29 Anon., 'Irish Women of Letters: Corinthian Club Banquet', *Irish Times*, 4 May 1910. 30 Martin Ross, letter to J.B. Pinker, *c*.May 1910, ms. TCD 3330–1/479, Trinity College, Dublin. Somerville and Ross felt 'justly indignant' when they weren't included as Irish writers but, at the same time, they perceived the Revival agenda as something that attempted to sideline their kind of writing: '[Heeney?]'s lecture on the "Irish Literary Renaissance" ... says that Martin and I, & Misses Edgeworth & Lawless, & Charles Lever, are not Irish writers! We are justly indignant ...' Edith Somerville, diary, 15 February 1919, Queen's University, Belfast, ms. 17/874.   31 Martin Ross, Diary, 2 May 1910, Queen's University, Belfast, ms. 17/874.   32 Edith Somerville, Diary, 4 May 1910, Queen's University, Belfast, ms. 17/874.   33 Jane Barlow et al., letter to the Editor of the *Irish Times*, *c*.December 1904 [published in the *Irish Times* on 5 January 1905], *Letters from Æ*, Alan Denson (ed.) (New York, 1961), pp 54–5.   34 Ibid.   35 Edith Somerville, Diary, 28 August 1919, Queen's University, Belfast, ms. 17/874. For a more detailed account of Somerville's marginal involvement in Irish national politics and her relationship with Plunkett and Russell see: Otto Rauchbauer, *The Edith Œnone Somerville archive in Drishane: a catalogue and an evaluative essay* (Dublin, 1994), pp 206–9.

The Workhouse Ward, Cathleen Ní Houlihan, The Rising of the Moon, and 'the much talked of' *Blanco Posnet*.[36] They were 'delighted' by Gregory's plays, 'disliked … very much' Synge's, and found *Blanco Posnet* to be 'most moral & melodramatic' and, given the fact that it was 'banned by the English Censor', 'quite harmless.'[37] One of Ross' last meetings with Gregory came in 1912 when she was, again, at Coole Park. Gregory had just returned from touring in America with the Irish players.[38] Despite her desire to take the local Castletownshend amateur theatre group 'barnstorming round England' with one of 'Lady Gregory's Irish plays', Somerville's relations with the Abbey Theatre and the Revival group (apart from Shaw) waned somewhat after Ross' death in 1915.[39]

This list is by no means exhaustive, limited as it is by the length of this essay, but it already forces several important conclusions. Somerville and Ross' active interest in the Revival movement is continually counterpoised by their repeated refusals to commit to it. It is also noticeable that they reserve their highest praise for the Fay brothers and aim their harshest comments at the Gaelicisation of Irish drama on the Abbey's stages, plus the Society's early employment of English actors. Given their approval and enjoyment of many of the plays they witnessed, their rather distinct anti-Gaelic streak of criticism seems to derive more from their disapproval at the ploughing up of Irish legends and Celtic history as a unique representative of contemporary Irish culture than anything else. Yeats and Gregory stated that their ambition for their theatrical enterprise was to: 'show that Ireland was not the home of buffoonery and easy sentiment, as it has been represented, but the home of an ancient idealism'.[40] But Somerville and Ross seem to have decided that Ireland as a home of ancient idealism was no home to them. What was perceived as national and authentic to one group of writers was not necessarily national and authentic to all. Frank Hugh O'Donnell's renowned pamphlet, *Souls for Gold! A Pseudo-Celtic Drama in Dublin*, launched a rather hysterical attack in 1899 on Yeats' play *The Countess Cathleen* and, among other criticisms, attacked the Irish Literary Theatre for creating its own version of stage Irishry.

Despite criticising the plays from a completely different political angle, the kind of abuse Somerville and Ross direct towards the Irish Revivalists is not unlike O'Donnell's. O'Donnell argued that what Yeats and others were promoting on the Abbey's stage was as misguided and misrepresentative as the blundering stage Irishmen of the London stage they were originally trying to oppose. The two authors continually exhibit a mocking hostility towards the way in which authenticity and nationalism become theatrical constructs in the Abbey's Celticized productions. Major Yeates, the narrator of the R.M. tales,

36 Edith Somerville, Diary, 25 August 1909, Queen's University, Belfast, ms. 17/874. 37 Ibid. and Martin Ross, Diary, 24 and 25 August 1909, Queen's University, Belfast, ms. 17/874. 38 Martin Ross, Diary, 12 March 1912, Queen's University, Belfast, ms. 17/874. 39 Edith Somerville, letter to Cameron Somerville, 3 December 1908, Edith Œnone Somerville Archive, Cork, ms. L.A.636.a–c. 40 W.B. Yeats and Lady Augusta Gregory, letter seeking financial assistance for the Irish Literary Theatre, quoted in Andrew Malone, *Irish drama* (New York, 1929), pp 34–5.

ANNE OAKMAN

rather tellingly reports that 'an Irishman is always the critic in the stalls, and is also, in spirit, behind the scenes.'[41] In their politics Somerville and Ross had little time for nationalist idealism and romanticism, despite their nationalist sympathies, and in literature they had even less tolerance for what they perceived to be the idealized and Gaelicized rural West of Ireland posturing as a representative symbol of Ireland.

The promotion of racial purity and active de-anglicization that accompanies such political and literary projects arguably erects an homogenous ideal of national unity that is increasingly difficult to penetrate. Monolithic national categories in Ireland were unable to encompass the anomalous position of the Anglo-Irish and hence the distinctly Anglo-Irish history and heritage that Somerville and Ross felt ought to be included in any discussion of Irish culture and nationality. Drawing on a Celtic past and envisioning a United Ireland future ignored a present that was less black and white in both political and cultural terms than Ireland's core of reactionary nationalists were willing to accommodate on the stage. O'Donnell's stage Irishman of the pseudo-Celtic drama sits at one end of an Irish national spectrum with the English stage Irishman at the other and a nebulous and changing concept of Irish nationality in the middle and it's at the continuum's mid-point of unstable national identities that I think the R.M. tales belong.

This is also a point where a distinction can and has to be made between Somerville and Ross' anti-Englishness and the Revival's efforts to de-Anglicize Ireland. Where Kiberd sees their disillusion with English culture and Empire politics in *The Silver Fox* as a signal that they may have been looking to join the other camp, I would rather conclude that this merely squashed them even more tightly in-between the two camps, looking to be a part of neither and yet desperately needing to maintain a link with both. This position is neatly paralleled by the Hiberno-English dialect Somerville and Ross were such masters at rendering and which all of their works are meticulously structured around. This pseudo-language is given its own unique and hybrid identity in the following passage by the two authors:

> Ireland has two languages; one of them is her own by birthright; the second of them is believed to be English, which is a fallacy; it is a fabric built by Irish architects with English bricks, quite unlike anything of English construction. The Anglo-Irish dialect is a passably good name for it, even though it implies an unseemly equality between artist and material, but it is something more than a dialect, more than an affair of pidgin English, bad spelling, provincialisms, and preposterous grammar; it is a tongue pliant and subtle, expressing with every breath the mind of its makers.[42]

41 E. Œ. Somerville and Martin Ross, 'When I met Dr. Hickey', *The Irish R.M.* (London, 2000), p. 31. All quotations from the *Irish R.M.* tales are taken from this edition. 42 Somerville and Ross, 'The Anglo-Irish Language' in *Stray-aways* (London, 1920), p. 184.

'Take of these elements all that is fusible,
Melt 'em all down in a pipkin or crucible,
Set 'em to simmer and take off the scum,
And a Heavy Dragoon is the resid-u-um!'[43]

Turning to the R.M. tales themselves, which arguably bring Ireland's second language to life, I want to briefly examine what I have been calling the tale's theatrical qualities. I am here using the term theatricality to refer to that which is easily adaptable to the stage and also that which is suggestive of the artificiality of performance and representation. Somerville metaphorically situates the tales within a theatrical framework when, in her last collection of essays published in 1946, she describes the feelings aroused when her and Ross completed their first R.M. story, 'Great Uncle McCarthy', in terms of an opening night at the theatre: 'We finished that first chapter feeling, I imagine, much the same sensations as must assail the man in the box-office on the night of a *premiere* before the doors are opened, and he knows there is a long queue outside, clamouring for admission. But their time was not yet.'[44] These comments not only metaphorically place the composition of the R.M. tales onto the theatrical stage, but they are also suggestive of the categorized audience that awaited their performance or publication. The tales were originally published in the London-based sporting monthly, *The Badminton Magazine*, and by appealing to this consistent magazine readership they were, as Somerville's comments suggest, writing for an eager, waiting, and predictable audience. Furthermore, this audience/author relationship was much closer to an audience/stage performance relationship than the reader/author relationship they had established through the work they had previously done in novel form. Somerville's allusion to the theatre exhibits an awareness of these relational differences and, like an interactive theatre audience, monthly magazine readers were afforded a space to create a dialogue, albeit a written one, between themselves and the authors of the columns they read. They were thus enacting a more distanced but nonetheless potent space of interaction between author and audience, and this is reflected in the fact that of all the works Somerville and Ross published, none produced more letters of comment than the R.M. tales.

The metaphorical framework of theatre practice that emerges in Somerville's later comments on the tales is also apparent in the text of the tales themselves. Yeates' narrative abounds with similes that describe his experiences in Ireland as if they had been played out on a popular stage, adhering to the conventions of fashionable theatrical forms such as farce and pantomime. People enter and exit the scenes of his narrative in pantomimic style and his encounters take on

43 Refrain from Gilbert and Sullivan's opera, *Patience*, which Somerville used to describe the creation of the characters in the R.M. tales. See E. Œ. Somerville, 'Étaples: where the Irish R.M. began,' *Happy days! Essays of sorts by E. Œ. Somerville and Martin Ross* (London, 1946), p. 70. 44 Somerville, 'Étaples', p. 70.

melodramatic proportions as if they were stage-managed to suit the occasion of their dramatic re-telling:

> I look back to that first week of housekeeping at Shreelane as to a comedy excessively badly staged, and striped with lurid melodrama.[45]

> Almost before I had time to realise what had happened, Flurry jumped through the half-opened window of the dining-room like a clown at a pantomime, and joined in the chase … 'Take me out of this!' howled Mr Flood hysterically, accepting my pantomime entrance without question.[46]

The emphasis of Yeats' narrative on the theatricality of events places them upon a stage of his own making and hence points out both the fictionality of the stories and their affiliation with popular theatrical forms. At the same time as allowing an element of the absurd to invade the narrative, Somerville and Ross strongly rely on the accuracy of recorded speech to maintain a level of authenticity and reality. The characters in the R.M. tales, however, also perform, they are effectively *staged* by Yeates' narrative and the theatrical language he uses, but the effect on national identity is unlike that produced on the Abbey's stages. First, Somerville and Ross draw on a much more popular and melodramatic tradition of the stage: pantomime, farce, and burlesque. Second, they use these models of theatrical form in a similar way to such early Irish dramatists as Charles Macklin in *The True Born Irishman* and Dion Boucicault, who challenged the melodramatic stage Irishman by reversing his foolish qualities onto the Englishman. In the R.M. tales and on the stage the familiar pattern of throwing an Irishman into the unfamiliar territory of an Englishman's society in order to watch him flounder and show up his ignorance and subservience is reversed. Somerville and Ross' R.M. tales allow us to laugh at the Englishman, Yeates, thrown into the unfamiliar social stratum of a parochial Irish county where his particularly English rules don't apply and he is left floundering in the wake of Flurry Knox's continual mischief. Ignorance and subservience comically fall upon the role of Yeates while the Irish are left to play with the traditional masks of the stage Irishman, throwing them on and off to their own advantage.

When Somerville and Ross chose Frank Fay to perform a reading of two tales in London they were essentially relying on his perfect grasp of English and Irish dialects to carry over both the humour and the seriousness of the tales. Fay reads one of Somerville and Ross' miscellaneous Irish hunting tales, 'A Patrick's Day Hunt', narrated by an Irishman, and 'Poisson D'Avril', narrated by Yeates from the second collection of the R.M. stories. As Ross remarks in her letter to Somerville on the event, the former story perhaps proved a little too 'esoteric' for some of the English audience. Somewhat surprisingly, the latter standard

45 Somerville and Ross, 'Great uncle McCarthy', p. 31. 46 Somerville and Ross, 'Lisheen races, second-hand', p. 96.

English narrated story is considered 'too Irish in idiom' and yet it seems to 'read much better in a general way' and the humour is more readily understood and responded to.[47] The fact that Ross tells us she has to laugh secretly at Fay's reading of 'A Patrick's Day Hunt' suggests the frequent stupefaction of their audience. Like Leigh Kelway and Maxwell Bruce, the English visitors to Ireland in 'Lisheen Races, Second-Hand' and 'The Last Day of Shraft', Fay's audience are also unable to comprehend this otherworldly realm of the British Union. Both Kelway and Bruce are attempting to categorize Ireland within a somewhat imperialist discourse. Kelway is a British Radical, in Ireland as the private secretary of an English lord collecting statistics on the 'Liquor Question in Ireland', and Bruce is making a tour of the Irish-speaking counties in order to collect and collate 'ancient' Irish tales and folklore. Major Yeates also tells his readers that Kelway 'further informed me that he thought of popularizing the subject in a novel, and therefore intended to, as he put it, 'master the brogue' before his return [to England]'.[48] Both projects, however, are somewhat thwarted. Kelway, due in most part to the liquor question, is left disgraced in front of his chief and with a story that would prove too hard to explain in his defence to popularize in a novel and he resolves to 'abandon Ireland to her fate'.[49] Maxwell Bruce meanwhile gets little further than managing to provide cover for the Brickley's shebeen, the illicit sale and consumption of alcohol without a license, and his tale takes a stab at the revivalist movement by mocking the practice of certain gentry folk who gathered tales and folklore from the homes of the Irish peasantry. Maxwell's eagerness for an 'ancient song' results in a local man's short limerick about his neighbour Ned Flaherty's drake, which he made up himself 'lasht year', and Phillipa's less than minimal knowledge of Irish is somewhat derided when hailed by her as 'one of the props of the Celtic movement.'[50] By the close of the tales, both Englishmen have been thoroughly duped by the Irish and the comic reversal of stage roles has been completed.

Fay's reading in London is delivered to a primarily English audience; 'Poisson D'Avril' and 'A Patrick's Day Hunt' reveal their own theatrical affiliations through Fay's performance and the interactive collaboration between author, actor and audience which may have altered the tale's meanings. Without any real knowledge of the reading itself it is impossible to assess the way in which Fay chose to dramatize the tales but the fact that Ross' notes largely applaud his attention to the minutiae of dialectical differences written into the text suggest that he successfully enforced the semblance of multivocality inherent in all of the R.M. tales. A reading of 'Poisson D'Avril' straddles the performative divide between speech and the written word which not only necessitates Fay's performance of Yeates but, in turn, Yeates' performance of his own stories, his own renderings of recorded speech, both standard and Hiberno-English. This oral presentation by Fay and self-presentation by Yeates destabilizes the text as

47 Martin Ross, letter to Edith Somerville, 12 June 1906, *SL*, p. 279. 48 'Lisheen races', p. 94. 49 Ibid., p. 108. 50 Somerville and Ross, 'The last day of Shraft', pp 347–8, p. 336.

written artefact and subjects the work to live or theatrical interaction and possible connotative modification, much as popular nationalist theatre in Dublin was subject to and partially formed by audience reaction. Moreover, Somerville and Ross write this overriding and guiding notion of theatricality or performance into the text itself. Yeates behaves as both player in and observer of the events he relates and this playfulness between actor and author, performance and text, brings out the stylistic and linguistic framework of theatricality governing the tales and which places them in direct contact and debate with Ireland's performance culture and the Abbey's stages.

CONCLUSION

Like the Revivalists, then, Somerville and Ross use their knowledge of popular stage Irishry to both satirize and combat this popular representation of Ireland on the stage. Somerville and Ross, however, are also using their knowledge of what went on on the Abbey's stages and they position themselves and the R.M. tales somewhere in between these two points allowing the Anglo-Irish a precious space of representation. They secure their position by having Yeates as both an actor and spectator/narrator of the tales he tells. This, in turn, allows Somerville and Ross the license to be both playwright and audience, creating the action of the tales and also governing their direction, as well as noting the sympathetic English reaction in the form of Yeates' narrative. Just as Ross secretly laughs at Fay's reading in London of 'A Patrick Day's Hunt', Yeates too can secretly laugh at Flurry's antics while his English hosts, like Kelway and Bruce, remain overwhelmingly perplexed.

Somerville and Ross, therefore, may have lived and worked in the increasingly isolated Big Houses of Ireland but their positive engagement with cultural revival and reform in the late nineteenth century arguably dispels any notion of isolationism in their literary output. The theatricality of the R.M. tales is not merely a stylistic catalyst that promotes farcical humour in the stories but an integral structural and metaphorical device that allows the tales to compete and engage with an Irish cultural revival heavily concentrated on the stage and the performative arts. While combating English stereotypes of the Irish both on and off the stage, it permits Somerville and Ross to place inside Yeats and Gregory's Celticized West of Ireland the hybrid identities of the characters who populate their Irish R.M. tales and who, in the eyes of Somerville and Ross, had a right to be included in any discussion of Irish national identity.

'Spain vanished, and green Ireland reappeared': Maria Edgeworth's patriotism in The Absentee (1812) and Patronage (1814)[1]

YURI YOSHINO, GOLDSMITHS COLLEGE,
UNIVERSITY OF LONDON

Maria Edgeworth's *The Absentee* (1812) is often categorised as an 'Irish Tale'. The text is, however, double-layered in the sense that it was originally written as an episode within *Patronage* (1814), an 'English Tale.'[2] This would mean that in theory the episode which became *The Absentee* had continuity with *Patronage* in terms of contexts and themes. *The Absentee* thus needs to be read against the English/British context of *Patronage* in addition to its own Irish/British context.[3] The two novels were written when the European intellectual and political climate was undergoing an ideological transition from Enlightenment cosmopolitanism to Romantic nationalism triggered by the French Revolution and its international aftermath of the Napoleonic Wars.[4] By exploring the intertextuality between *The Absentee* and *Patronage*, this essay aims to investigate potential conflicts between Edgeworth's ideal patriotism for the 'Anglo-Irish' landed class in *The Absentee* and the one for the English landed class in *Patronage*. The potential conflicts would substantiate a dimension of Edgeworth's 'Anglo-Irish' dilemma. This essay will be concluded by interrogating what Edgeworth viewed as the patriotic role of a woman writer from the Ascendancy.

Set mostly in England, *Patronage* revolves around the life of two English families, both in private and public spheres. The novel is preoccupied with the

1 I would like to thank the University of London Central Research Fund, the British Association for Irish Studies, and the British Federation of Women Graduates Charitable Foundation for their financial support for my doctoral research, an area of which is presented in what follows. 2 Marilyn Butler, Heidi Van de Veire, and Kim Walker (eds), introductory note, *The novels and selected works of Maria Edgeworth*, 12 vols (London, 1999–2003), v: *The Absentee* (1999), pp xv–xix. 3 W.J. Mc Cormack, 'The tedium of history: an approach to Maria Edgeworth's *Patronage* (1814)' in Ciaran Brady (ed.), *Ideology and the historians* (Dublin, 1991), pp 77–98 (pp 84, 95). See also Clíona Ó Gallchoir's comparative study of *The Absentee* and *Patronage* in terms of Edgeworth's representation of national characters in her 'Maria Edgeworth and the rise of national literature' (unpublished doctoral thesis, Cambridge University, 1998), pp 151–92. 4 Joep Leerssen emphasizes the distinction between 'patriotism' and 'nationalism' in the eighteenth century and nineteenth century European context, by pointing out that 'patriotism' in eighteenth century Europe did not necessarily mean exclusive commitments to a national group defined by ethno-cultural bonds. He argues that patriotism in eighteenth century Europe, especially 'Anglo-Irish patriotism', can be characterized as close to Enlightenment cosmopolitanism and needs to be distinguished from the cultural nationalism that became prominent in the nineteenth century. Following Leerssen's view, my reading of *Patronage* and *The Absentee* in what follows takes account of such resonance of the usage of the term 'patriotism'. See Leerssen, *Remembrance and imagination* (Cork, 1996), pp 8–32. See also Esther Wohlgemut, 'Maria Edgeworth and the question of national identity', *Studies in English Literature* 39 (1999), 645–58.

notion of 'legitimacy' as well as the notion of 'patronage', which it features as its title. The protagonist Mr Percy experiences a challenge to his legitimacy as the owner of his family estates, Percy Hall. The question of his and his family's legitimacy as patriots or guardians of the British nation is part of this theme. The novel opens with the shipwreck of a Dutch commercial vessel, which signifies potential financial loss and dislocation. The scene foregrounds the Dutch merchant passengers' concern about their merchandise and M. de Tourville's loss of diplomatic dispatches. This shipwreck contributes to the Percys' 'shipwreck' later in the novel. During the fire caused by a careless Dutch carpenter from the shipwreck, Mr Percy's deed for the Percy estates goes missing, and this incident enables his cousin Sir Robert Percy to deprive him of the estates. 'Shipwreck' was a haunting notion to the imagination of Edgeworth's contemporary readers, who witnessed the expansion of European countries' colonialism and the Napoleonic wars. Nautical operations were indispensable to these phenomena. It is notable, for instance, in the enduring popularity of the poem 'Shipwreck' (1762) by William Falconer (1732–1769) throughout the nineteenth century.[5] In *Patronage* 'shipwreck' is employed as a test of the Percys to see whether they are legitimate landowners and patriots.

Mr Percy is a benevolent landlord and man of letters with 'independence of mind'. He embodies the qualities desired in a country gentleman in *Essays on Professional Education* (1809), which was co-authored by Edgeworth and her father.[6] In *Advertisement to Professional Education* the Edgeworths widen the conventional definition of 'profession', which was confined to clergy, lawyers, physicians, and soldiers, to include 'Gentlemen', 'Statesmen', and 'Princes'. Their justification for this redefinition reads, '[I]n fact, Gentlemen, Statesmen, and Princes, exercise functions of the highest consequence in the state: and no word seems more proper to designate their occupations than the term Profession.' The Edgeworths' aim here seems to enhance the production and maintenance of the guardians of Britain who would 'function' for the interest of the state and their fellow countrymen. Within this framework, the country gentlemen who were considered as the leisured class are expected to manage their estates with professionalism so that they can contribute to the prosperity of Britain more responsibly.[7] Mr Percy's conscientious landlordship, backed by his rich legal knowledge, satisfies such criteria for the country gentleman as a professional.

Mr Percy's affinity for professionalism is mirrored in the education of his sons. They distinguish themselves by their self-exertion in their professions. Godfrey, the eldest son and heir of Percy Hall, serves a military campaign in the West Indies, defending the interest of the British Empire. This epitomizes Edgeworth's

5 William Falconer, *Shipwreck* (London, 1762). The poem was inspired by Falconer's own experience of a shipwreck off the Greek coast while he was serving on a merchant vessel. 6 Richard Lovell and Maria Edgeworth, *Essays on professional education* (London, 1809). Hereafter referred to as *Professional education*. 7 'Professionalism' is referred to as an attitude and practice in accordance with norms required for professional careers such as the mastery of relevant knowledge and/or skills, exertion, and discipline.

proposal in *Professional Education* that the heir of the landed family should experience a military service in times of war in order to share patriotic duties and learn about the world.[8] Godfrey's 'zeal for the interests of the service' is more than the educational treatise expects.[9] He wishes to pursue it as a long-term profession and almost regrets his hereditary right. Alfred, the second son, is a barrister and is shown to protect the interest of the British Empire by successfully representing the East India Company when the company had 'one of the greatest causes ever brought before our courts of law, relative to the demand of some native bankers in Hindostan against the Company.'[10] Alfred also rescues his father from a charge brought by Sir Robert. Having ruined his ancestral estates by degeneracy, Sir Robert exploits Mr Percy's loss of deed and takes Percy Hall into his possession. Sir Robert repeats his mismanagement and, with the assistance of a malicious solicitor, brings a lawsuit against Mr Percy in order to improve his situation. Alfred's achievement in having Mr Percy's landownership restored can, therefore, be interpreted not only as family affairs but also as the maintenance of order in the English landed system. The youngest son Erasmus is a physician struggling to build up his professional career despite partisan rivalry among his colleagues and tough working conditions. His professional pride is grounded on his belief that his medical career would be for 'the good of mankind.'[11]

In these ways, the Percy brothers' professional life is characterized by patriotic ends. Their independence of mind makes their professional commitments more disinterested than that of their colleagues.[12] They would defy patronage in order to be useful to their fellow countrymen. As Mr Percy's following remark indicates, patronage is defined as antithetical to patriotism in the text:

> I believe it [patronage] to be ruinous to my country … If the affairs of this nation were guided, and if her battles were fought by the corrupt, imbecile creatures of patronage, how would they be guided? – how fought? – Woe be to the country, that trusts to such rulers and such defenders! … – May such never be the fate of England! – And that it never may, let every honest independent Englishman set his face, his hand, his heart against this base, this ruinous system![13]

The Percy brothers mark a strong contrast with other characters in the same professions who would pursue self-interest through patronage and cause harm to the interests of the state and their fellow countrymen. Moreover, the Percy brothers' professionalism is employed with benevolence, a key notion of patriotism. Their benevolent professionalism transcends the boundaries of national groups. This is influenced by their father's belief. When Godfrey joins the Army, Mr Percy warns him against 'party-spirit' and national chauvinism.[14] Erasmus'

---

8 *Professional education*, pp 263–4. 9 *Works*, vi: *Patronage* (vols i & ii), Conor Carville and Marilyn Butler (1999), p. 55. 10 Ibid., p. 229. 11 Ibid., p. 65. 12 See also McCormack, 'Tedium', p. 93. 13 *Works*, VI, pp 108–9. 14 Ibid., p. 56.

compassionate care of the Irishman O'Brien, against his potential patron's instruction, would be a good example for these dimensions of the Percy brothers' professionalism. It also brings Ireland into the novel's agenda for the conceptualisation of patriotism. Edgeworth seems to designate such benevolent professionalism as the central component of her ideal patriotism.

There is another level where Edgeworth's ideal patriotism is entwined with professionalism. The novel has an ambitious linguistic theme drawing on seventeenth-century linguistics and cryptography[15] with reference to John Wilkins (1614–1672).[16] The theme is elaborate when coded Tourville papers fall into the hands of the Falconers and prime minister Lord Oldborough. The papers hold information on the treachery against Lord Oldborough and have immediate importance to British politics. The Falconers and Lord Oldborough attempt to decode them, but it is only Mr Percy who can complete the decoding.[17] By way of decoding, Mr Percy prevents the governmental crisis; the whole affair leads Lord Oldborough, partly corrupted by patronage, to retire from his political career. The novel thus features decoding as a means to protect national interests, like seventeenth-century linguistic publications, which were trying to meet the need for cryptography felt during the Civil War, and Richard Lovell Edgeworth's papers on the 'tellograph', which were inspired by Wilkins' works.[18] Accomplished decoding skills were equated with multilingualism in seventeenth century cryptography. In his book on cryptography, *Cryptomenysis Patefacta* (1685), John Falconer writes, '[I]f you once understand the Rules for Decyphering, in one Language, you may really, and without any Reservation, in a few hours, understand as much of any Language, as is needful to reduce it out of Cypher.'[19] Situated in this context, the implication of the plot would be that Mr Percy has real multilingualism.[20]

---

15 My reference to 'cryptography' covers 'cryptography' and 'cryptology' in modern usage. See David E. Newton's definition of the terms in his *Encyclopedia of cryptology* (Santa Barbara, 1997). 16 For Wilkins' life and work, see Vivian Salmon, *The study of language in seventeenth-century England* (Amsterdam, 1979). 17 My reference to 'decoding' covers what Edgeworth means by 'deciphering', since '[t]here is no sharp theoretical dividing line between codes and ciphers', according to David Kahn's *The codebreakers: the story of secret writing*, rev. ed. (New York, 1996), p. xvi. 18 John Wilkins, *Mercury; or, The secret and swift messenger* (London, 1641); *An essay towards a real character, and a philosophical language* (London, 1668); Richard Lovell Edgeworth, 'An essay on the art of conveying secret and swift intelligence', in *Transactions of the Royal Irish Academy* 6 (1797), 95–139; *A letter to the right hon. the earl of Charlemont, on the tellograph, and on the defence of Ireland* (Dublin, 1797). See also Salmon, *The works of Francis Lodwick: a study of his writings in the intellectual context of the seventeenth century* (London, 1972), p. 64. 19 John Falconer, *Cryptomenysis patefacta: or the art of secret information disclosed without a key* (London, 1685), quoted in Salmon, *Lodwick*, p. 65. The latest editors of *Patronage*, Butler and Carville, have identified the author as a potential model for the Falconers in the novel (*Works*, vi, 286). The historical Falconer's biographical details are hardly discovered, but, according to Kahn, he 'was a distant relative of the Scottish philosopher David Hume, was reportedly entrusted with the private cipher of the future King James II, and died in France while following James into temporary exile there' (p. 155). 20 'Multilingualism' is referred to in this essay as linguistic sensitivity and/or competence in more than one language and/or dialect. See John Edwards, *Multilingualism* (London, 1994), pp 33, 55–88; Suzanne Romaine, *Language in society: an introduction to sociolinguistics* (2nd ed. Oxford, 2000), p. 33; Romaine, *Bilingualism* (2nd ed. Oxford,

Meanwhile, the novel shows that Mr Percy's sons gain fluency or good understanding of dialects and/or modern languages relevant to their professions. For instance, Alfred writes, 'I begin to feel it difficult to write, speak, or think, in any but professional language. Tell my father, that I shall soon come to talking law Latin and law French.'[21] Edgeworth seems to regard such acquisition of the relevant professional dialect and foreign languages as an essential condition for the successful professional life. Alfred is eventually rewarded by professional success. Edgeworth's illustrations also seem to imply that professionalism could equip professionals with new dialects and languages relevant to their professions and therefore enable them to be multilingual.

From a twentieth century perspective, multilingualism is equated with multiculturalism.[22] The Edgeworths share such a view, as *Professional Education* reveals: 'Modern languages are absolutely necessary to a statesman, not only as the keys of books, but of *minds*' (my italics).[23] This extract can be read as a call for multiculturalism that appreciates foreign value systems and viewpoints through competent multilingualism. Multilingual/multicultural stances are addressed here for the benefit of direct interactions with people from different cultural backgrounds ('the keys of minds') rather than the benefit of reading experience ('the keys of books'). Some French expressions in *Patronage* are untranslated because they are said to be 'untranslatable'; universalism is denied, and cultural differences underlying specific languages are appreciated.[24] Since multilingualism and multiculturalism are regarded as two sides of the same coin, multilingual speakers could overcome language barriers and appreciate different language cultures and thus foreign values better. They could have an integral intercultural communication without resorting to a universalist viewpoint. Edgeworth seems to have conceived of such people with multicultural perspectives, benevolence, and professionalism as ideal patriots in order to negotiate with universalist cosmopolitanism and differential nationalism. Endowed with these qualities, the Percys are represented as true patriots who could connect with foreign people as well as their fellow countrymen from different social groups.

Edgeworth's affinity for professionalism is sustained until the end of the novel. Alongside Mr Percy's professional landlordship, the succeeding generation of the Percy family are oriented towards professionalism. The male members are successful professionals, and the female members are married to promising professional men. Apart from Godfrey, the young Percys have found legitimate partners, giving a prosperous outlook. Their counter-examples have attempted to abuse patronage or hereditary rights and are punished in the end of the novel. It is curious that Edgeworth chose not to introduce Godfrey's

1995), pp 11–12. **21** *Works*, vi, p. 193. **22** Edwards, p. 22. **23** *Professional education*, p. 388. **24** For example, the authorial voice refers to 'that undefinable, untranslatable French love of *succès de société*'. Carville and Butler (ed.), *Works*, vii: *Patronage* (vols iii & iv), (1999), p. 52. For the definition of 'authorial voice', see Susan Sniader Lanser's *Fictions of authority: women writers and narrative voice* (Ithaca, 1992), pp 15–18, 22.

future wife. One might regard this as a signal of a sterile future for Percy Hall and Edgeworth's departure from the landed system. The restoration of the organic community around Percy Hall in the end of the novel makes such a reading difficult. Rather, we may conclude that Edgeworth's hope for the future of Britain is invested in the alliance of professional meritocracy with benevolent landlords.

Edgeworth was well aware that professions would bring social mobility. The social climate under which *Patronage* was written saw successful professionals such as Nelson, whom the authorial voice in the text refers to as 'our naval hero', awarded with peerages for their achievements. The publication date of Robert Southey's *Life of Nelson* (1813), which appreciated the professional dimension of Nelson's life 'seriously', was close to that of *Patronage*.[25] Such awareness of Edgeworth is registered in Mr Percy's concern about his daughters:

> A man who has received a liberal education may maintain himself with honor by the exertion of his abilities in respectable professions, and in a variety of employments, which are allowed to be gentlemanlike … but a woman, by the caprice, the cruelty of custom, is degraded by the very industry which should obtain respect, and, if unmarried, she loses the prospect of being suitably established in life.[26]

We should note that the membership of professional meritocracy was not open to all men, since it required a certain level of financial support during the apprenticeship and early career, as Edgeworth illustrates in Buckhurst Falconer's episode. Buckhurst wishes to go into the Army but is forced to join the clergy since his father 'cannot afford to purchase [him] a commission, and to maintain [him] in the army.'[27] Edgeworth's redefinition of 'profession' and illustrations of professional life therefore do not necessarily subvert the politics of the class system based on primogeniture.

This quotation is also important in the sense that it draws attention to gender issues. It indicates that women are excluded from attaining social mobility through a professional life. It emerges that women of Edgeworth's period would have had difficulty in acquiring multilingualism because professional education/training was denied to them. *Patronage* suggests discreet literary education as an alternative means for women to fill this gap, which is reminiscent of the prescription for women's education in *Letters for Literary Ladies* (1795). The suggestion appears to encourage women to be sensitive to dialects rather than competent in foreign languages except for French, which was often regarded as acceptable as an accomplishment of genteel ladies.

This alternative kind of multilingualism is observable in the Percy women. In her dialogue with Lady Jane Granville, Mrs Percy shows her sensitivity to

25 Brian Southam, *Jane Austen and the navy* (London, 2000), p. 227. 26 *Works*, vi, p. 107. 27 Ibid., p. 32.

social dialects and unwillingness to conform to the dialect of fashionable society and the value system underlying it:

> 'But,' said Mrs Percy, 'allow me to ask, what you mean by happily married?'
> 'What do I mean? Just what you mean ... what every body means at the bottom of their hearts – in the first place, married to men who have some fortune.'
> 'What does your Ladyship mean by some fortune?'
> 'Why ... you have such a strange way of not understanding. – We who live in the world must speak as the world speaks ...'[28]

Edgeworth has represented linguistic tension between the English language, the French language, and the Dutch language in the dramatic scene of shipwreck earlier in the novel. In that scene, the English characters' encounter with the French diplomat M. de Tourville is initially registered in terms of language. The Frenchman's first appearance is made through his voice: 'But just as he [Mr Percy] gave the order for his boatmen to push off, a French voice called out – "Monsieur! – Monsieur l'Anglois! – one moment."'[29] In the depiction, linguistic rather than visual or other information is made to represent the foreign. The dialogue between Mrs Percy and Lady Jane above signals linguistic tension even within the English language. The comical effect of the dialogue lies in some sort of language barrier between the English speakers. Lady Jane presupposes the universality and prestige of the dialect used by what she calls 'the world' and expects Mrs Percy to adopt this as standard English. Mrs Percy does not allow this social dialect and the values underlying it to be universal. By drawing a language boundary, she seems to attempt to keep the Percys' value system nonconformist. It is significant in the additional sense that the act is done in front of her daughter Caroline as an example to be followed. The role of the mother in women's education is viewed as crucial in *Patronage*.[30]

This kind of alternative multilingualism found in exemplary women characters is seen to complement their marital partners' more extensive multilingualism with patriotic ends, as in the case of Caroline and Count Altenberg. Caroline's inheritance of sound linguistic sensitivity from her mother is enriched by literary cultivation. One of the moments when she and Count Altenberg perceive each other as her/his alter ego is when they share sentiments evoked by the lines about 'native land' from Scott's *The Lay of the Last Minstrel* (1805). It seems debatable whether Edgeworth believed in a prescription circumscribing women's roles since she was a successful woman writer with formidable multilingualism. One might ask where Edgeworth locates women, especially herself, in such a configuration of patriotism which revolves around the male-oriented class of professional meritocracy. This question will be interro-

---

28 Ibid., p. 125. 29 Ibid., p. 9. 30 See also Robert Tracy, *The unappeasable host: studies in Irish identities* (Dublin, 1998), p. 32.

gated in the end of this essay. Despite these limitations, the system of professional meritocracy still brings a certain degree of social mobility into Edgeworth's
ideal of patriotism. We are now beginning to question whether such a vision is
born out by *The Absentee*.

The Absentee operates around the notion of 'legitimacy' at some levels like
Patronage, but with different emphasis. The novel's opening portrays the uncomfortable position of the Clonbronies, an 'Anglo-Irish' absentee family, in the
fashionable society of London and invites the readers to overhear the gossip of
exclusive English socialites. By displaying a scene of Lady Clonbrony's lavish
but ill-received gala and touching on Lord Clonbrony's financial 'embarrass-
ments', Edgeworth points to the harms of their absenteeism, which would
require further investigation, from the outset. The legitimacy of the Clonbronies'
right to their landed estates in Ireland is thus questioned, but not so severely as
Mr Percy's landownership. The Clonbronies are never challenged through legal
procedures like Mr Percy. Given that Edgeworth dispossesses Mr Percy of his
estates and puts him into the prison despite his exemplary landlordship, this
seems to be a much softer approach. *The Absentee* instead concentrates on examining the potential of their son Colambre as the heir of the Irish estates and the
legitimacy of Grace Nugent, his future wife from England. Such a diversion
from the legitimacy of the Clonbronies' landownership would have been natural to Edgeworth, who belonged to the Ascendancy, since the 'Anglo-Irish'
landlords' landownership in Ireland was highly controversial.[31]

The notion of 'shipwreck' is hinted in *The Absentee*, as well, in terms of the
Clonbronies' mislocation in the London society and their financial crisis resulting from the mislocation.[32] The Clonbronies' 'shipwreck' justifies their return
to Ireland, without having the fundamental legitimacy of their landownership
investigated. While 'shipwreck' is used to test the Percys' legitimacy in *Patronage*,
it is employed in *The Absentee* primarily to support the Clonbronies' legitimacy.
The ironical gap between Edgeworth's handling of the Percys and the
Clonbronies may have been too large to be kept together within a single text.

So far we have observed that there is a gap between *The Absentee* and
Patronage in terms of narrative strategies despite the deducible continuity
between the two novels in terms of themes and contexts. One may well doubt
whether Edgeworth's prescription of ideal patriotism in *The Absentee* is consistent with that in *Patronage*. Colambre's eligibility as the heir of the Clonbrony
estates is explored in terms of patriotism in the novel, since Edgeworth represents preferred landlordship as residential commitments to improve the life of
the local people in the estates, especially, their socio-economic life. His English
education concluded at Cambridge provides him with 'the means of becoming
all that a British nobleman ought to be'.[33] Despite such 'British' orientation,
Colambre is 'attached' to his 'native country' Ireland by 'a sense of duty and patri-

31 McCormack, Introduction, *The Absentee* (Oxford, 1988), p. xvii. 32 See also McCormack,
'Tedium', p. 97. 33 *Works*, v, p. 20.

otism' and decides to visit the country.³⁴ His 'patriotism' is not represented as purely sentimental. Colambre perceives Ireland in economic terms as well as sentimental terms: 'I desire to become acquainted with it [Ireland] – because it is the country in which my father's property lies, and from which we draw our subsistence.'³⁵ Colambre's appreciation of Ireland as a place supporting the family's economic life and his attempt to understand its socio-economic structure are promising starts for him to become a benevolent landlord and patriot. Socio-economic ties between citizens rather than ethno-cultural ties, would have been an important basis for patriotism, according to Leerssen. Could we then find in Colambre such patriotism intertwined with multilingualism and professionalism as we found in the Percys?

Edgeworth's appreciation of professionalism is indicated in *The Absentee*, too. In Ireland Colambre meets officers and lawyers and is impressed with their 'taste for science and literature'; the professionals are characterized with enlightened perspectives. In a Dublin coffee house, he makes friends with Sir James Brooke, an English officer. Sir James is familiar with Ireland through his profession. It is he who introduces Colambre to the social changes in post-Union Ireland and gives him a list of readings on the country. Intriguingly, Edgeworth arranges an English professional rather than an Irish character as Colambre's primary guide to Ireland. Sir James' analytical description of Ireland sounds authoritative and brings in a colonial surveyor's perspective.³⁶ His introduction of the country to Colambre might not be precisely accurate, but it serves to transform Ireland from a sentimental place as Colambre's 'native country' into a socio-economic entity to which the Clonbrony estates belongs, in Colambre's perspective. Colambre is thus made ready to travel around the country in order to become a legitimate landlord and patriot. Besides, Sir James' motto 'Deeds not words' becomes a principle for Colambre's future landlordship.

The Gaelic aristocrat Count O'Halloran is an even more remarkable example of the profession. When Colambre consults him about a potential military campaign, the Count explains the role of the profession in the agenda of patriotism, paraphrasing the relevant lines from *Professional Education*:

> The life of an officer is not now a life of parade, of coxcombical or of profligate idleness – but of active service, of continual hardship and danger ... A martial spirit is now essential to the liberty and the existence of our own country. In the present state of things, the military must be the most honourable profession, because the most useful. Every movement of an army is followed, wherever it goes, by the public hopes and fears. Every officer must now feel, besides this sense of collective importance, a belief that his only dependence must be on his own merit.³⁷

34 Ibid., pp 8–9. 35 Ibid., p. 59. 36 For the colonial representation of Ireland through map-making and the Edgeworths, see Claire Connolly, 'Gender, nation and Ireland in the early novels of Maria Edgeworth and Lady Morgan' (unpublished doctoral thesis, University of Wales, 1995), pp 28–9. 37 *Works*, v, p. 172.

It is striking that the retired officer of the 'Wild Geese' appears to refer to Britain as 'our own country'. His integration into the public administration of Britain with his professional assistance via his nephew seems to be placed as a model example of patriotism. The Count also emphasizes the meritocratic system of the profession. There are counter-examples of officers in the novel, but the Count's observation about the military profession prevails. It kindles Colambre's yearning for 'a commission in a regiment going to Spain'. Colambre considers the commitments in order to be away from Grace Nugent. He wished to marry her but found her unacceptable as his wife since she was said to be an illegitimate child.

The Count also underscores that officers are now expected to be enlightened as well as conscientious: '[T]o go into the army, with the hope of escaping from knowledge, letters, science, and morality … was never, even in times of peace, credible; but it is now absurd and base.'[38] He is a man of letters himself, and his domestic space crammed with categorized curiosities echoes the encyclopaedia and thus the Enlightenment. Proficient multilingualism is also noticeable in him. His dialogue with Colambre gives us a glimpse into his fluency in the French language: "Heathcock, you know, is as good as another man for all those purposes: his father is dead, and left him a large estate. Que voulez vous? as the French valet said to me on the occasion, c'est que monsieur est un homme de bien: il a des biens, à ce qu'on dit.' Lord Colambre could not help smiling.'[39] Colambre enjoys sharing extensive multilingualism with the Count. On one occasion, he speaks to the Count in Latin: 'Emptum aprum!' said Lord Colambre to the count, without danger of being understood by those whom it concerned.'[40]

Colambre's multilingualism would surely cover Hiberno-English. At first Paddy's Hiberno-English in the London coach yard sounded to him 'so strange' that he 'could not help laughing, partly at, and partly with, his countryman.'[41] However, by mingling with indigenous peasants in Ireland, Colambre gets familiar with the regional dialect. For instance, he responds in Hiberno-English to Larry's explanation of the Garraghtys' cheating middle-man operation: "Do I make your honour sensible?' 'You make me much more sensible than I ever was before,' said lord Colambre.'[42] Colambre's multilingualism should be distinguished from Lady Dashford's competence in mimicking 'fourteen different brogues' and her familiarity with the French language. One may consider her to be multilingual, but her linguistic competence is sarcastic and exclusively to satisfy her anglocentrism; it fails to connect her to a multicultural perspective, unlike Colambre's.

The multilingualism and respect for professionalism observable in Colambre would qualify him as a legitimate patriot as defined in *Patronage*. Once Grace Nugent's legitimacy is proved, Colambre withdraws the plan for a Spanish commission quickly. He shows no hesitation in doing so, and the enthusiasm he had

38 Ibid., p. 172.   39 Ibid., p. 171.   40 Ibid., p. 94.   41 Ibid., p. 11.   42 Ibid., p. 110. This speech is translated in a footnote as: 'Do I make you understand?'

for the military service appears quite shallow. The authorial voice narrates, 'Joy and love returned in full tide upon our hero's soul; all the military ideas, which but an hour before filled his imagination, were put to flight: Spain vanished, and green Ireland reappeared.'[43] Even though Colambre's rejoicing is understandable, it would be natural to question why the text removes the military service from Colambre's outlook so easily. The way the authorial voice puts it sounds almost as if it were slighting the profession. The novel is set in time of war, and, according to *Professional Education* and *Patronage*, under such circumstances Colambre would be required to share the military defence of the country, like Godfrey Percy. Some conflicts may be detected between Edgeworth's prescription of patriotism for the English heir Godfrey and the one for the 'Anglo-Irish' heir Colambre.

The prescription for Colambre would sit uncomfortably in larger intertextual links, as well. The historical context suggests that Colambre's potential commission would have been set as part of the British operation against Napoleon during the Peninsula War. While the contemporary readers of *The Absentee* see Colambre disengaged from the military commitments so easily, publications featuring the 'Anglo-Irish' hero Arthur Wellesley's professional contribution to Britain's major victories during the Peninsular War were in circulation and preparation.[44]

Some implications may be gathered from Edgeworth's authorisation of Colambre's legitimacy as a landlord and patriot by his English education and first-hand learning on Ireland without the experience of the career of professional meritocracy. In regard to Colambre's choice of Grace Nugent over the military commission, it has been argued that in the framework of *The Absentee* Grace Nugent's support is essential to the validity of Colambre's residential landlordship in Ireland.[45] It may be added that Colambre's choice signals Edgeworth's awareness that benevolent landlordship in Ireland is as urgent a patriotic commitment as wartime military contributions. Alternatively, Edgeworth might have found the allowance of social mobility through the system of professional meritocracy to be too subversive in the context of post-Union Ireland, and thus taken a more conservative line in *The Absentee*.[46] The regrets concerning the 'confusion of ranks' in post-Union Ireland are repeatedly implied in the novel, and the return of an enlightened landed class is sought for.

Finally, Edgeworth's vision of her own patriotic role as a woman writer from the Ascendancy needs to be considered. Although her configuration of ideal patriotism may appear male-oriented, she had some of its constituents herself. A career in writing was the only acceptable profession to women around the

---

43 Ibid., p. 175. 44 For example, William Thomas Beckford, *Letters from Portugal and Spain; comprising an account of the operations of the armies under their excellencies Sir Arthur Wellesley, and Sir John Moore, from the landing of the troops in Mondego Bay to the battle at Corunna* (London, 1809); Francis L. Clarke, *The life of the most noble Arthur marquis and earl of Wellington* (London, 1812?). 45 Heidi Thomson, Introduction, *The Absentee* (London, 1999), pp xxii–xxv. 46 See also Ó Gallchoir, 'Maria Edgeworth's revolutionary morality and the limits of realism', *Colby Quarterly* 36 (2000), 87–97, 96.

period. As a woman writer, she could be affiliated with a professional meritocracy of letters. Her multilingualism is proven at the level of her narrative voice[47]
as well as the biographical level. Moreover, she prescribed patriotism throughout her writing career as she has done in *The Absentee* and *Patronage*. Her creative illustrations of patriotism were precisely the products of her background
as a member of the Ascendancy, who would be uneasy over the transition from
Enlightenment cosmopolitanism to Romantic nationalism. Edgeworth's ideal
patriotism is therefore highly compatible with her own identity and carves out
a place for herself to take a significant role in prescribing and disseminating
ideal patriotism as a multilingual/multicultural writer crossing the border
between nations, between social classes, and between genders.

Yellow: *Beckett and the performance of ascendancy*[1]

SEÁN KENNEDY, NUI, GALWAY

Samuel Beckett's *More Pricks than Kicks* (1934) depicts the solipsistic rebellion
of Belacqua Shuah, an errant son of well-to-do Protestantism in Ireland in the
early 1930s, against the strictures of a bourgeois upbringing. However, the failure of that rebellion is signalled early on, for we are told outright in Ding-Dong
that Belacqua later 'toed the line and began to relish the world'.[2] And, lest we
miss the point, the narrator insists that he had always been aware of the likelihood of a 'break-down in the self-sufficiency which [Belacqua] never wea-
ried of arrogating to himself'.[3] Guided by the narrator's acuity, we are conscious
throughout that Belacqua is little more than an 'indolent bourgeois poltroon',[4]
and proceed on the assumption that our hero will eventually capitulate to the
demands of his middle-class upbringing. In this way, the various sins against
propriety that are recounted in *Pricks* are coloured by our awareness of Belacqua's
impending collapse. In what follows, I wish to examine the manner in which
Belacqua's capitulation is presented in the penultimate tale 'Yellow', and to suggest that it is Beckett's ironic treatment of the perceived need among Ireland's
Protestant communities for an ongoing performance of ascendancy in the Irish
Free State.

47 For instance, the authorial voice in *Patronage* offers a self-conscious multilingual performance mimicking 'fashionable style' *Works*, vi, p. 241.   1 The author would like to acknowledge the assistance of
the Irish Research Council for the Humanities and Social Sciences, under whose auspices the research
for this article was carried out as part of a proposed doctoral dissertation entitled 'Beckett and the
End of Ascendancy'.   2 Samuel Beckett, *More pricks than kicks* (London, 1993), p. 39.   3 Ibid., p. 40.
4 Ibid., p.174.

By the performance of ascendancy I mean to advert to the manner in which the Protestant minorities responded to the gradual whittling away of the social and economic privileges that had characterized their position under British rule, and to their determination to make the best of it despite the apparently inexorable rise of the Catholic middle classes in Irish life in the twentieth century. As Roy Foster has observed, 'a modest, unofficial form of 'Ascendancy' lingered on' among the minority communities,5 and, since economic privilege no longer served to differentiate them from their Catholic neighbours, they were compelled to rely on essentially social means of maintaining their separateness in Irish life.6 Increasingly, being Protestant meant being seen to do certain things, in certain ways, and at certain times, and it is this overdetermined performance of social difference that I have termed the performance of ascendancy.

A notable feature of minority accounts of the ends of Protestant ascendancy in Ireland is the recurrence of the performative metaphor, suggesting that many writers were aware of the emerging audience at which much of this behaviour was being directed. As their position was progressively undermined, both by developments within Ireland and a British politics of expediency, many Protestants seemed to have felt as if they were merely acting out the spectacle of their own expropriation, and, when the show was over, felt relieved that the performance could be suspended once and for all. In Lennox Robinson's *The Big House* (1926), St Leger Alcock responds to the burning of the Big House at Ballydonal in revealing terms:

> I've felt for so many years like a bad actor cast for a part far too heroic for my talents ... I haven't in any way been big enough for it, the audience has realised at last what I realised years ago, it's hissed me off the stage and sitting here in the wings wiping off my make-up I'm feeling devilishly relieved, almost happy.7

Alcock's relief stems from the fact that there is 'no need to pretend ever again',8 and he looks forward to a less contrived future abroad, in exile. By contrast, his daughter Kate Alcock only really comes alive in her role on the Ballydonal stage when she is aware of the interest of her audience, vowing to rebuild the house and create a more assertive role for an emboldened minority in independent Ireland.

In Elizabeth Bowen's *The Last September* (1929), Lois also feels that she is caught up in a kind of performance: 'She could not hope to explain that her youth seemed to her also rather theatrical and that she was only young in that way because people expected it. She had never refused a role'.9 There is nothing for Lois in Danielstown except 'clothes and what people say',10 and the unre-

5 Roy Foster, *Modern Ireland, 1600–1972* (London, 1988), p. 534.   6 Kurt Bowen, *Protestants in a Catholic state: Ireland's privileged minority* (Montreal, 1983), pp 27–8.   7 Lennox Robinson, *Selected plays*, ed. Christopher Murray (Gerrards Cross, 1982), p. 192.   8 Ibid.   9 Elizabeth Bowen, *The last September* (London, 1998), p. 32.   10 Ibid., p. 49.

ality of Big House life is contrasted with the real business that is shaping Ireland's future over the demesne walls. What is most thrilling about Lois's encounter with the figure in the shrubbery inside Danielstown is its momentary intensity, and Lois is not the only figure in the novel longing for some 'crude intrusion of the actual'.[11] In Lois's eyes, authentic experience is almost always happening elsewhere, and to other people, whereas life in Danielstown is depicted as an absurd enactment of Anglo-Irish propriety that lurches from moment to moment. The conflagration at the end of *The Last September* brings down the curtains on the last performance of a doomed Anglo-Irish cast(e).

Memoirs of the time also refer to the idea of performing ascendancy. Brian Inglis recalls that when the Catholic middle classes took over the running of the country the ascendancy 'continued to behave as they had always behaved – as if determined to give an example to the lascars who had come up from the bilges to take over the ship'.[12] On one level, of course, this was an assertion of strength, intended to stiffen the resolve of the former ascendancy. However, as Inglis's comment makes clear, it was a performance that was also directed, in part, at the Catholic majority. Protestants continued to behave in a manner that suited them, but they were always also looking over their shoulder to ensure that the correct impression was being made on their somewhat presumptuous Catholic equivalents. The performance of ascendancy was not just a way of behaving; it was a signifier of difference, the assertion of a boundary.

The cultural anthropologist Fredrick Barth terms this the performance of identity. It is never sufficient, he argues, to simply claim an ethnic or cultural identity; one must also perform that identity successfully, and have that performance accepted by significant others.[13] Elizabeth Bowen was perhaps the most articulate observer of this phenomenon among Ireland's minorities, and she also used the language of performance to describe its dual import succinctly:

> Ascendancy cannot be merely inherited or arrived at; neither birth nor careerist achievement quite accounts for it; only by character is it to be maintained. Continuous action and demonstration, morale and energy are required.[14]

For Bowen, ascendancy is an ongoing performance requiring energy and morale; it is maintained by character rather than being merely achieved at birth. And the performance is both action and demonstration; it consists both of doing, and of intimating to significant others – in this case the Catholic middle classes – that this is the way in which things ought to be done.

Bowen elaborated on the social idea that governed this performance in her essay 'The Big House', published in *The Bell* in 1940. It was an idea that had 'raised life above the exigencies of mere living to the plane of art, or at least style':

11 Ibid., p.44. 12 Brian Inglis, *West Briton* (London, 1962), p. 12. 13 Fredrik Barth (ed.), *Ethnic groups and boundaries* (Boston, 1969), p. 23. 14 Elizabeth Bowen, *The mulberry tree,* ed. Hermione Lee (London, 1986), p. 175.

What is fine about the social idea is that it means the subjugation of the personal to the impersonal. In the interests of good manners and good behaviour people learned to subdue their own feelings ... Society, or more simply, the getting-together of people – was meant to be at once a high pleasure and willing discipline, not just an occasion for self-display.[15]

To this extent, the performance of ascendancy entailed a 'sort of impersonality'.[16] This was not an occasion for regret, but rather a display of willing discipline, a sacrifice made in the interests of social propriety. Here, Bowen was searching for a new role for the Anglo-Irish in Ireland, and she contended that what the Anglo-Irish had to offer was 'grace'.[17] An Anglo-Irish sense of grace and good manners would act as a sort of cultural inoculation against what she termed the 'naïve, positive gracelessness' of the Irish Catholic.[18] After all, she asks, 'are not humane manners the crown of being human at all?'[19]

The performance of ascendancy was all about propriety, sacrificing oneself to the performance of a social idea that identified you as a member of the social elite. It gave social expression to an innate sense of superiority, since many Irish Protestants felt that they were the only cultured element in Irish society. In 1929, Page L. Dickinson described the Anglo-Irish as having 'produced all that is valuable in Irish civilisation of the last thousand years',[20] and it was this kind of assumption that impelled the performance. Dickinson described the Irish political landscape starkly in terms of 'class and education against ignorance and lack of thought',[21] and the Anglo-Irish felt obliged to behave in a manner consonant with their superior gifts. 'I pity people who do not care for Society', Bowen wrote, somewhat sniffishly, in *Seven Winters*, 'they are poorer for the oblation they do not make'.[22]

The Protestant business classes, of which William Beckett was a member, also performed ascendancy. And the most significant aspect of their experience in the late nineteenth and early twentieth centuries was the fact that they were shadowed, at every level of city society, by a Catholic equivalent. Throughout the late nineteenth century a new Catholic middle-class had been growing steadily and, by the 1890s, they already outweighed their Protestant counterparts in terms of numbers and rivalled them in wealth.[23] This had the effect of engendering a more integrated society on both sides of the religious divide, and Protestants of the commercial classes were far more likely to come into regular contact with their Catholic counterparts. However, greater proximity also increased the likelihood of conflict between the two groups,[24] which led to an uneasy truce between them. Arthur Clery, a self-professed Irish

15 Ibid., p. 27, p. 29. 16 Ibid., p.27. 17 Ibid., p.29. 18 Elizabeth Bowen, *Bowen's Court and seven winters* (London, 1984), p. 37. 19 Bowen, *The mulberry tree*, p. 29. 20 Page L. Dickinson, *The Dublin of yesterday* (London, 1929), pp 1–2. 21 Ibid., p. 18. 22 Elizabeth Bowen, *Seven winters*, p. 43. 23 Jack White, *Minority report: The anatomy of the southern Irish protestant* (Dublin, 1975), p. 58. 24 Ian d'Alton, 'Southern Irish unionism: a study of Cork unionists, 1884–1914', *Transactions of the Royal Historical Society* 23 (Jan. 1973), 79.

Catholic of the upper middle classes, described how the two communities coped with this situation:

> In the market-place, in business life, men of all religions mingle freely. They become firm friends and appreciate each other's good qualities. They lunch together; they drink together; and in one sense they forget the religious question. Yet it is really present sub-consciously all the time. All the friendliness is to a certain extent like the 'fraternisation' of soldiers in opposing trenches, the inarticulate protest of human nature against conditions that are too strong for it. A single shot, a blast on the bugle, a tap on the drum, and they rush to take their places in the opposing firing lines.[25]

A degree of tolerance was good for business, but it was not indicative of any significant rapprochement between the two communities. This need for tolerance did not preclude the Protestant middle classes from espousing unionist politics, but merely from its overt expression. Many of them felt that any aggressive act on their part would be fatal to their commercial prospects, but their reticence should not be taken as an index of their sentiment. Protestant businessmen knew they would have to accommodate their Catholic equivalents in the market place if they were to continue to compete successfully in business, and it was for this reason that they exhibited a greater capacity for compromise than their landed counterparts.[26] While middle-class Protestants could not withdraw entirely from contact with their Catholic counterparts, they did tend to distance themselves socially as much as possible, leading to a kind of social apartheid. Life for the two communities ran on separate tracks, and religious affiliation in Ireland was an important social determinant of behaviour.[27]

The main way in which bourgeois Irish Protestants responded to the greater encroachment of the Catholic middle classes was by moving out into the suburbs. From about 1890 onwards, coincidental with an acceleration in the rise of the new Catholic middle-class and the growth of the Irish Ireland movement, well-to-do Irish Protestants tended to withdraw from Dublin city into secluded suburban enclaves where contact with Catholics outside of business hours could be minimized. Mary Daly confirms that 'religion operated in combination with social preferences and a growing feeling of political isolation to drive many [Protestant] families into the suburbs'.[28] They were increasingly drawn to quiet areas of Co. Dublin like Rathgar and Rathmines, or to exclusive new suburbs like Foxrock: 'areas developed by Anglo-Ireland for Anglo-Ireland'.[29]

As well as this, social distance was maintained by one's choice of activities. The minorities' social life revolved around a small number of well-recognized

25 Arthur Clery, 'The religious angle in Ireland', *Studies* (Sept. 1915), 434. 26 Alvin Jackson, 'Unionist politics and protestant society in Edwardian Ireland', *Historical Journal* 33.4 (1990), 857. 27 White, *Minority report*, p. 6; Clery, 'Religious angle', p. 433. 28 Mary Daly, *Dublin, the deposed capital* (Cork, 1985), p. 151. 29 Brian Kennedy, 'South county Dubliners and the building of independent Ireland' (Foxrock: Foxrock Local History Club, Pamphlet 22), p. 3.

institutions in Dublin, and in this manner it was possible that a Protestant should spend almost all his time, when not at work, among his own kind.[30] Terence de Vere White has described the typical Protestant businessman in Dublin at this time as:

> a quiet living and industrious fellow … principally concerned with the material welfare of his family and the safeguarding of his livelihood. In 1927 he was still firmly entrenched in the banking, commercial, and legal life of Dublin. Perusal of a Dublin directory at the commercial section … suggests that no change had taken place in Irish life since 1914. The ex-unionist lived as formerly, kept up his club membership … did not try to identity himself with the country, and his wife, who had servants then, played a great deal of afternoon bridge. If some sent their sons to St Columba's or Portora, many preferred an English public school, not always one of the top ones.[31]

Among the remnants of the ascendancy in Ireland, a lingering sense of pre-eminence was being socially enacted.[32] In this manner, the modest form of ascendancy described by Foster continued in middle-class Protestant society, and a discreet sense of distance from the Catholic majority was maintained/performed. Kurt Bowen is right to say that the Church of Ireland's middle-class community retained their material advantages, British loyalties, and an intense commitment to Protestantism up until the 1930s.[33]

The Beckett family moved to Foxrock in 1902 as part of the greater withdrawal of the Protestant middle classes from Dublin city centre at the turn of century. In choosing Foxrock, the Becketts moved even further out from the city than was common at the time. Foxrock was in its infancy as a development in 1902, and attempts were still being made to develop it as a smart new residential area. A free site was given to the Church of Ireland to build a church there, and it soon developed a reputation for exclusivity even among Protestants themselves.[34] Page L. Dickinson, for one, found the Foxrock community to be 'too remote and self-satisfied to add much to the activities of a bigger life than their own'.[35] According to Anthony Cronin, it was a boast in Foxrock that one could pass one's day without speaking to any Catholic other than the railway employees.[36]

Like most of his class, Bill Beckett lived much of his time apart from the Catholic community.[37] During the week, he drove to town in his Dion Bouton, parked at the Royal Irish Automobile Club on Dawson Street, and walked the short distance to Clare Street.[38] He would often take lunch at the exclusive

30 Robert McDowell, *Crisis and decline: the fate of southern unionists* (Dublin, 1997), p. 34. 31 Terence de Vere White, 'Social life in Ireland, 1927–1937', in Francis MacManus (ed.) *The years of the great test, 1926–39* (Cork, 1967), pp 20–1. 32 Of course, the Protestant minorities had always performed ascendancy, but the social aspects of that performance acquired especial significance in the altered social and political climate in Ireland in the twentieth century. 33 Bowen, *Protestants in a Catholic state*, p. 31. 34 Daly, *Dublin, the deposed capital*, pp 200–1. 35 Dickinson, *The Dublin of yesterday*, p. 202. 36 Anthony Cronin, *The last modernist* (London, 1996), p. 9. 37 Ibid., p. 9. 38 Cornelius

Kildare Street Club, 'the holy of holies in the Dublin social register'.³⁹ At week-ends, Bill played golf at the Protestant golf clubs at Carrickmines or Foxrock.⁴⁰ He was aware that an orthodox Protestant bearing was 'a social and personal necessity',⁴¹ and his two sons, Samuel and Frank, would have been expected to follow suit. Growing up in Foxrock, Beckett was surrounded by members of his own religion and class in an enclave whose social composition minimized the necessity for contact with Ireland's Catholic majority, and paved the way for a suitably orthodox Protestant upbringing.

Writing to his friend Thomas MacGreevy from the family home in Foxrock in 1932, Beckett included, with his letter, a humorous fragment describing his isolated situation:

> The pleasures of our country life: Far from our debtors; no
> Dublin letters; Not seen by our betters.⁴²

These ironic lines are a succinct description of the social situation of the Protestant middle classes in Dublin in the twentieth century, a tacit acknowl-edgement of the social pressures being felt by Dublin's suburban Protestant com-munities. They indicate that Beckett was aware of the motives behind his family's choice of home, since he highlights the self-enforced isolation of his 'country life', placing a certain discreet distance between these families and their places of business. If the need for trade compelled a kind of enforced camaraderie from businessmen on both sides of the religious divide, one can imagine that it would have been a relief finally to be able to relax 'far from one's debtors' in the con-fines of a Protestant enclave. Beckett's lines also include a gentle swipe at the emerging Catholic middle classes that had arisen steadily in Dublin after 1890, insofar as Beckett ridicules their desire for upward mobility by referring to them as 'our betters'. To be respectable was the aspiration that C.S. Andrews felt was endemic to the Catholic middle classes in Ireland at this period,⁴³ and Beckett is acknowledging those aspirations, but also adverting to the bemused manner in which they were viewed by the Protestant middle classes. This would not have been lost on Thomas MacGreevy.

Beckett's upbringing in Foxrock, then, implicated him directly in the overdetermined performance of ascendancy that I have described. And there are reasons to suspect that the atmosphere in Cooldrinagh may have been espe-cially tense. May Beckett, in particular, was intent on recreating the lifestyle that she had experienced as a girl growing up. May was born to a wealthy family of Irish Protestants living in Cooldrinagh House in Leixlip, Co. Kildare.

Smith, *The history of the Royal Irish Automobile Club, 1901–91* (Dublin, 1994), p. 47. 39 Inglis, *West Briton*, p. 19. 40 James Knowlson, *Damned to fame: the life of Samuel Beckett* (London, 1996), p. 11. 41 Cronin, *The last modernist*, p. 19. 42 SB to TM, undated 1932. All references are to the MacGreevy correspondence in Trinity College, Dublin (TCDMS10402). Further references are given as SB to TM, date. 43 C.S. Andrews, *Dublin made me* (Dublin, 1979), p. 11.

In the 1870s, they were exceedingly well to do, and May would have grown up with little expectation of having to work. The daily regime at Cooldrinagh was intended as an impeccable performance of ascendancy that would do justice to her Big House upbringing, and May ran her house in accordance with a form of 'prescriptive gentility' that was closely analogous to Elizabeth Bowen's authoritarian social idea of willing discipline.[44] Cooldrinagh was certainly a place where one learned to subdue one's feelings in the interests of good behaviour, and Beckett later claimed that he and Frank were brought up like Quakers.[45] There was 'little individuality displayed inside Cooldrinagh', and May 'worked deliberately to appear as a model of restraint and decorum'.[46] She was all too aware that sacrifices had to be made in order to maintain the necessary social front.

Knowlson's depiction of life at Cooldrinagh is instructive:

> Everyday life at Cooldrinagh was regulated as much as it was in May Beckett's power to control it. It reflected *le grand style*. Everything had to be properly done as she attempted to live up to the standards of the big house in which she had been brought up, although with fewer staff.[47]

The key to May's behaviour is its overdetermined motive: her attempts to live up to the standards of the Big House in which she had been brought up, but with fewer staff. Downward mobility gave an added urgency to the need for impression management, but the lack of resources made the continuous process of action and demonstration more difficult to achieve. The entire housekeeping regime was linked to an ongoing performance of propriety that was intimately linked to May's prior social position in Leixlip; Frank and Sam, for their part, were expected to perform 'all the social amenities before guests'.[48]

Beckett found the entire business extremely difficult, and he complained to MacGreevy of the mood of 'nervous comfort' in Cooldrinagh.[49] The subjugation of the personal to the impersonal did not come easily to the young author, especially when the standards of behaviour at Cooldrinagh were so patently obsessive. 'People's feelings don't seem to matter', he complained to MacGreevy, 'one is nice ad lib to all and sundry with an equanimity that never deserts one'.[50] This overarching concern with propriety seemed hopelessly outdated in Beckett's eyes. He despaired of the 'rigidity of home conditions',[51] and looked forward to the prospect of 'unclenchedness' elsewhere.[52] But Beckett's own behaviour did little to ease the tension. If ascendancy in Cooldrinagh was maintained by the strength of May Beckett's character, it was resisted in equal measure by the tenacity of Beckett's own. His decision to leave his post at Trinity dismayed

44 Knowlson, *Damned to fame*, p. 106. 45 Ibid., p. 22. 46 Deirdre Bair, *Samuel Beckett* (London, 1980), p. 18, p. 22. 47 Knowlson, *Damned to fame*, p. 20. 48 Bair, *Samuel Beckett*, p. 26. 49 SB to TM, 30 August 1932. 50 SB to TM, 8 August 1934. 51 SB to TM, 21 November 1932. 52 SB to TM, 5 August 1938.

both his parents, and his ongoing refusal to find gainful employment defied their expectations and incited their anger.[53] Again and again his father urged him to start teaching again, not least because it would lighten the atmosphere at home, but Beckett refused.[54]

All this time, Beckett was keenly aware that he was a disgrace to the family. He expressed his difficulties to MacGreevy:

> My parents do their best to be patient but the situation becomes more untenable every day for us all … [T]hey cannot help feeling that I am some-how behaving very badly and failing to pull my weight and letting myself down and them also … And there is no use explaining myself, not even to father. Because everything I do and reject doing, say and reject saying is an implied rejection of their values, or indifference, which is more offensive than a rejection.[55]

Beckett's behaviour is an embarrassment to all concerned, and threatens to undermine all of May Beckett's frantic efforts at impression management. Certain ways of behaving served to invigorate the value system being enacted, while others threatened to bring the whole thing down around one's ears. By refusing to perform ascendancy in the manner expected of him, Beckett was let-ting the entire side down.

Beckett's impatience regarding the performance of ascendancy was a main source of the conflict that persisted in Cooldrinagh throughout the 1920s and 1930s, and it received an oblique literary treatment in *More Pricks than Kicks*. Belacqua's solipsistic rebellion and his consequent recourse to pure blank move-ment in the stories are motivated by a desire to escape from the strictures of the family home: 'Was it not from sitting still among his ideas, other people's ideas, that he had come away?'[56] Belacqua is acutely aware of being 'sinfully indolent' in the tales,[57] and his indolence is a sin in the sense of that term described by Elizabeth Bowen: 'sin was most felt by me … as any divagation from the social idea'.[58] In other words, if you did not behave in the manner prescribed by your social position you were letting the side down. As we saw earlier, proper com-portment was to be maintained by character, and required the expenditure of energy and morale. Bogged in indolence, Belacqua displays little of either. The narrator convicts him of 'gratuity of conduct',[59] which is precisely the kind of thing that would have earned him the opprobrium of Brian Inglis and Elizabeth Bowen.

In the penultimate story of the collection, 'Yellow', Belacqua begins to behave in a manner consonant with his ascendancy background. About to undergo an operation, Belacqua exhibits a sudden concern to do right by the memory of his late family – 'the grand old family Huguenot guts'.[60] Belacqua tries to conceal

---

53 Knowlson, *Damned to fame*, pp 120–43. 54 SB to TM, 21 November 1932. 55 Ibid. 56 Beckett, *More pricks than kicks*, p. 42. 57 Ibid., p. 39. 58 Elizabeth Bowen, *Seven winters*, p. 47. 59 Beckett, *More pricks than kicks*, p. 95. 60 Ibid., p. 172.

his true feelings in order to put on a brave face, opting to laugh at everything in the manner of Democritus.[61] As Bowen points out, the Anglo-Irish instinctively 'place' a person who makes a poor mouth,[62] and Belacqua is suddenly keen to avoid such an eventuality: 'Now the good face was all that concerned him'.[63] His preoccupation with his own internal life has dissipated; 'his whole concern was with other people': 'these outsiders, the family guts and so on and so forth, all these things had to be considered'.[64]

Belacqua embraces Bowen's social idea completely, subjugating the personal to the impersonal in the interests of good manners and good behaviour. We are told that 'at every crux of the enterprise, he sacrificed his sense of what was personal and proper to himself to the desirability of making a certain impression on other people'.[65] According to Elizabeth Bowen, the social idea is an 'oblation',[66] and Belacqua is aware of the offering that is required: 'He must efface himself altogether and do the little soldier'.[67] He knows that his 'fortitude would be generally commended'. He refuses to cry before the hospital staff because 'he would be disgraced and, by extension, his late family also'.[68] He chats amiably to the nurses and congratulates himself that he managed to 'create a very favourable impression' on them.[69] This is his final capitulation, forgetting about his solipsistic revolt in an attempt to do right by the memory of his ancestors. Gratuity of conduct has been replaced by the kind of studied reticence that Bowen describes, and his entire demeanour is contrived to achieve the impression desirable for a 'dirty low-down Low Church Protestant high-brow'.[70]

In 1937, in the now famous German letter to Axel Kaun, Beckett wrote that grammar and style had 'become as irrelevant as … the imperturbability of a true gentleman. A mask'.[71] In 'Yellow', Belacqua tries to perform exactly the kind of simulated imperturbability that Beckett decries to Kaun, and the simile was probably suggested to Beckett by the ongoing need for just such a display in the family home at Cooldrinagh. In *Pricks*, of course, Beckett writes as an 'ironist who criticizes' an earlier manifestation of himself in the person of Belacqua,[72] and the fact that Belacqua capitulates to the demands of the performance of ascendancy in 'Yellow' is a wry variation on Beckett's own failure to do so. While writing *Pricks*, Beckett complained to MacGreevy of the 'ridiculous old itch to grub up your guts for publication',[73] and the stories that emerged as a result of that itch were a fictionalized description of Beckett's own ongoing rebellion against 'the grand old family Huguenot guts'.[74]

61 Ibid., p. 177. 62 Elizabeth Bowen, *The mulberry tree*, p. 29. 63 Beckett, *More pricks than kicks*, p. 173. 64 Ibid., p. 173. 65 Ibid., p. 176. 66 Elizabeth Bowen, *Seven winters*, p. 47. 67 Beckett, *More pricks than kicks*, p. 176. 68 Ibid., p. 177. 69 Ibid., p. 179. 70 Ibid., p. 184. 71 Samuel Beckett, *Disjecta* (London, 1983), p.171. 72 Lawrence Harvey, *Samuel Beckett: poet and critic* (Princeton, 1970), p. 41. 73 SB to TM, 1 November 1933. 74 Beckett, *More prick than kicks*, p. 172.

Joyce and postcolonial literature: creating an inclusive Irish identity

THOMAS F. HALLORAN, MIC, UL

History is what gets written down in books by life's winners and *tradition* is what gets remembered and told among the common people.[1]

HISTORY AND THE VICTOR

The postcolonial theoretical approach to literature involves more connections with history than most literary and cultural theoretical methodologies.[2] History, in a traditional Western academic sense, is reduced to linear time-line testimony, aimed at providing an unambiguous narrative, a reductive representation of the past through the historians' reconstruction. However, history in postcolonial theory is too large to be all-inclusive and too random to be conformed to a scientifically recorded set of events, constructed upon the idea of progress. In fact, the very idea of a universal truism such as 'progress' is suspect within the postcolonial paradigm. Western philosophy assumes that the nation state is the successful fulfilment of a universal aspiration, the national developmental process of nationhood. By this method there is only one strand of history that is analysed, that being the path to nation-statehood.[3] However, postcolonial critics have questioned this universalism because this notion of history not only is a Western presentation but more importantly a Eurocentric force that proselytizes the others' perspective into accepting the Western notion of history. This destabilizing imperative has prompted critics of postcolonial theory to question the relevance of any theory that cannot answer to such finite problems as: 'when is a postcolonial period ever set to begin or end?'[4] As a theoretically driven discourse, postcolonial theory is constantly critiquing its own givens and assumptions. However, this very question illustrates the possibility of an alternative non-linear narrative that could be realized to incorporate multifaceted representations of the past.

History is a principal tool of academic learning and a fundamental source of knowledge, but historical study must be interrogated in terms of its assumptions if it is to do justice to the complexity of perspectives that require to be taken into account. The ideal tactic proffered for creating authority and legitimising power is history, as by few other means can claims be made in Western thinking than through the power of verified historical fact. History therefore

1 Declan Kiberd, *Inventing Ireland* (London, 1996), p. 15. 2 David Lloyd, *Ireland after history* (Cork, 1999). 3 Ibid., p. 24. 4 Anne McClintock, 'Angel of progress: pitfalls of the term "post-colonialism"' *Social Text* 31/32, p. 5.

becomes the breeding ground of nationalism through 'monoculturalism, ancestry, purity of race and lineage.'[5] These ideological constructs of the old European world served as justification for the colonial project and the domination of the other. The nation with colonial aspirations needs to legitimize its claims through history, and this promotes the interpretative histories that only seek to benefit one nation's cause.[6] To return to the opening quote from Kiberd, however, there is another area through which identity can be enunciated, and that is the realm of literature and tradition. The issue arises, then as to whether there is any superior approach to the question of nationality and identity for the former colonies than through the institution of literature? Edward Said notes:

> The main battle in imperialism is over land, of course; but when it came to who owned the land, who had the right to settle and work on it, who kept it going, who won it back, and who now plans its future – these issues were reflected, contested and even for a time decided in narrative.[7]

Said's quote promotes literature as one of the prime methods for the post-colonial nation to achieve autonomy of identity: to write in response to the colonizer or to ignore the colonizer and return to the pre-colonial, are the postcolonial nation's only options. However, to ignore history and specifically the history of colonialization, not only denies reality, it also denies modernization in a vain and stubborn refusal to acknowledge the altering consciousness of the national populace. The postcolonial nation has little to gain by ignoring the past and much to lose by ignoring what is a shared national experience of colonization. For the postcolonial writer, realizing this situation offers an opportunity to give voice to the previously unrepresented people to 'hear' their own perspective.

The problem with offering a voice to the newly liberated is that the voice is also speaking to Europe and as a result is forced to speak in the colonizer's language. The damage that the colonizer's language has left on a national pride, psychology and development is a seminal factor in the psyche of all former colonies, and the postcolonial writer in the colonizer's language often suffers through this situation, neither a part of the colonizing process, nor a traditional version of the national artist. For this reason the postcolonial writer in English is often the first to take up the role as a hybrid.

ENGLAND'S ENGLISH

Prior to postcolonial studies, writing in English from the colonies of the former Empire was located at the periphery of English literature and culture. Literature in English from abroad was meant to fit into the canon if it emulated the tech-

5 Bill Ashcroft, *The empire writes back: theory and practice in post-colonial literatures* (London, 1989), p. 154.   6 Edward W. Said, *Culture & imperialism* (London, 1994), p. 16.   7 Ibid., p. xiii.

nical qualities of its English contemporaries and could be valued by the standards of traditional literary criticism. While these categorizations not only undermine the artistic integrity of postcolonial writing, they also ignore the multi-cultural possibilities that could be incorporated into the tradition of prose fiction. Postcolonial writers deal with the obstacle of using the English language because the 'main feature of imperial oppression is control of language.' The control of language leads to the standard version of metropolitan England's English being installed in the educational system of the colonial nation, this development ensconces standard English in the postcolonial nation as the ideal instrument of communication and self-definition. Furthermore, this develops a hierarchy of class that is arranged in relation to the idealized centre, which of course is England.

This problematic aspect of metropolitan English language develops substantially when applied to literature, as the standard version of English, as a normative value, begins to effect the position in which national literatures are evaluated. What is more, Ashcroft details the problem with standardizing the English version of English language:

> Through the literary canon, the body of British texts that all too frequently still acts as the touchstone of taste and value and through Received Standard English, which asserts the English of South-East England as a universal norm.[8]

The postcolonial writer must first advocate a reworking of literature in English to provide a voice for their nation, to first make the English language their own, and then to make English their nation's language, and so to create a literature that would be independently specific to their nation, and not merely an offshoot of, or subject to, English traditions and standards while still being a part of the English language.

RE-VISIONING 'ENGLISH' LITERATURE

The creation of postcolonial studies is designed to re-vision that which has been made the non-western world of 'otherness' and exoticism. The creation of 'other', has justified damaging rationalizations for international affairs. Postcolonial literature is in the re-telling of history from the opposing perspective, giving readers the opportunity to find a balance between the multiple perspectives. Through this method, not only is history reclaimed by the post-colonial nation, but also national consciousnesses are envisioned and the institution of English literature is expanded into a medium of transformative communication rather than viewed as merely one nation's literature.

Furthermore, Denis Walder explains, the aim 'of postcolonial theory, whatever its origins, is to aid, not hinder critical understanding of a proliferating area

8 Ashcroft, *Empire*, p. 7.

of literary creativity, as well as the reinterpretation of text from a newly aware position.'⁹ Postcolonial theory, like postcolonial literature, is founded on the goal of freeing literature in English from a restrictive notion of English tradition and rules, thus making the language something of a shared medium between nations while never belonging exclusively to any one nation specifically. Walder's quote also mentions the questions of reinterpretation. With the newfound postcolonial novels adding to the discussion of the traditional cannon, the traditionally canonized novel must be re-evaluated in respect to the postcolonial novel.

Creative growth from the postcolonial national writer is not only in the form of re-vision, but also in a vision itself, as in, the ability to see the future of the nation in terms previously unimagined. What a writer like W.B. Yeats or Joyce can do is to ignore the colonial occupation, the actual colonial setting, and thereby settle in the imagination that dreams of a new setting:

> Art in this context might be seen as man's constant effort to create for himself a different order of reality from that which is given to him: against the ability to imagine things as they are, it counterpoises the capacity to imagine things as they might be.¹⁰

Kiberd focuses on the question of re-imagining Ireland from a postcolonial theoretical perspective, in a manner similar to Joyce, who imagines an Ireland unconnected to an exclusive vision of the past, as is the case when Stephen Dedalus attempts to fly by the nets of nationality, language, and religion.¹¹

'AN ÉIRINNEACH NÓ SASSANACH TÚ?'

Here ensues the apparent difficulty of the Irish situation in terms of the canon of English literature. Unlike African and Asian colonial writers who were at the periphery of the English canon of literature, the colonial United Kingdom claimed Irish born and Irish specific writers as their own. Even fellow Caucasians and English descendants like the American, Canadian, Australian and New Zealand born or based writers wrote as specific to their location and nation or colonial state. However, the Irish writers, although subjects of the UK, no different in name than other colonial subjects further afield, were consistently anthologized as English writers. James Joyce famously derided what might have been intended as a compliment from the English perspective, his inclusion into their cannon:

> And in spite of everything Ireland remains the brain of the United Kingdom. The English, judiciously practical and ponderous, furnish the over-stuffed

---

9 Dennis Walder, *Post-colonial literatures in English: history, language, theory* (Oxford, 1998), p. 79. 10 Kiberd, *Inventing Ireland*, p. 118. 11 James Joyce, *Portrait of the artist as a young man* (New York, 1993), p. 220.

stomach of humanity with a perfect gadget-the water closet. The Irish condemned to express themselves in a language not their own, have stamped on
it the mark of their own genius and compete for glory with the civilised
nations. This is then called English literature.[12]

Joyce's sarcastic comments highlight Ireland's unwillingness to be made English,
or to be exploited like other colonial nations. Adding to Joyce's frustration is
the inclusion of Ireland's identity with England, subverting the literature that
seeks to liberate Irish identity.

By adding the language question into this statement, Joyce not only links
the Irish experience with that of the other colonials, but further insults the
English canon of which he does not wish to be a part. The language question
is exploited here to draw attention to the differences between national identities. Yet despite the refusal to be English by law, definition, style or subject even
contemporary scholarship continues to link the separate and independent
nations. Perhaps then, it is best to briefly consider the role of Ireland as a critical text of postcolonial theory.

IRISH POSTCOLONIALISM

The Empire Writes Back was the seminal students' guide to postcolonial theory;
however, the study insensitively portrayed the Irish nation's understanding of
its own history as involving a somewhat lacklustre membership of the United
Kingdom. From the opening chapter of the study's discussion of models of postcolonialism, it is suggested that Ireland's 'subsequent complicity in the British
imperial enterprise makes it difficult for colonized peoples outside Britain to
accept their [Irish] identity as post-colonial.'[13] There is no objection to be made
that the Irish colonial experience was different compared to their African and
Asian counterparts, or that the Irish at times benefited as a result of their closer
colonial ties with England than those of other colonial states, but to overlook
the Irish resentment at, and challenge to, colonization is to disregard a significant aspect of Irish history and national development. By the nature of the quote
and the absence of any reference to Irish writers outside of Yeats (who is essentially viewed as an English writer by the study), the problem of Ireland's position with respect to postcolonial legitimacy begins.

Perhaps because of the length of the English stay in Ireland, the geographic
and racial proximity, and some similarities in culture (despite constant polariza-
tion based on binary oppositional definition of each other), the Irish are often
regarded as English in the international community. In spite of this, the identity
debate that exists within the culture of the two islands has often dominated their
relationship. Irish identity, particularly before and just after independence was

12 Richard Ellmann, *James Joyce* (New York & London, 1959), p. 226.   13 Ashcroft, *Empire*, p. 33.

largely based on what was not English or what was Gaelic. This line of thinking not only seems to comply with Franz Fanon's ideas of postcolonial development, but also strengthens the legitimacy of Irish postcolonial claims. Essentially Ireland has developed in parallel with England, but has also developed differently, due to historical circumstances, and the two nations cannot be joined by the colonial history to the extent that an Irish writer could represent England.

Ireland fits into the postcolonial concept if for no other reason than because its writers, say so. The Irish national consciousness has long seen itself as oppressed by its English colonizer and despite differences between the types of oppression in other colonies, Ireland will always maintain a history that includes the story of British oppression. Ireland's politics, from the Act of Union through de Valera's economic war, has centred around the Irish-English relationship that had until 1922 been voiced in Westminster. Even Irish independence has failed to distance the nation's identity questions. The nationalist movement that led to independence, that created the free state, also refined the nation's political interests to those that shared a confining nationalist and religious position, effectively based on a converse of English rule. Furthermore, Ireland since the English arrival has seen unprecedented transformations in culture. Perhaps only the Caribbean colonies have seen greater changes and more forced hybridism than Ireland. Although not all of these changes in Irish culture can be attributed to colonialism, the changes began with English influence.

THE IRISH ROLE IN POSTCOLONIAL STUDIES

Irish postcolonial status may have been overlooked because of the unique conditions of postcoloniality in Ireland. Declan Kiberd explains: 'The Empire Writes Back passes over the Irish case very swiftly, perhaps because the authors find these white Europeans too strange an instance to justify their sustained attention.'[14] Whatever the reasons for the Irish exclusion, the case not only for Irish inclusion can be made but the case for Irish inclusion must be made. Irish writers who have been written into the English tradition have provided inspiration for the more recognized postcolonial writers. Examples of Irish inspiration include Achebe's Things Fall Apart, which was inspired from Yeats' 'The Second Coming',[15] while J.M. Synge's Playboy of the Western World is not only equated to Franz Fanon's ideal of the decolonising text, but the play was later adapted by Mustafa Matura in Trinidadian as The Playboy of the West Indies.[16]
Perhaps the most fundamental of errors in terms of excluding Ireland's writers as postcolonial pioneers, is the case in Empire Writes Back where Jamaican novelist, Wilson Harris' novel Assent to Omai (1970), is given credit for pioneering the use of the English language in a free way, apart from the tradition of binary bases,

14 Kiberd, Inventing Ireland, p. 5.   15 Walder, Post-colonial literatures in English, p. 15.   16 Kiberd, Inventing Ireland, pp 185–8.

dismantling literature, language, history and time.[17] This summary not only undermines Harris' work, but also is factually incorrect, as the methods described above were not first published in Jamaica, but in Paris, by an Irishman, James Joyce. The problem this distinction creates for the argument of *The Empire Writes Back* is a serious one. Essentially, the postcolonial writers of the Caribbean, Asia and Africa did not discover their own voice and perspective within the English language and literature, but merely copied a style that originates from a member of the centre, the United Kingdom's James Joyce and his novels *Ulysses* and *Finnegans Wake*. The importance here lies in admitting Joyce's role as outsider, maybe not in the same context as Achebe, Rushdie or Harris, but none the less, as a hybrid on the border between the colonizer and colony.

JOYCE AND POSTCOLONIAL STUDIES

Joyce studies have expanded to all reaches of literary and cultural theory, to the extent that Joyce can be made to represent conflicting sides of a given argument. Joseph O'Connor gives a humorous take on Joyce studies when he states:

> It was clear that you could make James Joyce say whatever you wanted him to say. He was like an academic version of a ventriloquist's dummy. Depending on whose hand was up him on which day, what he had to say would change substantially.[18]

O'Connor's point could be expanded by recognizing that what Joyce has to say could change substantially as well, by what is left out of the reading. In the decisive work to deal with Joyce and postcolonial theory, Vincent Cheng's *Joyce, Race, and Empire*, argues that Joyce has been too long regarded as an apolitical writer, to the point where he can be given a place in the English literary canon.[19] By placing Joyce into the canon of English Literature, Cheng rhetorically asks:

> Are we not, indeed, effectively muting and blunting (even ignoring) the power of the key motivations behind his writings, which were most frequently attempts to resist and defy the authorized centrality of canons, empires (especially England), and totalising structures?[20]

Indeed, the misreading of Joyce as an English writer was examined earlier for its consequences on postcolonial literature, and here Cheng shows that it is by such an apolitical reading that Joyce can be interpreted into the English canon. Therefore reading the implied political message of Joyce's text both locates Joyce

17 Ashcroft, *Empire*, pp 49–50. 18 Joseph O'Connor, *The secret world of the Irish male* (Dublin, 1994), p. 149. 19 Vincent J. Cheng, *Joyce, race, and empire* (Cambridge, 1995), p. 2. 20 Cheng, *Joyce, race, and empire*, p. 3.

at the beginning of the postcolonial writing movement as well as opens Joyce
to interpretations left undone by previous critics who assumed Joyce apolitical.

A DESCRIPTION OF COLONIAL DUBLIN

To discuss Joyce's relation to colonialism is to consider the evolution of a career
and philosophy divided appropriately enough by publication, ultimately developing towards the deconstruction of the English language, literature, tradition
and culture in *Finnegans Wake*. While *Ulysses* and *Finnegans Wake* would seek
to liberate Ireland of any debt or subservience to England's literature through
deconstruction of language and binary philosophies, Joyce's *Dubliners* would
subtlety declare an initial need for decolonisation. Consider the mask of a capital that is Dublin; the centre of paralysis which when articulated by the details
of the lives of those characters, could initiate the description of the colonized
and thereby portray the need for decolonisation.

From 'The Sisters' to 'The Dead', *Dubliners* is a narrative of colonial life.
The characters are able to visualize another place, another life, but only in fantasy as they are repeatedly defeated by either a disappointment in reality or dis-
illusionment in terms of their inability to realize their aspirations. This overly-
ing feature of the collection figures as the first challenge to any independent
Irish identity because action seems futile in the colonial setting where one is
always subservient. These lives are overshadowed by politics, religion, poverty
and limited vision, and may seem gratefully oppressed, but the text seeks to
describe the discontent that lies dormant or unexplained within them. Although
at no one point do the characters overtly make their grievances about colonial
subjection clear, the frustrations are most blatantly and concisely stated in a crucial scene from 'The Dead' in which Gabriel comes so close to explaining the
frustration that many characters feel:

> – O, to tell you the truth, retorted Gabriel suddenly, I'm sick of my own
> country, sick of it! – Why asked Miss Ivors. Gabriel did not answer for his
> retort had heated him. They had to go visiting together and as he had not
> answered her, Miss Ivors said warmly: – Of course you've no answer.[21]

Gabriel is unable to answer because he is torn between a desire to be a part of
modern continental Europe as evidenced by his goloshes, associations with the
conservative British press and interests in continental holidays, and also between
his desire to identify with the tradition that the 'fathers have handed down to
us and which we in turn must hand down to our descendants.'[22] Gabriel, with
perhaps more foresight than other characters, wishes for Irish identity to expand

21 James Joyce, *Dubliners* with an introduction and notes by Terence Brown (London, 1992), p. 190.
22 Joyce, *Dubliners*, p. 204.

to incorporate other cultures, and yet his feelings are in conflict with the resentment of the colonial state. These feelings of divergence continue to muster
nationalistic attachment to the tradition and ideal of an autonomous state built
in the mode more favoured by Miss Ivors' brand of nationalism, which by nature,
shuns the multiculturalism and openness of an Irishness that would be more
inclusive of continental and British values or opinions.

Momentary images of the 'ragged' poor are scattered throughout *Dubliners*.
These portrayals of the unfortunate are brief and these characters are almost
never given a voice. Yet their inclusion highlights the division in Irish society
considering the overall poverty of almost all characters. However, beyond Irish
society, poverty in Ireland, when compared to the economic strength of the colonial powers, further highlights Irish colonial stature. Demonstrating this occurrence where the impoverished Irish are contrasted to their colonial masters is
the story 'After the Race', where the reader is reminded of this disparity of wealth
and power:

> Sightseers had gathered in clumps to watch the cars careering homeward
> and through this channel of poverty and inaction the Continent sped its
> wealth and industry. Now and again the clumps of people raised the cheer
> of the gratefully oppressed.[23]

This intricate description portrays the Irish as exploited outsiders, passively
watching the colonial powers flex their affluence and superiority. In fact, the
term 'careering' is used to describe the movement and pace of the cars, but of
course the word's other meaning would allude to a vocation or a profession,
which then brings about an image of the continentals making a livelihood out
of the colonial enterprise and at the expense of the Irish.

The word choice in this passage is not only poetic in terms of the 'careering' *double-entendre*, but also the contrast in the shape of the sightseers who are
merely 'clumps', formless masses rather than individuals in comparison to the
sleek design of the speeding race cars. Essentially, the colonial subjects have
come to perceive the colonial power's wealth and industry as attractive, something that these oppressed masses are happy to applaud from a spectator's position, as they are used as a catalyst to help speed their oppressors towards even
greater success.

This treatment would seem to agree with the traditional postcolonial narrative that could describe colonial subjection as leading to poverty, lowered self-
esteem and eventually a manipulation of the values that belonged to the nation
before colonialism. While these aforementioned aspects may be exhibited in
Dubliners, the inability of the Irish masses to show disdain at such a display of
affluence and exploitation in the face of poverty complicates a postcolonial interpretation. These colonial Irish subjects are actually 'grateful' for the oppression.

23 Ibid., p. 35.

Characters like Doyle and Corley will even strive to learn from the oppressor and profit in the exploitation of their own people. Few mentions outside that of the narrator's voice draw attention to the essential postcolonial problem of oppression. In this regard, *Dubliners* presents a traditional decolonisation message about the disparity of the masses while simultaneously giving an anti-nationalist and condemning vision of Irish complacency and willingness to turncoat.

A VISION FOR POSTCOLONIAL IRELAND

Joyce views colonialism and nationalism as having equally perverted the nation's ability independently to create a national consciousness. In *A Portrait of the Artist as a Young Man* and *Stephen Hero*, the reader finds Stephen as the first character in Joyce's writing to seize control of his situation, and therefore, Stephen figures particularly important in the allegory of Irish identity as the instance of genius or epiphany. By imagining himself outside of the confines of nationalism and oppression, Stephen may become an independent person or in terms of the analogy, nation.

Illustrating the importance of liberation from nationalism and foreign oppression, Stephen can be a metaphor for the Irish nation, as he attempts a solution to the problems that were merely illustrated in *Dubliners*. Although Stephen is initially frightened into conformity, he possesses a realisation of his responsibility to speak. Because Stephen is self-conscious enough to see the danger of losing a critical perspective, and even though he temporarily regrets having to be forced to the realization that he controls his own fate, Stephen is ultimately rewarded by embracing this understanding that gives him the rationalization to forge change. A more mature Stephen will once again find the strength to change when he realizes that by controlling his own fate he need not necessarily give way to the systems that seek his subservience. It is in this vein that Stephen famously utters, 'You talk to me of nationality, language, religion. I shall try to fly by those nets.'[24] If Stephen may be accepted as a metaphor for the nation, then consider the forwardness of his decision to shed his own past and his nation's history; to break the mould of the existing Irish consciousness and create another definition.

Free of those constrictive forces of nationality, language and religion, Stephen seems poised to define a new identity and future for himself and metaphorically the nation. Yet Stephen falls short of creating the consciousness of his race because he essentially is flustered by the defeatist history of Ireland that he internalizes. Fortunately, the vision that Stephen could not advance is already practiced by Bloom, whose attributes offer a counter point to Stephen's failures. Bloom represents the otherness that already exists in Ireland. Bloom's otherness affords an alternative perspective from which to view Ireland's culture and impor-

24 Ibid., p. 220

tantly, Bloom takes an avid interest in Ireland and actively tries to understand the aspects of the culture that are foreign to him, which gives the text an opportunity to objectively criticize the culture and propose a solution.

A solution for Ireland's crisis of identity can be found in Bloom's understanding of his own identity. Bloom essentially allows for a flexibility that makes absolute definition impossible. In contrast to characters that represent fixed sides of a binary identity, Bloom endorses 'botheration.'[25] Botheration is meant to advance the idea that Bloom can maintain both sides of a binary philosophy at one time. Examples of Bloom's botheration abound, such as his extreme positions of sexual identity, where at one moment he can be aggressively male as he objectifies the woman outside the Grosvenor Hotel with his desire to 'possess her once take the starch out of her',[26] while later in the 'Circe' episode, Bloom may become entirely female as he admits, 'O, I so want to be a mother.'[27] These are but two examples of the binary extremes that Bloom's identity is equally capable of accepting.

Furthermore, Bloom can occasionally identify with Ireland as his nation and yet just as well identify with England or Hungary. Of course religiously, Bloom has been inducted to three religions, a testament to his embrace of plurality and his aversion to the constrictive forces of fixed identity that colonialism, nationalism and religion all impart. Bloom's flexible identity is ultimately the direction that Joyce's writing advises Ireland to embrace as a means of circumventing a binary choice of colonialism or exclusionary nationalism. This simple philosophy of rejecting binary identity groups places Bloom in a unique role, whereby he can independently demonstrate why a fixed definition of Irish identity should never have been the search for the Irish to embark on.

Joyce and Beckett: epiphany, the subject, and the comic

LYNNE MAES, UNIVERSITY OF CALIFORNIA AT SANTA CRUZ

> The bitter laugh laughs at that which is not good, it is the ethical laugh. The hollow laugh laughs at that which is not true, it is the intellectual laugh. Not good! Not true! Well well. But the mirthless laugh is the dianoetic laugh, down the snout – Haw! – so. It is the laugh of laughs, the *risus purus*, the laugh laughing at the laugh, the beholding, the saluting of the highest joke, in a word the laugh that laughs – silence please – at that which is unhappy.[1]

25 James Joyce, *Ulysses*, Annotated students edition with notes by Declan Kiberd (London, 1992), p. 421. 26 Joyce, *Ulysses*, p. 89 27 Ibid., p. 614. 1 Samuel Beckett, *Watt* (New York, 1959), p. 48.

A recent conversation about how many readers have been tutored to comment on Joycean 'epiphany' provoked a colleague to reminisce about his first reading of Joyce. Having gotten hold of a used copy of *Dubliners* as a very young man, he mainly recollects having been completely perplexed by the mysterious word 'epiphany' carefully written over and over in the margins.[2] Despite the exaggerated emphasis often placed on this feature of Joyce's texts, my latest reading of Samuel Beckett's play *Krapp's Last Tape* (1958) drew me back to one of the most famous epiphanies in *Portrait*: Stephen Dedalus' sighting of the 'bird-girl' – a scene that marks the moment of his metaphoric birth as an artist. *Krapp's Last Tape*, I discovered, offers a parody of Stephen's epiphany that, while paying homage to Joyce, performs the literary equivalent of the Marx Brothers' hat trick in *Duck Soup*.[3] In *Krapp's Last Tape*, Beckett offers a critique of how language seems to work in *Portrait* to metaphorically engender the artist, and questions the artist's power to approach a complete or totalizing narrative of the subject. Beckett then returns to this problem in *Film* (1963).[4] Though *Film* eliminates language almost completely, it remains focused on issues of subjectivity – and what it means, finally, to attempt to entirely eliminate the subject. As my reference to the Marx Brothers suggests, I would also like to explore the implications of Beckett's comic strategies in *Krapp* and *Film*. Grounding my study in Jean-Luc Nancy's essay on *Witz* and Tyrus Miller's theoretical elaboration of the role of laughter in late modernist text, I propose that Beckett's wit and his strategic turn toward silent comedy invokes the possibility of the dissolution of genre in terms of comic form, and exposes the permeability of language, subjectivity, and textuality.

In the fourth section of *Portrait of the Artist as a Young Man*, Stephen is invited to join the Jesuit order, and as he meditates on why he has refused what he once considered his future he articulates his artistic destiny, asserting himself as a secular priest who will use words to 'recreate life out of life.'[5] The passage that initiates his epiphany, in which he encounters a group of Christian Brothers crossing a footbridge, hints at one of the dominant features of Stephen's interest in language: how words *work*.[6] 'Idle' is the term that pulses through this section: 'it was idle for him to tell himself …', 'idle for him to move himself … to tell himself …', 'Idle and embittering, finally, to argue.'[7] Stephen's response

2 James Joyce, *Dubliners*, 1914 (New York, 1992).   3 Samuel Beckett, '*Krapp's last tape 1958*' in *Collected shorter plays* (New York, 1984).   4 Samuel Beckett, *Film*, Dir. Alan Schneider (Grove Press, 1963). 5 James Joyce, *A portrait of the artist as a young man*, 1916 (New York, 1992), p. 186.   6 I am indebted to Tom Vogler's graduate and undergraduate courses on James Joyce for this crucial aspect of Joyce's project. As Professor Vogler points out, how words work is a constant preoccupation not only of Stephen, but also of many of the characters in *Dubliners*. The protagonist in 'The Sisters' opens his narrative with the meditative repetition of three words, *paralysis*, *gnomon*, and *simony*, which lay out the themes of the rest of the text, while also making language itself a focal point. Part of the opening paragraph of *Dubliners* is worth quoting, as it explicitly introduces the notions of work and idleness in connection to language: 'He had often said to me: *I am not long for this world*, and I had thought his words **idle** … Every night as I gazed up at the window I said softly to myself the word *paralysis* … I longed to be nearer to it and to look upon its deadly **work**' (1, italics Joyce's).   7 Joyce,

to the rhetorical, idle language he feels burdened by is to invoke language that he perceives as having some power: 'He drew forth a phrase from his treasure and spoke it softly to himself: – A day of dappled seaborne clouds.'[8]

This phrase inaugurates Stephen's series of revelations. His name is encoded within the phrase, and marks his metaphoric birth as an artist: the 'name of the fabulous artificer' becomes 'a symbol of the artist forging anew in his workshop out of the sluggish matter of the earth a new soaring impalpable imperishable being.'[9] His sighting of the 'bird-girl' follows, and Stephen invests it with a similar symbolic weight: 'On and on and on and on he strode, far out over the sands, singing wildly to the sea, crying to greet the advent of the life that had cried to him.'[10] This scene, drawing as it does on religious imagery, is often characterized as a secular annunciation, Stephen's artistic ordination, and is literally engendered in and by words.

The main character of *Krapp's Last Tape* is also bound up in the moment in which his metaphoric birth as an artist takes place. The allusions to Joyce's text are numerous and explicit: both 'epiphanies' take place near water; Krapp characterizes his experience as 'the vision' that has come 'at last'; both use imagery of fire or flame both women carry marks on their thighs and the exchange of gazes is foregrounded in both. Samuel Beckett, however, takes the hallmark of Stephen's artistic philosophy – the very possibility that language has the power to initiate a pure genesis – as one of the central points in his critical parody of Stephen's epiphany.

If we read Stephen's epiphany as a conventional narrative of his birth as an artist, Beckett's text would seem to intentionally subvert the totalizing narrative implied by Stephen's epiphany.[11] What the viewer witnesses in *Krapp* is an ever-diminishing retrospective: Krapp in his late twenties filtered through Krapp at 39, which is in turn filtered through Krapp at 69. Though Joyce's *Portrait* is also filtered through the artist in the present (Joyce himself, who marks his authorial presence in the text in the final line of the novel *Trieste 1914*), Krapp's retrospective moves forward and backward indiscriminately. He manipulates the voice we hear, switching it on and off at crucial moments, supplementing it with journal entries he reads aloud, or speaking back to himself. The technological aid of the recording device makes it possible for him to wind forward and backward in time, but also to avoid beginnings, middles, and ends, perpetually deferring the narrativizing possibilities of language.

The term epiphany implies direct, unmediated knowledge, and refers to the light of intuition – an immediacy that is somehow outside of time and space.

Portrait, p. 180. 8 Ibid. This phrase has the delightful quality of prefiguring his name, of encoding it phonetically: 'A day of dappled seaborne clouds' = de-da-lus/ 9 Ibid., p. 183. 10 Ibid., p. 186. 11 In order to avoid an overly reductive reading of Joyce's text, however, I will also point out that the very skeptical rereading of *Portrait* that *Krapp* provokes is not without its counterpart in Joyce's own fiction, and that in fact the final paragraphs of 'The Dead', once suspended alongside Stephen's epiphany in *Portrait*, bear an uncanny resemblance to the subjective past, present and future telescoped through the figure of Krapp.

Beckett's parody of Stephen's linguistic epiphany invokes and then disavows the possibility of unmediated experience and unmediated self: the voice is rendered materially by the recording machine, yet it highlights the unrecoverable distance between the corporeal subject and the disembodied voice.

Beckett's exploration of another technological medium, film, demonstrates his continued interest in the problems of origin and subjectivity, though this time with an eye to reversing the metaphoric birth of the artist and attempting to expunge the subject entirely. Beckett describes *Film*'s plot (for lack of a better term) as a 'search of non-being in flight from extraneous perception breaking down in inescapability of self-perception' and, accordingly, the protagonist is 'sundered in object (O) and eye (E), the former in flight, the latter in pursuit.' It is clear by the end of the film that the 'pursuing perceiver is not extraneous, but self'.[12] This final epiphany of *Film*, in which O (Buster Keaton) realizes he cannot escape from self-perception, is preceded by his perusal of a series of photographs of himself, a scene that stages the complex relationship between memory and subjectivity.

Opening an envelope, O takes out seven photographs: a mother and infant; the same woman and child, now a toddler; the young boy with his dog; the young man at his commencement ceremony; the young man with his fiancée; the man, now older and in uniform, holding his own child; and, finally, a photo of O himself staring out at the camera, wearing the black cloak we've seen from behind throughout the film and an eye patch over his left eye. O's actions in this sequence remind us of Krapp, listening to himself on tape over and over again. The crucial difference is that O goes through the series of photos from beginning to end and then from end to beginning, and finishes by systematically destroying each photograph. As in *Krapp's Last Tape*, we are witnessing a character with the ability to manipulate time and narrative with the aid of technology. The photographs narrate the events of a life instantaneously, and the character's power to alter or reverse that narrative – or to destroy it altogether – is only conceivable with the technological aid of the camera.[13] Beckett's parody of Joyce thus comes full circle, as each 'portrait of the artist as a young man' is obliterated.

II

Any examination of Beckett's film and play is incomplete without a look at the comic strategies in both works. Krapp's clownishness is emphasized from the opening of the play: eating a banana very deliberately and exaggeratedly, and

12 These quotations are taken from Beckett's notebook describing his original project for *Film*, which has been reprinted in Samuel Beckett, *Collected shorter plays*, p. 163. 13 My reading of this scene was inspired by Sidney Feshback's 'Unswamping a backwater: on Samuel Beckett's *Film*', in Lois Oppenheim (ed.), *Samuel Beckett and the arts: music, visual arts, and non-print media* (New York & London, 1999), pp 333–63.

nearly slipping on the skin, Krapp performs an instantly recognizable vaudevillian routine. Like Watt's meditation on the word 'pot', Krapp's interactions with his journal and tape-recorded self occupy the territory of the absurd, and Beckett's choice of name for his character extends the absurdity: Dedalus, the 'great artificer' has been replaced by Krapp, the constipated artificer.

The difficulty inherent in discussing the comic nature of Beckett's text stems partly from the difficulty of defining the nature of the comic itself, and this is not a task I propose to undertake here. Instead, my approach to this aspect of Beckett's text will draw from Jean-Luc Nancy's essay 'Menstruum Universal', which offers a discussion of *Witz* that seems most appropriate to thinking about how Beckett's text operates comedically.[14] Nancy argues that *Witz* – he uses the German word due to the central theoretical position it occupies within German Romanticism – is essential to both literature and philosophy, and yet is 'a subject that has been virtually neglected in the history of literature and philosophy.' Nancy writes:

> *Witz* is barely, or only tangentially, a part of literature: it is neither genre nor style, nor even a figure of rhetoric. Nor does it belong to philosophy, being neither concept, nor judgment, nor argument. It could nonetheless play all these roles, but in a derisive manner. Yet it can also occupy strategically decisive positions in all seriousness: on rare but noteworthy occasions in history *Witz* has, in fact, appeared in such crucial positions. In his preface to *Tristram Shandy*, Sterne argues against Locke in the name of Wit, and in doing so ascribes to it the essential property of the entire philosophical genre. The founders of German Romanticism … made *Witz* a dominant motif, indeed made it the principle of a theory that claimed to be aesthetic, literary, metaphysical, even social and political, all at the same time.[15]

What Nancy suggests is that *witz* is a 'universal solvent' (*menstruum universal*) that melts away the boundaries separating literature and philosophy. The 'hero' of *Witz*, according to Nancy, is Tristram Shandy, whose very origin is attributed to accident, or, as Sterne writes, the 'unhappy association of ideas which have no connection in nature.'[16] This brings up two key notions for our understanding of *Witz* and of Beckett's Krapp: heterogeneous combination and 'uncontrolled birth.' In attempting to discover an origin of *Witz*, Nancy points out that we are compelled:

> to go back to the first known forms of grotesque and carnivalesqe literature, beyond the Latin *satura* and its mixture of genres and prosodies, beyond the scraps of texts of the Cynics, with their witty saying and their parodies of philosophy, beyond the wordplays sprinkled throughout Plato's dialogues, beyond the very genre of the dialogue, a sophistic genre and the favorite

14 Jean-Luc Nancy, 'Menstruum universal', *SubStance* 21 (1978), 21–35. 15 Ibid., pp 248–9. 16 Ibid., p. 254.

haunt of 'witticisms' and thus as far back as the first mimes and the birth of comedy *and* tragedy, as far as the *Witz* of their 'strange combination' … The lesson is clear: in such an endeavor we could never reach an origin, or we would reach it as a *Witz*, by a genesis taking the form of vicious circles …[17]

Krapp's Last Tape reveals its *witzig* character by combining slapstick clownishness and tragic impotence and by playing out a series of inconclusive self-representations that foreclose the notion of a singular identifiable genesis. Krapp's circular and fragmented 'epiphany' has as its central theme the origin of the artist, yet this origin never achieves the status of a definable event.

Embedded in this fragmentation is a critique of the *cogito*, a topic frequently explored in Beckett criticism.[18] Nancy's formulation of the *cogito* in *witzig* terms seems particularly apt in Krapp's case, and gestures uncannily to Beckett's choices regarding lighting and stage directions:

> the Cartesian act of the *cogito* splits itself in two and produces its own double: *l'homme d'esprit*, the man of wit. Instead of being unique and unitary like the cogito, the double proliferates and immediately becomes a multiplicity of figures. The courtier … the man of taste … the woman of *esprit*, all these constitute the polymorphous character of the subject of judgment who finds his certainty within himself. He differs from his double in that he does not find this certainty by the light of intuition, but in the penumbra that is the product of a natural gift; in that he does not discover it as the truth, but only as an entity as precise as a glance or strategy can guarantee … in that he does not propose any *Meditations*, but rather works of the genre 'miscellany', where, by means of dialogue, fable, or aphorism, the saying [*sentence*] always reigns supreme.[19]

It is impossible not to associate the physical appearance of the stage with the penumbra that Nancy mentions here. Beckett's stage directions specifically place a 'strong white light' at its centre leaving the surrounding area in darkness, a choice that explicitly figures uncertainty, and simultaneously parodies the play of light and dark in an epiphany. Nancy's adoption of the penumbra as a metaphor suitable for the 'multiplicity of figures' created by the *cogito* lends itself in turn to a description of Krapp, a figure defined by his very multiplicity, existing half in shadow, half in light.

Though Beckett himself warned us: 'Let's not muddle our genres or we might as well go home and lie down', his texts gesture toward the dissolution of boundaries between literature and philosophy by way of their insistence on *Witz* as their playing field.[20] That each of the texts I've explored here brushes up against the genre of autobiography pulls my argument in a similar direction.[21]

---

17 Ibid., pp 254–5. 18 See for example Richard Begam, *Samuel Beckett and the end of modernity* (Stanford, 1997). 19 Nancy, 'Menstruum universal', p. 257. 20 Cited in Catharina Wulf (ed.), *The savage eye/l'oeil fauve: new essays on Samuel Beckett's television plays* (Amsterdam, 1995), p. 164. 21 The notion of the *doppelgänger* also helps to make sense of the relationship between these texts. By

Paul de Man's look at autobiography in *The Rhetoric of Romanticism* reverses our usual conception of how this genre functions. Although I don't have space here to delineate the contours of his argument, he suggests that the figure (or the medium through which the life is depicted) may determine the referent, rather than the other way around, and that there is an inherent instability that affects the study of autobiography. What intrigues me about his argument is his invocation of the reader. According to de Man, whether the text is read as autobiography or as fiction is dependent on the reader (that is, I may choose to read a particular sequence of events as having generated a character's epiphany, or, the other way around: that the need to establish an epiphany generated the chain of events leading up to it) and thus autobiography ceases to be a distinct genre so much as a figure of reading or understanding.

The three texts I am attempting to put in conversation with one another share an interest in memory, its reconstitution, or its deconstruction. *Krapp* and *Portrait* both invoke a particular memory whose reconstitution provides, to a greater or lesser extent, the occasion for the writing (or re-membering) of the text. *Film* and *Krapp* take this one step further, reflecting on memory *itself* rather than on a memory of one particular event, and thus suggest a distinct intersubjective relationship with the reader of Beckett's texts. As O, in his attempt to eliminate the self, eliminates the memories (textually) by ripping up the photographs, an uncanny transference is made onto the reader who is familiar with the recurring images and themes in Beckett's texts. The viewer is already sharing the subject position occupied by E (thanks to the camera as mediating technology), but as the photographs that feature the mother and child appear, the reader/viewer is invited to recall the recurring presence of the severe mother in so many of Beckett's texts (*KLT, How It Is, Company*).[22] The reader/viewer, in discerning the connections and repetitions engendered within these texts, may thus lend a stability of sorts to texts that are indeterminate. The active reader of Beckett's texts may move between and among the texts, integrating images and events in a way that may not be possible from the vantage point of a single

conceiving of these texts as doubles for one another, we may explore them dialogically, while still maintaining our hold on their inassimilable differences. Sylvie Debevec Henning, in her essay 'Narrative and textual doubles in the works of Samuel Beckett' *Substance* 29 (1980), 97–104, provides an invaluable discussion of the relationship between *Krapp* and *Film*, one that relates the generic differences to the gap that is inevitable in the search for self-identity: 'Although man's doubles, his past selves as well as the multiple aspects of his present character, are all similar they are not identical. Some differences always remain that cannot be integrated into an all-encompassing whole' (97). She argues for a relationship between the different texts that is supplementary rather than complementary, and goes on to argue that the indeterminacy, or rejection of totalization that each text provokes, opens up a particular kind of space in which it may inscribe or be inscribed by other texts. A crucial connection to *Portrait* is also made possible in her citation of Beckett's own understanding of the creative process as "a step forward' that is 'by definition, a step backward.' Such a step back necessarily involves an encounter with tradition(s), and what tradition has repressed' (103).
22 Ciaran Ross' discussion of the mirror stage in Beckett's work provides some useful details regarding the images of the mother across different texts. See Ciaran Ross et al. (eds), *Lectures d'une oeuvre: en attendant Gottot, fin de partie de Samuel Beckett* (Paris, 1998).

text only. In *Film*, despite O's attempt to destroy memory, the traces of these memories remain legible to the reader/viewer, who can recreate the labyrinthine course of many of these images throughout the corpus of Beckett's work.[23] This permeability returns us to the *witzig* figures of Krapp and E/O, and to an understanding of the very permeability (or dissolution) of the subject, of genre, of the text itself. The possibility of theorizing this permeability in terms of Beckett's comic strategies shifts our attention back to *Film* and to a final exploration of the function of laughter in late modernist works.

In *Film*, the cloaked figure of Buster Keaton, recognizable in his pork-pie hat, scuttling along the wall and causing bystanders to take pratfalls, instantly invokes early slapstick and silent comedies. The formal structure of *Film* also explicitly recalls the silent comedies of the twenties: it is shot in black and white, and eliminates sound (though there is an audible 'shhh!' spoken by the dowager figure in the first scene that serves only to emphasize the silence surrounding it).[24] In a classic silent comedy sequence, O is faced by an undersized dog and an oversized cat, who stare at him unblinkingly, and torture him with a carefully orchestrated scene in which each time he opens the door to eject one, the other scoots in again. The 'chase scene' we view is aptly described by Enoch Brater who is one of the only critics to note the continuity between Keaton's own 1924 film *Sherlock Jr.* and *Film*: 'the routines Beckett incorporates in *Film* parody the precision and timing of Keaton's successful acrobatic comedy. The chase-and-escape gags resemble the crisis mimed in *Sherlock Junior* (1924).'[25] Brater, unfortunately, focuses on the pessimism of *Film*. He doesn't realize that the routine with the mirror (Keaton covers it with a cloak, and has the opportunity to showcase his exquisite timing as he quickly ducks each time the cloak falls off) and that the 'crucifying picture of God the Father, strategically located near a nail' is meant to provoke (grim) laughter, as is the reversal of hierarchization that marks the scene in which O is tortured by his perception of the comically grotesque animals staring at him.[26]

The silent comic strategies that Beckett deploys in *Film*, in particular his decision to cast one of the most important silent film comedians, highlights the crisis of subjectivity already figured in *Krapp's Last Tape*. As Tom Gunning writes in 'Buster Keaton or the Work of Comedy in the Age of Mechanical Reproduction':

> Keaton ... devised a style of physical performance in which the human body seemed possessed by the machinelike rhythms and manic tempo of modern

23 This possibility was suggested to me by Marek Kedzierski's speculation regarding the viewer's lack of referential links in *What where* in his essay 'Beckett and the (un)changing image of the mind' anthologized in Wulf, *The savage eye*, pp 149–59. 24 Enoch Brater, in his article 'The thinking eye in Beckett's *Film*', notes these similarities, while also drawing out the allusions to early surrealist films. He persistently chooses to undermine the comedic nature of this film, however, reading malevolence everywhere I read hilarity. 25 Enoch Brater, 'The thinking eye in Bekett's *Film*', *Modern Language Quarterly* 36 (1975), 166–76, 172. The structure of *Film* as a whole may be seen as different phases of one continuous chase scene (E pursuing O in a series of three different settings), and thus as an invocation of the *iterative*, or cyclical, structure of narrative in Beckett's work. 26 Ibid., p. 174.

life … The fascination of Keaton's universe, the absurdist aspect of its vast, recessive spaces and oversized props, lies in adapting a vaudeville humor of nonsequitors to a truly modern, environmental art form.[27]

Gunning's article points out the special significance Keaton brings to the subtext of *Film*: in a work that hinges on subjectivity (problematically) captured by technology, and wrapped up inextricably with that technology, Keaton's determination to 'push [cinema's] unnerving mechanical possibilities', is quite appropriate for Beckett's own project.[28] The tinge of anxiety that is always lurking in Keaton's own films is exploded in *Film*, and yet the comic dimension remains.

Tyrus Miller's theoretical elaboration of the way laughter operates in late modern texts helps us see the significance of *Film*'s comic dimension, and its relationship to this omnipresent anxiety. In *Late Modernism: Politics, Fiction, and the Arts Between the World Wars*, Miller develops the concept of 'self-reflexive laughter' as a crucial thread of continuity among late modernist texts.[29] In contrast to more traditional modes of satire, in which the authorial subject maintains a stable position with regard to social norms, values or morals, an author whose position is marked by indeterminacy generates the late modernist text. 'Self-reflexive laughter' functions to 'shore up – to 'stiffen' – a subjectivity at risk of dissolution' and late modernist texts that provoke this laughter exhibit what Miller calls 'a major loosening of symbolic unity.'[30] The grotesque body comes to occupy a central role in the relationship between laughter and subjectivity in Miller's argument, and is worth quoting at length, as Beckett's work is at its centre:

> Images of tics, fits, convulsions … plaguing Beckett's characters … abound in late modernism as instances of 'limit-experience.' They stand as figures of an unthinkable and unrepresentable threshold: a pure laughter in which all subjectivity has been extinguished … Late modernism, finally, presents an image of subjectivity 'at play' in the face of its own extinction. It prepares the literary ground for the anthropological 'endgame' Beckett would betray to the world in the 1950s – the theatricalized gestures of the Western subject, rehearsing its final abdication.[31]

Though both of the Beckett texts I examine here fall outside the period considered late modernism, and may already have crossed the 'unthinkable threshold' of pure laughter, Miller highlights dominant features of both *Krapp* and *Film*, and recalls the relationship I have attempted to establish with Joyce's *Portrait*.[32] As my discussion of the parodic doubling of Krapp and Stephen has demonstrated, the place Stephen holds with respect to language and art, his sense of mythic unity

27 Tom Gunning, 'Buster Keaton or the work of comedy in the age of mechanical reproduction', *Cineaste* 21:3 (1996), 14–16, see 14. 28 Ibid., p. 15. 29 Tyrus Miller, *Late modernism: politics, fiction, and the arts between the world wars* (Berkeley, 1999). 30 Ibid., p. 63. 31 Ibid., p. 64. 32 It is worth remarking here that both *Krapp* and *Film* revert to an earlier materiality (present in the late modern *Watt*) that had been abandoned in the trilogy.

with Daedalus the 'great artificer' stands him 'always in good stead.' Krapp's comic fumblings and returns to the notebook and recording mechanism (another send-up of Stephen's diary at the end of *Portrait*) participate in the shaking loose of this 'symbolic unity', while O's obsessive attempt to shield himself from extraneous perception provokes laughter whose very occasion is the subject's 'own extinction.' Even the seemingly obvious use of Krapp's banana peel, which we so easily dispensed with as a reference to vaudeville routines, takes on a more significant function when examined through the lens provided here on laughter: Krapp's obsession with bananas not only points out the fragility of his body, but the self-reflexive laughter provoked by the play of his name and the bananas' effect – constipation – can now be read as a (mirthless?) instance of the function of laughter to 'stiffen' the self (the body) against the possibility of its dissolution.

Nancy's *Witz* and Miller's 'self-reflexive laughter' supplement one another, framing the comic in Beckett, and making sense of the role laughter plays in his texts. Whereas Nancy focuses on how *Witz* (discursively) puts aesthetics, literature, philosophy and politics in play, Miller's theoretical elaboration of the way laughter operates in the text pushes the notion of solvency, or dissolution, into the realm of the subject, the body, the text.

That Samuel Beckett begins with a parody of Joyce opens up a series of issues that I have only just begun to explore here. As two writers grappling with the problematics surrounding the inscription of the self in writing, on tape, and on film – though one works towards the symbolic unity of the artist's consciousness and the other towards its very negation – their relationship bears further examination on the level of comic form, and how questions of identity, framed by grim hilarity, may be operating in Irish literature since the advent of Joyce.

'There must be combustion. Plot depends for its movement on internal combustion.'[1] Compass, map and palimpsest: plotting the internal combustion of Elizabeth Bowen's The Last September.

EDWINA KEOWN, TRINITY COLLEGE, DUBLIN

Elizabeth Bowen wrote in her essay 'Notes on writing a novel', 'Novelist must have one foot, sheer circumstantiality, to stand on, whatever the other foot may be doing ... There must be combustion. Plot depends for its movement on inter-

---

1 Elizabeth Bowen, 'Notes on writing a novel' in *The mulberry tree* (London: 1999), p. 39.

nal combustion.'[2] Bowen's poetic statement for her creativity contains a paradox of fixity and combustible motion. Her image of the novelist with one foot rooted someplace, and the other foot moving elsewhere in an alternative past, present or future space calls to mind the stiff twin-legged compass used in geometry for drawing circles or plotting co-ordinates across a map. I attended a lecture[3] on the poetry of John Donne and his conceit of a twin-legged compass to describe the movement of two lovers in 'A valediction forbidding mourning':

> If they be two, they are two so
> As stiff twin compasses are two;
> Thy soul, the fixed foot, makes no show
> To move, but doth if the other do.[4]

Donne's conceit called to mind Bowen's viewpoint that a writer must have a fixed foot and a moveable one and led me to visualize Bowen, in the process of writing, as a compass with one foot rooted in Irish soil and the other foot with the pen attached to it moving across the pages and topographies of her novels. Further, the trope of the compass exemplifying the unity of two individuals can be used as a metaphor for Bowen's psychological connection with some of her characters, and the connections between certain characters themselves that subtextually embody Bowen's writing process. Finally I am working with the concept that Bowen's novels have the characteristics of a map and palimpsest. In her work she merges the various topographies of Ireland, England and Europe, modelling her locations upon personal memories. Her novels are not only two dimensional maps of the world at Bowen's present moment of composition, but three dimensional maps showing historical depth through time. In this they are palimpsests - manuscripts on which later writing has been superimposed on effaced earlier writing; traces of the old are still evident beneath the new. This paper will explore the imagery of compass, map and palimpsest in *The Last September*, Bowen's second novel, written in Oxford in 1928 and published in London in 1929, and show how the characters and setting are moved by Irish politics. In particular this paper will use the compass metaphor to reveal how the connection in *The Last September* between writing, Lois Farquar, Marda Norton, Danielstown, North Cork and Kent textually embodies Bowen's own writing process. Linking the trope of the writer as a twin-legged compass with that of *The Last September* as a map and palimpsest, I will show how Bowen plots a course through her novel.

The Last September is set during the Anglo-Irish war and spans September 1920 to September 1921, the final year in the life of a fictional Anglo-Irish big

2 Ibid., pp 36–9. 3 Lecture on John Donne, one of a series of lectures on seventeenth-century English poetry given by Professor Andrew Carpenter, University College Dublin, 15 October 2002. 4 John Donne, 'A valediction forbidding mourning' in Margaret Ferguson et al. (eds), *Norton anthology of poetry* (4th ed. London, 1996), p. 276.

house, Danielstown in North Cork. Bowen's biographers[5] and critics believe that Danielstown is modelled on her family home, Bowen's Court, which was built in Farahy near Mitchelstown in 1776, and was sold by Bowen and subsequently demolished in 1959.[6] The story focuses upon the passage from adolescence to womanhood of the novel's heroine, Lois Farquar, who is the orphaned niece of Lord and Lady Naylor, the owners of Danielstown. Lois has just finished boarding school in England. The same age as the century, twenty years old, she is living at Danielstown and wondering what she should do with her life, whether to marry, become an artist or something else. The coinciding visits of the rootless Hugo Montmorency, a former lover of her mother's, and Marda Norton, an Anglo-Irish woman living in England who is ten years older than Lois, further disrupts Lois and propels her into an unsuitable engagement to a British soldier, Gerald Lesworth, who is stationed with his regiment near Danielstown on active service against the local Irish Republican Army. Lois is drawn towards Marda, who voices alternatives to marriage or life as the lady of an Anglo-Irish big house and marks a life-path beyond the confines of the Anglo-Irish community in Ireland, but it is a life-path at risk. Danielstown is a microcosm of Anglo-Irish and Catholic-Irish society in North Cork, and their entangled history preceding the novel that is affecting the future. The house is a meeting point for dispossessed Anglo-Irish visitors, such as Hugo and Francie Montmorency, Lois and her cousin Laurence, the local Anglo-Irish community and the British militia. *The Last September* ends with the return of Marda Norton to Kent, the death of Gerald Lesworth in a skirmish with the IRA, the departure of Lois for art school in London and the burning of Danielstown in February 1921.

The structure of *The Last September* echoes the Irish landscape and big houses where memories of past occurrences influence the present. But the novel achieves more than this; it captures the past and present of Irish lives, the land and its history, in an atemporal space of permanence. The essence of the characters, Irish history, Danielstown and the political tension in Ireland in 1920 are kept alive within the text in perpetuum, outliving the actual events they are based upon, indeed outliving the author. Bodies are interred in Irish soil; they dissolve and with the passage of time are usually forgotten unless specifically appropriated and remembered for political or cultural purposes. The rota of daily duties necessary to run an Anglo-Irish big house can impose a sense of entombment upon its inhabitants. The novel does not inter or entomb its characters, but incubates

5 Hermione Lee believes that *The last September* (1929) equals the semi-autobiographical *Bowen's Court* (1942) as a study of Bowen's Court, 'Both her books about Bowen's Court were written from a distance, in place and time. *The last September* was written in Headington, in 1928, about County Cork in 1920: 'Ireland seemed immensely distant from Oxford … another world.' Bowen's Court, which takes the history of the family up to 1914, was started in the summer of 1939 and finished in December 1941.' *Elizabeth Bowen: an estimation* (London, 1991), p. 17.   6 Bowen writes of the sudden demise rather than protracted death of her family home, 'It was a clean end. Bowen's Court never lived to be a ruin.' In *Bowen's Court & seven winters* (London, 1999), p. 459.

them and Munster in 1920 as the dynamic between the narrative and the reader perpetually gives birth to the characters and the setting within the novel. In this way *The Last September* becomes a cartographer's ideal - a map drawn in the aorist tense with no duration at all, not out of synchronicity but free from time.[7]

The Last September, its Danielstown setting and the Irish landscape share the characteristic of being a palimpsest. The story of Ireland is a retelling of narratives from different perspectives, which record the possession, and repossession of Irish land. Bowen's fictional topography is a commingling of old Gaelic Ireland, eighteenth century Ireland and modern twentieth century Ireland. Lois and Hugo return to Danielstown after visiting a neighbour and view it from the height of a mountain road. For the first time Lois perceives the vulnerable relationship of the big house to its Cork surroundings. Here are a few lines taken from the extensive paragraph describing the altered perspective:

> Single trees, on a rath[8], at the turn of a road, drew up light at their roots ...
> The house became a magnet to their dependence ... There was Viola's square
> blue temperate envelope on the table. There was nothing more but some gloves
> Lady Naylor had worn in Cork, some English papers, a box of tennis balls.[9]

The narrative maps North Cork; more importantly the paragraph length manifests the depth of Irish soil with its historical stratum, and acts like a plumb line. The novel takes the form not only of a map but also a palimpsest as the marks of previous settlements and words are discernable beneath the new. In the space of a page the narrative unearths the history of Ireland from the old Irish rath, the now redundant fortified home of an Irish tribal chief, to the construction of Anglo-Irish homes upon land that once belonged to the Irish chieftains, through to the blue envelope on the table from Lois's English school friend Viola and the English newspapers denoting the modern world of literature, print and the distribution of information connecting dispersed people and nationalities. The subtext is a map of Ireland without duration as ruins and memories are not moribund but sentient. The English papers juxtaposed between Lady Naylor's gloves that she had worn in Cork and the tennis balls that had been used on the courts of Danielstown bring the presence of British politics into the local history of Cork, panning out to encompass the broader history of Irish and English relations and the political situation in the world in the 1920s.

7 Denis Wood in his chapter 'The interests lies in signs and myths' relating to cartography and mapping writes, 'The map employs a code of tense, concerning its temporal topology, and a code of duration, which concerns its temporal scale. Tense is the direction in which the map points, the direction of its reference in time. It refers to past, to present (or a past so immediate as to be taken as a present), or future, relative, of course, to its own temporal position ... and the allegorical map (the map of matrimony, the Gospel temperance, railroad map, the road to hell) that proclaims itself atemporal or eternal and, thus, presumes the aorist of the Greek', in *The power of maps* (London, 1993), p. 126. 8 A rath is an archaeological term, originally Irish, denoting the strong circular earthen wall forming an enclosure and serving as a fort and residence for an Irish tribal chief. *Oxford English Dictionary* (Oxford, 2001). 9 Bowen, *The last September*, pp 67–8.

Danielstown itself is a palimpsest as its interior of accumulated bric-a-brac records and stores the memories of past lives as well as accommodating the present generation. More than a storage space it becomes an atemporal meeting space for all generations of Naylors and the wider Anglo-Irish community. Previous lives are not completely overwritten and obscured by the present as manifested in the dinning room during evening dinner:

> The distant ceiling imposed on consciousness its blank white oblong, and a pellucid silence, distilled from a hundred and fifty years of conversation, waited beneath the ceiling. Into this silence voices went up in stately attenuation.[10]

A weighty atmosphere of past conversations and stories, almost a miasma, inhabits the house. Utterances rise to join the clear silence that holds past words and voices. The layers of existence within the house (and the novel) are semi-transparent as past conversations and actions are heard and felt, mingling with or commenting upon the present. Over dinner the Naylors and their guests discuss the current political instability in Cork: guns buried in the grounds of Danielstown, subversive manoeuvres by the local Irish Republican Army and surveillance by the British militia. Family servants who are Irish-Catholic and probably have relatives in the local IRA wait upon them. The diners refer back in time to personal memories of stability and garden parties at the start of the twentieth century. By 1920 the tension and hostility mounting outside has penetrated the house and moved into the dining room. Bowen envisaged this mounting hostility, arising from the change during the nineteenth-century in the native Irish sense of themselves as a political entity, as a tide that momentarily halted at the demesne walls of Anglo-Irish big houses.[11] In her semi-autobiographical history of her home, *Bowen's Court & Seven Winters,* she refers to the living emptiness that is a watching presence, 'No, it is not the lack of people that makes the country seem empty. It has an inherent emptiness of its own.'[12] In *The Last September* homes, whether Anglo-Irish or Irish-Catholic, become besieged targets or surveillance engines. Michael O'Connor's farmstead takes on the attributes of a submarine, 'its furze-thatched byres, sank slowly under the curve of a hill. Looking longest after them, like an eye, a window glittered.'[13] The inherent emptiness is the record of warfare between the Catholic-Irish and the British and Anglo-Irish, interspersed with spans of exhausted peace. The ghosts of previous Naylors, listening to the bravado of the diners, bear witness to the fact that Ireland's unstable past has not been filed away in history but is

10 Ibid., p. 20. 11 Bowen asserts Daniel O'Connell's role in forging amongst the Catholic-Irish a sense of themselves as a political community and power, 'Even where the Liberator had not been, he was felt. The psychological change he brought about in the people remains as important as anything that he did. (This had been the change Big George had felt in the Kingstown tenants; it was hostile to his power, not to his life.) An altered Ireland came, in the course of the eighteen-twenties, to live at the big house gates': *Bowen's Court & seven winters*, p. 266. 12 Ibid., p. 5. 13 Bowen, *The last September*, p. 65.

still living in the flux of the present. The novel as a map and a palimpsest marks the historical, current and future perspectives of the different groups, Anglo-Irish, Catholic-Irish and British, and of the individuals within those general groupings, in a never-ending story.

The Last September seems to be telling two stories of the same location from two perspectives of time, like a double exposure. In fact there are three time perspectives at play in the novel. The first is an easily identifiable exterior one of a narrator, in a dateless present, telling the story of Lois Farquar and past events, 'In those days, girls wore crisp white skirts and transparent blouses clotted with white flowers.'[14] The other two perspectives of time located within the interior of the novel are harder to discern. Initially the reader believes the novel is structured as a chronology of events between 1920-1 that will culminate in the burning of Danielstown, 'By next year light had possessed itself of the vacancy, still with surprise.'[15] Upon a closer look the novel's interior perspective is the actual burning of Danielstown in February 1921. The text is littered with kindling ashes:

> Exhausted by sunshine, the backs of the crimson chairs were a thin light orange … Behind the trees, pressing in from the open and empty country like an invasion, the orange bright sky crept and smouldered … She [Lois] could not forgo that intensification, that kindling of her personality … dusk would stream up the paths ahead, lie stagnant over the lawns, would mount in the bank of garden, heightening the walls, dulling the boarders like a rain of ashes.[16]

The fiery timber and masonry of Danielstown form the framework upon which the events of September 1920 are hung and superimposed. Lois acts as a conductor for Danielstown's embattled relationship with the land it inhabits. After the evening dinner Lois walks alone through the demesne and experiences a preternatural fear of and even threat from the vegetation of her home:

> Her fear of the shrubberies tugged at its chain; fear behind reason, fear before birth; fear like the earliest germ of her life that had stirred in Laura … High up a bird shrieked and stumbled down through dark, tearing the leaves. Silence healed, but kept a scar of horror.[17]

Nature is hostile to Lois. This fear that the soil and shrubbery of her home will hurt and damage her is an essential part of Lois' being. It is depicted as an Anglo-Irish gene that is passed from parent to child, part of an inheritance in conjunction with the big house. In the grounds of Danielstown the bird is unable to fly and unnaturally stumbles through the dark, tearing the leaves. Lois' existence, as she blindly stumbles through the narrative, is equated with the bird. In the political climate of September 1920 Lois cannot feel at home in

14 Ibid., p. 6.   15 Ibid., p. 206.   16 Ibid., pp 10, 22 and 67.   17 Ibid., p. 33.

Danielstown yet is unable to escape. Silence maintains the 'scar of horror' that marks the contested nature of the big house's relationship to the Munster soil down the centuries. This silence can only momentarily heal and speaks of an interregnum before the final assault. Returning to the house after her nocturnal walk through the shrubbery Lois perceives that she and Danielstown are connected to the shifting Irish soil:

> Inside, they would all be drawing up closer to one another, tricked by the half-revelation of lamplight. 'Compassed about,' thought Lois, 'by so great a cloud of witnesses …' Chairs standing round dejectedly; upstairs, the confidently waiting beds; mirrors vacant and startling; books read and forgotten, contributing no more to life; dinner-table certain of its regular compulsion; the procession of elephants that throughout uncertain years had not broken file.[18]

'Compassed about' is an interesting image for Lois to use to describe herself and her family, enclosed within the walls of Danielstown and its history. A twin-legged compass has two joined parts; a leg that stays rooted in the page and a leg with a pen attached that draws a circle upon the page, around the embedded point. When the leg with the pen moves to draw the circle the embedded leg at the centre rotates with it. So Lois and her family's position and sense of being are connected to and dependent upon Danielstown, its past and its relationship to Irish soil. When the house is removed by Irish politics, so too are they.

Marda Norton is a rootless Anglo-Irish woman aged twenty-nine, engaged to an Englishman living in Kent who has broken all his connections to Ireland. To Lois' perspective Marda brings a kinetic chemistry to Danielstown that resettles the rooms and inhabitants:

> At half-past five Lois went to the top of the house with her drawing-books, paused for confidence, tickled a panel of Marda's door. Coming into the changed and vivid room, she tipped her drawing-books disengaged on to a window-seat. Marda sat on the writing table engaged in manicure … And the pink smell of nail-varnish, dresses trickling over a chair, flash of swinging shoe-buckle, cloud of powder over the glass, the very room with its level stare on the tree-tops, took on awareness, smiled with secrecy, had the polish and depth of experience. The very birds upon the frieze flew round in cognizant agitation.[19]

Danielstown has been invaded and occupied by Marda's fluidity and unconventionality as she rearranges the social spaces that regulate Anglo-Irish decorum by sitting upon the writing table. By doing this she disrupts the text and draws attention to Bowen's creative writing process. Danielstown and Lois are

18 Ibid., p. 34.   19 Ibid., p. 96.

linked as two parts of a twin-legged compass with the big house the leg embedded in the countryside of North Cork and Lois the leg with the pen expanding away from Danielstown with her schooling in England, drawings and desire to sample life elsewhere. There is the fear that the house will be removed by the mounting violence in Cork, uprooting Lois and leaving her suspended and directionless. The sub-textual link between Marda, Lois and Danielstown is important for Bowen's development as an author because all three personify aspects of her psyche. The move from Dublin to Kent at the age of seven birthed the writer in Bowen. She was drawn to the new landscape and English villas in which she and her mother lived during her father's illness.[20] They brought Bowen's Court furniture with them to these villas. Although physically the two locations ran counter to each other,[21] the landscape of Cork and Dublin obtruded into her vision of Kent so that her child's play superimposed the newness of England upon her memories of Ireland.[22] Marda Norton personifies Bowen's Cork and Kent origins. About to begin married life in Kent, Marda has an emotional and historical tie to Danielstown having visited it since childhood and lost an engagement ring there. *The Last September* merges the topographies of Cork and Kent, linking Bowen's childhood memories with her present moment of composition in Headington, Oxford in 1928.

Lois has brought her pen and ink drawings upstairs for Marda sitting on the writing table, to review both the work and Lois' half-formed view of herself. At this point in the novel Lois is trying to choose a life-path for herself and oscillates between a big house existence, marriage to an English officer or vague ideas about travel. Indeterminate, she falls back on her drawings that have been informed by the art of Aubrey Beardsley (1872–98), an English artist associated with art nouveau and the Aesthetic movement who was known for controversial illustrations such as those for Oscar Wilde's *Salome* (1894):

> The drawings in black ink, illustrated the Morte d'Arthur and Omar Khayyam. They remembered Beardsley. Lois, away at a window, heard Marda rustle the tissue paper: she watched the rain intently. Beyond the demesne trees, a farm cart rattled along the road. Marda, conscientious, turned back to the title-page. Here she paused, for Lois had printed out, in uncertain Gothic:

> 'I am a painter who cannot paint;
> In my life, a devil rather than a saint;
> In my brain, as poor a creature too:

20 Bowen writes, 'She and I, who had been anxious in Georgian rooms, together developed a personal love of villas – villas with white balconies … In those Kent-coast years we lived in many such villas', in *Bowen's Court & seven winters*, p. 419. 21 'The blotting out of all my visual past was so total as to become giddying. What had to be bitten on was that two entities so opposed, so irreconcilable in climate, character and intention, as Folkestone and Dublin should exist simultaneously, and be operative, in the same life time, particularly my own: Elizabeth Bowen, *Pictures and conversations* (ed.), Spencer Curtis (London, 1976), p. 34. 22 'a cleft between my hereditary and my environment – the former remaining in my case, the more powerful': ibid., p. 23.

No end to all that I cannot do!
But do one thing at least I can -
Love a man or hate a man
Supremely -
Lois Honoria Farquar: Her book.[23]

Lois' poetry is influenced by the English poet Robert Browning (1812–89), in particular his two dramatic monologues 'Fra Lippo Lippi' and 'Andrea del Sarto' who were Italian Renaissance artists.[24] Lois permits an English education system, its art and literature, to define her instead of crafting her own definition. Marda informs Lois the drawings are limiting and suggests writing or travel, ideas Lois is impotently attracted to, 'There was just 'abroad': she always wondered how long the feeling lasted … if she went to Cook's could they look out all the trains for her, in Spain and elsewhere?'[25] The drawings and poetry are insubstantial artistic moulds and do not anchor Lois who needs to build a solid identity composed of her childhood in England and her family home. But she needs co-ordinates to move from the interior of Danielstown to the unfilled spaces of abroad and the future without becoming lost and dispersed among the flux of modern culture and travel in the 1920s.

While Marda scrutinizes the drawings Lois is at the window intent upon the Irish weather and life. As part of a twin compass whose fixed foot is Danielstown, Lois, with pen attached, is embedded in the Irish rain that falls indifferently upon all of the landscape of Ireland, both the demesne trees and the farm cart rattling on the road that signify the territory of the Anglo-Irish and Catholic-Irish. The house provides Lois with anchorage and scope to write and connect with Marda Norton. At this point in the novel the bond between Danielstown, Lois, Marda and Bowen's poetic imagination intensifies. Referring back to the start of this paper Bowen believed, 'Novelist must have one foot, sheer circumstantiality, to stand on, whatever the other foot may be doing.' The tropes of the writer as a twin-legged compass and the novel as a map and palimpsest links Danielstown, Lois and Marda to each other and Bowen through the writing process, on three levels: plot, subplot and Bowen penning the novel at her desk.

Writing will enable Lois to branch out from Cork to elsewhere. To reach London, she requires co-ordinates and a penetrative audience such as Marda. Danielstown and the Irish climate intervene to connect Lois and Marda as potential writer and audience:

Marda said nothing; once or twice she changed her attitude, shifting the book from knee to knee. Soot, dislodged by the rain, sifted sharply on to the

23 Bowen, *The last September*, p. 97. 24 Both poems were published in *Men and women* (1855). Each has a painter's vision: Fra Lippo for the dramatic and Andrea for tonal harmony and draughtsmanship, yet both are flawed as Fra Lippo is controlled by his emotions whereas Andrea is emotionless: Leonard Burrows, *Browning the poet: an introductory study* (Perth, 1969), p. 187. 25 Bowen, *The last September*, p. 98.

paper fan in the grate, startling them to an exchange of glances. Then she said deliberately, closing the drawing-book:

'I think you are cleverer than you can draw, you know.'

'Oh – '

'You don't mind do you? Look - have another cigarette. Why can't you write or something?'[26]

At this critical point the house makes its presence felt. It awakens the characters to each other and the power of writing as a method of preservation and a vehicle to construct an identity sourced from personal memories but not limited to them. By turning her self and Danielstown into words upon the page Lois will conserve the embedded foot of her compass. The exchange of glances marks the first time someone has perceived Lois wholly. The subplot links Lois to Marda as subject matter and author. Marda, sitting upon the writing table and shifting the book from knee to knee, reviews and recreates Lois who, 'received the imprint of each look as though her sensibility were the paper.'[27] It is as if Marda is now moving the twin-legged compass that is Lois and Danielstown across the page, urged on by the burning house. Marda, with her connection to both Kent and Danielstown, embodies Bowen in the act of writing *The Last September*. The soot dislodged onto the paper fan reminds the reader that the primary narrative is the burning of a big house. The subtext points to the fact that Bowen's writing process arises from her childhood in Bowen's Court and England, and her experience of the Anglo-Irish war. Bowen was not personally at Bowen's Court when the house was threatened with burning in 1921. She was in Italy at Lake Como, having been sent there by her family to halt an unwise engagement to a British officer, where she taught herself to visualize the burning of her home in the lake waters. Her father kept her informed of the bloodiness of the Anglo-Irish war and the burning of neighbouring homes to theirs.[28] Bowen's Court survived but the fear of its loss psychologically scarred Bowen. In writing *The Last September* she transforms a potential act of destruction into artistic construction.

Bowen insisted that when writing a novel, 'There must be combustion. Plot depends for its movement on internal combustion.' Danielstown operates as both a symbol of Bowen's family origins and the molten structure upon which all the narratives within *The Last September* are written, becoming the dynamism

---

26 Ibid., p. 98. 27 Ibid. 28 'Between the armed Irish and British troops in the country, reprisals and counter-reprisals - tragic policy raged. Fire followed shootings, then fires, fires. In the same spring night in 1920, three Anglo-Irish houses in our immediate neighbourhood – Rockmills, Ballywater, Convamore - were burnt by the Irish … Henry VI [Bowen's father] had watched this pointless campaigning, more with moral distress than fear of loss. He now wrote to me – I was in Italy – telling me what was latest … I read his letter beside Lake Como, and looking at the blue water, taught myself to imagine Bowen's Court in flames. Perhaps that moment disinfected the future: realities of war I have seen since have been frightful; none of them have taken me by surprise', in *Bowen's Court & seven winters*, pp 339–440.

and mutable form for her creativity. Writing a novel composed from the per-petually burning structure of an Anglo-Irish home with its topographical and historical record of Ireland empowers Bowen to preserve her origins, recreate herself and expand her sphere of being.

'A self-sustaining tension in space': tradition, history, myth and John Banville

BRENDAN MC NAMEE, UNIVERSITY OF ULSTER, COLERAINE

In his book of essays, *The Irish Mind,* Richard Kearney puts forward the idea of a specifically Irish mode of thought which he sees as 'a counter-movement to the mainstream of hegemonic rationalism which Jacques Derrida has named "logocentrism".'[1] He defines the chief characteristic of this mode of thought thus: 'In contradistinction to the orthodox dualist logic of *either/or*, the Irish mind may be seen to favour a more dialectical logic of *both/and*: an intellectual ability to hold the traditional oppositions of classical reason together in creative confluence'.[2] This definition bears a close family resemblance to the *OED* def-inition of the adjective 'Irish': 'Irish in character or nature … used of seemingly contradictory statements.' The *Shorter OED* takes the further step of commenting on this phenomenon, which it describes as '*offensive*', the offence presumably being taken by anyone accused of thinking or speaking in such a fashion. We know instinctively, I think, why this should be so, but in any case, the *OED*, defining the term 'bull', clears the matter up for us: 'an expression containing a manifest contradiction in terms or involving a ludicrous inconsistency unper-ceived by the speaker.' In a country with such a delicate and uncertain sense of its own identity as Ireland, the idea that such self-contradictory statements were 'unperceived by the speaker' has been too readily accepted – no doubt because it chimed so closely with such derogatory stereotypes as the 'thick Irish' or the 'thoughtless, over-imaginative Celt' – and this acceptance was then followed by an immediate rejection of the whole idea of such bulls as having anything to do with real Irish identity, so anxious were we to prove ourselves as logical and ratio-nal as any country on earth – especially the one lying off the east coast. Kearney's point, of course, is that such a tradition is one of immense value, calling into question as it does the presumed certainties of language as a way of describing the world, or of conveying truth. Today, such certainties have been severely bat-tered by the various post-isms of modern theory, and John Banville has been

1 Richard Kearney, *The Irish mind: exploring intellectual traditions* (Dublin, 1985), p. 9. 2 Ibid.

well to the forefront of that particular assault. But the thing about Banville that I want to stress in this paper is the way that he manages to inhabit (or haunt) both camps at once. He stresses the futility of language to represent reality, and in one and the same movement goes a long way towards overcoming that limitation. Overcoming the inability of language to encompass reality could perhaps be described as literary art's *raison d'être* to begin with, but Banville's approach can, to some degree, be clarified with reference to the philosophy of Martin Heidegger, and particularly to his concept of truth as *aletheia*, or 'unconcealedness'. Rather than attempt an initial, and, given space restrictions, necessarily inadequate explication of this complex term, I would prefer that it come into clearer focus through elucidation of its relevance to Banville's work.

Banville has sometimes been accused of not being a proper 'Irish' writer because of his failure to address specific Irish problems or follow any obvious Irish tradition, and in interviews he has indeed derided the whole idea of national literatures.[3] Nevertheless, in his fiction, albeit in a very oblique fashion, he has interesting things to say about the idea of tradition, and about how tradition relates to myth and history. I want to approach the subject through two passages: one from the novel *Ghosts*, the other from *The Newton Letter*. Both passages describe purely individual experiences, and say nothing directly about tradition, myth or history, but are all the more intriguing for that, because they show how universal metaphysical concerns of the type that preoccupy Banville are intimately connected with more tangible questions of history and tradition. And they show, too, how both these areas of enquiry grow naturally from intense pre-linguistic experience.

To begin with the Ghosts passage: as so often with Banville, the narrator is speaking of a recurring memory from childhood, one of those 'emblematic fragments from the deep past that seem mysteriously to constitute something of the very stuff of which I am made':

> It is a summer afternoon, but the room is dim, except where a quartered crate of sunlight, seething with dustmotes, falls at a tilt from the window. All is coolness and silence, or what passes for silence in summer. Outside the window the garden stands aghast in a tangle of trumpeting convolvulus. Nothing happens, nothing will happen, yet everything is poised, waiting, a chair in the corner crouching with its arms braced, the coiled fronds of a fern, that copper pot with the streaming sunspot on its rim. This is what holds it all together yet apart, this sense of expectancy, like a spring tensed in mid-air and sustained by its own force, exerting an equal pressure everywhere. And I, I am there and not there: I am the pretext of things … Without me there would be no moment, no separable event, only the brute, blind drift of things.[4]

3 See, for instance, Ronan Sheehan's conversation with Banville and Francis Stuart in *The Crane Bag* 1:3 (1979), 408–16.   4 John Banville, *Ghosts* (London, 1998), pp 39–40.

History and myth are traditionally seen as very different, though related, concepts. History is what actually happened; myths are the stories we form around what happened to suit our own purposes, be they personal, social, political or cultural. But there is no such thing as pure history in this respect. 'There are no facts', Nietzsche said, 'only interpretations'. Myth is implicated in history from the very beginning by dint of the ordering consciousness that, like Banville's 'sense of expectancy', 'holds it all together yet apart', and without which there is 'only the brute, blind drift of things.' History is as much a constructed narrative as is myth. So is it all lies? One of the fascinating aspects of the passage quoted above is that in answer to this question (in true Irish fashion!) it says both yes and no. The passage hints at a stillness, a silence that seems to verge on the kind of silence sought so ardently by writers such as Beckett, a fusing of the world without with the consciousness within. And yet consciousness is forming this pattern; in a very real sense the pattern is not there (though all the remembered fragments are there) without the controlling consciousness. Consciousness seems at once to be the source of the pattern, an integral part of the pattern, but also, in its sense of itself as an individuated 'I', irrelevant to the pattern, a mere pretext, 'there and not there'. The result is a strange tension that echoes far beyond the circumstances of the described incident, and seems to hold history and the imagination, the flow of time and the timelessness of myth, in perpetual balance, hinting that life as we perceive it, the eternal interaction between the passing phenomenal world and the busy consciousness forming it into coherent narratives as fast as it arrives, is itself a form of artistic creation, or would be if only we could get the balance right. Banville has actually described the artistic process proper in very similar terms:

> Before I put down even a note for a novel, there exists in my mind, or just outside it somewhere, a figure, not geometrical, exactly, … more a sort of self-sustaining tension in space, tangible yet wholly imaginary, which represents, which in some sense *is,* the completed thing. The task is to bring this figure out of the space of the potential and into the world, where it will be manifest yet hidden, like the skeleton beneath the skin.[5]

This is consistent with Banville's postmodern rejection of the traditional novel's claim to represent reality. Following Beckett, his novels try, not to be *about* things, but to be the things themselves. (In this, strictly ideal, sense, the novelist can be seen as standing to the novel as the narrator stands to the phenomenal world in the passage from *Ghosts*: without him/her there would be no novel, but when

5 John Banville, 'Making little monsters walk', in Clare Boylan (ed.), *The agony and the ego: the art and strategy of fiction writing explored* (London, 1993), p. 109. Banville's articulation of his artistic wellsprings recalls another Heideggerian term, *Grundstimmung*, meaning a fundamental or ground tone. Timothy Clark elucidates the idea thus: 'Provisionally, the *Grundstimmung* can be related to the fact, attested by many poets, that in the emergence of the poem a sense of the whole precedes and determines the individual parts': Timothy Clark, *Martin Heidegger* (London, 2002), p. 112.

the novel exists, the novelist becomes 'like a passageway that destroys itself in the creative process for the work to emerge';[6] he/she is both there and not there, 'the pretext of things'.) But they *are* novels, and the essence of the novel form is that it deals with people in society, people in time. (Beckett tried to escape this, but in escaping it, he had to abandon the novel and resort to fragments.) In the same essay quoted above, Banville went on to say, 'Will it now seem paradoxical, in the light of what I have said so far, if I now insist that the only way to portray life in art is to be as lifelike as possible?'[7] He gets around the bind by making use of a kind of Derridean self-erasure. Speaking once of his own methods in relation to Joyce and Beckett, he said, 'Joyce put everything in, Beckett took everything out. I put everything in, and then deny it all'.[8] In artistic terms, putting everything in and then denying it all is a way of, in Joyce's phrase, 'having two thinks at a time.'[9] It is both recognising the phenomenal world (through its re-creation in the fiction), but refusing to let it settle in the mind into a definite historical shape (in terms of personal response, into the boredom of habit; in broader historical terms, into fixed ideologies and dead traditions); it is maintaining that 'sense of expectancy, like a spring tensed in mid-air and sustained by its own force'. Eliot's 'Burnt Norton' contains the lines: 'Except for the point, the still point, / There would be no dance, and there is only the dance'.[10] Banville's art is aimed at keeping alive the silent dialogue between the 'still centre' and 'the dance', without which the dance turns into a series of grotesque, mechanical jerks.

From this angle, it is worth looking more closely at something Richard Kearney, in an essay on Beckett, says about tradition: '[T]he very idea of an 'Irish' or 'French' writer is a contradiction in terms, for national identities and traditions are themselves no more than impostures of language. We are the voices that speak us. Language precedes existence. It determines who and what we are.'[11] If language determines who and what we are, what is it that determines how and why we change?

The obvious answer would be the force of history itself acting on and reforming (or deforming) the perceptions and myths of a society; an ongoing, and healthy, process of continual renewal. As Kearney himself says elsewhere (echoing Hugh in Brian Friel's *Translations*), 'We must never cease to keep our mythological images in dialogue with history; because once we do we fossilise'.[12] But can this be the full story? Is the essential conflict between two different modes of perception, both mediated through language? If so, where does this leave Beckett's yearning for silence, for an absence of the division of life into subject and object which language by its nature entails? And where does it leave

---

6 Clark, *Martin Heidegger*, p. 40. 7 Banville, 'Making little monsters walk', p. 7. 8 Quoted in Gary Ferguson, 'Modernist influences on the fiction of John Banville' (DPhil, UU, Jordanstown, 1997), p. 318. 9 Kearney, *Irish mind*, p. 10. 10 T.S. Eliot, *Four quartets* (London, 1959), p. 15. 11 Richard Kearney, *Transitions: narratives in modern Irish culture* (Dublin, 1988), p. 65. 12 Richard Kearney, *Myth and motherland* (Derry, 1984), p. 24.

Banville's 'self-sustaining tension in space, tangible yet wholly imaginary'? The gist of the work of both these writers could be said to entail a rejection of the possibility of an absolute reality independent of language (Banville has explicitly declared as much in interviews), yet their writing, it could be argued, derives the main of its power from this very absence.[13]

The idea of absence brings us to the second passage from *The Newton letter*. The narrator is here imagining Isaac Newton's reaction to the legendary fire at his rooms in Cambridge that is thought to have destroyed some of his papers:

> The joke is, it's not the loss of the precious papers that will drive him temporarily crazy, but the simple fact that *it doesn't matter*. It might be his life's work gone, the *Principia* itself, the *Opticks*, the whole bang lot, and still it wouldn't mean a thing ... Someone beats out the flames. Someone else asks what has been lost. Newton's mouth opens and a word like a stone falls out: *Nothing*. He notices details, early morning light through a window, his rescuer's one unshod foot and yellow toenails, the velvet blackness of burnt paper. He smiles ... The fire, or whatever the real conflagration was, had shown him something terrible and lovely, like flame itself. *Nothing*. The word reverberates. He broods on it as on some magic emblem whose other face is not to be seen and yet is emphatically there. For the nothing automatically signifies the everything.[14]

Newton's devastating insight is that structures erected in the phenomenal world, whether of science or language (and 'language' here would include myths, histories and traditions), regardless of their utility or their self-evident correspondence with tangible aspects of that world, are somehow, despite their overwhelming presence, not *real*. It is the Nietzschean insight that '[o]ur true experiences ... could not communicate themselves even if they tried. That is because they lack the right word. Whatever we have words for, that we have already got beyond.'[15] Later in the novel, Banville has Newton write a fictional letter to John Locke, some of which is borrowed from Hugo Von Hofmannsthal's *Ein brief* ('The Letter of Lord Chandos'). Speaking of his encounters with tradesmen around Cambridge, he writes, 'They would seem to have something to tell me; not of their trades, or even of how they conduct their lives; nothing, I believe, in words. They are, if you will understand it, themselves the things they might tell. They are all a form of saying.'[16]

13 The power of absence is a strong strain in modern writing. Jacques Derrida, speaking of his denial of 'pure presence' as a 'Necessity', says, 'Because ... there is no such thing [as pure presence], because there is this Necessity, it is because of that that there is a desire for presence and intimacy. So, I try to articulate the Necessity that urges me, compels me to write ... and this articulation means that it's *because* there is no pure presence that I desire it', in Michael Payne and John Schad, *Life after theory* (London, 2003), p. 10. The French mystic, Simone Weil, expresses a similar idea in religious terms: 'God can only be present in creation under the form of absence', in *Gravity and grace* (London, 2002), p. 109. 14 Banville, *The Newton letter* (London, 1984), pp 30–1. 15 Walter Kaufmann, *The portable Nietzsche* (New York, 1976), p. 530. 16 Banville, *The Newton letter*, p. 59.

It is here that the Heideggerian notion of *aletheia* comes to the fore. Heidegger resolutely set his face against an idea of truth that has dominated the Western metaphysical tradition since the time of Plato, the idea of truth as *mimesis*, as a correspondence between words and their referents, and as a corollary of this, the conviction that the division between subject and object is fundamental, and that it is the purpose of the subject (human consciousness) to appropriate and dominate the object (the world). Instead, he favoured the idea of truth as *aletheia*, a Greek word meaning, literally, 'uncoveredness' or 'unconcealment.'[17] This kind of truth is more about acceptance, about being-in-the-world (consciousness as 'the pretext of *things*')[18] than about appropriation and dominance, which characterize the idea of truth as mimesis (and which constitute postmodernism's chief criticism against the Enlightenment); and it is towards this kind of truth that Newton is tending when he speaks of people being 'themselves the things they might tell'.

When these two versions of truth are related back to ideas of tradition, myth and history, it may be seen how our blind acceptance of truth as mimesis, and of the fundamental division of subject and object, have contributed hugely towards the creation of the horrors and the nihilism of the twentieth century. Tradition exists to give us a sense of home, and of identity. The word 'home' conjures up many images – warmth, security, peace – words which have, not only opposites (cold, insecurity, agitation), but negative concomitants – suffocation, boredom, stagnation. The word 'completion', however, encompasses all of the above terms and, though it has an opposite – incompletion – it lacks a negative concomitant. In short, completion is perfection, paradise. And paradise is not of this world. That is why, whenever we are tempted to build it, within the warmth and security of a tradition, or by way of a unifying grand narrative, it turns sour. Taken to extremes, it can turn into blind terror. The French novelist and philosopher, Michel Tournier, proposes an interesting contrast between the words 'purity' and 'innocence' that throws much light on this idea:

> Purity is the malign inversion of innocence. Innocence is love of being, smiling acceptance of both celestial and earthly sustenance, ignorance of the infernal antithesis between purity and impurity … Purity is horror of life, hatred of man, morbid passion for the void … A man hag-ridden by the demon of purity sows ruin and death around him. Religious purification, political purges, preservation of racial purity – there are numerous variations on this atrocious theme, but all issue with monotonous regularity in

17 Clark, *Martin Heidegger*, p. 22. 18 This resonates with some lines from Rilke's Ninth Duino Elegy, which Banville has cited as encapsulating his own artistic stance: 'Are we, perhaps, *here* just for saying: House, / Bridge, Fountain, Gate, Jug, Fruit tree, Window, – / possibly: Pillar, Tower? … but for *saying*, remember, / oh, for such saying as never the things themselves / hoped so intensely to be,' in 'John Banville, a talk', *Irish University Review* 11:1 (Spring 1981), 15. 19 This recalls a distinctly biblical sentence from Kafka: 'He who seeks will not find, but he who does not seek will be found,' Pietro Citati, *Kafka* (New York, 1990), pp 183–4.

countless crimes whose favourite instrument is fire, symbol of purity and symbol of hell.[19]

A concept central to tradition is identity. Like all of life's essentials, identity comes most sharply into focus in its absence, that is, in its *felt* absence. But its absence is only felt because of our fixation on mimesis, on truth as graspable fact: there must be an identity that we can define. Conversely, to drop this demand and simply live, to be in the world and to look outward onto it, is to create (and eternally re-create) an identity. Identity then would arise naturally from this being-in-the-world, but without being fixed or defined in directly referential language.[20] Paradoxically, this outward-looking, this 'smiling acceptance of both celestial and earthly sustenance', also conceives of identity as an absence (but, importantly, not a felt absence), in that there is no consciously defined set of characteristics or attitudes that one feels must direct one's life. It is, to return to Eliot, that 'still point of the turning world' without which 'There would be no dance, and there is only the dance.' Looking outward, responding to life as openly as possible and without preconceptions, is what Tournier means by 'innocence', and what Banville's Newton fears his obsession with science has robbed him of. It is narrowing the gap between consciousness and the phenomenal world, reaching for that point where, in Yeats's words, 'We are blest by everything, / Everything we look upon is blest.'[21] By contrast, looking inward, hungering for a defined identity, demanding *presence*, widens that gap and leads to 'purity', leads to questions such as, 'Am I being sufficiently Irish (English/ American/German etc) in this activity?' (whatever it may be), or 'Should I approve/disapprove, according to such and such set criteria, of this or that writer or work of art?' and leads, as Tournier points out and as history relentlessly demonstrates, to political, religious and racial purges.

It can be seen, then, that Banville, like Beckett before him, firmly rejects the Enlightenment ideal of truth as correspondence between words and referents, as graspable concepts and facts, but the course taken by Banville provides an interesting variation on Beckett's rejection. In 1949, Beckett laid out an artistic credo that his subsequent work focused on with ever more concentrated passion: the idea that the artist has 'nothing to express, ... together with the obligation to express.'[22] Along the way, he jettisoned all the 'realistic' trappings of traditional prose fiction. As already mentioned, Banville brings them all back, but ironises them, and in doing so, transforms them. Far from being a merely playful, typically postmodernist ploy, this is a recognition that even though all our attempts to create 'truth' or 'reality' by wrapping ourselves in myths and traditions are doomed to failure, these narratives are, literally, all that we have. We

20 This recalls a distinctly biblical sentence from Kafka: 'He who seeks will not find, but he who does not seek will be found,' ibid. 21 William Butler Yeats, 'A dialogue of self and soul', in Daniel Albright (ed.), *The poems* (London, 1994), p. 286. 22 Samuel Beckett, *Proust and three dialogues with Georgess Duthuit* (London, 1999), p. 103.

do not have to take them seriously (in fact, we cannot afford to), but we do have to take them, and, as Kearney adjures us, continually remake them. We have to recognize them for what they are – 'supreme fictions'.[23] This path has the advantage of *neither accepting nor rejecting* the idea of an ultimate truth. To reject the concept outright is to inhabit the same mental universe as is entailed by its acceptance, and down that road, as we have seen, lie rigid terror (acceptance) or nihilistic despair (rejection). Conversely, by adopting the Heideggerian notion of truth as *aletheia*, the idea loses the force of its demand for a definite yes/no answer, it remains suspended in a kind of psychic mid-air, providing the source of that 'self-sustaining tension in space, tangible yet wholly imaginary'. If this tension is cast aside, we are left with either the 'brute, blind drift of things', or a delusional and dangerous belief, so beloved of tradition-builders, that truth, home, paradise, is attainable here on earth. The only home we can have is accepting that we can never have a home, because this mythical home never existed except in our yearnings for it. This, I think, is what Kearney means when he says that 'we will go on telling stories, inventing and re-inventing myths, until we have brought history home to itself.'[24] Bringing history home to itself is bringing it into its proper relationship with myth, which means steering consciousness between the Scylla and Charybdis of changing, unsettling realities, and the essential, if dangerous, comfort of myth.

By this means, the past and the present are brought together, locked in an ongoing dialectic which infuses temporality with a *frisson* of timelessness, which necessary *frisson* is a way of maintaining a reverence towards life without either closing it down in definitions or diffusing it through a vaporous ether of relativism; it is a way of maintaining a kind of informed, ironic innocence. Eliot's definitions are useful here:

> [T]he historical sense involves a perception, not only of the pastness of the past, but of its presence ... This historical sense, which is a sense of the timeless as well as of the temporal and of the timeless and of the temporal together, is what makes a writer traditional. And it is at the same time what makes a writer most acutely conscious of his place in time, of his own contemporaneity.[25]

This is a good description of Banville as a writer. He is the most contemporary of novelists, acutely aware of and engaged with postmodern influences (though with restraint and a sense of anguished playfulness), but is also quite traditional, relying mostly on (fairly) conventional narrative forms (he has referred to this aspect of his work as 'fighting the system from within.'[26] In addition, Banville conflates past and present in much of his work. He does this in two ways: one, by a subtle use of intertexuality which gives the sense that his work is intrinsi-

23 Wallace Stevens, *Selected poems* (London, 1965), p. 85.   24 Kearney, *Myth*, p. 34.   25 T.S. Eliot, in John Hayward (ed.), *Selected prose* (London, 1953), p. 23.   26 Banville, *The Crane Bag*, p. 81.

cally connected with works of the past, that all are aspects of one great work comprising the entire European tradition, and two, through the idiosyncratic use of quotations from and references to modern writers and thinkers in his historical novels. This creative confusion of time and timelessness is also, I believe, part of what Banville is getting at when he talks of art as being 'a mode of objective knowledge of the world, not an expression of the subjective world.'[27] The true path to experiencing the wonder of art, as of the world, is not to search for its hidden meanings – to do that is simply to reduce it to a set of familiar linguistic concepts – but to marvel at its very existence: 'The world and being in it are such a mystery that the artist stands before it in a trance of bafflement, like an idiot at High Mass.'[28] Banville could be said to be proposing, in his oblique fashion, that the world look on its myths and traditions as he looks on his art, as 'analogues, parallel microcosms, tiny models of the huge original with which the mind may play in earnest'.[29] And it is this aspect of earnest play, I would suggest, that, while in one sense marking Banville as a postmodern writer, also lifts him above the aura of nihilistic frivolity with which that movement (if that is not too definite a term for it) is often characterized. While being in no sense a traditional writer, as that word is usually understood in either its Irish sense of being concerned with issues of Irishness, or its more general sense of taking the external world as a given, Banville has much to say that both these positions could profit from hearing.

Warming the other side: Trevor, Cixous, and facing a new direction

SIÂN WHITE, UNIVERSITY OF NOTRE DAME

The automatic association of 'Irishness' with certain stereotypes, emergent from long-standing power struggles, has gone on long enough: the stereotypes are anachronistic and reflect an essentialist view of the Irish that is entirely too limiting. The images of the feminized people of Mother Ireland, in which Hibernia is robbed of her lands by John Bull England and left to wander in search of someone to defend her, arguably reflect the struggle shared by women and the colonized. While postcolonial and feminist critics have challenged the power structures that perpetuate these stereotypes, the images nevertheless persist in contemporary Irish literature. William Trevor's *Felicia's Journey* presents two protagonists whose relationship personifies the opposition between England and

27 Banville, 'Making little monsters walk', p. 108. 28 Ibid. 29 Ibid.

Ireland.[1] The opposition is meaningful only for those who would have it be; arguably the acknowledgement and subsequent analysis of these recurring images encourages the associations that allow the stereotypes to persist. What makes the stereotypes dissatisfying at best and offensive at worst is the association of symbolic genderisation with feminist, colonial, and nationalist politics. To accept that association as fixed or necessary is to allow the reductive images to endure. French feminist Hélène Cixous, whose theory examines the relationship between gender and power structures in language, provides a tool for investigating the significance of binaries in literature. Using her theory of the 'couple,' I intend to examine *Felicia's Journey* first as a linguistic work that employs binaries – detached from immediate cultural association – and, second, as a historically situated text. Seen through this interpretation, Trevor's novel provides a launching point for a new view that disengages the ways of reading that keep Irish literary studies rooted in the debate about the 'significance' of the historical past.

The imagery traditionally used to represent the clash between England and Ireland has a substantial history. In his critical work, *Inventing Ireland*, Declan Kiberd addresses the relationship in terms of dichotomies, in a section entitled, 'Ireland-England's Unconscious?':

> By Arnold's day, the image of Ireland as not-England had been well and truly formed ... if John Bull was industrious and reliable, Paddy was held to be indolent and contrary; if the former was mature and rational, the latter must be unstable and emotional; if the English were adult and manly, the Irish must be childish and feminine.[2]

The associations that Kiberd highlights here connect Ireland with traditionally feminine characteristics, demonstrating how the colonial relationship can be linked with gender stereotypes. In her article, 'De-colleenizing Ireland: William Trevor's *Family Sins*,' Mary Fitzgerald-Hoyt remarks:

> The identification of Ireland with female icons – Hibernia, Erin, the old woman, the colleen – has for centuries been a potent and pernicious tendency. Curiously, these stereotypes have been embraced by Irish and English alike: the metaphor of Ireland as oppressed woman or occasionally as militant standard-bearer fueled Irish nationalist posters and political cartoons. Conversely, the image of weeping, pliant Hibernia was juxtaposed with the simian-appearing Fenian to indicate to English Victorian audiences the difference between good (i.e., tractable) Irish and bad (i.e., rebellious) ones.[3]

By comparing the opposition of two nations with the opposition of the sexes, the oversimplified labels connect postcolonial and feminist theories. That is, to

1 William Trevor, *Felicia's journey* (New York, 1994). 2 Declan Kiberd, *Inventing Ireland* (Cambridge, MA, 1995), p. 30. 3 Mary Fitzgerald-Hoyt, 'De-colleenizing Ireland: William Trevor's *Family sins*', *Notes on Modern Irish Literature* 5 (1993) 28.

problematize these stereotypes of Ireland is to challenge the power structures delineated by both 'colonizer' and 'patriarch.'

Felicia's Journey sets up an opposition between Felicia and Mr. Hilditch that seemingly aligns with traditional stereotypes; Felicia is an Irish female, and Hilditch an English male. Felicia is impregnated and abandoned by her Irish boyfriend, who leaves to serve in the English army. She must choose whether to remain in Ireland, where her father calls her a 'dirty hooer', and her familial obligation is to care for her hundred-year-old great-grandmother, widowed of a husband killed fighting for Ireland.4 The congruence of the nation's history with her familial history sets her up as a symbolic figure. Literally pregnant by Johnny and figuratively impregnated by the past, she instead travels to England searching for her boyfriend and thus represents oppressed Ireland seeking reparations for what has been done to her. In England Mr. Hilditch, a corrupt Englishman whose obsession with control positions him as a representation of imperial power, preys upon her.

His obsession manifests throughout the novel in a number of domestic rituals. He habitually reads several newspapers in their entirety, listens each night to songs on his gramophone, and cleans his house often and thoroughly. The narrator's insistent listing of these activities in specific detail – in the form of headlines, song titles, and shopping lists – calls attention to Hilditch's meticulous and deliberate manner. Similarly, throughout the novel much attention is paid to Hilditch's eating habits; the narrator describes in considerable detail what, when, and how often he eats. The descriptions emphasize Hilditch's privileged station in life, in which his financial security affords him access to a reasonably comfortable lifestyle. In this degree of privilege he can be seen as analogous to the colonizer; he can afford not only to be satisfied but also to be greedy.

While he is portrayed as a fat man, however, he is not characterized as gluttonous. Like the abovementioned practices, his eating behaviour is not compulsive but intentional. His every act is calculated, particularly when it comes to his relationship with Felicia. When he lies to her and steals her money, he positions himself as her only resource. By the midpoint of the novel, Hilditch is in a place of power: he has the money, the food, the shelter, the information about Johnny's whereabouts, and – most significantly – Felicia's trust. Her acceptance of his hospitality reveals her dependence. In a traditional postcolonial reading of the novel, then, Felicia is a symbol of post-Famine exile, deprived of resources and land, displaced by misfortune and maltreatment. In contrast, Hilditch is the imperial figure that governs with an aim to possess all information, to organize as he sees fit, and to administrate all resources and decisions from a position of domination.5

4 Trevor, *Felicia's journey*, p. 60. 5 For a lengthier discussion of the relationship between Irish nationalism, the Famine, and the transition from the traditional to the modern as it manifests in the relationship between the Irish and English, see the chapter entitled, 'National character', in Seamus Deane's *Strange country* (Oxford, 1997), pp 49–99.

What might be considered to be the obvious political undertones of the novel are adeptly explored by critics Liam Harte and Lance Pettitt in the article entitled, 'States of Dislocation: William Trevor's *Felicia's Journey* and Maurice Leitch's *Gilchrist*.'⁶ The essay not only demonstrates parallels between Johnny and Hilditch, explaining Hilditch's homicidal actions, but also executes a sophisticated postcolonial reading. Focusing on Felicia's symbolic significance, it addresses the connection between postcolonial and feminist interests:

> In addition to being a compelling psychological thriller, the novel may be read as a postcolonial critique of the ideologies of British colonialism and post-independence Irish nationalism. Felicia suffers a double oppression on account of her gender and nationality. In Ireland, she is a victim of patriarchal nationalism; in England, she is oppressed by the embodiment of a malign residual colonialism.⁷

To assert that this or any other postcolonial interpretation is the definitive reading of the text, however, is to risk honouring outdated and reductive stereotypes. After all, the more literary critics emphasize the traditional stereotypes – whether literature evokes those images to legitimize or debunk them – the more they reinforce the associations that keep them rooted in historical origin. Stereotypes solicit postcolonial readings and postcolonial readings perpetuate stereotypes.

Instead, Harte and Pettitt's work invites a supplemental reading that moves beyond the standard postcolonial interpretation by posing Felicia as a 'migrant figure [who] acts as both a disruptive presence upon the inherited identities available to postcolonial subjects and as a transformative agent engendering hybrid identities.'⁸ If Felicia is released from the 'inherited identities', then a reevaluation of her corresponding character, Mr. Hilditch, reveals that the novel develops the opposition between them through several traits – not simply those that rouse political controversy. In addition to being female and Irish, Felicia is also young, unemployed, homeless, and poor. In contrast, Hilditch is middle-aged and fitted with a middle-class home, substantial occupation, and comfortable lifestyle. These oppositions are not inherently political; they assume political significance only when read that way. Examining binaries for their linguistic rather than political function enables an interpretation that extends beyond stereotypical meaning. In her essay, 'Sorties,' Cixous suggests that oppositions are tied to linguistic hierarchy:

> Thought has always worked through opposition ... Through dual, hierarchical oppositions. Superior/Inferior. Myths, legends, books. Philosophical systems. Everywhere (where) ordering intervenes, where a law organizes

6 Liam Harte and Lance Pettitt, 'States of dislocation: William Trevor's *Felicia's journey* and Maurice Leitch's *Gilchrist*', in Ashok Bery and Patricia Murray (eds), *Comparing postcolonial literatures: dislocations* (New York, 2000), pp 70–80. 7 Ibid., p. 73. 8 Ibid., pp 71–2.

what is thinkable by oppositions (dual, irreconcilable; or sublatable, dialectical). And all these pairs of oppositions are *couples*. Does that mean something? Is the fact that Logocentrism subjects thought – all concepts, codes and values – to a binary system, related to 'the' couple, man/woman?[9]

Though Cixous couches her analysis in terms of gender (which could undermine any discussion that aims in part to degenderize power relationships) the paradigm itself addresses simultaneous symbiosis and conflict within the binary, regardless of gender or national associations. Morag Shiach restates Cixous' argument in different terms, in which 'subjectivity requires the recognition of an Other, from whom the individual differentiates him- or herself. Yet this recognition is experienced as threatening, and the Other is immediately repressed, so that the subject can return to the security and certainty of self-knowledge'.[10] The otherness, while frequently associated with notions of marginality that characterize postcolonial and feminist theory, refers generally to the hierarchy that ultimately manifests in any power struggle. The 'couple' only exists with both terms or partners; yet the threat that is the Other causes the conflict that breaks the couple apart. When repression results in destruction, the entire system ceases to exist: 'Each couple is based on the repression of one of its terms, yet both terms are locked together in violent conflict. Without 'nature', 'culture' is meaningless, yet culture must continually struggle to negate nature, to dominate and control it, with obviously deadly results.'[11] Arguably the equation works in the other direction, as well: when the relationship ceases to exist, the result is death to one party.

Cixous' 'couples' theory, when applied to *Felicia's Journey*, permits an examination of binary opposition on the level of language rather than politics. The idea that Felicia and Hilditch have equally represented points of view invites a reading that examines their balance of power. When Felicia literally foresees her death, she abandons the power relationship in which she has unwittingly engaged with Hilditch. As Cixous' paradigm indicates, Hilditch's existence depends, at least symbolically, upon that relationship. When the conflict dies, the result is deadly for him. The novel ends with Felicia, the migrant figure, living homeless in England. She reflects on the souls in heaven whose ranks she might have joined had she not escaped the powerful relationship with Hilditch, and decides: 'the certainty she knows is still what she would choose. She turns her hands so that the sun may catch them differently, and slightly lifts her head to warm the other side of her face.'[12] The power balance has not shifted; it has ended.

On the national level, the conflict of power between England and Ireland must die, and the role of history in dictating the future – on the literary and political levels – must be negated. Bearing in mind that the use of labels such

9 Hélène Cixous, 'Sorties: out and out: attacks/ways out/forays' in Catherine Belsey and Jane Moore (eds), *The feminist reader* (2nd ed., Malden, MA, 1997), p. 91. 10 Morag Shiach, *Hélène Cixous: a politics of writing* (London, 1991), pp 7–8. 11 Ibid., p. 7. 12 Trevor, *Felicia's journey*, p. 213.

as 'England' and 'Ireland' grossly oversimplifies the national relationship – omit-
ting, for example, any discussion of the region of Northern Ireland – the use of
these terms nevertheless can reiterate the importance of eliminating reductive
labels and exemplify the value of applying Cixous' binaries. The 'couple' composed of England and Ireland faces a collapse similar to the destruction of the
relationship between Felicia and Hilditch. As an economically and technolog-
ically progressive Ireland slips out of the binary, no longer recognizable as the
feminized or repressed nation that once maintained its half of the couple, the
corresponding England must die. Ultimately, the entire system will cease to
exist, particularly as progress towards peace (since the Good Friday Agreement)
suggests and invites a revision of the political ties between England and Ireland.

To apply Cixous' theory to Irish literary studies requires a return leap from
observing power struggles within linguistic binaries in the text back to regarding the literary text as a representation of politics and possible vehicle for change.
As Edna Longley notes, 'It has grown harder to discuss Irish literature without
being drawn into arguments about culture and politics. No doubt historical
necessity is to blame.'[13] To suggest an apolitical way of reading raises two objections: first, that to read without politics in mind is to negate the experience of
those disenfranchised by the literal oppression by colonialism and patriarchy as
well the figurative oppression imposed by reductive stereotypes; and second,
that to suggest a reading without politics is to propose the impossible. In order
to demonstrate how a reading of *Felicia's Journey* through Cixous might apply
on the level of criticism, we must first address these two protestations.

In her article, entitled, 'Antagon*isms*: Revisionism, Postcolonialism and Feminism in Ireland,' Rebecca Pelan provides working, though admittedly oversimplified, definitions of 'revisionism' and 'postcolonialism.'[14] If 'revisionists' urge that 'a
re-reading and re-writing of the national mythology [be] undertaken to allow for
a more politically sophisticated/objective version of history to emerge,' then 'postcolonialists' might retort that setting aside the 'hurts of the past' denies 'a step in
the decolonization process whereby the inequities and injustices of a colonial history are dealt with.'[15] By Pelan's characterization, postcolonialism seeks reparations
for the tangible political, economic and social effects of colonization on the society, a compensation denied them by revisionist intentions to 'move on.'[16] It is the
latter group that might argue against the value of an apolitical way of reading. Just
as Felicia must abandon her quest to seek reparations in order to escape the dangerous power struggle with Hilditch, however, so must those postcolonialists – as
Pelan identifies them – consider that continuing to identify Ireland with victimization prevents the potential liberation from the symbolic opposition to England.

More delicate and theoretical is the second argument, that it is impossible to
suggest an apolitical reading. According to New Historicism, not only are texts

13 Edna Longley, *The living stream: literature and revisionism in Ireland* (Newcastle upon Tyne, 1994),
p. 9. 14 Rebecca Pelan, 'Antagon*isms*: revisionism, postcolonialism, and feminism in Ireland', *Journal
of Commonwealth and Postcolonial Studies* 7 (2000), 127–47. 15 Ibid., p. 127. 16 Ibid.

inescapably situated, but critics themselves are just as historically and contextually situated as the texts they critique. In 'Professing the Renaissance: the Poetics and Politics of Culture,' Louis Montrose points out that, as critics and as authors, 'our analyses and our understandings necessarily proceed from our own historically, socially, and institutionally shaped vantage points; that the histories we reconstruct are the textual constructs of critics who are, ourselves, historical subjects.'[17] If this is true, however, then history is constantly being revised as each text and critic changes the contextual landscape. For Irish studies, the text and the critic need only be freed enough from the fixed stereotypes and static conception of history to venture a new reading. Furthermore, to employ Cixous' theory is not to imply that the examination of linguistic trends allows for the possibility of transcending society, for which deconstructionism has been criticised. This reading simply requests a temporary suspension of political associations.

At the risk of assuming political affiliations, this proposed reading most closely aligns with Pelan's characterization of revisionism, although it does not suggest a 're-writing of the national mythology.' Seamus Deane's oft quoted statement that 'everything, including our politics and our literature, has to be re-written' – i.e. re-read – in order to 'enable new writing, new politics, unblemished by Irishness, but securely Irish,' attempts to acknowledge the existence of an identifiable Irish identity even as that identity tries to break free of anachronistic connotations.[18] Although he is criticised as asking for contradictory impossibilities, [Longley argues that 'Deane tries to have his Nationalist history and eat it, to deconstruct and canonize in the same gesture'],[19] Deane's statement suggests that, though there is a shared experience that is identifiably Irish, the essentialist notions of Irishness that conjure up reductive stereotypes no longer serve critical studies or Irish identity – if they ever did.

Deane's proposal articulates on the level of literary criticism that which this essay has tried to demonstrate on the textual level in *Felicia's Journey*: although, historically, the binary oppositions associated with England and Ireland have been charged with political meaning, by denying that those associations are fixed, Irish literature and its critics can surpass outdated and reductive ways of reading. To acknowledge the possibility of re-writing history is not to abandon it completely, to ignore stereotypes, or to deny wrongs done. It simply frees us to revisit what Longley identifies as a trend in Irish literary criticism: she says, 'Irish history emerges as the author of Irish writing, rather than *vice versa*.'[20] When the past no longer is viewed as a fixed truth, it ceases to constrain reading and writing, so that the literary text might contribute to the ever-changing face of history. As Montrose remarks, 'to speak of the social production of 'literature' or of any particular text is to signify not only that it is socially produced but also that it is socially productive: that it is the product of work and that it

17 Louis A. Montrose, 'Professing the Renaissance: the poetics and politics of culture', in H. Aram Veeser (ed.), *The new historicism* (New York, 1989), p. 23. 18 Seamus Deane, *Heroic styles: the tradition of an idea* (Derry, 1984), pp 17–18. 19 Longley, *The living stream*, p. 26. 20 Ibid., p. 27.

performs work in the process of being written, enacted, or read.'[21] As an economically and politically 'new' Ireland emerges, the historical and symbolic
'truths' that have diluted Irishness can be absorbed into the dynamic past, while
a liberated Ireland 'slightly lifts her head to warm the other side of her face.'[22]

Hibernicizing the bohémien: the Irish Revival and fin-de siècle Paris

MARY BURKE, KEOUGH INSTITUTE FOR IRISH STUDIES,
UNIVERSITY OF NOTRE DAME

W.B. Yeats's *Where There is Nothing* (1902) concerns a seditious country gentleman who marries a 'tinker' girl as a political statement, while John Millington
Synge's *The Tinker's Wedding* (1907) centers on the nullification of an agreement
between a priest and a 'tinker' clan that leads to violence against the clergyman.
The ubiquitous artistic representation of the *bohémien* in nineteenth-century
France, based upon a narcissistic imagining and containment of the 'Gypsy' as
illustrative of 'cultural vagabondage',[1] was a superficially subversive fad to which
sporadic Paris residents, Yeats and Synge, were undoubtedly exposed. As Synge's
biographer, W.J. McCormack, suggests:

> The entire spiritual milieu of the Parisian 'Bohème' derived not from Czech-
> speaking Bohemia, but from the gypsies (cf. Synge's tinkers) who formed
> part of its population. There were links between Parisian care-freedom and
> Irish subsistence. Synge's later equation of the beggar and the artist did not
> spring from nowhere.[2]

The modernist bohemian myth was only superficially subversive of the normative order and the commodified artistic realm.[3] An establishment artist such
as Gustave Courbet could write: 'In our oh-so-civilized society it is necessary
for me to lead the life of a savage ... To that end, I have just set out on the

---

21 Montrose, 'Professing the Renaissance', p. 23   22 Trevor, *Felicia's journey*, p. 213   1 '[T]he terms
"gypsy" and "bohemian" frequently became interchangeable in nineteenth-century French literature ... the gypsy began to lend his name to all those artists and other supposed cultural vagabonds
who chose to lead a creative life outside the mainstream of bourgeois society': Marilyn R. Brown,
Gypsies and other bohemians: the myth of the artist in nineteenth-century France (Ann Arbor, Michigan,
1985), p. 2.   2 W.J. McCormack, *Fool of the family: a life of J.M. Synge* (London, 2000), p. 149.   3
'The bohemian subject provided the artist, and the artist provided the bourgeois with a needed
stimulation. In the marketplace the artist was to the bourgeois what the gypsy was to the artist, and
the linked chain of appropriation eventually led to sound art investment': Brown, *Gypsies and other
bohemians*, p. 6.

great, independent, vagabond life of the gypsy'.⁴ In like fashion, when George Moore came into his patrimony in 1873, 'he made straight for Paris to study painting – or at any rate to enjoy the *vie d'artiste* – at the expense of his tenants in County Mayo.'⁵

Synge's unconventional dress style, often remarked upon by family members, is interpreted by McCormack as 'the reaction of a gentleman no longer possessing any country estate on which to potter about in a briar-torn jacket.'⁶ The dramatist 'almost became a Frenchman, so his mother said when his hair was affected by his illness and he took to wearing a black wig and a soft hat in French style.'⁷ Yeats constructed Synge as 'the Celtic incarnation of Arnold's scholar gypsy', and cast the 'apprentice Irish Protestant bohemian' as romantic vagrant-artist in his account of their first meeting: 'He had wandered among people whose life is as picturesque as the Middle Ages, playing his fiddle to Italian sailors, and listening to stories in Bavarian woods.'⁸ The dramatist appears to have been remembered as a carnivalesque bohemian: in Paris, where he sporadically resided between 1895 and 1902, Synge played the violin 'to friends at night with (as someone who heard him writes) 'the wild passion of a gypsy', one Aran islander recalled him simply as someone who 'used to play the fiddle, and was a great conjurer', and on a visit to the von Eiken sisters in 1894, he appeared with the family in a 'tableau of a gipsy camp.'⁹ According to family history, John was destined to be musical: 'The surname Synge was originally a kind of nickname or by-name: according to tradition, John Millington, a 'canon' or precentor of the Chapel Royal, sang so sweetly that King Henry VIII bade him take the name of Sing or Synge.'¹⁰ Synge's nephew situated his uncle's 'Tramp' persona within the *fin-de siècle* art world's appropriation of 'Gypsy' identity: 'He used the tramp or tinker as his symbol of the artist ... because he saw an analogy between the relation of the vagrant to peasant society and that of the artist to the educated, bourgeois class.'¹¹ In 'The Vagrants of Wicklow', Synge, whose brothers and brothers-in-law were conventionally successful, explicitly links underclass vagrancy and middleclass creativity:

> In the middle classes the gifted son of a family is always the poorest – usually a writer or artist with no sense for speculation – and in a family of peas-

4 Gustave Courbet, quoted in Brown, *Gypsies and other bohemians*, p. 4. 5 Vivian Mercier, in Eilís Dillon (ed.), *Modern Irish literature* (Oxford, 1994), 329–30. 6 McCormack, *Fool of the family*, 139. Synge had 'fifty pounds a year and a new suit when I am too shabby.' Lady Gregory, *Our Irish theatre*, 3rd ed. (Gerrards Cross, 1972), p. 77. 7 Katharine Worth, 'Synge', *The Irish drama of Europe from Yeats to Beckett* (London, 1978), p. 138. 8 Mary C. King, 'Synge's use of language', in Edward A. Kopper, Jr (ed.), *A J.M. Synge literary companion* (Westport, Conn., 1988), p.191; Roy Foster, 'Good behaviour: Yeats, Synge and Anglo-Irish etiquette' in Nicholas Grene (ed.), *Interpreting Synge: essays from the Synge summer school 1991–2000* (Dublin, 2000), p. 46; W.B. Yeats, 'Preface to the first edition of *the well of the saints': essays and introductions* (London, 1961), p. 298. 9 Maurice Bourgeois, *John Millington Synge and the Irish theater* (London, 1913), p. 47, p. 80; Edward Stephens, in Andrew Carpenter (ed.), *My uncle John: Edward Stephens's life of J.M. Synge* (London, 1974), p. 91. 10 Bourgeois, *Synge and the Irish theatre*, p. 3. 11 Stephens, *My uncle John*, p. 156.

ants, where the average comfort is just over penury, the gifted son sinks also, and is soon a tramp on the roadside.[12]

At the time Maurice Bourgeois was writing his biography of Synge (c. the 1910s), he notes that a legend had arisen 'which represents him as suffering the pangs of poverty, sleeping in ditches, and, like Goldsmith, his fellow-countryman, earning a livelihood by playing his fiddle to peasants. This he was never obliged to do.'[13] Honoré de Balzac's *Prince of Bohemia* suggested that 'Bohemia' enfolded all ambitious, unknown and fleetingly insolvent artists who carefully cultivated the semblance of poverty: 'Bohemia ... is made up of young men between the ages of twenty and thirty, all of them men of genius in their way; little known as yet, but to be known hereafter, when they are sure to be distinguished.'[14] Although Synge did not live long enough to reap major financial awards from his professional success, and lived on a less than bountiful allowance from his mother while in Paris, he once boasted to his early love, Cherie Matheson: 'I am a poor man, but I feel that if I live I shall be rich. I feel there is that in me which will be of value to the world.'[15]

The transgressive 'tinker' of Yeats' *Where there is nothing*, Synge's *The Tinker's Wedding*, and James Stephens's novel, *The Demi-Gods* (1914), where angels befriend roguish tinkers, encoded the bohemian values with which the *literati* narcissistically identified. The exoticising British *Journal of the Gypsy Lore Society* (1888 –) briefly promoted the concept of the archaic origins of the Irish tinker and his language, *Shelta*. Irish-born *JGLS* grandee John Sampson's entry on Shelta in the 1893 edition of *Chambers's Encyclopedia* defined it as 'a secret jargon of great antiquity spoken by Irish tinkers ... descendants of the ... bards.' Contemporary race theory underpinned the journal's obsession with cataloguing the 'disappearing' culture of 'ure-blooded' British Romanies of Indian origin. (Enlightenment ethnography purported to expose the 'Oriental' origins of European gypsies, consolidating the discourse of the exotic, heathenish gypsy.)[16] Although noting that tinkers were of indigenous origin, the journal nevertheless exoticized the minority, and the Revival fashion for depicting 'tinkers' as the antithesis of the expanding bourgeoisie emerged. The increasingly commodified and Orientalized bohemian myth mediated the 'perceived diametric opposition of bohemian vs. bourgeois',[17] or, in the case of the 'Tramp', as Synge signed his love-letters, the chasm between those he moved amongst and their perpetual awareness of his social status. Synge admits that he brought his fiddle on later trips to Aran in

12 John Millington Synge, 'The vagrants of Wicklow', in Robin Skelton (ed.), *Collected works*, 4 vols (London, 1962–68), ii, p. 202.   13 Bourgeois, *Synge and the Irish theatre*, p. 32.   14 Honoré de Balzac, *Un prince de la bohême* (1840). Quoted in Brown, *Gypsies and other bohemians*, p. 10.   15 C.H.H. (Cherie Matheson, a.k.a. Mrs. Kenneth Houghton), 'John Synge as I knew him', *Irish Statesman*, 5 July 1924, 534.   16 Mary Burke, 'Eighteenth-century European scholarship and nineteenth-century Irish literature: Synge's *Tinker's Wedding* and the orientalizing of "Irish Gypsies"' in Betsy Taylor FitzSimon and James Murphy (eds), *The Irish revival re-appraised* (Dublin, 2004).   17 Brown, *Gypsies and other bohemians*, p. 4.

order to 'have something new to keep up the interest of the people',[18] with whom he increasingly found it difficult to gain common ground.

Synge framed both the tinker and the islander depicted in *The Aran Islands* within the discourse of susceptibility to the supernatural and apartness from a homogenous sedentary or mainland majority. The islanders are bohemianized by the erratic nature of Aran's climate: 'The continual passing in this island between the misery of last night and the splendour of to-day, seems to create an affinity between the moods of these people and the moods of varying rapture and dismay that are frequent in artists.' Even the island's 'scattered cottages' reminded Synge of 'places I have sometimes passed when travelling at night in France or Bavaria.' The instinctively sophisticated islanders are uncannily quick to pick up the French phrases Synge teaches, an interest reciprocated by the French philologists they observe visiting their island. The Gallic spirit hovers over every aspect of Aran: if the islanders' innate sophistication links them to Paris, then their attractively primitive superstitions recall Brittany, one of the more 'quaint' districts of France. The surprisingly independent nature of the Aran women is compared to that of the bohemian females 'of Paris and New York', and one young woman is surprised by the draw she feels for the independent lifestyle of bohemian Paris.[19] Moreover, to Synge, the beggar's life embodies the antithesis of bourgeois and sedentary values, and the 'true' artist intuitively gravitates towards the 'authenticity' of the vagrant lifestyle:

> In all the circumstances of this tramp life there is a certain wildness that gives it romance and a peculiar value for those who look at life in Ireland with an eye that is aware of the arts also. In all the healthy movements of art, variations from the ordinary types of manhood are made interesting for the ordinary man.[20]

The *Irish Independent* review of *The Shadow of the Glen* that suggested Synge was inspired not by the Western Isles, but by 'the gaiety of Paris', and Arthur Griffith's accusation that it reeked of 'the decadent cynicism that passes current in the Latin *Quartier*'[21] are oddly perceptive. Bourgeois, Synge's French biographer, suggests that the Revival drama's glorification of the vagabond and the wandering fiddler was an importation of *fin-de-siècle* theatre Synge may have been exposed to: 'not only in Synge, but in the whole contemporary Anglo-Irish drama, we find a romantic glorification of the tramp and the fiddler, not unlike, it seems, that in M. Jean Richepin's *Chemineau*.' Le chemineau (*The vagabond*) was first produced at the Ódeon Theatre, Paris, on 16 February 1897, and Synge, who was in Paris from October 1896 to May 1897, might have seen Richepin's play.[22] Jean Richepin (1849–1926) was a poet and dramatist, best

---

18 Synge, *The Aran Islands*, *CW*, ii, p. 151. 19 Ibid., pp 74, 127, 60, 80, 102, 143, 114. 20 Synge, 'The vagrants of Wicklow', *CW*, ii, p. 208. 21 Quoted in David H. Greene and Edward M. Stephens (eds), *J.M. Synge 1871–1909*, rev. ed. (New York, 1989), p. 159. 22 Bourgeois, *Synge and the Irish theatre*, p. 150; p. 150n.

known for poems about tramps and vagabonds that employed the canting language of the underworld.

British influence on Synge's own writing or Irish letters in general is diluted within a broad European context (he writes of 'Dante and Chaucer and Goethe and Shakespeare')[23] or bypassed altogether. Artistic and intellectual influence is seen to flow to and return from France and the continent: Synge stresses the importance of Irish pseudo-historian Geoffrey Keating's studies in Bordeaux on his formation as a scholar, while both the Irish and contemporaneous Breton-language theatre revivals are products of the 'Celtic imagination'.[24] Synge was exposed to the theories of d'Arbois de Jubainville at his time at the Collège de France, which connected ancient Ireland to Homer's Greece. He also reviewed R.I. Best's translation of d'Arbois de Jubainville's 1883 study of the medieval Gaelic pseudo-history, *The Book of Invasions*, which pointed to manifold comparanda in classical and Oriental mythology, a thesis that the dramatist found 'suggestive.'[25] Synge attempted a verse play on Ireland's first inhabitants based on the Gaelic chronicles. Orientalizing traditions that pre-Gaelic peoples from 'the East' such as the Fir-bolg and Tuatha Dé Danann were a long-lasting presence in Ireland and inflect both his belief that 'tinkers' were a 'semi-gipsy' class with 'curiously Mongolian features' and his exoticisation of Aran islanders; a pair of girls Synge meets spoke in 'a sort of chant', and the *outré* roots of the island's *sean-nós* singing is implied by its comparison with a 'chant' Synge 'once heard from a party of Orientals.'[26]

Such Orientalization derived both from a Gaelic mytho-history tradition in which the arrival of the Milesians (Gaels or Celts) was constructed as the culmination of the ancient plantations, and a seventeenth-century theory that Phoenician was the mother tongue of all non-Romance languages of Europe, avidly promoted by Patriots challenging the claim that English culture derived from classical civilisation.[27] The nationalist charge of Synge's reference to the supposed archaic, non-classical ancestry of the islanders derives from the Patriotic antiquarian emphasis on Ireland's circumvention of Roman dominion (for Roman dominion, read English dominion), an implicit claim unchallenged by the Synge critic, Weldon Thornton.[28] The dramatist abhorred what he understood to be the England-obsessed parochialism that fired Gaelic League campaigners: 'Was there ever a sight so piteous as an old and respectable people setting up the ideals of the Fee-Gee because, with their eye's glued on John Bull's navel, they dare not be Europeans for fear the huckster across the street might call them English.' The

23 Synge, 'Various notes', *CW*, ii, 347–8. 24 Synge, 'An Irish historian', *CW*, ii, p. 36; Synge, 'A Celtic theatre', *CW*, ii, p. 393. 25 Henri d'Arbois de Jubainville, *The Irish mythological cycle and Celtic mythology*, trans. R.I. Best (Dublin, 1903). Synge's review appeared in *The Speaker*, 2 April 1904. 26 Synge, 'People and places' *CW*, ii, p. 198; Synge, *The Aran Islands*, *CW*, ii, p. 52; p. 141. 27 Joep Leerssen, 'On the edge of Europe: Ireland in search of oriental roots, 1650–1850', *Comparative Criticism* 8 (1986), p. 95. 28 'Aran culture was prehistoric and untamed, a Celtic / Indo-European survival owing nothing to Greco-Roman-influenced European culture': Weldon Thornton, 'J.M. Synge', in Richard J. Finneran (ed.), *Anglo-Irish Literature: a review of research* (New York, 1976), p. 51.

'fraud and hypocrisy' of the League's language policy will only be swept aside, Synge suggests, when Ireland learns 'again that she is part of Europe.'[29] Synge's *Aran Islands* deliberately veils the problematic incongruities of Aran's long evolution. The dramatist situates the islanders within a pseudo-historical frame by his intimation that they were descended from a pre-Celtic people: during a trip to Dun Aengus, he props his book on 'stones touched by the Fir-bolgs.'[30] Synge ignores the intriguing fact, cited in a near-contemporaneous account of Aran, that the islanders were partially descended from the soldiers of a Cromwellian garrison.[31] This suggests that the English language was not as recent an arrival on Aran as Synge would have readers assume. Throughout the text, Synge subtly implies that he was taught Gaelic on the island, obscuring the irony that Trinity, where he formally studied the language, instituted the study of the subject in order to prepare clergymen such as his uncle, Alexander Synge, Aran's first Protestant missionary.[32] The ambiguities of centuries of religious and linguistic contact problematize Synge's picture of islands mercifully lacking in British and English-language influence, but intuitively in possession of a whiff of Gallic sophistication and an innate sympathy for all things French.

Yeats famously wrote that on meeting Synge in 1896 he told him: 'Give up Paris ... go to the Aran Islands. Live there as if you were one of the people themselves; express a life that has never found expression.' In fact, Yeats did not advise Synge to give up all things French; he continued to urge his reviews of French literature. Synge was the cosmopolitan Yeats wished himself to be: the dramatist wrote notebooks in French, was almost bilingual, and translated Villon.[33] Altogether, Synge's time in Germany and France is often subtly dismissed, as if 'he had taken a wrong turn and his creative life only began when he returned to Ireland.'[34] Rejecting the attention paid to Yeats' dismissal of Synge's Paris experience, Mark Mortimer states that Synge's time in the French capital is central to understanding his formation as an artist:

> In Paris, he read widely and retained what was appropriate to his own intellectual and aesthetic growth, ... attending the lectures of d'Arbois de Jubainville on Celtic civilization and languages, he returned to a study of the Irish language and acquired a knowledge of, and a love for, Irish mythology ... and learned the trade of writing.[35]

Synge's debt to the French capital 'was deliberately underestimated by George Moore and Stephen McKenna'; Moore believed that he himself was the one

29 Synge, 'Can we go back into our mother's womb?' *CW*, ii, p. 400. 30 Synge, *The Aran Islands*, *CW*, ii, p. 69. 31 Arthur Symons, 'The isles of Aran', *The Savoy* (8 Dec 1896), p. 78. 32 Trinity founded a Professorship of Irish in 1838, and the first four holders of the chair were Church of Ireland clergymen. The fourth in line, the Revd James Goodman, gave Synge his first lessons in Irish. Eilís Dillon (ed.), *Modern Irish Literature: sources and founders* (Oxford, 1994), p. 82. 33 See Roy Foster, 'Good behaviour', p. 45. 34 Worth, 'Synge', p. 121. 35 Mark Mortimer, 'Synge and France', in Joseph McMinn (ed.), *The internationalism of Irish literature and drama* (Gerrards Cross, 1992), pp 92–93.

Irishman capable of interpreting France, whilst McKenna played down Synge's French 'to defend him against the charge of being "Frenchified" ... levelled by extreme nationalists and smug pietists in Dublin' outraged by *The Shadow of a Glen* and *The Playboy of the Western World.*[36] The nationalist conviction of the derivative 'foreign' decadence of Synge's drama led William Bulfin to accuse the dramatist of being a kind of literary Dr Frankenstein, 'hunting for slimy, clammy, hideous things ... gleaning odds and ends of humanity from graveyards and dead-houses and making a monster!' Unsurprisingly, Bourgeois feels the need to defend his subject with the assurance that Synge was 'one of the few Irish writers who europeanized Ireland with degaelicizing it.'[37] In various journal and newspaper articles, Synge outlined French art, theatre and literature to the Irish reading public, and interpreted the Irish Literary Revival for the French. The dramatist partook of a long continuum of Irish literary contact with Paris,[38] and admitted to the influence of French literature in a 1907 draft Preface for the Cuala Press edition of his poems. '[T]hey were written from five to eight years ago and, is obvious enough, in Paris among all the influences of the so-called decadent and symbolist schools.'[39]

Sampson stated that 'one of the earliest and most gracious traits' of the Gypsy was his 'love of music', which appears to be biologically determined: 'The only authentic name for a Gypsy, the word *Rom*, identical with Indian *Dom*, means, if etymology may be trusted, 'professional musician.'[40] Representations of the ambulant musician, the tramp, the brigand, the beggar and the urban *flâneur* – such a list reads like an inventory of Syngean *dramatis personae* – were located within the pliable 'set of meanings the *bohémien* could occupy.'[41] Douglas Hyde's *The Tinker and the Fairy* (1905), which concerns the affair of the musician 'king of the tinkers' with a fairy woman, reinforced the apolitical stereotype of 'innate' tinker musicality. The fiddle came to be considered the most 'patriotic' instrument of the Revival,[42] and the theme of the uncanny influence or compulsion to wander of the fiddler was popular in plays produced in many of the major Irish theatres during the opening years of the twentieth century: Rutherford Mayne's *The Turn of the Road* was produced by the Ulster Literary Theatre in 1906; Pádraic Colum's *The Fiddler's House*, a revised version of *Broken soil* (1903),

36 Mortimer, 'Synge and France', p. 87.   37 Bourgeois, *Synge and the Irish theatre*, p. 63.   38 In the previous decade, Wilde had visited Paris, and, whilst there, wrote his French-language play, *Salomé*; Moore was part of the Parisian impressionism and literary scene; later, Joyce settled in the French capital and wrote *Ulysses*, while Beckett adopted both France and its language. See Mortimer. 'Synge and France', p. 88. Patrick Rafroidi demonstrates the impact of writers such as Thomas Moore, Charles Maturin, Lady Morgan, the Banims and Maria Edgeworth on French Romanticism in his *L'Irlande et le Romanticisme: la litterature Irlandaise-Anglaise de 1789–1850 et sa place dans le mouvement occidental* (Paris, 1972).   39 Quoted in Jon Stallworthy, 'The poetry of Synge and Yeats', in Maurice Harmon (ed.), *J.M. Synge: centenary papers 1971* (Dublin, 1972), p. 153.   40 Eileen Lyster, 'Introduction' in John Sampson, *The gypsy life of Betsy Wood* (London, 1926), p. x.   41 Brown, *Gypsies and other bohemians*, p. 3.   42 'It is good news that in many parts of Ireland the people are taking to the fiddle again, where their fathers were content with the melodeon and its crude noitses.' Robert Lynd, *Home life in Ireland* (London, 1909), p. 316.

was staged in March 1907; E.K. Worthington's unpublished one-act play, *The Burden*, was performed by the Cork Dramatic Society on 11 May 1910.[43] In like manner, Synge attempted an opera based on the tale of Eileen Aroon, who is enticed away from her wedding by a musician lover.[44]

In his youth, Synge cultivated the artistic self-image of a bohemian fiddler, and describes his performance on the fiddle for the benefit of islanders wishing to dance in *The Aran Islands*. Music may have pioneered the cultural revival, a theory that places Synge in a vanguard 'later outmanouevred by Yeats and company.'[45] Incidentally, a certain number of composers and librettists have been inspired by Synge's work: Ralph Vaughan Williams chose *Riders to the Sea* as a libretto, and Joyce's friend, Carlo Linati, adapted *The Shadow of the Glen* as *La Veglia*. Music was by Arrigo Pedrolo.[46] I have also found references to William E Hart's *Synge's first Symphony: The Aran Islands*, and James Adair's *The Tinker's Wedding: a Comic Opera in Two Scenes*. Mary C. King sees Synge's preoccupation with the musician as of a piece with the boundary-dissolving obsessions of contemporary art movements.[47] Such collaboration links some of those surrounding Synge: Hyde's musical collaborator on *The Tinker and the Fairy* in 1910, the Dublin-based composer Michele Esposito (1855–1929), was chief piano professor at the Royal Irish Academy of Music where Synge studied violin, composition and theory while simultaneously enrolled at Trinity.[48] The cult of the 'tinker' had become so pervasive in Irish artistic life by the time of Esposito and Hyde's collaboration that it encompassed both pupil and teacher. Esposito too, had lived in Paris for a time.

The Romantic period in music, as conventionally considered, collided with the rise of the 'Gypsy' as a popular and ubiquitous trope of wildness and sensuality in European letters, and the experimental and passionate Franz Liszt (1811–86) welded both trends in his study, *The Gipsy in Music* (1859), an 'overgrown preface' whose aim was to elucidate his *Rhapsodies Hongroise*.[49] Like Synge after him, Liszt sojourned in Paris, and there studied music formally, but later immersed himself in Gypsy culture, the source of what he considered '*real music*':[50] in its endeavour to express the 'soul of the nation', Romantic music tended to appropriate the 'colourful' and the ethnic. To Liszt, the music of the putatively non-intellectual, uncivilized and child-like Gypsy musician expressed pure emotion and instinctive poetry, and his musical skills were innate rather than learnt.[51] The *gitan* is the quintessential tormented, otherworldly Romantic: 'the Gipsy's

43 Bourgeois, *Synge and the Irish theatre*, p. 11. 44 Greene and Stephens, *J.M. Synge 1871–1909*, p. 38. 45 Harry White, *The keeper's recital: music and cultural history in Ireland, 1770–1970* (Cork, 1998), p. 7; McCormack, *Fool of the family*, p. 84. 46 Ann Saddlemyer, 'Synge's soundscape', *Interpreting Synge*, p. 185. 47 Mary C King, *The drama of J.M. Synge* (Syracuse, 1985), p. 163. 48 Douglas Hyde, Libretto. *The Tinker and the Fairy, Op. 53*. 1910. Music by Michele Esposito (London, 1910). 49 Franz Liszt, *The Gipsy in Music*, trans. Edwin Evans, 2 vols (London, 1926), i, p. xiii. 50 Ibid., i, p. xv. 51 'In the very act of passing the bow across the violin-strings a natural inspiration suggested itself [to the Gypsy musician]; and, without any search for them, there came rhythms, cadences, modulations, melodies and tonal discourses.' Ibid., i, p. 13.

sufferings, after all, are caused by his habit of too much feeling without thought too much dreaming without calculation, and too much imagining without judgement.' Liszt constitutes the nineteenth-century discourse of the peripatetic artist as Gypsy vagabond when he notes that he himself 'led the life of a wandering virtuoso, precisely as [Gypsies] do.' However, fellow Paris bohemians can never 'penetrate' the mystery of Gypsy expression because they do not have the Gypsy's 'passion for Nature.'[52] The Romantic stereotype of the vagabond musical genius was actually grounded in the reality that in nineteenth-century Spain, Hungary and Russia, Gypsies became part of an alternative artistic aristocracy, such was the respect they earned for their prowess as musicians; Queen Victoria's harpist was a Gypsy, as was the nineteenth-century violinist Palaczinta, who was honoured in her native Romania with a commemorative postage stamp.[53] The nineteenth century saw an upsurge in interest in the subject of the Gypsy among formal composers, the most famous being Bizet's *Carmen*.

'Étude morbide' (*c.*1899), described by the author himself as 'a morbid thing about a mad fiddler in Paris', was a veiled autobiographical account of Synge's life. It concerns a musician who has a breakdown after a failed concert, and Synge later exhorted Yeats not to publish it in a letter written prior to his surgery in mid-1908. The fervent, Romantic authorial voice was embarrassing to the older Synge: 'My nervousness is increasing. ... I read of men who have gone mad and slain their kindred ... if I go among the streets I fall in with wretched beings on the brink of total alienation.'[54] Although there is no evidence to suggest that Synge had read Liszt either in the French original or the German translation, the saturation of 'Étude morbide' with Lisztean ideas indicates the degree to which Liszt's folk musician-as-noble-savage paradigm had permeated artistic discourse: All art that is not conceived by a soul in harmony with some mood of the earth is without value .... Music is the finest art, for it alone can express directly what is not utterable.' The troubled hero of 'Étude morbide' burns his trite, insincere 'sonnets written in Paris', finding that the only poetry he is 'only able to read' is 'the songs of peasants.'[55] (Similarly, in 'Moods and Memories', a series of pieces describing artistic Paris published in *Dana*, George Moore describes his perplexity at the discordant music 'of the younger generation', and suggests that 'truth' is to be found in the singing of a vagrant).[56] Synge was a member of the student orchestra, an experience of 'ecstasy' and 'magical beauty' he treasured:

> No other emotion that I have received was quite so puissant or complete. ...
> One is lost in a blind tempest [of music] that wails round one with always
> beautiful passion, the identity is merged in a ... symmetrical joy, cathedrals
> build themselves about one with the waves of purple storm.[57]

52 Ibid., i, p. 113; I, p. 129; ii, pp 228–9. 53 Angus Fraser, *Gypsies* (Oxford, 1992), p. 203; Donald Kenrick, *Gypsies under the swastika* (1995), p. 16. 54 Synge. 'Étude morbide.' *CW*, ii, p. 29. 55 Ibid., *CW*, ii, p. 35. 56 George Moore, 'Moods and memories', *Dana* 3 (July 1904), p. 76. 57 Synge, *Autobiography*, *CW*, ii, 14.

Synge's immersion in Irish folk traditions and his self-conscious fostering of a Lisztean European artistic sensibility collide in the account of a dream he has on Aran in which he is made frenzied by mysterious music against his will:

> It came closer to me, gradually increasing in quickness … the sound began to move in my nerves and blood, and urge me to dance with them …Then the luring excitement became more powerful than my will, and my limbs moved … I was swept away in a whirlwind of notes … till I could not distinguish between the instruments and the rhythm and my own person or consciousness.[58]

This passage invokes the folk belief, exploited by many Revival writers, that 'the little people' lured humans for a brief time to an inverted, alluring world by their beautiful playing, or could be coaxed by consummate human musicians. (Intuitively utilising the vocabulary of the era, Synge's mother considered her son to be 'bewitched with music', a path she believed would inevitably lead to 'mischief').[59] By referring to the presence on Aran of Fir-bolg, Synge implies that the islanders are their descendants, since folkloric belief suggested that the pre-Celtic peoples ultimately fled to Aran or descended underground to become those afterwards known as 'the little people'. The association of the putative descendants of pre-Celts with fairies allies the islanders with 'tinkers' as a people apart from the majority of 'Gaelic' mainlanders, and reveals Synge's identification, as a non-Catholic of English descent, with those constructed as non-Gaelic, in an era when the terms 'Gael', 'Catholic' and 'Irish' were increasingly conflated. A Catholic commentator was to state in the wake of the attempted expurgation of Protestant and British traditions from the post-1922 state: 'The Irish nation is the Gaelic nation; … its history is the history of the Gael. All other elements have no place in Irish national life, literature and tradition.'[60]

Sympathy towards islanders, seafarers, tinkers, and tramps is revealed at every turn in the dramatist's prose writings, in particular. One Wicklow beggar Synge eulogizes was a well-travelled sailor whose life embodies the antithesis of bourgeois and sedentary values:

> all wanderers have finer intellectual and physical perceptions than men who are condemned to local habitations … The slave and the beggar are wiser than the man who works … Every industrious worker has sold his birthright for a mess of pottage, perhaps served him in chalices of gold.[61]

The identification of skilled musicianship with a putative non-Gaelic caste promulgated in the Revival text is, like the supposed exotic nature of the 'Irish

---

58 Synge, *The Aran Islands*, CW, ii, pp 99–100. 59 Mrs Synge to Robert Synge, quoted in Greene and Stephens, *J.M. Synge, 1871–1909*, p. 23. 60 *Catholic Bulletin* 14. 4 (24 April 1924), p. 269, quoted in Terence Brown, *Ireland: a social and cultural history, 1922–1985* (London, 1985), p. 63. 61 Synge, *People and places*, CW, ii, p. 196.

Gypsy', a seemingly recent stereotype that actually has roots in centuries of exclusionary constructs of ethnicity. Cambrensis' concession that the flawed Irish were skilled musicians at least, is preceded by the following Gaelic myth-historic classification of remnants of vanquished pre-Celtic peoples: 'All who are fair-haired, vengeful, large, every plunderer, all who are musical, professors of music and entertainment, those who are adepts in all druidical arts, they are descended from the Tuatha Dé Danann in Ireland.'[62] Synge bicycled the neglected and serpentine eighteenth-century roads of Wicklow, routes known by few but 'the tinkers who camped on the wide grass margins';[63] the positive stereotype of the male Irish tinker that had solidified in popular discourse by the mid-twentieth century had gathered Syngean accretions of knowledge of Irish literature and immersion in the Irish landscape. The tinker 'has ... a magnificent command of the traditional tales of Irish folklore' and 'the soul of a poet. He plays the fiddle divinely. He has never, I am sure, stolen money or clothes or personal property. But he is an inveterate and highly skilled poacher' and 'knows more about the ways of the wild creatures of the countryside than any other man I have known.'[64] Ultimately, Synge's work and that of certain of his contemporaries is instrumental in the constitution of the double-edged discourse of Ireland's non-sedentary and non-mainland peoples as carriers of 'authentic' musicianship and intuitive bohemianism, rhetoric that supports calls for recognition of separate identity and culture, but simultaneously reinscribes Otherness.

Reforming the savage: the Ireland and England of Pedro Calderón de la Barca

ANITA HOWARD, NUI, CORK

Written in the tradition of Spanish *comedias de santos* or hagiographical dramas, Pedro Calderón de la Barca's 1628 play *El purgatorio de San Patricio* ('St Patrick's Purgatory') seems outwardly to reflect a definition of Irishness as a passionate and unpredictable condition. Its pagan Irish setting is chiefly represented by the character of Egerio, Ireland's fiercely proud and impetuous king, whose self-destructive passions resist Patricio's Christian counsel from his first moments onstage to his death at the end of the second act.[1] On the face of it, the play seems a straight-

---

62 Duald MacFirbis (Dubhaltach Mac Fhirbhisigh), *Book of genealogies*, qtd in Eoin MacNeill, *Phases of Irish history* (Dublin, 1919), p. 79. 63 Stephens, *My uncle John*, p. 32. 64 Brian Seymour Vesey-Fitzgerald, *Gypsies of Britain: an introduction to their history* (1944), (Newton Abbot, 1973), pp 184–5. 1 Throughout this paper, I will refer to the widely-known leading characters of the plays by Calderón's versions of their names: Patricio for St Patrick, Enrique for Henry VIII.

forward tale of the evangelisation of a savage realm through the stoical and austere Christianity personified by Patricio. But it proves as much a celebration of the
possibilities of Ireland as an untamed land as a cautionary tale about a savage 'other'.

The life of St Patrick was a popular theme of Spanish Counter-Reformation
literature and drama.[2] While the spiritual significance of the Patrician theme
was clear, it was also of political relevance in a country which, by the 1620s, was
home to many Irish exiles from political and religious unrest, whose descendants transferred their loyalty to the nation sheltering them. For many Spaniards,
and Irish exiles, Ireland's unpredictable climate and terrain offered points of tactical and ideological advantage. It was a place of military possibility, as a ground
from which to launch attacks on England; it also had a spiritual resonance, being
a land of embattled Catholicism. The ideological heart of Calderón's play develops a point of visionary connection between the natural and supernatural worlds,
a realm that provides the gateway to spiritual fulfillment.

This point of connection is represented by the institution of St Patrick's
Purgatory, one of the best-known legends of medieval Christianity. There already
existed a substantial amount of visionary literature by those who claimed to have
journeyed from the natural world to the state of purgatory.[3] As a favourite theme
of early modern spiritual literature, the same Patrician legend had been taken
up by such political figureheads of Ireland in exile as Philip O'Sullivan Beare
and Thomas Messingham, superior of the Irish College in Paris.[4] But at the
time Calderón wrote the play, the status of St Patrick's Purgatory as a shrine of
Catholic spirituality in Ireland was becoming obsolete through religious disputes and unrest.[5] It was a time when faith needed to be stated strongly.

Calderón's play tells how the purgatory, a cave on Saints' Island in Lough
Derg thought to lead penitents through the infernal regions to salvation, is instituted miraculously in order to demonstrate divine approval of Ireland's conversion. Its first decisive role in Calderón's plot is to serve as a hell's mouth for

---

2 Calderón found a main source in the novel *Vida y purgatorio de San Patricio* ('Life and Purgatory
of St Patrick'), by Juan Pérez de Montalbán, published in Madrid in 1627. An immediate bestseller,
it was also adapted for the stage by Lope de Vega, then the more established dramatist, as the play
El mayor prodigio y purgatorio de la vida ('The greatest wonder and purgatory of life'), again within
a year of its publication. 3 The legend of St Patrick's Purgatory was conveyed through at least three
medieval texts of this kind, the best known being Henry of Saltrey's twelfth-century *Tractatus de
purgatorio S. Patricii*. 4 Montalbán used O'Sullevan Beare's 1621 *Historiæ catholicæ Iberniæ com-
pendium* and Messingham's 1624 *Florilegium insulæ sanctorum* as source material. The voices of two
prominent Irish political exiles of the time thereby contributed to Calderón's play: Victor F. Dixon,
'St Patrick of Ireland and the dramatists of golden age Spain', *Hermathena* 121 (1976), 142–4. 5 Shane
Leslie records how Miler Magrath, owner of the Lough Derg purgatory site, surrendered it to
Elizabeth I in 1597. Magrath was the first Protestant bishop of Clogher, and simultaneously Catholic
bishop of Down and Protestant archbishop of Cashel for nine years. His career reflects the need to
disguise or compromise personal ideologies in order to retain prosperity at a time when England
was turning its energies for political and religious reformation towards Ireland. When Magrath's
son James inherited the purgatory site in 1610 he made it over to the Protestant Archbishop
Spottiswoode of Clogher, who destroyed it in 1632, four years after the first performance of Calderón's
play. Cf. Shane Leslie, *St Patrick's purgatory: a record from history and literature* (London, 1932).

Egerio, who enters it as a defiant unbeliever in a final dismissal of Patricio's new creed: 'que ni temo su horror, ni a su Dios temo' ('for I fear neither his horror nor his God').⁶ Calderón's trademark causal structure brings Egerio to the violent and incendiary fate predicted from the opening moments of the play: 'muera rabiando quien rabiando vive' ('Let him die raging who lives raging').⁷ It seems that the cave of enlightenment discovers little more than innate savagery in Ireland's monarch. But in a revealing error, the earliest printed versions of *El purgatorio* list Egerio, as 'rey de Ingalaterra', or king of England.⁸

This suggests that the young court dramatist was making a conscious or unconscious association between his Irish play and a drama of his performed the year before about an historical English monarch far more recent and controversial than the fictional construct Egerio. Calderón's 1627 *La cisma de Ingalaterra* ('The schism of England') portrays Henry VIII's divorce of his Spanish queen and remarriage to Anne Boleyn, an act which, in Counter-Reformation perspective, instituted England's Protestant Reformation. Drawing on the account of a Jesuit historian writing in stringent defence of the Counter-Reformation, Calderón portrayed these historical events as the loss of a nation's soul through the moral collapse of its monarch.⁹ Yet his Ireland finds its soul through religious and political upheaval, despite the unapologetic depravity of its king. Both these early Calderonian plays place on or near centre stage the figures of impassioned kings who resist the moderation of Christianity and thus bring upon themselves similarly inevitable consequences.

Calderón never visited Ireland or England, but he would have been aware of the presence of Irish and English visitors and exiles, in Madrid and further afield. For instance, *La cisma de Ingalaterra* was probably strongly influenced by the Spanish Match controversy, which, to judge from contemporary accounts, was a time when Irish exiles had to be kept apart from the entourage of the Prince of Wales and Duke of Buckingham on their unscheduled trip to Madrid.¹⁰ Attempts to forge direct alliances between Spain and Ireland had fre-

6 All Spanish quotations from the plays throughout this paper are taken from the following editions: José María Ruano de la Haza (ed.), *El purgatorio de San Patricio, by Pedro Calderón de la Barca* (Liverpool, 1988); Anne Mackenzie (ed.), *La cisma de Ingalaterra, by Pedro Calderón de la Barca* (Warminster, 1990). In subsequent footnotes I will refer to these editions of the plays as *Purgatorio* and *Cisma*, respectively. The quotation from *Purgatorio* cited in this footnote is from p. 132, line 2082. All English translations from the plays throughout this paper are mine. 7 Calderón de la Barca, *Purgatorio*, p. 74, line 8. 8 Egerio is cast-listed as king of England in the first collected edition of Calderón's plays, printed in Madrid in 1636 and in two subsequent Madrid editions of 1640. The 1636 edition, compiled by Calderón's brother, appeared in the year of the playwright's appointment to Spain's prestigious military Order of Santiago. Both events were a sign that Calderón's work had earned him high royal favour, and prominence as a court dramatist. Accidental or otherwise, the confusion of pagan Egerio with heretical Enrique was a detail to reinforce rather than challenge the political and spiritual ideologies of a ruling establishment that had bestowed one of its highest honours upon Calderón. 9 Calderón's main source for *La cisma de Ingalaterra* was the first book of Pedro de Rivadeneira's 1588 prose work *Historia eclesiástica del cisma del reino de Ingalaterra* ('An ecclesiastical history of the schism in the kingdom of England'). This portrays Henry VIII's divorce of Catherine of Aragon as the abandonment of a legitimate marriage, resulting from the king's surrender to the sensual wiles and political manipulation personified by Anne Boleyn and Cardinal Thomas Wolsey. 10 Philip O'Sullevan Beare,

quently led to Spain's military humiliation at such ventures as the 1601 battle of Kinsale: with Spain's international influence beginning to decline, Calderón would not have been expected to write a warlike play about Ireland.[11]

But it was in Spain's interest to approve of Ireland, as it was in England's interest to depict Irishness as uncivilized and inconstant. Spain's Irish exiles, especially the *guzmanes* descended from those who left in the Flight of the Earls, were building up a reputation for bravery and loyalty to their new country.[12] As foreign reinforcements went, they were judged to be among the more desirable and reliable allies. Many *arbitristas*, or political theorists, nonetheless supported the Tacitean view that foreign forces were apt to behave in a primitive and uncivilized manner.[13] It is noticeable that the nations they most frequently accused of producing such soldiers were those leaning towards Protestantism, such as Germany, Ireland and Poland, cited as Spain's most loyal allies by Philip IV's chief minister Olivares, had remained predominantly Catholic. Calderón's Ireland was essentially the territory of the subjective mind, used to reflect personal progression, with the invigorated Irishness of conversion portrayed as a condition his own declining nation might envy.

Calderón's Irish play, then, portrays salvation; his English play explores the decline of a schismatic soul directing itself towards damnation. The Irish and English kings promise these different trajectories of fate from their opening moments. In Egerio's first appearance, he rushes onstage maddened to the point of suicide by the horror of a dream in which he saw both his daughters incinerated by the flame that leapt from a slave's mouth. His customary dress of animal skins reflects this irrational behaviour. Even awakening from the nightmare cannot end the king's torturous sense of his own powerlessness:

> Nada podrá alegrarme.
> Tanto pudo el dolor enajenarme
> de mí, que ya sospecho
> que es Etna el corazón, volcán el pecho.[14]

> [Nothing can cheer me.
> So far did the pain distance me from myself
> that I still suspect
> my heart is an Etna and my breast a volcano.]

Proposición de la conquista de Irlanda ('A proposal for the conquest of Ireland'), ms., République Française Archives, Paris, p. 233. In this treatise, addressed to Philip IV of Spain, O'Sullevan Beare sets out his plan for a possible Spanish invasion of Ireland, reminding the king that, at the time the Prince of Wales was in the Spanish court, he had been advised by another Irish exile close to Philip 'to keep away from the English or run the risk of your wrath'. This translation from O'Sullevan Beare is mine.   11 As historian R.A. Stradling put it, Ireland's significance to Spain was essentially idealistic: '… orthodoxy of religion was just about the only aspect of western civilisation which [the Irish] had successfully adopted.': R.A. Stradling, *Spain's struggle for Europe, 1598–1668* (London, 1994), p. 260.   12 Ibid., p. 258, p. 262.   13 Ibid., pp 259–60.   14 Calderón de la Barca, *Purgatorio*, p. 75, lines 69–72.

We hear similar sentiments from the English king Enrique as he confesses his forbidden passion for Anne Boleyn to Cardinal Wolsey, his chief minister. But it has taken Enrique a full act to reach Egerio's intensity of passion:

Todo el infierno junto	[The whole of hell
no padece en su llanto	in its lamentations does not suffer
pena y tormento tanto	as much pain and torment
como yo en este punto,	as I do over this question
porque, en muerte deshecho,	for undone by death my heart
si es Etna el corazón, volcán el pecho.[15]	is an Etna, my breast a volcano.]

Yet Enrique has also been affected by a significant dream in the opening moments of his play. The setting is far from wild: he is first seen fulfilling his intellectual and spiritual prowess by writing a treatise against Luther in the original spirit of his papal title of Defender of the Faith. But he falls asleep, and is joined onstage without warning by the figure of Anne Boleyn, entering to distract his sleeping soul and telling him that 'yo tengo de borrar cuanto tú escribes' ('All that you write is for me to erase').[16] While *El purgatorio de San Patricio* dramatizes and describes various apparitions and miracles in order to illustrate the divine favour invested in Patricio, no other moment of *La cisma de Ingalaterra* portrays a supernatural event. There is no rational explanation for Anne's presence at court.

Such baroque patterns of language and action are identified by some critics as reflecting disorder in the realm of *El purgatorio de San Patricio*.[17] They seem, when first applied to Henry VIII's court, to represent the opposite of this instability: a political harmony attainable only through the preservation of the social hierarchies and moral absolutes which seem to portray court life as the model of civilized existence. But the Calderonian kingdoms of Ireland and England oppose each other in a deeper sense than the political. Calderón's Gongorine descriptions of pre-Christian Ireland as a place defying the baroque contrasts of supreme order do reflect a popular image of a land both pastoral and untamed. Yet it is portrayed less as a geographical reality than as the uncertain territory of mind and soul: an archipelago that can be pagan and purgatorial in equal measure. The playwright's version of the English court of the previous century is a more measured and disciplined environment, all passions literally contained within the formalities and ceremonies of royal life. By the end of the English play, however, the religious and political ideologies of that realm will be as unpredictable as the geography of Calderonian Ireland.

15 Calderón de la Barca, *Cisma*, p. 120, lines 1511–16. 16 Ibid., p. 48, line 6. 17 Ángel Valbuena Briones, 'La extraña contrariedad en la armonía del mundo' ('The strange opposition in the harmony of the world'), in Josep M. Sola-Solé, Alessandro Crisafulli and Bruno Damiani (eds), *Estudios literarios de hispánicos norteamericanos dedicados a Helmut Hatzfeld* ('Literary studies of North American hispanists dedicated to Helmut Hatzfeld') (Barcelona, 1974), pp 312–13.

England's new political landscape will also be more barren than that of Ireland. The desolate landscape of Calderón's Ireland may reflect the 'watery wilderness' referred to as the likely reality of the land at the time of its Christianisation.[18] However, pre-Christian Ireland was a place far richer in cultural and spiritual enlightenment than the wilderness Calderón seems at first to suggest. It was a landscape in which the physical and metaphysical worlds were seen as interdependent. The institution of shrines like Patrick's purgatory in this land linked Celtic votive mythology to Christian faith.[19] Egerio's greatest limitation is his inability to accept the possibility of such a connection between materialistic and spiritual dimensions. It would suit Calderón's didactic purpose to portray the Irish as devoid of spiritual belief or hope of salvation at the start of the play, in order to heighten their difference from Patricio and to make their course towards Christianity appear a choice of moral certainty. The conflict between Egerio and Patricio exemplifies the dichotomy of physical and metaphysical worlds.

When Egerio first encounters Patricio as the refugee from a shipwreck he rebels instinctively at the mention of Christianity, making the correct association between Patricio and the slave of his terrifying premonition. He throws the future apostle of Ireland to the ground and promotes Ludovico Enio, the lapsed Christian adventurer whose life Patricio saved when both were shipwrecked. Ruthless in ambition, Ludovico is more to Egerio's taste than Patricio. But in an irony typical of Calderonian drama, Egerio's efforts to escape his fate steer him directly towards it. The enslavement of Patricio to the most isolated reaches of Egerio's realm strengthens his faith to the point where he can carry out the mission of evangelising Ireland. Meanwhile, the favours granted to Ludovico embolden him to seduce the princess Polonia, heir to Egerio and intended wife of Filipo, the king's lieutenant and Ludovico's master.

Egerio's deposition of Patricio might be regarded as an act of hopeless savagery if a similar scene had not taken place in the English play, showing Enrique's struggle to forget the effects of Ana's intrusion into his dreams. He has received letters from the Pope and from Martin Luther, a more modern political version of the dichotomy of good and evil represented by the shipwrecked Patricio and Ludovico in the Irish play. Trying to demonstrate his sincerity of faith by throwing Luther's writings to the ground and placing the Pope's counsel on his head, he confuses the letters and finds himself trampling on the words of Leo X. The confusion of the academic and spiritual ideas, the moral and political certainties of Enrique's realm, is not as dramatic as that of Egerio's realm with its storms and portents, but it is all the more devastating for the restraint with which it is portrayed.

After all, the advantage of Egerio's Ireland is that it contains no comparable certainties. Egerio argues from the outset that his realm is not even a pagan

18 Liam de Paor, *St Patrick's world: the Christian culture of Ireland's apostolic age* (Dublin, 1993), p. 23.
19 Ibid., p. 29.

place: he believes in no gods, and accepts no certainties beyond those of birth and death. In this regard, he is similar to the prince Segismundo in Calderón's later play *La vida es sueño* ('Life is a dream') which portrays in Everyman style the transformation of a man maddened by lifelong incarceration into a balanced and triumphant ruler. The play is set in Poland, but its context is universal as the prince Segismundo's wilderness of inexperience is conquered through internal and external strife.

Incarcerated to spare his kingdom the consequences of the moral depravity his astrologer father foretold for him, Segismundo first appears in surroundings as wild and remote as those of Egerio's realm and Patricio's exile, dressed in the skins of beasts to reflect his savage temperament. Like the untried Segismundo, Egerio seems to understand only the power-centred aspects of kingship, with none of the ideals of exemplary self-government. He admits this with proud defiance to the newly-arrived Patricio and Ludovico:

El traje,	[I wear clothing
más que de rey, de bárbaro salvaje	more suited to a wild barbarian than a king
traigo porque quisiera	because I want to seem
fiera ansí parecer, pues que soy fiera.[20]	a wild beast in this way, since I am wild.]

The word 'fiera' refers to the wildness of animals, but also to the wild energy of an untamed spirit. Egerio certainly behaves in a savage and pitiless manner, reacting violently to any challenges and threatening to destroy even the heavens when they do not conform to his will. He rules his small realm with defensive jealousy, seeing nothing but the likelihood of overthrow and destruction. Other Irish characters, such as his heir Polonia, comment on his 'fiera condición' or wild condition.[21] He himself complains from his first moments onstage that he can never find peace of mind because he carries the torments of hell within him, 'que yo mismo a mí mismo me hago guerra' ('so that I myself am making war on myself').[22]

However irrational he sounds, Egerio makes very deliberate and clear evaluations of his behaviour. He seems less a beast incapable of understanding any but the most basic of motivating urges than a man, as passionate about unbelief as Patricio is about faith. That surely makes him a more honest figure than Enrique, who institutes fundamental schism to satisfy his illicit passions under the guise of an exemplary defender of the Catholic faith responding to a Biblical tenet which seems to pronounce his marriage illegitimate. The reality is that Enrique's theological knowledge could easily justify the apparent irregularity of his marriage to Catherine, but he has given up his exemplarity to follow his passion for Anne Boleyn. What is more, he has lost his independent judgement by allowing himself to be manipulated by corrupt counsellors:

20 Calderón de la Barca, *Purgatorio*, p. 78, lines 164–7. 21 Ibid., p. 105, line 1134. 22 Ibid., p. 74, line 18.

Confieso que estoy loco y estoy ciego,
pues la verdad que adoro es la que niego;
pero si un hombre el daño no alcanzara
aunque errara, parece que no errara.

…

Bien sé que me ha engañado
Volseo, y que he quedado
de su falso argumento satisfecho,
y es, que el fuego infernal que está en el pecho
hace que, ciega mi turbada idea,
niegue verdades y mentiras crea.[23]

[I confess that I am mad and blind,
for I am denying the very truth that I worship;
but if a man is oblivious to the harm he does,
though he do wrong, it does not seem like wrongdoing.

…

[I know well
that Wolsey has tricked me, and that I have allowed myself
to be satisfied with his false arguments
and this is because the hellish fire
which is now in my breast makes
my disturbed reason blindly deny truths and believe lies.]

Within the disciplined young academic a 'fiera condición' is developing, all the more dangerous for not being acknowledged. The concept that hell or heaven could be carried within an individual was a commonplace of early modern literature, and the internal battle for a soul between the forces of good and evil, or *psychomachia*, was especially conducive to drama. The souls of the Irish and English kings thereby become microcosms of their realms. In his outrage at the news that Patricio is returning to Ireland as bishop to spread his Christian faith, Egerio warns that he will not easily escape alive from 'este sucinto mapa, / esfera de mi rigor' ('this brief map, sphere of my rigour').[24] This is not the first time he has linked Ireland's geographical smallness to the harshness of his regime: he introduced the realm to Patricio as 'pequeño porque es mío' ('small because it is mine').[25] Ireland is the soul of Egerio, a mental territory of passionate unbelief.

But Egerio's is a soul on its way to oblivion. The immortality of the soul is a doctrine he cannot bring himself to accept, even when faced with the ultimate miracle in Patricio's resurrection of his murdered daughter Polonia. When Patricio tries to convince him that purgatory after death will offer a chance to purge the soul of its sinfulness, he demands, on pain of death for the apostle, more certain proof than words. Ireland needs something real, that everyone can

23 Calderón de la Barca, *Cisma*, p. 126, lines 1623–6, 1629–34. 24 Calderón de la Barca, *Purgatorio*, p. 108, lines 1228–9. 25 Ibid., p. 78, line 162.

touch: 'no todos sean / entes de razón' ('let them not all be entities of reason').[26]
He insists that all miracles are witchcraft designed to destabilize his power. The
Good Angel who announces the institution of the earthly purgatory assures the
apostle that he will prove the authority of this miracle by bringing the impassioned king of Ireland to the infernal abyss 'porque se atormenten dentro / su
envidia y veneno mismo' ('that he may be tormented within by his own jealousy
and venom').[27] This plausible description of the fate awaiting the damned seems
an exact reflection of Egerio's approach to self-government and kingship. It
seems that he will indeed die as he has lived.

Nonetheless, Egerio's hubris gives him 'a certain tragic stature' of which he
himself seems increasingly aware.[28] He now shows himself capable of deeper
thought and tenderness than was at first apparent. From the beginning he had
disliked Patricio because the voice of the young man moved him in a way he
had not previously experienced:

Calla, mísero cristiano,	[Be silent, miserable Christian,
que el alma, a tu voz atenta,	for my soul, attentive to your voice,
no sé qué afecto la rige,	is mastered by I know not what affection
no sé qué poder la fuerza	and forced by I know not what power
a temerte y adorarte.[29]	to fear you and adore you.]

The religion for which Egerio professed nothing but fear and hatred has therefore moved his soul from the beginning of the play. One senses that he would
have been the more likely candidate for the journey through Patricio's purgatory to a condition of passionate and austere faith, as described in the third and
final act. However, it is the reformed murderer Ludovico Enio who undertakes
this pilgrimage. His account of visionary salvation completes and justifies the
play, but this conclusion is made possible by the sacrifice of Egerio.

Though he seems tyrannical, Egerio is capable of inspiring loyal service from
such equally passionate and proud characters as Ludovico and Filipo. Prejudice
against Christianity, and the fundamental changes it would bring to his realm,
is always behind his worst excesses in the play, contributing to Ludovico's vengeful murder of Polonia. When Patricio comes to Ireland as bishop, his mission
supported by full papal authority, Egerio has just discovered the violated corpse
of his daughter, who symbolized his hopes for the realm's future and his closest chance of immortality. In such circumstances, another violent and defensive
response to Patricio would be understandable. But the three years since Patricio's
escape from slavery have taught Egerio the futility of such behaviour. In the
midst of his rage and despair, Egerio moves beyond physical contest to reasoned
disputation. Following his daughter's restoration to life, the Irish king might

26 Ibid., p. 125, lines 1853–4. 27 Ibid., p. 128, lines 1941–2. 28 Ruano de la Haza (ed.), *El purgatorio de San Patricio, by Pedro Calderón de la Barca*, pp 36–7. 29 Calderón de la Barca, *Purgatorio*, p.
83, lines 348–52.

have been expected to embrace Christianity as impulsively as he rejected it. But at this most emotional of moments, his first words are addressed to his people:

¡Que tenga un engaño fuerza,   [That a trick should have the power
pueblo ciego, para hacer   blind people, to create
maravillas como éstas,   wonders like these,
y no tengas tú valor   and that you should have no courage
para ver que la apariencia   to see that you are being deceived by appearances!]
te engaña! [30]

Egerio still does not trust Christianity, and avoids exemplary conversion as a dangerous path for his realm. He refers to Polonia's resurrection as a mere 'aparencia' or appearance, a word applied to the increasingly elaborate stage props and effects of the seventeenth-century Spanish theatre. At a moment of spiritual intensity Egerio reminds his subjects, and through them the audience, that truth is not easy to recognize. Spain's religious Counter-Reformation was informed by the awareness that supernatural experiences should not be automatically credited as spiritual or miraculous until the individual had closely questioned their source. Calderón's Ireland is Egerio's soul in microcosm, but as a dramatized realm it becomes an emblem of an early modern commonplace of Christian kingship and stoical self-government. As exemplary human beings, monarchs were expected to cultivate their power of discernment between life's external ceremony and the internal moral and spiritual values needed by rulers and subjects alike.

In that spirit, the ferocity and inconstancy of Egerio's *psychomachia* abates to reveal that the Irish king has a questioning intelligence similar to that of his English counterpart Enrique. His probing of the schoolmen's doctrines for materialistic proof could be likened to the development in Calderón's time of natural philosophy, or the experiential knowledge of scientific research:

¿Qué quieres,   [What is it
que así los mares y tierras   that you alter the sea and earth
de mi estado, con engaños   of my state in this way,
y novedades alteras?   with novelties and tricks?
Aquí no sabemos más   Here we know no more
que nacer y morir. Esta   than birth and death. This
es la doctrina heredada   is the doctrine passed on to us
en la natural escuela   in the natural school
de nuestros padres. [31]   of our fathers.]

Egerio reminds us with a dignity not previously heard from him that Ireland has an ancient culture which, however inferior in spiritual terms, stands to be

30 Ibid., p. 123, lines 1743–8.   31 Ibid., p. 120, lines 1656–64.

displaced by Christianity. Responding to Patricio's sympathy and lyrical lamentation for Ireland, he seems at last more of a noble savage than a figure of irrational fury. However, gentle words will not be enough to persuade him to accept a changed vision of life. He acts now as a representative of his people, for whom he has always provided the traditional protection of a warrior-king.[32] Having defied a God in whom he believes, Ludovico Enio is in a better condition for exemplary repentance. But for Egerio, the purgatory is a testing-ground where the unbeliever must either expose deception or be undone by the force of the truth he denied. His final words to Patricio are defiant, but also call proudly on his ancestors: '¿Piensas, Patricio, que a mi sangre debo / tan poco, que me espante ni me asombre, / o que como mujer temblando muero?' ('Do you think, Patricio, that I owe so little to my blood that this should frighten or amaze me, or that I should die trembling like a woman?')[33]

These are words of resigned courage: while Egerio's life is often irrational, his last moments indicate that it was far from amoral. The king must realize that his refusal to acknowledge the supremacy of Patricio's God will lead him to the fate foretold in his terrifying dream. But without his sacrifice, Patricio's words will not be endorsed and the Irish people will not accept Christianity. There can be no regeneration of the realm without the death of its king. Egerio does die as he lived, but in a more heroic sense than the opening scene suggested. Far from self-destructing, he sacrifices himself for his people, allowing Christian belief in the immortal soul to replace the confused despair he personified. This regenerates his nation from passionate unbelief to a faith that proves as intense as it is austere.

In this regard Egerio's character can be linked to the most ancient traditions of classical kingship, particularly those of the *Rex Nemorensis* or 'King of the Wood'. This sacral king of the shrine to Diana at Nemi traditionally came to prominence by challenging and killing his predecessor, and reigned with the knowledge that he would die at the next king's hand.[34] Nemi's pastoral significance in the midst of Roman imperial civilisation is reminiscent of Ireland's idealistic importance to Spain.[35] Calderón's naming of his Irish king may indicate an even more direct association with this place, since the water nymph Egeria was a figure of great spiritual importance at Nemi and was believed to have influenced the establishment of laws for Rome through her relationship with the wise king Numa.[36] Egerio's life and death will similarly influence the establishment of a Christian code of belief in Ireland.

Enrique, by contrast, has lost nobility and authority by the end of his play, bringing decline to his realm rather than spiritual progress. He deconsecrates the truths to which Egerio sacrifices himself, and becomes tyrannical in an attempt to defend his position. In the long term, he has proved himself precisely

32 De Paor, *St Patrick's world*, p. 29. 33 Calderón de la Barca, *Purgatorio*, p. 131, lines 2067–9. 34 J. G. Frazer, *Lectures on the early history of kingship* (London, 1905), pp 9–10, p. 16. 35 Ibid., p. 15. 36 Ibid., p. 22.

the 'docto ignorante' or learned ignorant man he is dubbed in the closing lines.[37] The Irish king, who appeared the least civilized at the start of his play, eventually overcame blind aggression to articulate his need for guidance. But the central figure of English royalty and political supremacy betrays the intellectual and spiritual idealism he carried so confidently at the opening of his play. Unflinchingly, Calderón shows that the savage passions of limitless pride and ambition can prove more difficult to conquer behind the façades of court ritual than within the disordered elements of a pagan and primitive realm.

The constancy and magnanimity Egerio tries to attain in his debate with Patricio are completely lost to Enrique, who finds himself cuckolded by the woman for whose sake he repudiated his wife and his faith. Having ordered Anne Boleyn to be executed Enrique asks for divine guidance, after which a stage direction allows him a moment in which he becomes 'suspenso': astounded, or suspended.[38] This, one suspects, is the closest he can now come to the revelations granted to Polonia, Ludovico and others while they were in the purgatorial state of suspension between heaven and hell. He is enlightened into despair: that moment of silent revelation made him decide to return to his first wife, but almost immediately he discovers that she has died and there is no way he can make amends. The spread of England's schism cannot be halted, and his traumatized daughter Mary's stubborn loyalty to Catholicism is turning into a fanaticism that promises the realm a legacy of political and religious turmoil. Enrique is fully aware of his errors, but no longer has the authority to repudiate them; even the sacrifice of Egerio is denied to him by the necessity of maintaining what remains of his kingdom's political stability. It is all he can do to control his daughter, with the following lines:

Callad y disimulad,	Be silent and dissimulate,
que tiempo vendrá en que pueda	for a time will come when that zeal
ese celo ejecutarse,	will be fulfilled
ser incendio esa centella.[39]	and this spark will be a blazing fire.

These words reduce Enrique's England to the same condition as Egerio's Ireland: a hopeless and unbelieving country awaiting the fire of conversion. But this England has already known the light of true faith and has chosen to give it up. Therefore its position at the close of *Cisma* seems far more confused and hopeless than that of Ireland at the close of *Purgatorio*. Indeed, the metaphor of fire used at this moment in the play could easily be read as a wry reference to the most horrific earthly purges of Mary's historical reign.

Thus the cave of purgatory, linking physical and metaphysical realms, replaces the study from which Enrique defended his faith. From the moment he allowed his soul to be invaded by lust in this same theatrical space, the English king

37 Calderón de la Barca, *Cisma*, p. 190, line 2894. 38 Ibid., p. 178, between lines 2651 and 2652. 39 Ibid., p. 190, lines 2880–3.

began a painful journey towards redemption. In the Irish play, Patricio's miraculous cave becomes a discovery space in every sense of the word; however, Ludovico's revelations of afterlife are not dramatically portrayed as they are in Lope de Vega's play. He simply recounts them at some length. Critics have questioned the dramatic effectiveness of Ludovico's extensive monologue, citing it as an example of Calderón's close reliance on his printed source.[40] However, the elaborate materialistic proof of afterlife as demanded by Egerio would be implausible in this play, which dramatizes Augustinian divine illumination within the individual soul and thereby subjects readers or spectators to the same individual challenge as Egerio: 'to solve the mystery of the cave so that we may arrive at our own personal solution.'[41] The discoveries of Calderón's Ireland are subjective rather than collective.

The Calderonian purgatory of St Patrick may be linked to Segismundo's cave in *La vida es sueño*, since a savagely impassioned individual emerges from it invigorated and chastened, converted to a life of Christian restraint. But Segismundo's cave, like the allegorical cave of Plato's *Republic*, is one that blinds humans to full enlightenment. It is a cave of incarceration and deprivation. Patricio's cave becomes in itself the place of enlightenment, transforming the perspectives of those who take shelter there. In this respect it is more reminiscent of the oracle of Trephonius, or, in a contemporary context, the 'cave of Montesinos' episode from Cervantes' *Don Quixote*.

Ludovico's experience in the purgatory fits at least two of the categories of mysticism: it is transient, noetic, and may have been passive. But it does not prove ineffable, as Ludovico ends the play with a detailed account of his visions and experiences. The moment when Enrique realizes the irreversibility of England's schism carries greater mystical intensity. But this conveys the earthly fall of a nation. Ireland, by contrast, is being shown as the focus of divine salvation. Calderón imagines it as a universal theatre in which mystery can meet reality and consume the figure who represented doubt; Enrique's England, dispensing with spirituality, becomes a world of chilling confusion, passing slowly beyond the Christian civilisation discovered, and in some cases rediscovered, by the Irish.

Calderón's handling of Ireland, a land offering Spain opportunities rather than the hostility and uncertainty reflected in *La cisma de Ingalaterra*, prepared him to explore the themes of enlightenment and self-government in a more universal context than that of the Irish play. It is significant that Polonia, whose resurrection is Egerio's first confirmation of his own fate and his realm's destiny, is given the name of Poland. This was the country Olivares had named alongside Ireland as Spain's most trusted ally, which would in due course provide the setting for Calderón's masterpiece of political drama, *La vida es sueño*. *La cisma de Ingalaterra* moves towards the dramatic environment of that play,

40 Dixon, 'St Patrick of Ireland and the dramatists of golden age Spain', p. 150.　41 Ruano de la Haza (ed.), *El purgatorio de San Patricio, by Pedro Calderón de la Barca*, p. 43.

exploring the expediency and idealism of a nation's political and religious upheaval in a more universal 'cave' than the one of earthly purgatory instituted by Patricio. But Calderón's dramatic realms of England and Poland were moulded from the idealistic territory of his Irish setting. What seemed at first to be savage and alien to Spain's Christian civilisation therefore became an exemplary model of national regeneration, as exiled Ireland laid claim to a renewed spiritual and moral identity.

George Moore and the 'martial outside': concealed complexity on the route to literary freedom[1]

MARY PIERSE, NUI, CORK

'We'll have a swashing and a martial outside' [*As You Like It.* I.iii.123]

This paper will argue that there are several complementary elements in the strategy employed by George Moore in his pursuit of literary freedom during the last two decades of the nineteenth century and that, despite a common perception to the contrary, there is a fascinating and substantial actuality underlying his public positioning and the perception of him as daring and fighting Irishman in England's literary battles of that period. The 'swashing' side of Moore confronted the near-monopoly in book distribution and challenged the flawed justifications for its censorship of novels; the creative literary man expanded novelistic horizons in subject, treatment and form. His innovations were frequently obvious and controversial but some of what can be deemed his most significant achievements in the enrichment of the novel were not immediately apparent – they were subtly woven into the fabric of his prose and their existence emerges only in close examination of the texts. One of the more surprising aspects of this, almost hidden, expansion of permitted literary possibilities is the existence of a strong 'New Woman' element in two of the most unlikely places: in the story of a servant in *Esther Waters* (1894),[2] and in the story of 'John Norton', one of the three tales of *Celibates*.[3] Together, the overt and covert strands of Moore's resistance to imposed literary limitation form a purposeful and intricate approach, one that had implications for the

1 This paper arises from an aspect of wider research into the work of George Moore, a study that was generously funded by a Government of Ireland Scholarship awarded by the Irish Research Council for the Humanities and Social Sciences (2001–2003). That assistance is very gratefully acknowledged.   2 George Moore, *Esther Waters* (London, 1894).   3 George Moore, *Celibates* (London, 1895).

contemporary book world and bequeaths a legacy of unexpected tactics and achievements.

An awareness of the prevailing literary climate of the 1880s and 1890s – one which produced many diverse authorial responses to its repressions – is essential to any adequate evaluation of English prose in the period. Rather ironically, the last decade of the nineteenth century which was the epoch of particular battles in the world of the novel, is remembered as 'the gay nineties' and 'the naughty nineties', whereas it was indeed a time of political, social, and literary conservatism when moral police patrolled the boundaries and auto-censorship was far from unknown. Opposition to such restriction was evident in the obvious and flamboyant contributions from Oscar Wilde, Aubrey Beardsley and Joris-Karl Huysmans; it was also apparent in public debate and polemic. The literary war was waged between authors, between authors and critics, and between various parties including some or all of authors, critics, publishers, booksellers, librarians, readers and other custodians of public morality. They tangled over separate spheres, hypocrisy concerning matters sexual, preservation of strict class hierarchies, and the freedom of authors to write realistically – all matters that were closely bound up with questions of power, authority and economics. The degree of the problems for writers was very clearly indicated by the appearance in *The Yellow Book* of a meandering and circumlocutory article by Arthur Waugh in which he argued for 'reticence' in literature and against the realism of recent French writing, which he likened to 'the outspoken brutality of Restoration drama.'[4] That such a piece should appear in what would be considered a liberal and *avant garde* publication was indicative of the centrality of the issue; that it should be followed in the succeeding number of the magazine by a response that was almost equally cautious in its prose if not in its sentiment, can be taken as doubly reinforcing the existence of considerable literary difficulties.[5] Under threat from publishers and circulating libraries, both George Gissing and Thomas Hardy removed scenes and phrases from novels and, weary of the excesses of censorship and puritanical criticism, Hardy finally abandoned fiction.[6] Gissing complained that Thackeray 'wrote below the demands of his art to conciliate Mrs Grundy ... the same thing is done by our living novelists every day.'[7] Henry James asked, 'how can a novel be worth anything that deals only with half of life?'[8] On the state of the English novel, he asserted: 'nothing but absolute freedom can refresh it and restore its self-respect.'[9]

4 Arthur Waugh, 'Reticence in literature', *Yellow Book* 1 (April 1894), 201–19. 5 Hubert Crackenthorpe, 'Reticence in literature: some roundabout remarks', *Yellow Book* 2 (July 1894), 259–69. Crackenthorpe's use of the word 'roundabout' is indicative of the very indirect and cautious way in which both he and Arthur Waugh couched their contributions. 6 Although Hardy did not desert fiction until after the publication of *Jude the obscure* in 1896, it is clear from his autobiography that he felt moved to quit in the wake of reaction to *Tess of the d'Urbervilles*. His diary entry of 15 April 1892 reads: 'Well, if this sort of thing continues no more novel-writing for me. A man must be a fool to deliberately stand up to be shot at.' Thomas Hardy, *Tess of the d'Urberville* (ed.), Scott Elledge, (3rd ed. New York, 1991), p. 336. 7 George Gissing, Letter, *Pall Mall Gazette* 15 Dec. 1884. 8 George Moore, *A mere accident* (London, 1887), p. 32. 9 Henry James, 'Address to be read at a summer school

In that atmosphere, one of Moore's tactics was to generate a public debate that might possibly expose the nature of the limitations imposed on novelists, and galvanize readers into demanding something more true-to-life than the standard formulaic and romantic fiction. His contributions to those open arguments, conducted in newspaper columns and in pamphlet, focused on what was proper and appropriate to literature and on the deficiencies, as he saw them, in the prevailing system. Seeing controversy as a means to defeat conservatism in the lending libraries and publishers, Moore was much more direct than Arthur Waugh had been, and he was never less than provocative. The immediate impulse behind his pamphlet, *Literature at Nurse* (1885), was the banning of his novel *A Mummer's Wife* (1885) by Mudie & Co. In his pamphlet, Moore disputed the right of 'a mere tradesman' to exercise censorship 'over the literature of the nineteenth century' and he contrasted extracts from fashionable novels that Mudie had published with the section from his novel which had been deemed immoral.[10] The presentation of the case is palpably taunting and confrontational, especially so since after each extract, Moore poses a question for the publisher and lending library: 'tell me Mr Mudie, if there be not in this doll just a little too much bosom showing, if there be not too much ankle appearing from under this skirt? Tell me, I beseech you.' The difference between any morality depicted in the novels circulated by the libraries and in the paragraphs quoted from *A Mummer's Wife*, appeared to substantiate Moore's case that his prose was less guilty of offence against the letter and spirit of the unwritten Victorian laws. The six lines of restrained prose that provoked that Mudie ban bear reproduction, if only to illustrate their relative discretion and innocence:

> Strong arms were wound about her, she was carried forward, and the door was shut behind her. Only the faintest gleam of starlight touched the wall next the window; the darkness slept profoundly on landing and staircase, and when the silence was again broken, a voice was heard saying, 'oh you shouldn't have done this! What shall I tell my husband if he asks me where I've been?' 'Say you've been talking to me about my bill, dear. I'll see you in the morning. [11]

The apparently disproportionate reaction to a brief literary allusion further illustrates the contemporary problems for writers who wished to expand the novelistic horizons beyond those permitted to 'virgins and boys'.[12] Yet, despite the accusation that *A Mummer's Wife* featured immorality, the intimation was that it was really Moore's transgression against some other code that led to the ban on his books. Although it came nearly a decade later, Waugh's identification of realism in French writing, and his equation of such a style with brutality, was

on the novel', 1889. 10 George Moore, *Literature at nurse* (London, 1885), p. 17. 11 George Moore, *A mummer's wife* (London, 1886), p. 115. This version was actually published in 1885; some subsequent editions, such as the authorised American one of 1903, preserve the brevity of the incident and the darkness, but omit the verbal exchange between Dick and Kate. 12 George Moore, *A mere accident* (London, 1887) 32.

the articulation of a real dread that had underpinned some censorship and condemnation. France, where greater literary freedom had been achieved some decades earlier in the *bataille littéraire*,[13] was home to the naturalist novel and its main theoretician, Émile Zola, and it was those two names that were most frequently mentioned as the foreign influences that should not be permitted to enter the world of English fiction.

The tone of comment was exaggerated, with Robert Buchanan labelling naturalist literature 'the diabolic adumbration of a disease which is slowly but surely destroying moral sentiment and threatening to corrupt human nature altogether.' He compared its effect on society to that of Jack the Ripper and made specific mention of 'the tribe of Zola'.[14] Such opinions were fairly widely held – for example, W.B. Yeats forbade his sisters to read *A Mummer's Wife*, but he did not impose such restrictions on himself.[15] Moore's purposeful association of himself and his prose with Zola and with French influences was both a risky and a rewarding stratagem: it created publicity for him as the alleged, and scandalous, imitator of Baudelaire and Zola; it would furnish him with examples of novelistic innovation and development from which he would pick, choose, discard and refine. However, while the conflict brought his name before the public in 1885 – as it had done previously, and would do again – the resultant notoriety excluded him from the main channels of book distribution for a period and risked tarnishing his literary image for a certain readership. Moreover, it facilitated identification of him with a literary label that was inappropriate for much of his subsequent writing, and it hindered appreciation of the many subtleties that he injected into the novel form.

In *A Mummer's Wife*, the account of Kate's adventures with the travelling players, and of her asthma, cirrhosis and terminal convulsions, are naturalist in their detail and progress. The same tag would be affixed to *Esther Waters* (1894), partly as a term of abuse and, to an extent, because it was judged to follow a scientific pattern in its study of a servant's life. However, on closer inspection, the same book can be seen to lack many qualities associated with naturalism, but can be seen to incorporate the essentials of a New Woman novel. There is a certain piquancy in the combination of some of Moore's achievements in that text: he had aggravated conservative literary and social opinion by the innovation of making a servant the main character in a novel, a development that was viewed as unsuitable and undesirable; Esther's flouting of Victorian moral codes, effectively minimized in the story by her success in rearing a son, was another cause for complaint; the brief references to Esther's seduction and to the labour ward

13 Alain Pagès, *La Bataille Littéraire* (Paris, 1989) provides a detailed and well-referenced account of this period. 14 Robert Buchanan, *Universal Review*, 18 Mar. 1889. 15 This seems ironic in view of his subsequent defiance of ecclesiastical censorship of the theatre in Ireland when, according to Richard Ellmann, George Moore was apparently willing to compromise. At that time, Yeats said that 'literature is the principal voice of the conscience and that it is its duty age after age to affirm its morality against the special moralities of clergymen and churches, and of kings and parliaments and peoples'. Richard Ellmann, *Yeats: the Man and the masks* (London, 1987), p. 134.

resulted in lengthy debates in newspaper columns. Had it, in addition, occurred to any of the critics or complainants that Esther was a 'New Woman', it would have been read as according an unthinkably high social status to a kitchen maid, or perhaps the suggestion would have been greeted with disbelief. It is not an identification that was made at the time, or in the century following the book's publication, but the case seems very strong.

As described by Kate Flint, New Woman fiction covered a wide range of material but was often seen as a symptom of social decay.[16] It was perceived as causing women to question the desirability of marriage and children, and to dispute any attribution of natural instinct towards either. It frequently featured protest against any restrictions on education or other opportunity for women and stressed the importance of their struggles and what they achieved in their working lives. It tended to privilege childhood in a nostalgic way, marriage was rarely put forward as a solution and the double standard of sexuality was interrogated. In form, this literature was rarely complex or suspenseful but was regularly a *bildungsroman*. Other characteristics of the form were the focus on woman's life as a learning process that was sometimes difficult and painful, and the expectation that readers would take seriously the representations of reading within the text and be moved to re-evaluate society and seek out new literary experiences. Flint identifies the 'relatively downbeat endings' of the novels as calculated to avoid total identification with the central character, but to encourage awareness of the options taken and rejected by her and so sensitize readers to their own societal position. Finally, the writers of such fiction used the readers' emotional responses to the central character as a catalyst to such desired reaction.

When measured against that template, the tale of Esther, superficially a most unlikely 'New Woman', seems to have an uncommonly good fit. It is significant that, of nine or more distinguishing features of the New Woman novel genre, the majority can be found in *Esther Waters*. It is also rather surprising that this clear evidence should have remained unremarked for so long. Esther's life is depicted as a struggle and her survival as an achievement against the odds: she is worked to the bone, employers dismiss her, she is reduced to the workhouse, what remains of her family abandon her. Her childhood appears as a simple and happy time, never to be recovered: she clings to its memories (pictures of shepherd and shepherdess, prayers) and associations (the unread collection of her mother's books). After Jackie's birth, she does not see marriage as a goal nor does it turn out to be the security for him that had been promised: 'she hadn't a young man, and did not want one'[17]; 'She didn't want to marry anyone'; to William's assertion that they should marry because 'There's no other happiness. I've tried everything else,' Esther's immediate response is: 'But I haven't.' Esther is envious of Miss Rice's single state but says 'you've to chance it in the end … Not the likes of you, miss, but the likes of us.'[18]

16 Kate Flint (ed.), *The woman reader*, 1993 (Oxford, 1995), pp 294–7. 17 Moore, *Esther Waters*, p. 177. 18 Ibid., pp 213, 222, 231.

Marriage has not led to happiness for many of the novel's other characters either: Mrs Barfield, although married, is rather alone in that state and pursues her life with purpose, without depending on a man; Mrs Randal and Mrs Saunders suffer as result of their marriages. In contrast, the unmarried Miss Rice, an author and a reader of French naturalist novels, is a quiet and dignified lady whose existence is depicted as comfortable, peaceful and independent, and whose conduct would be deemed impeccable by Victorian standards. It is made quite clear that reading such literature has not had the deleterious effect threatened by Buchanan, Waugh and others. While Miss Rice is educated and economically privileged, Esther's opportunities are limited by her lack of education (not just in reading but in cookery), and by the arbitrary barriers to employment associated with height, age or good looks in women.[19] The double standard in sexuality becomes apparent in relation to Ginger and William on the one hand, and to Esther and Margaret on the other; it is unobtrusively confirmed by the contrast provided in the depiction of young men, in evening dress, soliciting.[20]

The novel elicited considerable empathetic response from the public at large: Gladstone approved *Esther Waters* as a moral book, other influential voices praised it as a treatise against gambling, one woman set up a fund to establish The Esther Waters Home for single mothers. The book's survival in print for over a century, and its initial and ongoing appeal, must be attributed to its power to engage the sympathy and interest of readers.[21] The ending of the story could fairly be described as 'downbeat', even if Moore might prefer the term 'in minor key': Esther returns to Woodview, her future is uncertain and her son has joined the army. Although often perceived as an achievement for Esther as a mother, 'to bring him up to man's estate', and for him to reach that career, such a judgement ignored the harsh reality of Moore's additional sentence: 'the possibility that any moment might declare him to be mere food for powder and shot.'[22] The concluding pages are not triumphal.

In the matter of stimulus to reading, several dissimilar models are offered in *Esther Waters*, and in their disparity, they would tend to generate reflection in the readers' minds. In the Barfield home, destined to decline and decay in economic and moral terms, the library has 'bookless' shelves. When William Latch describes Sarah Tucker, the upper-housemaid and 'wonderful reader', it is quite clear that her literary diet in *Bow Bells* falls into the category castigated by Moore in *Literature at Nurse*: 'English fiction now consists of either a sentimental misunderstanding, which is happily cleared up in the end, or of singular escapes over the edges of precipices, and miraculous recoveries';[23] Sarah 'can tell you which lord it was that saved the girl from the carriage when the 'osses were tearing like mad towards a precipice a 'undred feet deep, and all about the baronet for whose sake the girl went out to drown herself in the moonlight'.[24] Sarah's path to ruin,

19 Ibid., p. 168, p. 171. 20 Ibid., p. 169. 21 *Esther Waters* was one of the first books published in Penguin, subsequently published in Dent's Everyman series and then in Oxford World's Classics. 22 Moore, *Esther Waters*, p. 377. 23 Moore, *Literature at nurse*, pp 19–20. 24 Moore, *Esther Waters*,

prostitution, theft and imprisonment can be seen to relate to the romantic unreality of her reading material. Taking all these factors into consideration and relating them to the criteria laid down by Flint, the startling fact emerges that, whether as a forerunner or as a literary fellow-traveller, George Moore has fashioned *Esther Waters* in the manner of a slightly camouflaged New Woman novel.

Perhaps it is even more unexpected that the story of 'John Norton' in *Celibates*[25] could also be considered in relation to the qualities of a New Woman novel. The very idea runs contrary to John's attitude and beliefs but yet, under several criteria, the elements are comparable: John's antipathy to marriage and children; his denial that there is such a universal instinct towards either;[26] the resultant impossibility of any suggestion from him that marriage might be a solution to anything; the inconclusive ending. In addition, his behaviour and his voiced opinions would tend to diminish, for any female, the attraction of marriage with him or one of his ilk. Nonetheless, the societal expectation is seen to exert some pressure on him to marry and to fit into the country groove. On the other hand, he has full access to education, travel and money, and his opportunities appear unlimited; there is no struggle for him in those areas. In contrast to Esther's, his childhood is not portrayed in a happy light, nor are his subsequent actions or thoughts typical of a *bildungsroman*. There cannot be constructive emphasis on what he achieves. As his character is depicted, there is strong disincentive for the reader to follow the example of John's book choices so that a spur to new literary experience or reassessment of society is more likely to arise in repulsion rather than from attraction. Any interrogation of double standards in sexual matters would not emerge from John's actions or opinions, nor from narratorial or other comment within the text, but it could easily be read from the nightmare sequence and its evidence of Kitty's internalized strictures. Kitty is not the central personage in the story but her fate is certainly capable of sensitising the reader to the injustice of a prevalent societal belief concerning the rape victim. The thrust of the tale is not to establish John as either New Woman or New Man, nor does it do so. However, at least six of the Flint norms can be discerned in the ensemble of the characters and events. The ingredients that the story shares with the New Woman novel are, plausibly, sufficient to put it into that category. If it is not irrevocably classified as such, it is undeniable that the issues are more than 'hovering' in the wings.

The camouflaged nature of George Moore's construction of the New Woman element, in both *Esther Waters* and 'John Norton', is in sharp contrast to his courting of controversy, both by public debate and by obvious espousal of a naturalist pattern and precedent. Ironically, the hidden development of the novel was too well concealed and while *Esther Waters* has very frequently been described as naturalistic in style, it has never been referred to in connection with the New Woman. Both the former identification and the latter omission sug-

p. 5.   25 George Moore, *Celibates*.   26 Ibid., p. 345, pp 368–9.

gest that the Moore programme for novelistic development backfired, to some extent. It seems likely that the social status of the central character and the mention of forbidden matter combined to attract the label of naturalism when any objective scrutiny must reveal that *Esther Waters* is not a determinist text. Rather, Esther defies and defeats the fate that would have overcome her in any naturalistic tale. The unpleasant associations of such prose are clearly absent, as comparison with the supposed French precedents of Goncourts' *Germinie Lacerteux* and Zola's *L'Assommoir* would show. *Germinie Lacerteux* had dealt with a servant's gradual descent into depravity, it was outspoken in a way that had not been part of recent literature and its physical descriptions of drunkenness and the sexual voracity of a woman caused a furore.

This tradition of candour was continued by Émile Zola and in his theory of the naturalist novel, nothing was to be left unsaid. The descriptions provided in *Esther Waters* lack the interminable and so-called scientific detail of Zola's models, rather they are painted in artistic fashion and much is left to the imagination. This is borne out by the two episodes in *Esther Waters* that had caused offence, the seduction and maternity hospital scenes. The contemporary objections concerning certain detail in the book mentioned its 'unpleasant hospital details and wished for 'some little respite from "the sex question"'.[27] W.H. Smith claimed to have banned the book 'on account of its blemishes' and, in comparing it to *Tess of the d'Urbervilles*, said that 'Tess is delicately inferential; Esther is precisely positive. What is merely delicately inferred in the one, is bluntly told in the other'.[28] But, as had been the case with *A Mummer's Wife* nine years earlier, the seduction was recounted briefly:

> One evening, putting his pipe aside, William threw his arm round her and whispered that she was his wife. The words sounded delicious in her ears, but she could hardly hear what he said after; a sort of weakness seemed to come over her. It must be the beer she had drunk. She wished she had not taken that last glass. She could not struggle with him.[29]

Complaints about depiction of the maternity hospital centred on similarly fleeting reference to the presence of male medical students and female nurses in the labour ward, to a single phrase 'the steel instruments on the round table and the basins on the floor', and to the administration of chloroform. Moore had claimed a full six years earlier that he had moved away from naturalism[30] but the memory of *A Mummer's Wife* facilitated the inaccurate diagnosis in the case of *Esther Waters* and Moore's pugnacity and coat-trailing ensured that the derogatory label was applied with venom rather than with accuracy.

27 Malcolm MacColl, 'The clergy and fiction', *The Speaker* (5 May 1894), 492–3. 28 William Faux, Interview, *Daily Chronicle* (2 May 1894), p. 3. Faux was the representative of W.H. Smith. 29 Moore, *Esther Waters*, p. 69. While this version appears in the 1894 edition, there is no reference to beer in later editions. 30 George Moore, *Confessions of a young man* (London, 1961), p. 111, p. 118.

Yet, he also won over a large audience to the relative frankness that was to be a part of the new English novel. Part of his clever approach was, at every turn, to cajole sympathy and support for Esther, the single mother, despite any transgression of traditional novelistic rules and patterns. By spotlighting the difficult choices that faced Esther, several of which were patently caused by the hypocrisy of the upper classes, he took the sharp focus off objective features of the story, ones like Esther living with a married man, helping him to run a pub and an illegal gambling business. Instead, readers remembered her touching success in managing to keep her illegitimate son alive and her struggle to support him. The overall manipulation of emotion achieved by Moore meant that a greater number of readers, probably to their surprise, opted for the pragmatic choice rather than the moral rulebook. Moreover, they acquiesced in the daring of having a servant as the central figure of a novel without having her story treated from the hauteur of the high moral ground or the viewpoint of the upper-class author. Neither did they object to the ultimate relationship between Mrs Barfield and Esther, one of almost equality between mistress and servant. Moore's achievement was revolutionary, but very quietly so.

Moore's injection of a New Woman strain into his stories continued in a second tale in *Celibates*. In 'Mildred Lawson', any reading of Mildred's conduct tends to evoke the appellation 'New Woman', if only as the reaction to be expected in the 1890s. In evaluating the story for New Woman criteria, the first standards appear to be met by Mildred's questioning of the suitability of marriage and childbearing for herself, and hence the denial of universal disposition thereto. Mildred does not put the married state forward as any kind of solution; the characters of Morton Mitchell and Ralph clearly view it in ways that were not socially approved; even Harold is 'in no hurry.'[31] However, childhood is not nostalgically recalled by any of the characters. Moreover, while Mildred's life is seen as a learning process that is often problematical, it is hardly one in which education achieves an acceptable result for her, although it appears to do so for Mrs Fargus. The latter's reading of Comte could conceivably direct the reader towards such texts and thus stimulate interest in the structure of society and the possibility of its reform. While the question of double standards in sexual morality may arise, it does so in a way opposed to the aims of New Woman. In the subdued conclusion, there is the unspoken invitation to the reader to reject Mildred as a rôle model and, possibly, since Mildred had no interest in such things, to join the suffragettes and promote the advancement of women. Overall, the story possesses sufficient of the requisite characteristics to qualify as New Woman literature, but, ironically, it can also be read as delivering an antithetical message.

As the extracts from *A Mummer's Wife* and *Esther Waters* show, it is all too easy today to pass over such passages without even seeing them, let alone giving them a second glance. Their rather earth-shattering properties for society in the 1890s are now well nigh invisible and hence, the artistic strategies and achieve-

31 Moore, *Celibates*, p. 262.

ments of their author could well remain misunderstood, unseen and/or under-valued. That the topic of 'immoral literature' could be one of the four subjects that occupied most space on the comment pages of newspapers and periodicals, from 1885 to 1895, reinforces the perceived magnitude of the forces facing writers of English literature at the time, particularly in connection with power and morals. It helps to explain the varied reactions of authors, from Hardy's withdrawal from the novel to George Moore's confrontations, provocations and subtle expansions of the novel's subject and treatment. This was bound to be a decade when, under pressure, various different literary subterfuges and styles were likely to emerge. In 1890, Edmund Gosse wrote that 'the experimental or realistic novel is mainly to be studied in America, Russia, and France … it has no direct development in England, except in the clever but imperfect stories of Mr George Moore.'[32] By 1896, the literary critic D.F. Hannigan could assert that the English novel had 'recently thrown out vigorous shoots; and in the future, no hybrid romance can flourish even on the soil where hypocritical prudery has reigned so long'.[33] George Moore's New Woman ingredient was just one of the elements he used to enrich the English novel and, like several of his other innovations, the manner of its insertion demonstrates an interesting quality that, despite Gosse's article, has not been generally noticed, or identified as a valuable contribution to literature. In his campaign for literary freedom for all authors, it was rather Moore's 'swashing and a martial outside' that caught the eye. His works, and probably those of other writers of the period, now merit further investigation and re-evaluation for the concealed subtleties and treasures that lie therein.

Robert Lowell and the 'lace-curtain Irish': identification and identity

ANN WALSH, NUI, CORK

For several weeks in April 1946, Jean Stafford, the American novelist and at that time wife of the poet Robert Lowell, worked day and night to redecorate their house at Damariscotta Mills, Maine. Lowell was furiously angry at the result, a reaction which in 'An Influx of Poets', her thinly disguised fictional account of that era, Stafford attributes to his belief that her home-making impulses were

32 Edmund Gosse, 'The limits of realism in fiction', in George J. Becker (ed.), *Documents of modern literary realism* (Princeton, 1963), 385. The article was originally published in June 1890. 33 D.F. Hannigan, 'The Victorian age of literature and its critics', *Westminster Review*, 145 (1896), 525.

'plebeian, anti-intellectual, and lace-curtain Irish.'[1] If the reliability of Stafford's 'nakedly autobiographical narrator'[2] has been called into question by a recognition of the writer's persistent tendency 'to get the spirit of the thing right but to inflate or wittily distort the events', this discussion accepts the spirit of Stafford's account in its argument that Lowell's reported conflation of these attributes evokes the spirit of an attitude to Irishness which resounds consistently through his poetry.[3] It will examine the relevance to this issue of the poet's temporary conversion to Roman Catholicism, the religious affiliation of the vast majority of the Irish-American community, and will reveal a direct relationship between the poet's perspective of Irish identity in the twentieth-century American context and his personally problematic self-identity as direct descendant of and ideological heir to the original New England Pilgrim settlers.

As is well-documented, Lowell was of long-established New England stock, descended on his mother's side from the *Mayflower* Winslows, and through his father from those Lowells who arrived in Massachusetts in 1639, early enough to make the list of Massachusetts first families. The influence and status of both families was considerable in the ongoing development of the state, and the poet's Lowell antecedents were notable for their contribution to American education and letters: James Russell Lowell and Amy Lowell were respectively his great-uncle and his cousin. Yet Paul Mariani, the poet's biographer, attests to what he calls Lowell's 'marvellous New England patrician manner of underplaying his pedigree: 'I never knew I was a Lowell until I was twenty', the poet once recalled.[4] This remark, from the retrospective stance of the mature poet, suggests a desire to distance himself a little from some of the more burning issues of his youth for, in April 1940, aged twenty-three, in the course of an acrimonious correspondence with his parents about his future, he was writing 'I am heading exactly where I have been heading for six years. One can hardly be ostracised for taking the intellect and aristocracy and family tradition seriously.'[5] Here, contrary to Mariani's point, the young poet's assertion suggests a full awareness of the significance of his pedigree, and offers a striking oppositional resonance with the characteristics of Irish identity specified in Lowell's response to Stafford's attempt at interior decor.

Mariani's account of the poet's remark (made during an interview with Ian Hamilton) is illuminating in another respect. Although the later biographer had never met his subject, he insists on Lowell's 'patrician' bearing, an inference of the poet's innately aristocratic nature manifest in many other analyses. Norman Mailer, for example, in his account of the October 1967 anti-Vietnam march on the Pentagon, describes Lowell as 'at once virile and patrician', who even in conversational pose with an old friend, resembled 'one Harvard dean talking to another, that same genteel confidential gracious hunch of the shoulder toward

1 Jean Stafford, 'An influx of poets', *New Yorker* (6 Nov. 1978), 43–60, see p. 51. 2 Ian Hamilton, *Robert Lowell: a biography* (London, 1982), p. 78. 3 Ibid., p. 80. 4 Paul Mariani, *Lost puritan: a life of Robert Lowell* (New York, 1994), p. 28. 5 Hamilton, *Robert Lowell*, p. 73.

ANN WALSH

each other' and yet managed 'to give off at times the unwilling haunted saintliness of a man who was repaying the moral debts of ten generations of ancestors'.[6] It might be suggested that here Mailer offers his reader a glimpse of his personal insecurities rather than an objective perspective of Lowell, but his comments offer further evidence of the undoubted fascination of the poet's lineage for his American public.

This effect is manifest also in the critical response to the poetry, as witnessed in Philip Hobsbaum's reading of Lowell's poem 'Sailing Home from Rapallo', which describes Charlotte Lowell's coffin: 'her *Risorgimento* black and gold casket / was like Napoleon's at the *Invalides*'[7] and 'in the grandiloquent lettering ... / *Lowell* had been mispelled *LOVEL*'.[8] Hobsbaum comments on these lines: 'the name on the Napoleonic coffin has been mispelled 'Lovel', a reversion to what may have been the authentic name of the family, found in the Battle Abbey Roll of early Normans'.[9] Hamilton informs us of an unpublished autobiographical fragment which specifies the misspelling as 'Lowel', and muddying the water even further, that the poet's contemporaneous letter to Blair Clark reports the inscription's misrepresentation as 'Winslon' in place of 'Winslow', Charlotte Lowell's maiden name.[10] The historical facts are unverifiable, but what is pertinent to this argument is that Hobsbaum's critical response to the poet's deliberate archaicisation of the family name is to make a leap of faith, transposing the Lowell lineage's traceable origins to early Norman England, and granting it aristocratic roots beyond its American context. Michael Hofmann has written of the attitude to Lowell's ancestry: 'In England, where social distinction is far more plentiful and arguably counts for far less, it is hard to get any sense of how this background could be overplayed and resented by Lowell's unsympathetic readers and rivals in America'.[11] Hofmann's observation is valid of some commentaries, but may be inverted to suggest that, as evidenced above, the poet's background has also been overplayed and mythologized by some of his more sympathetic readers and critics. If the reaction to Lowell's family origins varies between these two extremes, it is consistently seen as integral to his poetic, in a manner unparalleled in the response to the work of other twentieth century American poets.

This issue is raised by Elizabeth Bishop, in a letter to Lowell about his family poems, in which she claims (and complains) that: 'I feel that I could write in as much detail about my Uncle Artie, say – but what would be the significance? ... Whereas all you have to do is put down the names! And ... it seems significant, illustrative, American'.[12] Here Bishop identifies two salient aspects of this topic. Firstly, the names *do* matter; the New England Lowells have a signifi-

6 Norman Mailer, *The armies of the night* (New York, 1968), p. 30, p. 83, p. 99. 7 Robert Lowell, *Life studies* (London, 1968), p. 77. 8 Ibid., p. 78. 9 Philip Hobsbaum, *A reader's guide to Robert Lowell* (London, 1988), p. 86. 10 Ibid., p. 203. 11 Michael Hofmann, 'Introduction', in *Robert Lowell: poems selected by Michael Hofmann* (London, 2001), pp ix–xvi, see p. xi. 12 Elizabeth Bishop, *One art: the selected letters*, ed. and introd. Robert Giroux (London, 1994), p. 351.

[265]

cance in the American social context not attainable by anybody's Uncle Artie.
This fact is acknowledged by the British writer Anthony Powell who has argued
that: 'Lowell is an interesting instance of the American self-deception as to class
existing in the U.S.; Robert Lowell never on any occasion being mentioned
without his precise status within the Lowell family, as a Lowell aristocrat, albeit
a minor one, being gone into.'[13] In 'putting down the names', Lowell moreover
acknowledges his personal belief that they do matter, that they are significant
and illustrative and, particularly, that they are American in a way that other
names are not. In spite of the poet's reported early lack of awareness of his illus-
trious relatives – he insists on another occasion that 'I really didn't know I'd had
them until I went to the South' – the poems suggest rather a clear recognition
of the fact of his ancestry, and a recurring ambivalence about the relevance of
that legacy.[14]

Stafford alludes to this ambivalence in her depiction of Theron Maybank,
the fictionalized version of the young Lowell:

> Although Theron appeared to have repudiated all the luxuries and limita-
> tions of his Bostonian breeding and totems, he had in fact not done so at all;
> he was as vain as a peacock that Copley had painted his distant cousin
> Augustus' family.[15]

Stafford's contention is borne out by many of the poems in *Life Studies*. The
poetic depiction of Lowell's grandfather, for example, which we will look at later,
emphasizes his exceptional European education, 'his high school at *Stukkert am
Neckar*'[16], and his walking cane 'carved with the names and altitudes /
of Norwegian mountains he had scaled'.[17] All is elevated, pertaining to the heroic,
establishing this figure as archetypal representative of a tradition that sees itself
as the aristocracy of American liberal democracy.

This ambivalent tone re-echoes in the disingenuous ring of Lowell's poetic
account of a conversation with T.S. Eliot, which opened with the older poet's
question: 'Don't you loathe to be compared with your relatives? / I've just found
two of mine reviewed by Poe/ he wiped the floor with them ... and I was
delighted.'[18] The sonnet purposefully emphasizes the notion of a shared burden
of inherited and depreciated glory, bestowing on Eliot an ambivalent attitude
to his forebears mirroring Lowell's own; for the speaker introduces the topic of
the very ancestors whom he claims to deplore, and subtly establishes their literary significance in having been reviewed by no less a figure than Poe. Lowell's
contribution to the mythical image of his family's status is indisputable; if his
youthful conversion to Catholicism and his transfer from Harvard to Kenyon

13 Nancy Schoenberger, *Dangerous muse: a life of Caroline Blackwood* (London, 2001), p. 145. 14
Frederick Seidel, 'The art of poetry: Robert Lowell', in Jeffrey Meyers (ed.), *Robert Lowell: interviews and memoirs* (Ann Arbor, 1988), p. 64. 15 Stafford, 'An influx of poets', p. 50. 16 Lowell, 'My
last afternoon with Uncle Devereux Winslow', in *Life studies*, p. 67. 17 Ibid., 'Dunbarton', p. 74.
18 Robert Lowell, *Notebook* (London, 1970), p. 71.

College are generally recognized as attempts to distance himself from his aristocratic background, the poetry repeatedly exploits this same background in its interrogation of twentieth-century American experience.

The notion of an American aristocracy is not the paradox that it might seem. In his book, *The Protestant Establishment: Aristocracy and Caste in America*, the sociologist E. Digby Baltzell offers a definition in the American context of the term 'aristocracy' as:

> a community of upper-class families, whose members are born to positions of high prestige and assured dignity because their ancestors have been leaders for one generation or more; ... these families are carriers of a set of traditional values which command authority because they represent the aspirations of both the élite and the rest of the population; and that this class continue to justify its authority a) by contributing its share of contemporary leaders and b) by continuing to assimilate in each generation the families of new members of the elite.[19]

In a situation where this upper class protects its privileges and prestige, but fails to contribute to leadership, or refuses the assimilation of new élite members on grounds of racial or ethnic origins, Baltzell refers to 'the process of caste'.[20]

Writing in 1964 as Lowell's contemporary, Baltzell offers a sociological perspective of an issue which was a particular preoccupation of the poet's and which seems, as I will demonstrate, to have a direct relation to his poetic depiction of Irishness. For Lowell's poetry is haunted by a pervading personal sense of lost inheritance, exemplified by his elegiac poems set in Dunbarton, his grandfather's New Hampshire estate and by other poems which mourn the abandoned ideals of early America. His bleak perspective of the modern American nation is consistently underpinned by a sense of lost opportunity, of a birthright squandered by successive generations of Americans of his own background. Baltzell's thesis concerns itself with this very issue, arguing that after the Civil War the American upper classes responded to the enormous increase in immigration by refusing the social absorption of 'new' Americans, as had been the practice up to the middle of the nineteenth century. Thus even the most gifted and able members of immigrant groups – especially Jewish and Catholic, and other obviously hyphenated Americans – found assimilation into the nation's élite progressively more difficult. The traditional White Anglo-Saxon Protestant began to focus more on the pursuit of wealth and the creation of social enclaves rather than continuing to lead the nation politically and academically.

Lowell's poetry acknowledges that aristocratic America of which he sees himself the self-elected representative voice has, through its increasing reluctance to renew its authority in the practice of civic responsibility, and in its fail-

19 E. Digby Baltzell, *The Protestant establishment: aristocracy and caste in America* (New York, 1964), p. 8. 20 Ibid., p. 9.

ure to pursue the role of leadership, degenerated to what Baltzell calls the process of caste, a closed upper class whose 'all-too-prevalent attitude has been in this twentieth-century America, to succeed rather than to lead.'[21] This latter point is an issue for the poet in his elegy for his maternal grandfather 'In Memory of Arthur Winslow.' Here Lowell suggests that the mercenary impulse which had impelled Winslow to Colorado – to make the fortune which financed Lowell's upbringing – was misguided, and argues that capitalist expansion was not the way to revive the lost ideals of New England:

> for what else could bring
> You, Arthur, to the veined and alien West
> But devil's notions that your gold at least
> Could give back life to men who whipped the British King?[22]

This is the poem, which, in its second stanza, offers us Lowell's earliest reference to the Irish:

> Grandfather Winslow, look the swanboats coast
> That island in the Public Gardens where
> The bread-stuffed ducks are brooding, where with tub
> And strainer the mid-Sunday Irish scare
> The sun-struck shallows for the dusky chub
> This Easter, and the ghost
> Of risen Jesus walks the waves to
> Run Arthur upon a trumpeting black swan
> Beyond Charles River to the Acheron
> Where the wide waters and their voyager are one.[23]

The rather overblown image, with its mixed mythical metaphors of Arthur Winslow escorted by 'the Ghost / Of risen Jesus ... upon a trumpeting black swan', vies in this scene with the more mundane elements of the Boston Public Gardens, 'the bread-stuffed ducks' and 'the mid-Sunday Irish', who 'with tub/ And strainer scare the sun-struck shadows for the dusky chub/ This Easter.' Written soon after Lowell's conversion to Catholicism, at the height of his religious fervour, these lines offer a wry commentary on the Sabbath observances of his Irish co-religionists, and on the cultural and social inappropriateness demonstrated by their ineffectual angling equipment.

The Irish are not the only immigrant group whom Lowell identifies as striking this jarring note in the American milieu. The poem 'Christmas in Black Rock' offers a parallel depiction of irreligiosity and inappropriate social behaviour where the 'drunken Polish night shifts walk / Over the causeway and their

---

21 Ibid., p. 78. 22 Robert Lowell, 'In memory of Arthur Winslow' in *Lord Weary's castle* (New York, 1946), p. 27. 23 Ibid., p. 25.

juke-box booms/ *Hosanna in excelsis Domino.*'[24] Overwhelmingly, however, it is the Irish whom Lowell chooses as the representative element of the immigrant tide which transformed America and dispossessed its original settlers. And so in '91 Revere St', the autobiographical prose section of *Life Studies*, the poet recollects his Boston childhood as follows:

> I'd loiter by the old iron fence and gape longingly across Charles St at Boston Common, a now largely wrong-side-of-the-tracks park. On the Common, there were mossy bronze reliefs of Union soldiers, and a captured German tank, filled with smelly wads of newspaper. Everywhere there was grit, litter, gangs of Irish, Negroes, Latins.[25]

Lowell's classification of the detrital elements of the modern Boston Common thus identifies the Irish – and only the Irish – by nationality, demonstrating their particular relevance to the poet's view of the twentieth-century dissolution of the American dream.

II

Other factors complicate this issue. Lowell's awareness of the waning relevance of his own caste was compounded by his awareness of the related phenomenon – that, as H.L. Mencken observed in 1924, 'if the descendants of the first settlers ... tend plainly to move downward, mentally, spiritually, even physically ... the descendants of the later immigrants tend more generally to move upward'.[26] Upward mobility along any parameter is not always easily achieved, even in a land of opportunity, and it has been noted that minority groups in America often attempted to attain this end by different means. Baltzell points out that 'the Irish ... tended to dominate both the Church and the urban political machine which was largely responsible for keeping the Democratic Party alive during the years of Republican rule between the Civil War and the New Deal.'[27]

The issue of Irish domination of American Catholicism is particularly relevant for Lowell because of his personal experience of that religion. Raised as an Episcopalian, he converted to Catholicism in 1941, against the wishes of his family and against the grain of his own inherited prejudices. Peter Taylor, a lifelong friend of the poet, has recalled that, as a student:

> [Lowell] had now and again teased him about his own interest in Catholicism. He called it 'a religion of Irish servant girls' – remembering here his mother's advice to an Irish maid who wanted to become

24 Ibid., p. 12. 25 Lowell, *Life studies*, p. 41. 26 Baltzell, *The Protestant establishment*, p. 223. 27 Ibid., p. 49.

Episcopalian: 'No, you have your church and we have ours, and it's better to keep it that way.'[28]

Notwithstanding this attitude, Lowell did convert, possibly motivated by a desire to distance himself in a concrete fashion from his family and what they represented, but primarily influenced in this decision by his mentor Allen Tate, whose search for an antidote to what he perceived as the toxicity of secular modernity led him not only to agrarianism, but to neo-Thomist scholastic philosophy. Although Lowell's manic-depressive disorder was an undoubted factor in the fervour of his religious observance, his conversion, after exhaustive theological studies, seems to have been based on a sincere spiritual position. During the early years of his allegiance to Catholicism, he paid several visits to the Trappist monastery in Rhode Island, 'attending' as Stafford records 'all services, including Vespers, Compline and Benediction [in a] chapel with a real del Robbia and a Van der Weyden Madonna.'[29]

If this was the kind of Catholic expression that had prompted the poet's conversion, mainstream American Catholic experience was very different. Lowell found himself aligned with a community of co-religionists and their clergy, very many of whom were either Irish or American-Irish and very many of whom failed to live up to his idealized vision of Catholicism. This position is exemplified in Stafford's account of their parish at Damariscotta:

> a stone's throw from the house was St Patrick's, the oldest Catholic church in Maine ... a red-brick structure which was too beautiful to believe ... full of paintings purloined from Spanish churches, an altar-piece three hundred years old, and a heavenly bell made by Paul Revere. But the pastor, Fr Lynch, turned out to be a disaster, being anti-intellectual and interested mainly in prize-fights.[30]

The association of Catholicism with anti-intellectualism, as personified by the hapless Fr. Lynch, will be directly articulated in the poems discussed next, illustrating the poet's linkage of Irish and Catholic identity as a representative type of the new American.

Two poems in *Life Studies*, 'Waking in the Blue' and 'Memories of West St and Lepke', recount Lowell's experience as a psychiatric patient. Each, like 'Arthur Winslow', juxtaposes members of New England's traditional élite with Americans of other origins. 'Waking in the Blue' is set in Boston's McLean Hospital, a large private psychiatric hospital; the speaker's fellow-inmates are 'Stanley, now sunk in his sixties',[31] once a Harvard all-American full-back, with 'a kingly granite profile in a crimson golf cap', and 'Bobbie/ Porcellian '29/ a replica of Louis XVI/ without the wig'.[32] Significantly, 'Bobbie' was the name by which the poet was

28 Hamilton, *Robert Lowell*, p. 55. 29 Mariani, *Lost puritan*, p. 115. 30 Ibid., p. 126. 31 Lowell, *Life studies*, p. 95. 32 Ibid., p. 96

known within his own family. These demented personae must defer in the order of their appearance in the narrative to the poem's opening figure, 'the night attendant, a BU sophomore / rouses from the mare's nest of his drowsy head / propped on *The Meaning of Meaning.*' The fact that the attendant is a student at Boston University, carries significant connotations; after World War II, Boston University was notable for its enormous intake of ex-servicemen under the auspices of the GI Bill, enabling, in their thousands, members of ethnic and racial minority groups including Irish and Irish-Americans, to receive an education which would have been otherwise beyond their reach. His relevance is heightened when we note the intimation that, in spite of his on-going education, this student appears doomed to remain in the ranks of the anti-intellectuals. For the 'the mare's nest of his drowsy head', which offers a pessimistic perspective of his intellectual ability, is 'propped' on *The Meaning of Meaning*, I.A. Richards' book on psycholinguistics, the merely physical contact between text and student refuting his chances of mastering this topic.

This defining attribute of the attendant, his innate intellectual deficiency, contrasts pointedly with the defining attributes of the speaker's fellow-patients, for Stanley (with his 'kingly granite profile') and Bobbie (the 'replica of Louis XVI') possess a genetically determined nobility which persistently transcends their physical and psychological decline. It is a quality shared by the senile Mary Winslow, a tragicomic figure cared for by her Irish maids, whose apartment even after her death, remains a 'four-roomed kingdom'.[33] These poems thus emulate 'In Memory of Arthur Winslow' in the consistent oppositional contrast achieved by juxtaposing the degenerate, but intrinsically noble original settler, and the culturally incongruous and anti-intellectual newcomer.

This opposition is re-worked in 'Memories of West St and Lepke', in which the speaker specifies even more clearly the significant aspect of the attendants' identity :

> In between the limits of the day
> Hours and hours go by under the crewcuts
> And slightly too little nonsensical bachelor twinkle
> Of the Roman Catholic attendants.
> (There are no Mayflower
> screwballs in the Catholic Church)[34]

Statistically, there is no evidence that the incidence of mental illness is higher in the descendants of America's Pilgrim settlers. Indeed, it is reasonable and pertinent to suggest that state institutions and other psychiatric hospitals less exclusive than McLean would show a correspondingly higher proportion of immigrant and less affluent patients, thus redressing this alleged epidemiological imbalance. These lines are also noteworthy for their intimation that

33 Lowell, *Lord Weary's castle*, p. 31.   34 Lowell, *Life studies*, p. 96.

American Catholicism's good fortune in its scarcity of 'Mayflower screwballs' is offset by the deficiencies intimated in the 'slightly too little nonsensical bachelor twinkle' of the Roman Catholic attendants.

There are two recognisable stereotypical concepts at work in these poems. Firstly, that there exists in twentieth-century America some kind of pure and undiluted *Mayflower* line – descendants of New England's first settlers who are psychologically unsound, and unable to meet the responsibilities of their aristocratic heritage – of which Lowell repeatedly offers his own mental illness and chaotic personal life as metaphorical representation. Against this is pitted a second stereotypical construct, that of the immigrant population who are represented in contrast as psychologically robust but culturally inappropriate and intellectually challenged. It is relevant that in spite of their reiterated shortcomings, these figures, as nursing maidservants and hospital attendants, are now the custodians of the former American aristocracy. The poetry thus acknowledges the empowerment of these new Americans in modern America, while at the same stressing their intellectual and cultural limitations in this role.

In this binary opposition we can thus recognize that the new American – as epitomized by those of Irish (and Catholic) immigrant stock – represents for Lowell a significant Other, a manifest antitype of his own caste. Hayden White has explored this representational tactic in general terms in his essay 'The Forms of Wildness', where he defines it as 'the technique of ostensive self-definition by negation.' White writes of this concept:

> In times of socio-cultural stress, when the need for positive self-definition asserts itself, but no compelling criterion for self-identification appears, it is always possible to say something like: 'I may not know the precise content of my own felt humanity, but I am certainly *not* like that' and simply point to something in the landscape that is manifestly different from oneself.[35]

White adds that this move 'appears as a kind of reflex action in conflicts between nations, classes, and political parties, and is not unknown among scholars and intellectuals 'seeking to establish their claims to élite status against the *vulgus mobile*.'

This brings us to a recognition of the crux of Lowell's dilemma: his attempt to locate a viable sense of self-definition in modern America is blocked on the one hand by the awareness that his own caste has been dispossessed, even of those qualities which might allow them to redress their disinheritance – all they possess now is that sense of inherited status which in their present context is valueless. The poems demonstrate a typical Lowellian ambivalence to the significance of this inherited status; his persistent reference to this quality becomes

---

35 Hayden White, 'The forms of wildness: archaeology of an idea', in Edward Dudley and Maximillian E. Novak (eds), *The wild man within: an image in western thought from the Renaissance to Romanticism* (Pittsburgh, 1972), pp 3–38, see p. 4.

in effect an interrogation of its irrelevance. On the other hand, he cannot or will not find satisfactory self-definition among what White terms the *'vulgus mobilé'*, the Irish and Catholic immigrant group, whose cultural and intellectual inadequacies demonstrate their ineligibility for the position of power that they occupy. It is in fact the inadequacies of these new Americans which justify the poet's lingering fascination for that lost patrician inheritance which, even in the recognition of the disintegration of his own tradition, allow him to regret its passing. It is interesting to consider that such assertion of difference has historically been an important rhetorical device in the justification of colonisation and other processes of oppression. Here we see Lowell employ it for an inverse purpose: for the twentieth-century dispossession of America's aristocracy can be seen to represent in the poet's eyes a form of re-colonisation of that nation, the disinheritance of its original settlers, and an appropriation of the landscape by an alien group.

III

This discussion would be incomplete without a reference to another facet of Lowell's depiction of the Boston Irish, to his poetic references to the Kennedys. The poet had some slight acquaintance with John F. Kennedy, and one of his more notorious manic episodes in the sixties was marked by an obsession with the dead President's widow. But it was with Robert Kennedy that Lowell had a more significant relationship, stemming from the poet's growing politicisation in his opposition to the Vietnam War, and it was in memory of the younger Kennedy that three sonnets were published in the various *Notebook* volumes, and later amalgamated and republished as two separate sonnets in the *History* sequence. As has been noted by his biographers, Lowell was fascinated by Robert Kennedy, whom he envisaged as 'a driven fated prince',[36] a view articulated in the sonnet 'R.F.K':

> Doom was woven in your nerves, your shirt
> woven in the great clan; they too were loyal
> and you too were loyal to them, to death.
> For them, like a prince, you daily left your tower
> To walk through the dirt in your best cloth.[37]

Unlike the innate royal attributes of the *Mayflower* descendants, Robert Kennedy's princely attributes are simulated – and simulated, moreover, specifically for the benefit of his doomed 'great clan' – 'for them, like a prince, you daily left your tower.' Tellingly, Lowell locates the Massachusetts senator within an archaic tribal system of political allegiance, an intimated anachronism in the

36 Hamilton, *Robert Lowell*, p. 376.   37 Lowell, *Notebook*, p. 118

modern political arena. Here the poem resounds the nativist accent of the poems discussed above, voicing an attitude to second and third generation Americans that, thirty years earlier, had prompted Joseph Kennedy, the senator's father, to ask: 'How long does our family have to be here before we are called Americans rather than Irish-Americans?'[38]

There is an intriguing epilogue, also with a colonial underpinning, to Lowell's poetic identification of the Boston Irish as representative dispossessors of the natural heirs to the American nation. In the last years of his life, he formed a connection with a very different Irish tradition, which as we shall see, facilitated a poetic re-kindling of some of the concepts that have just been discussed. For in 1972, the poet married his third wife, Caroline Blackwood, daughter of the Anglo-Irish peer, the marquis of Dufferin and Ava, and heiress to part of the Guinness family fortune, whose childhood home was at Clandeboye, an estate of 3,000 acres in Co. Down. By the time she married Lowell, her third husband, she was living in London and attempting to find her voice as a writer. His marriage to Blackwood, in other words, brought Lowell into a sphere of landed historical privilege – an exaggerated form of his own New England origins.

With the exception of the reference in 'Fourth of July in Maine' to his summer house at Castine, none of Lowell's verse after the Dunbarton poems of *Life Studies* finds an affirmative setting in his place of habitation until he relocates a sense of groundedness in the aristocratic tradition of Blackwood's Anglo-Irish background. Writing from her eighteenth-century Palladian house ('Milgate') in Kent during their relationship, the poet articulates that sense of poetic identification with a landed tradition, which he had relinquished after *Life Studies*. Several poems in *The Dolphin* celebrate Milgate: 'Milgate kept standing for four centuries / Good landlord alternating with derelict / Most fell between',[39] and: 'A sweetish smell of shavings, wax and oil / blows through the redone bedroom newly aged; / the sun in heaven enflames a sanded floor'.[40] (If, in his poetry, Lowell exploits the historical connotations of his wife's residence, it is interesting that Blackwood reciprocates that action: her fictionalized memoir 'Great Granny Webster', an over-rated book which was shortlisted for the 1977 Booker Prize, re-names Clandeboye, her childhood home and calls it Dunmartin, echoing the lost Dunbarton of Lowell's youth.)

In 1977, however, their relationship under strain, Blackwood sold Milgate and moved her family to Castletown House, Co. Kildare. Castletown is the setting for one of Lowell's final marriage poems, 'Last Walk?', the interrogative voice of the title conveying his more than tentative awareness that this relationship is almost concluded. The poem resonates with the 'Walk' sonnets of *Notebook*: 'Ice on the Hudson', 'Mexico' and 'The Walk', each of which articulates a parallel regretful awareness of foundering sexual relationships. 'Last Walk' is Lowell's only poem with an overtly Irish setting, and as in his

38 Baltzell, *The Protestant establishment*, p. xiii.   39 Robert Lowell, *The dolphin* (New York, 1973), p. 30.   40 Ibid., p. 59.

American poems, he offers the personal turmoil of his life, and the sudden disintegration of his marriage as metaphor for the state of the nation which in this instance is Ireland beset by terrorist attacks: 'explosion is growing common here.'⁴¹ Appropriately enough for the poem's locale, 'Last Walk?' manifests a conspicuous manipulation of several Yeatsian tropes in its composition. The speaker recounts: 'we walked to an artificial pond / dammed at both ends to reflect the Castle – / a natural composition for the faded colorist.' This is no Yeatsian tower, no haven for the poet and his descendants, but rather an acknowledged anachronism in a modern environment. There is, however, a lingering and typical Lowellian ambivalence at play here – the artificiality of the pond and the punning of 'dammed at both ends' are offset by the perceptible bulk of the 'Castle', its higher case punctuation at the couplet's end asserting its persisting significance. Lowell's river may call to mind the racing waters of 'Coole and Ballylea 1931', but the treacherous flow of 'the Liffey, torrential, wild / accelerated to murder' carries a very different potential. Nor are Lowell's swans of the Yeatsian mould, 'unwearied still, lover by lover': the Castletown birds are about to dispel the myth that swans mate always for life, reneging on their 'the misleading promise / to last with joy as long as our bodies.'⁴² In this poem, Lowell thus integrates an Anglo-Irish setting with the re-appropriation and subversion of some of the most familiar images of Anglo-Irish poetry. It is an approach to the Yeatsian poetic, moreover, which is paralleled in Lowell's account of the American-Irish: for Yeats' mythologising of the native Irish population is inversely mirrored in the way that Lowell, as we have seen, takes this same group, in its fresh identity as American immigrant, and creates of it a very different mythic construct, as adjunct to an on-going mythologising of his own caste.

This point brings us to an aspect of 'Last Walk?' which highlights the ease with which Lowell taps into the implications of the Anglo-Irish backdrop, and the way in which this setting resonates for him with his own lost heritage. For these swans, like the Boston Winslows, and the patrician lunatics of McLean Hospital, display an inbred nobility which overrides their other traits. He introduces this concept with a declaration of its contemporary irrelevance: 'yet everything about the royal swan / is silly, overstated, a luxury toy / beyond the fortunate child's allowance'; and yet this quality, albeit a burden to the possessor, must be acknowledged. Thus, the mother swan sits 'enthroned like a colossal head of Pharaoh / on her messy double goose-egg nest of sticks', and 'the male swan … / … gallanted down the stout-enriched rapids to Dublin / as if to show that a king had a right to be too happy.' There is an intimated abnegation of instinctive responsibility in the image of the female with her 'messy double goose-egg nest' and her gloriously gallanting mate which resonates with Lowell's earlier portrayal of his own degenerating New England caste. In this Irish context, very different from its original sounding, the Lowellian speaker thus articulates his

41 Lowell, p. 13   42 Robert Lowell, *Day by day* (New York, 1977), p. 14.

re-location of that sense of aristocratic identity pertaining to his American roots, voicing an ambivalence regarding the legacy of that identity unaltered and unresolved since its first expression thirty years earlier.

Lowell's sense of familial identification with the American aristocratic tradition represents a thematic cornerstone of his most popular verse, and its expression can be recognised as a persistent facet of his entire *oeuvre*. The poetry demonstrates the not inconsiderable significance of Irishness as a particular and distinct ethnic identity in the context of twentieth-century American experience, in the continually evolving synthesis of American national identity. His poetic utilisation of the American-Irish as antithetical foil to his own élite New England community forms part of the poet's complex account of a rapidly changing society, where the influence of a massive tide of immigration had eroded the authority of the old order. In his last collection of poems, Lowell's encounter with another old order, that of Anglo-Ireland, elicits a resounding of the complex undertones of that lost entitlement.

Anne Walsh acknowledges that publication of material from Robert Lowell's manuscripts, shelf mark bMS Am 1905 (2906), was made available due to the permission of the Houghton Library, Harvard University.

Rimes of the ancient mariner:
a reading of the plural poem

COILÍN Ó HAODHA, NUI, GALWAY

JCC Mays is the seventh editor of the collected poetical works of Samuel Taylor Coleridge, published in 2002.[1] His work has two principal aims: to document and collect as many poems written by Coleridge as is possible, and to establish a revision of the standard definitions of the poetic to accommodate and justify his additions to the poet's body of work. Each successive edition of Coleridge's works since the poet's death has included more material than the last contained. Mays has added three hundred poems to his edition; one hundred of these are published for the first time. Since the new edition contains just over seven hundred poetical works, Mays's additions amount to an expansion of the poet's oeuvre by almost one half.[2]

1 *The collected poetical and dramatic works of Samuel Taylor Coleridge*, ed. and introd. J.C.C. Mays, is Volume 16 in the Bollingen Series Collected Coleridge published by Princeton UP (Princeton, 2001). The volume comprises three books; there are two parts to each book, published separately. Volume 16, Book 1, Parts i and ii contain the Reading Text of the poems; Book 2, Parts i and ii, the Variorum Texts; Coleridge's dramatic works are reproduced and annotated in Book 3, Parts i & ii. Citations in the text follow the standard order: CC [Collected Coleridge], Volume, Book, Part, Page number. 2 *Biographia literaria*, ed. and introd. by James Engell and W. Jackson Bate, is Volume

Many of Coleridge's poems exist in several versions that exhibit minor and substantive variations in theme, style, language and punctuation. Mays rejects the notion that a poem that exists in several versions can be reduced to a single 'corrected' text without significant loss. In his 'Editor's Introduction', he registers the difference between cleaning a text to reveal its original, authoritative form and correcting the text to produce the (or an) intended form.[3]

The standard mode of presentation of poems in a variorum edition has been to provide a reading text of the poem, with footnotes and endnotes inserted to alert readers to variant possibilities. Mays abandons this format in his variorum text of Coleridge's poems in order to show as clearly as possible the relations between variants as they occur, and to make the work of reconstruction of whole versions – the work of the critical reader – less laborious. He hopes that the format in which he presents the texts of each poem – printing each line in the chronological order of composition or publication, as changes occur – will enable a reader to hold in mind a sense of the way 'the poems move, as they often do, simultaneously in several planes: that is, the way the poems move laterally, as a series of independent versions, and vertically, as one version overlays and succeeds another.'[4]

Chronological ordering by date of composition has become the norm in collected editions. It is attractive to Mays and adopted by him because it embodies his revision of the poetic: different poems are included as they were written, in the order in which they were written, without prior distinctions of type or value. Short or long silences in the record of time frustrate easy attempts to read the poems from beginning to end into a meaningful order. However, it is precisely because a chronological order of poems retains the blanks and mysteries, which the poet's taste in selection or the editor's in his arrangements might seek to explain away or to endow with significance, that such an order is valuable: it neither sets up nor satisfies expectations in readers unfamiliar with the poet, nor does it easily gratify the anticipations of a reader familiar with Coleridge's writings.

My thesis is that the expression the 'plural poem' can be used to approximate both the modes of poetic composition availed of by the author and the states of textual decomposition that editors and critics can encounter or provoke. The expression is first of all a descriptive one: it accounts for the multiple appearances of one poem in manuscript and print, and acknowledges the differences between these various appearances. However – and this is where description tends toward definition – the existence of a plurality of versions can no longer be regarded as an anomalous state of a single text to be established by the industry of an editor. The ongoing editorial and critical debates about the 'best' or 'correct' text of a poem, for the purposes of interpretation, might be resolved more fruitfully (if not finally concluded) through the development of strategies of reading that take into account all the extant, authoritative versions of the poem.

7 in the Bollingen Series Collected Coleridge published by Princeton UP (Princeton, 1983). Citations in the text follow the standard order: CC [Collected Coleridge], Volume, Book, Page number. 3 Ibid., 16, 1, i, p. lxxxii. 4 Ibid., 16, 1, i, p. cxxiii.

The description of the plural poem offered here is one attempt to initiate the development of such a strategy. The poem is not identical to one textual version in the history of its composition; it is not a text carefully restored, *post mortem*, from the available variant possibilities: the poem is the plurality of its versions. The two key elements in establishing meaningful relations among versions are time – times of writing, times of revising – and the place or places of publication. The presentation of the poem as a plural phenomenon does not disguise the way that a plurality of versions can render any definitive reading of the poem as a singular text problematic; on the contrary, the description of the poem as plural is an attempt to derive a positive reading of textual instability. In the case of Coleridge, it is particularly noteworthy that there appears to be a correlation between textual instability and the canonical status of his major poems within his own oeuvre and in the literary canons more generally; that is, the more unstable the text, the higher its critical standing and significance. 'The Rime of the Ancient Mariner' is a case in point.

Secondly, the plural poem can be used as a descriptive term for poems whose authority cannot be limited to a single, named author. The poetic transactions of suggestion, revision, correction and criticism between Coleridge and Wordsworth are very well documented. Similar forms of negotiation are evident among these two and other poets of same period – especially Charles Lamb and Robert Southey. Poetic transactions of this type informed in a fundamental way Coleridge's revisions of his poems. The plural poem encompasses the practices of collaborative composition, or a plurality of authorship. The existence of the plural poem, as it is proposed here, exposes the absence of a singular origin for literary authority (and, incidentally, spells the end of the peculiarly Romantic – though enduring – myth of the poet as solitary genius).

The final definition of the plural poem that I offer arises from both the consideration of textual instability and the equivocal sense attributed to literary authority. Mays intends the complexity of Coleridge's collected works – the continuities and discontinuities in the chronological order of the poet's writings and the many abrupt changes in style and form – to stand as a representation of the poet's mind.[5] The definition of the plural poem expands to encompass the entire collected works: in so far as it can be known, the mind of the poet is the body of his work. The image of the poet in the reader's mind is significant because it informs his reading of the poems as surely as Coleridge's shifting perception of himself as a poet informed his diverse writings.[6]

What gives this final understanding of the plural poem special significance in the case of Coleridge is that the author undertook a similar project in *Biographia literaria*.[7] The *Biographia* began its long and complicated life in Coleridge's mind as a preface to a definitive collection of his poems, which would

5 Ibid., 16, 1, i, p. cxx.   6 Ibid., 16, 1, i, p. xcv.   7 The edition of *Biographia literaria* cited here is Volume 7 in the Bollingen Series *Collected Coleridge*. Citations in the text follow the standard order: *Collected Coleridge*, Volume, Book, Page.

attempt, in his words, 'to define with the utmost impartiality the real poetic character of the poet'[8] – 'What is poetry? [he says] is so nearly the same question with, what is a poet? that the answer to the one is involved in the solution of the other.'[9] By the time the *Biographia* came to be written, however, the poetic character in Coleridge's own mind was not himself, but Wordsworth.

Each of these ideas finds a precedent in the history of criticism. Jack Stillinger[10] has questioned the functions and value and usefulness of critical definitions and the establishment of a single, authoritative text in his study, *Coleridge and Textual Instability: the Multiple Versions of the Later Poems*; and in *The Book of Yeats' poems*,[11] Hazard Adams has argued that a reading of the collected works of Yeats produces a narrative of the poet from which the poetic character of the poet may be inferred. What is distinctive in this discussion of the plural poem is that these ideas, first, are drawn into interpretative relation with one another; and second, that they are brought to bear on an author whose critical writings have definitively shaped characterisations of the authority of the poet and of the nature of the poem that have endured in various forms to the present day.

The history of its textual versions shows the poem coming into existence in revised forms, repeatedly and at discrete moments in time. These moments in time are occasions of reading: for the author, reading as a prelude to re-writing, for the reader, reading as a prelude to new understanding.

The temporality of the poem leads to a conception of each version as a text for performance. The word 'performance' is being used here in a very broad sense to include the recitation of a poem, the private publication of a poem in notebooks or letters, and the official publication of a poem in a newspaper, a review, an anthology or a book. Mays remarks that 'separate versions [of Coleridge's poems] are for the most part consistent with themselves, and have their own justification almost as separate performances might',[12] and this functional analogy has been allowed a more general application by Stillinger in an essay entitled 'A Practical Theory of Versions': 'To an extent, the branching out of textual versions of poems can be likened to performance versions in music.'[13] To describe the poem as a plural phenomenon, and then to figure its plurality in performative terms is to underline, as a starting-point for further critical reading, the interpretative work that has already been done by the author through the production of several versions of his poem.

To put textual version and performance on either side of a tentative equation also results in a less absolute definition of literary intentions, one that accords more closely with the writer's practice and the readers' experience. Furthermore, the idea of performance includes the presence of an audience; if the text of a poem can be described as similar in some respects to the notation of a musical score, acts of literary interpretation share some common ground with a musi-

---

8 *Collected Coleridge*, 7, i, p. 5. 9 Ibid., 7, 2, p. 15. 10 Jack Stillinger, *Coleridge and textual instability: the multiple versions of the later poem* (Oxford, 1994). 11 Hazard Adams, *The book of Yeats's poems* (Florida, 1990). 12 CC, 16, 1, i, p. lxxxvi. 13 Stillinger, 'A practical theory of versions', p. 123.

cian's interpretation of the composer's concerto. The analogy has a special congruity in the case of Coleridge. Many of the versions of his major poems and above all 'The Rime of the Ancient Mariner' demonstrate that Coleridge's revisions centre on the sound of the text, rather than on semantics or structure. Moreover, Coleridge earned a considerable reputation for his recitations of his own poems and the poems of others.

THE RIME
OF THE
ANCYENT MARINERE,
IN SEVEN PARTS

Are these her naked ribs, which
    fleck'd
The sun that did behind them
    peer?
And are these two all, all the crew,
That woman and her fleshless
    Pheere?

Lyrical ballads (1798)

THE RIME OF THE ANCIENT
MARNER.
IN SEVEN PARTS.

And its ribs
are seen as
bars on the
face of the
setting Sun.
The spectre-
woman and
her death-
mate, and no
other on board
the skeleton-ship.

Are those her ribs through which
    the Sun
Did peer, as through a grate?
And is that Woman all her crew?
Is that a Death? and are there two?
Is Death that woman's mate?

Poetical Works (1834)

The ANCIENT MARINER.
A POET'S REVERIE.

Are those her Ribs, thro' which
    the Sun
Did peer, as thro' a grate?
And are those two all, all her crew

That woman and her Mate?

Lyrical ballads (1800)

The Rime
of the
Ancient Mariner.
IN SEVEN PARTS.

And its ribs
are seen as
bars on the
face of the
setting Sun.
The spectre-
woman and
her death-
mate, and no
other on board
the skeleton-ship.

Are those her ribs through which
    the Sun
Did peer, as through a grate?
And is that Woman all her crew?

Is that a DEATH? and are there two?
Is DEATH that woman's mate?

Sibylline leaves (1817)

What follows is a brief discussion of the textual history of 'The Rime of the Ancient Mariner' as an illustration of the ideas outlined above. Wordsworth had a determining influence on Coleridge's work; therefore, particular attention is paid to his direct and indirect roles in the history of the poem. A strong emphasis is also placed on the fact that the history of composition and revision is not a straightforward process of clarification of meaning; the process of revision is more complex and wide-ranging than the elaboration of a single authorial intention or set of intentions. 'Coleridge was well aware that, for him, revision ('correcting') was an essential part of the creation of poetry … In a letter to Daniel Stuart of 7 October 1800, he writes that 'his taste in judging' is 'far more perfect than [his] power to execute.'[14]

The specific examples referred to in the discussion are taken from the four versions of one stanza in the poem,[15] which are displayed above. The last three versions of the poem, published by Coleridge in his *Poetical Works* of 1828, 1829 and 1834, are not dealt with in detail here. The changes they display, while not insignificant, are largely typological variations on the *Sibylline Leaves* text (1817). Mays prints two reading texts of the 'The Rime of the Ancient Mariner', the first version (1798) and the last (1834), in deference to the fact that it is in many respects Coleridge's most famous and important work, and that it is the poem that undergoes most substantive revision over the course of Coleridge's career. His variorum treatment of the 'Ancient Mariner' takes in eight printed versions of the poem; there is no complete manuscript extant.

The first four versions of 'The Rime' come from the four editions of *Lyrical Ballads*, the first of which was published in 1798. On Coleridge's insistence, the volume was published anonymously and as though its contents were the work of a single author. The revolutionary preface to *Lyrical Ballads*, while undoubtedly drawn up and written on the basis of discussions between the two poets, articulates a vision of poetry that was and would remain Wordsworth's. The preface's central tenets – on the naturalness of poetic language and form, and on the importance of truth to nature and ordinary emotion – cannot be readily discerned in the ballad of the 'Ancient Mariner'.

Wordsworth, along with early critics of the volume, was quick to see that 'The Rime of the Ancient Mariner' detracted from (if it did not contradict) the poetic vision expounded in the preface. In a letter to the publisher Joseph Cottle on 24 June 1799, Wordsworth wrote: 'From what I can gather it seems that The Ancyent Marinere has upon the whole been an injury to the volume, I mean that the old words and strangeness of it have deterred readers from going on'.[16] Nevertheless, the first edition of *Lyrical Ballads* had sold out, and the publisher soon proposed a second edition, revised and expanded to two volumes.

Coleridge carried out a comprehensive revision of the 'Ancient Mariner' for the 1800 edition: he removed most of the archaic language and deleted a number of stanzas. He initially thought to place the poem at the beginning of the second volume, and to include a new poem, 'Christabel' – like 'The Rime of the Ancient Mariner', a ballad – which he felt succeeded in his intentions where the 'Ancient Mariner' had failed. Wordsworth, whose role in the preparation of the second

14 Stillinger, *Coleridge and textual instability*, p. 104.   15 *CC*, 16, 2, ii, pp 185–9.   16 William Wordsworth (& Samuel Taylor Coleridge), *Lyrical ballads*, ed. R.L. Brett and A.R. Jones (1963, repr. London, 1988), p. 273

edition was minimal (but crucial), insisted that the 'Ancient Mariner' be moved to the end of the first volume, where it might draw less critical attention, and at a very late stage in the process, demanded that 'Christabel' be removed altogether. Moreover, in a late addition to the revised preface, which Coleridge did not see until it had been printed, Wordsworth appended a note on the poem which reads: 'the Author was himself very desirous that [the 'Ancient Mariner'] should be suppressed. This wish had arisen from a consciousness of the defects of the Poem, and from a knowledge that many persons had been much displeased with it.'[17] That Wordsworth refers to himself so confidently as the author indicates his increased sense of ownership of the collaborative collection. However, his statement also has factual basis because, despite the editorial arguments that accompanied the second edition of *Lyrical Ballads* to the press, Coleridge insisted that it be published under Wordsworth's name alone.

In response to Wordsworth's criticism in the revised preface, Coleridge introduced a further change to the text of the poem. He changed the title to 'The Ancient Mariner. A Poet's Reverie.' For the first time Coleridge displays what will become an almost reflex response to criticism. The new subtitle concedes Wordsworth's view of the poem's strangeness and lack of purpose by re-categorising the work as a reverie, a dream, whose only claim to poetic status is that it is the dream of a poet. This reflex can be seen in a more extreme form in the preface to 'Kubla Khan', where Coleridge seeks to pre-empt any and all criticism of the poem by claiming that 'Kubla Khan' is not a poem at all, and that if it is a poem, it is not finished.

After the publication of the second edition of *Lyrical Ballads*, Coleridge effectively abandoned the poem as a text for publication, although his interest in its narrative and his personal investment in the character of the 'Ancient Mariner' as a fitting image of himself deepened. He had little or no involvement in the production of the third and fourth editions of *Lyrical Ballads*, in 1802 and 1805. In 1815, Coleridge engaged a publisher to print a book of his poems. In the intervening years, his personal and poetic relationship with Wordsworth had deteriorated, been broken entirely for a time, and was then uneasily restored. Nevertheless, there is a Wordsworthian connection to the proposed new book. In 1815, Wordsworth produced an edition of his collected poems. Coleridge's initial plan was to publish a book that was all but identical to Wordsworth's: a two-volume collection, prefaced by an author's note on the nature and art of poetry. He even negotiated with the publisher about replicating exactly the print typeface used in Wordsworth's book.[18] His authorial note, he wrote at the time, would be 'a critical essay on the uses of the Supernatural in poetry, and the principles that regulate its introduction,' a much-delayed reaction, perhaps, to the *Lyrical* preface.[19] Like many of Coleridge's plans, however,

17 Ibid., p. 276.   18 Richard Holmes, *Coleridge: darker reflections* (London, 1998), p. 390.   19 *CC*, 7, 1, p. 306.

this one came to nothing: no such preface has survived, and there is little evidence to suggest that his thought went any further than the note cited above. After a torturous gestation period, a single volume of poetry, *Sibylline Leaves*, was published in 1817. *Biographia Literaria*, which began its life as the preface to the collection, was published as a full-length prose work in the same year.

There are several reasons to stress the significance of the version of 'The Rime of the Ancient Mariner' that appears in *Sibylline Leaves*: it is the first time that the poem appears outside *Lyrical Ballads*, and thus beyond the shadow of Wordsworth's influence; it is the first time Coleridge puts his name to the poem in print; and finally, it contains Coleridge's most radical revision of the poem from its original form. Coleridge reverts to the original title of the poem in *Sibylline Leaves*, which betokens a new-found confidence in what he has written. The location and presentation of the poem in the new collection suggests as much: after two short, 'juvenile' poems – to use Coleridge's descriptive – 'The Rime of the Ancient Mariner' opens the collection. The distinctive typeface of the title and the inclusion of the prose marginal gloss hark back to late medieval precedents. The authority of antiquity is thus claimed for defects in the poem's style; that is, the (feigned) antiquity of the text explains and seeks to justify what critics had pointed to as the poem's worst defects: the 'old words' and the 'strangeness' of its narrative. A general tension is inaugurated here, which Coleridge will never (and perhaps never wanted to) resolve. The antique character of both typeface and gloss render the perceived defects of the poem as natural effects of its style; however, Coleridge is simultaneously engaged in the removal of the archaic forms of language and expression that had prompted the initial criticisms of the poem's 'defects'.

This revisionary tension is found also between the title and the beginning of the revised poem. Coleridge's 'Argument', a brief summary of the plot and themes of the 'Ancient Mariner', which is present in some early versions (1798 and 1800), is replaced in *Sibylline Leaves* by a quotation from a book entitled *Archaeologiae Philosophicae*, which concludes 'we must take care to keep to the Truth, and observe Moderation, that we may distinguish certain from uncertain Things, and Day from Night.'[20] Despite this professed concern for certainty, however, the epigraph has a much more ambiguous relationship to the poem than the original authorial 'Argument'.

The narrative effect of the marginal gloss – to explicate and comment on the poem – acts on one level as a response to criticism of the poem's disorder, the lack of a clear line of cause and effect. At the same time, the gloss amounts to the addition of a further level of complexity to the poem's narrative structure. 'The Rime of the Ancient Mariner' is a framed narrative – the poet recounts the tale of an Ancient Mariner telling a tale – with all the semantic ambiguity such a structure generates. The addition of a further frame deepens rather than

20 *CC*, 16, 2, i, p. 371.

resolves this narrative ambiguity. Moreover, the relationship between particular gloss notes and the lines or verses to which they refer is often less than straightforward.

There is a similar effect at work in Coleridge's calculated use of capitalisation. In revising the poem for *Sibylline Leaves*, Coleridge almost entirely drops the use of capitals with common nouns, which had been a feature of the earlier versions. At the same time, there is a systematic capitalisation of certain nouns throughout the text – the Ancient Mariner, the Wedding Guest, the Woman, Death, the Sun and the Moon – to signal their status in the poem and, in some cases, to suggest their possible symbolic functions in the narrative. At the same time as he is ostensibly engaged in a naturalisation and clarification of the poem, Coleridge imputes a supernatural character to natural elements within it.

As has already been mentioned, Coleridge pruned most of the archaisms from the 1798 text for the second edition of *Lyrical Ballads* in 1800: for example, the pun in 'Pheere' was lost to an ordinary 'Mate'. Linguistic modernisation of this kind continues in his preparation of the *Sibylline Leaves* edition: the spelling of 'thro' is lengthened to its conventional form, 'through'. Changes like these, considered in isolation, may appear to be minor, but their effect – even their visual effect – over all 620 lines of the poem is cumulative. The modernisation of language extends in *Sibylline Leaves* to an attempt to give 'The Rime of the Ancient Mariner' a more natural rhythm and tone. This process was begun in the revision of 1800: for example, the awkward inversion that frames the question expressed in the first two lines of the stanza in the 1798 version, 'Are these her naked ribs, which fleck'd / The sun that did behind them peer?'[21] is smoothed away without the introduction of a change in meaning in the 1800 version: 'Are those her Ribs, thro' which the Sun / Did peer, as thro' a grate?'[22] In the later revision for *Sibylline Leaves*, an emphatic repetition in the verse, one of the stylistic features of the poem of 1800, is removed as part of a more substantial revision of the stanza's meaning: 'And are those two all, all her crew'[23] becomes in the 1817 version, 'And is that Woman all her crew?'[24] This process of naturalisation is carried on typographically in versions of the poem after *Sibylline Leaves*: Coleridge revised the full capitalisation – in 'Death' – and abandons italics – in 'her' – as forms of emphasis in the edition of the poem printed in 1834.

Connected to all of these changes is a modulation of the poem's emotional tone. Like the addition of the gloss and Coleridge's system of capitalisation there is a double effect at work: things may be said more clearly in the *Sibylline Leaves* text of 'The Rime of the Ancient Mariner', but what they might mean is made less clear. Taking this stanza as an example, two questions have become five, and all asked with barely a pause for breath.

Coleridge's revisions of this poem, over a period of time that spans the length of his poetic career, exemplify the material instability of the text to be inter-

21 CC, 16, 2, ii, pp 185–6. 22 Ibid. 23 CC 16, 2, i. p. 187. 24 Ibid.

preted. This textual instability arises from the poet's equivocal sense of literary authority, and is reflected in the plurality of versions of the poem. The figuration of the plural poem – the eight versions of 'The Rime of the Ancient Mariner', for example – in terms of texts for performance helps to demystify a textual situation that has long been regarded as a problem to be resolved. Each succeeding version overlays the one(s) prior to it with another layer of meaning: the author's composition and revision of each version is both an act of interpretation and invitation to interpret further. The production of a stable text need not be the elusive object of a project of critical remedy; indeed, there can be no resolution of textual instability that does not involve more or less significant interference with some or all of the authoritative versions of the poem. A definitive text of 'The Rime of the Ancient Mariner' cannot by established by conclusive argument or without substantial loss. A reading of all the authoritative texts of the poem, and of the relations between them, on the other hand, opens up all the horizons of the poem's meaning and the shifting breadth of its thematic and stylistic concerns.

Index